TALIESIN;

OR,

THE BARDS AND DRUIDS OF BRITAIN.

A Translation

OF THE

REMAINS OF THE EARLIEST WELSH BARDS,

AND AN

EXAMINATION OF THE BARDIC MYSTERIES.

BY

D. W. NASH,

MEMBER OF THE ROYAL SOCIETY OF LITERATURE.

LONDON:

JOHN RUSSELL SMITH,

36, SOHO SQUARE.

M.DCCC.LVIII.

London :
F. Pickton, Printer,
Perry's Place, 29, Oxford Street.

Od oes prydydd wydd diwysg,
O Gymro hen digamrwysg,
Attebed vi.

SION KENT.

If there is a poet possessed of knowledge without bias,
An old Welshman free from perverseness,
Let him answer me.

PREFACE.

It has been so generally represented that the remains of the old British Bards are so obscure, and clothed in so obsolete and almost unintelligible a language, that a translation of these poems by an Englishman, acquainted with the Welsh only as a dead language, may very reasonably induce some hesitation in admitting the correctness of the following translations.

This feeling has induced me to add to the size of this work by the publication of the originals as they are found in the *Myvyrian Archæology*, so that the correctness of the translation may in every instance be tested by comparison with the original poem.

It is to be expected that many errors will be discovered, and that the construction given to many passages may be disputed; but I believe that, so far as regards the tenor and contents of these compositions, the translations given will meet with the approbation of the majority of Welsh scholars. In truth, the translation of these poems is a work of much less difficulty than would at first sight be supposed.

Some years since, the writer of the following pages, while endeavouring to obtain some insight into the early history of Britain, found that a great store of information on that subject was supposed to be contained in the works of the old

British poets of the sixth and following centuries, contemporaries, or nearly so, of Vortigern, Hengist, and Arthur, and of the great events of their era.

The translations of the Rev. Edward Davies and Dr. Owen Pughe revealing but little of what appeared to be history, it became necessary to examine the documents themselves. The difficulties presented by the language of the majority of these poems, appeared to demand more time and labour than the writer had at his disposal. The task was therefore thrown aside as hopeless. M. De la Villemarqué's translation of the *Gododin* in 1850, showed, however, that a sensible version of these poems could be obtained, and that they probably did not contain the mythological jargon extracted from them by Mr. Davies.

The admirable Essay of Mr. Stephens on the Literature of the Kymry, and Mr. Williams ab Ithel's critical translation of the *Gododin*, offered invaluable assistance, while the publication of the *Grammatica Celtica* by Zeuss, in 1853, rendered it apparent that the difference between the form of the language of these poems and that of the glosses ascribed by Zeuss to the eighth or ninth century, was so great, that they could not possibly have been written in their present form in the sixth or even in the tenth century, and that there could be no great difficulty in their translation to any one who could read the Welsh version of the Bible. The *Mabinogion,* so admirably translated by Lady Charlotte Guest, supplied the key to a considerable number of the allusions to persons and events; and it soon appeared that the greater part of the obscurity which prevails in these poems arises from the extremely corrupt state of the MSS. in which they have been preserved, owing, no doubt, to the circumstance that they were first written down from the dictation of the minstrels, by whom they had for some time been preserved by oral tradition only. The difference between the condition of the songs of the " History of Taliesin " in the *Mabinogion*, which were, if we may use the expression, " edited " by Thomas ab Einion in the thirteenth century, the songs on the Battles of Argoed Llwyfain, and Gwen Ystrad, and some others, which have also been carefully rewritten, and that of such as the " Prif Gyvarch," which have not received that attention, supplies the explanation of the extremely corrupt state of some of these compositions.

However strange it may at first appear, the compositions to which so remote a date has been attributed are far less difficult to read than many of those of the known bards of the twelfth, thirteenth, or fourteenth centuries. The explanation of this fact is, not only that many of the Taliesin ballads are later in date than the twelfth century, but that they were the compositions of comparatively unlettered and unskilled persons, and therefore comparatively simple and inartificial in structure, while the higher class of Bards whose works have been preserved, prided themselves upon a difficult and complex system of metrical composition, in which a process of alliteration is carried to a wonderful extent. This, and their " cynghanedd " or peculiar system of rhythm, have been made of such importance that they have rendered their works in many instances very obscure, by a forced adherence to their very artificial and most ingenious elegancies of composition.

The necessities of alliteration cause them at times to string together epithets without number, to the omission of the connecting links of their sentences, and without regard to the obscurity in which their meaning might be involved. The beauty, extent, and flexibility of the Welsh language, and the great skill of the writers in making it subservient to their purposes, are undoubtedly made manifest; but the labour employed is somewhat too visible—they had not acquired the " ars celare artem."

In the preparation of the following pages I have endeavoured to make myself acquainted with all that has been written on the subject of the old Welsh poems. My views may differ from those of more accomplished Welsh scholars than myself; but on such a subject there can but be a common desire to ascertain the truth, and, according to the motto of the Bardic Chair of Taliesin himself,

"MYN Y GWIR EI LE."

CHELTENHAM,
October, 1857.

TABLE OF CONTENTS.

CHAPTER I.

PAGE

INTRODUCTION: Early British History—The Ancient Druid—The Hyperboreans—Religion of the Druids—The Arch Druid—The oldest Welsh MSS.—The Black Book of Caermarthen—The Red Book of Hergest—The Myvyrian MSS.—The Bards—their social position—The Laws of Howel—Bardic Congresses—Regulations of Gruffyd ap Cynan—Different kinds of Musical Composition—The Cler, or Strolling Minstrels . 1—33

CHAPTER II.

PERSONAL HISTORY OF TALIESIN: Legends relating to him—Aneurin and Taliesin—The evidence furnished by the Gododin—Connection of Taliesin with Urien Rheged—History of Urien Rheged—his date and locality—Poems attributed to Taliesin—The Myvyrian Collection—Opinions of Welsh Scholars—Classification of these Poems by Mr. Stephens—their date—Translations of Taliesin—The Poems of Merlin—The Gododin—Christianity of the Gododin—The corrupt state of some of the Taliesin Poems—Explanation of—The " Prif Gyvarch," or First Address of Taliesin—The Cyff Cler—Exaggerated notions of the Antiquity of these Poems—The Englynion Marchwiail—The supposed Pictish Stanzas . . . 34—80

CHAPTER III.

THE HISTORICAL POEMS: The Elegy on Cunedda—The Gorchan Adebon—The Songs of Gwellawg ap Lleenawg—Stanzas on his death—The Battle of Gwenystrad—The Battle of Argoed Llwyfain—The Spoils of Taliesin—Songs to Urien—The Reconciliation of Lludd the Less—The Genealogy of Urien Rheged—Age of these Poems . . . . . . 81—121

CHAPTER IV.

PAGE

THE MYTHOLOGICAL POEMS: Their supposed Arkite Mysteries—
Mr. Davies's Translations—Supposed Hymn to the God Pryd
—Dr. Meyer's Translation—The Elegy of Aeddon—its true
character—The Celtic Metempsychosis—The Statements of
Edward Williams, or Iolo Morganwg—His Lyric and Pastoral
Poems—His Doctrine of the Barddas and Bardic Triads—The
Cyfrinach Beirdd—its real contents—The Elegy on the Thou-
sand Saints—The Romance or Mabinogi of Taliesin—Tales of
Magic and Mystery—The Goddess Ceridwen—her Cauldron
—The Mysterious Birth of Taliesin—Songs which probably
formed part of the Romance—The Song of the Ale—The
Cadeir Taliesin, &c. .   .   .   .   122—238

CHAPTER V.

OF NEO-DRUIDISM AND THE DRUIDICAL PHILOSOPHY: Opinions
of Mr. Herbert—Supposed Evidences of the Worship of
Mithras in Britain in the sixth century—The Song of the
Horses—Songs relating to Alexander the Great—The Ape of
the Sanctuary—The Mystery of the Gwyddvedd—Worship of
Hu—The views of the Archdeacon of Cardigan—his Discovery
of Heathen Deities in the Welsh Poems—The Egyptian Apis
—Castor and Pollux—The Philosophy of these Poems—The
Songs of the World—The Angar Cyvyndawd—Religious Poems
—The Divregwawd Taliesin, Awdyl Vraith, &c. .   .   239—306

CHAPTER VI.

OF THE WORSHIP OF HU GADARN THE SOLAR GOD, AND THE
DRUIDISM OF THE WELSH IN THE TWELFTH, THIRTEENTH,
AND FOURTEENTH CENTURIES .   .   .   .   .   307—320

CHAPTER VII.

THE WELSH ROMANCES: Irish and Scandinavian Legends—The
Welsh and Irish Druids—Absence of Welsh Tradition respecting the Druids—The Bardic Mystery—Conclusion   .   321—341

TALIESIN;

OR,

THE BARDS AND DRUIDS OF BRITAIN.

———◆———

CHAPTER I.

INTRODUCTION.

THE cloud of fable which has settled on the early history of Britain, is with difficulty to be penetrated. Her earliest monuments, rude and unsculptured, afford little assistance to the historian; and her most ancient written documents are composed in a language, sealed to the majority of inquirers. Unfortunately, also, many of those most competent, from a native acquaintance with the still existing dialect of the ancient language of Britain, to undertake the investigation, have suffered themselves to be led into relating as history, the most extravagant fables, and asserting the most unreasonable claims to antiquity.

The romance of Geoffrey of Monmouth, with its line of Trojan-British kings, and the fables of the Welsh Triads, with Hu Gadarn or the Mighty, " who first conducted the nation of the Cymry from Deffrobani, that is, the place where Constantinople now stands," to the Isle of Britain, and Dyfnwal Moelmud, a legislator who lived 400 years before the Christian era, have each in turn been represented as containing genuine historical materials for the history of Ancient Britain.

The opinions generally maintained by the Welsh writers and historians on the subject of the origin of the Cymry, may be summed up in the words of a learned and judicious writer

1

on Welsh literature, Mr. Stephens,[1] "that the modern Welsh, or Cymry, are the last remnant of the 'Kimmeroi' of Homer, and of the Kymri (Cimbri) of Germany, that great people whose arms struck terror into the Roman legions, and whose virtues Tacitus held up for the imitation of his countrymen. From the Cimbric-Chersonesus (Jutland) a portion of these landed on the shores of Northumberland, gave their name to the county of *Cumberland,* and in process of time, followed the seaside to their present resting-place, where they still call themselves Cymry, and give their country a similar name. Their history, *clear, concise, and authentic,* ascends to a high antiquity; their language was embodied in verse, long before the languages now spoken rose into notice; and their literature, cultivated and abundant, lays claim to being the most ancient in modern Europe."

Without attempting to discuss the merely conjectural part of this statement, the derivation of the modern Cymry or Welsh from the Cimbri or Kimmeroi, or inquiring whether these latter were a Teutonic or Celtic people, or how it happened that they were not known by the name of Cymry to the Roman writers on the affairs of Britain, we may pass to the interesting and important inquiry, the claims of the Welsh to the possession of a cultivated and abundant literature, the most ancient in modern Europe, and to a clear, concise, and authentic history of great antiquity: a history which should of course include the important transactions of the Cymric nation, their rise and fall in Britain—their wars and struggles, with their native, Roman, and Saxon enemies.

If, in order to reduce the difficulty of this inquiry, we abandon any attempt to tread the labyrinth of an antiquity prior to the establishment of the Roman power in this island, and confine ourselves to the more recent period of the two centuries which succeeded the final departure of the Romans

---

[1] *Literature of the Cymry;* a Critical Essay on the Language and Literature of Wales during the twelfth and two succeeding centuries: to which was awarded the prize given by H. R. H. the Prince of Wales at the Abergavenny Eisteddfod in 1848.

from Britain, we find that even this era, though a period full of events of the greatest interest and importance, most deeply and intimately affecting the fortunes of the British nation, is involved in the greatest doubt and obscurity.

This period, from the commencement of the fifth to the close of the sixth century, presents, as it were, a debateable ground between history and romance. It comprises the almost unknown history of the struggles of the wealthy and civilized Roman and Romano-British inhabitants of the great cities and fortified towns of Britain, against the ceaseless inroads of the native tribes, relieved from the pressure of the Roman power, and alike allured by the wealth and attracted by the comparative weakness of the citizens; and the history, little more authentic, of the transactions which resulted in the establishment of the Saxon dominion.

It comprises the drama of Vortigern and Rowena; the story of the fatal advent of Hengist and Horsa in their three ships with their band of Saxon sea-rovers; of the treacherous massacre of Stonehenge; and of all the long series of obstinate combats between the Christian tribes of Britain and their Pagan invaders. Moreover, it includes the wonderful romance of the renowned Arthur, " begirt with British and Armoric knights," whose era, commencing with the reign of Aurelius Ambrosius, in the early days of the Saxon invasion, closes with the fatal battle of Camlan, and the destruction of the flower of British chivalry in A.D. 542.

How much of what passes for history in the relation of the important events which mark this era, deserves that title, it is difficult, if not impossible, to determine; for the documentary evidence adduced in its support, affords but little aid in unravelling the tangled web of tradition and fable of which it is composed. " Our knowledge of the affairs of Britain, previous to the introduction of Christianity among the Anglo-Saxons " (that is, the commencement of the seventh century), says Sir Francis Palgrave,[1] " is derived from the most obscure and

---

[1] *Rise and Progress of the English Commonwealth*, pp. 389-483.

unsatisfactory evidence. The early Cymric chronicles scarcely even furnish us with the means of computing time. 'Annus,' 'annus,' 'annus,' is repeated in succession, but no era is marked. The entire absence of dates baffles all attempts which may be made to regulate their chronology, or to knit their fragments into a consistent story. The Welsh, in the days of Giraldus, easily accounted for the loss of all memorials of King Arthur, by asserting that Gildas cast his 'authentic history' of this renowned prince and his nation into the sea; but the same misfortune appears to have fallen on all the British annals of the next three centuries. British history, during this period, is therefore a mere hypothesis; and in this truly Cimmerian darkness, we can neither admit nor deny the assertion, that all the Cymric principalities, from Alcluyd to the mouth of the Severn, were united under the dominion of Einion Urdd, son of Cunedda; nor are we possessed of the data which could enable us to trace the advance of the Saxon power towards the Severn."

It is again admitted by one of the most competent and learned writers on early Welsh history,[1] that the interval between the termination of the Roman dominion in Britain, and the close of the seventh century, is a historical blank; " for it must be confessed that the Welsh, though possessed of a variety of records relating to that time, have not preserved a regular and connected history of their ancestors, who rose into power upon the departure of the Romans, and who, notwithstanding their dissensions, maintained a longer and more arduous struggle against the Saxons, than the continental parts of the empire did upon the irruption of the Goths and Vandals. In the middle ages, these records, to which was added a large store of tradition, attracted the attention of the romance writers, who gradually invested them with a cloud of fable, which at last, when arranged and regularly digested, was suffered to usurp the place of history. When the *Armorican Chronicle*, usually attributed to Geoffrey of Monmouth,

---

[1] Rees, *Essay on the Welsh Saints*, 1836. Preface, p. vii.

was brought from Brittany to Wales by Walter de Mapes in the twelfth century, its contents were found to be so flattering to national vanity, that it was soon received as an authentic record of facts, to the disadvantage of other records of a less pretending nature. For a long time, implicit faith was given to the story of the Trojan-British kings, and the superhuman actions of Arthur and his valorous knights commanded the admiration of Europe, few caring to question the truth of tales which suited the taste of the age, and filled their readers with delight. The criticism of later years has, however, determined the race of Trojan-British kings to be a pure fabrication, and most writers are contented to commence the history of Britain with the invasion of Julius Cæsar, following the Latin authorities until the termination of the Roman power in the island, when, for want of more satisfactory information, they are obliged to have recourse to records which they know not when to trust, or, leaving the affairs of the Britons in that darkness which they could not dispel, they have confined their researches to the Saxons."

Notwithstanding this acknowledged deficiency in the true sources of history, it is still maintained by the very latest writers on this topic, that there are extant in the Welsh language, compositions as early in date as the sixth century at the least, in which are preserved the traditions if not the history of the Britons, for this obscure period of the fifth and sixth centuries.

"It may be asked," says the Rev. Archdeacon Williams,[1] "how has it come to pass, if great events marked the epoch between the departure of the Romans and the death of Bede, that the whole history is so obscure, and that no literary documents remain to prove the wisdom of the teachers and the docility of the people? The answer is very plain. Such documents do exist: they have been published for more than half a century, but have hitherto wanted an adequate interpreter."

[1] *Gomer: a Brief Analysis of the Language and Knowledge of the Ancient Cymry.* London, 1854.

It has been, moreover, strenuously and repeatedly asserted, that these literary remains of the earliest British writers contain the most distinct and conclusive evidence, of the persistence, down to at least the close of the sixth century, of the doctrines and mysterious lore of the ancient Druidical priesthood, such as it is represented to have existed in Gaul and Britain, by Cæsar, Pliny, and other Roman authors. It is said by the author above quoted, that in the remains of the early British Bards "we have ample proof that during the Arthurian period (that is in the fifth and sixth centuries), and probably long before, certainly long after it, there flourished two schools of literature: the one essentially heathenish in creed, although often nominally Christian, and blending with Druidical doctrines, the worship of many of the Pagan idols of Greece and Rome, and of their own peculiar mythology. Specimens of this school are to be found in the remains ascribed to Taliesin, the Caledonian Myrddin, and in certain tales of the Mabinogion, as well as other anonymous works." The opinion that the poems of the celebrated Taliesin and other bards of his era, contain Druidical doctrines and Pagan superstitions of some unknown antiquity, is by no means an uncommon one. It is shared by almost all writers on the early periods of British history. Even Sir Francis Palgrave has been misled by the generally received opinion, to which the difficulty of consulting the original documents, and the audacious misinterpretation of portions of them in support of particular theories, have given a fictitious value. " Taliesin," he observes,[1] " hardly conceals his belief in the religion of his forefathers; and the Druidical worship, which was still recollected in Strathclyde and Cumbria, was so strong and vigorous on the opposite shores of Deira, that the British inhabitants not only preserved their priesthood, but had induced the Anglo-Saxon conquerors to embrace their faith; for the name of Coifi the Pontiff (in Gaelic, Coivi, Cuimhe, or Coibidh), by whose per-

---

[1] *Rise and Progress of the English Commonwealth*, p. 154.

suasion Edwin embraced Christianity in A.D. 627, is no other than the title of the chief of the Druids."[1]

The principal source of these opinions is the Rev. Edward Davies, who, in his two monuments of misapplied learning, his *Celtic Researches*, and the *Mythology and Rites of the British Druids*, maintained most perseveringly, and certainly not without great erudition, the Druidical character of the works of the British or, rather, Welsh Bards. "Ancient and authentic documents," he says (with reference to these poems), "of the opinions and customs of the old Britons, have been preserved, though long concealed by the shades of a difficult and obscure language." "The mystic lore of the Druids, and those songs which are full of their old mythology, were extant and in repute during the ages immediately subsequent to the times of Aneurin, Taliesin, and Merddhin," and that "the ancient superstition of Druidism, or at least some part of it, was considered as having been preserved in Wales without interruption, and cherished by the Bards to the very last period of the Welsh princes; that these princes were so far from discouraging this superstition, that on the contrary they honoured its professors with their public patronage."

In fact, according to the statements of this author, this Druidical superstition, which was actually publicly proclaimed and patronized in Wales down to the time of Edward I. in the thirteenth century, was a Helio-Arkite worship, in which the bull, the horse, and the element of fire, were prominent emblems, and King Arthur the representative of Noah; while a certain Hu Gadarn, whose history is to be found in the Welsh Historical Triads, was also an impersonation of the Patriarch, deified and worshipped by Welshmen in the thirteenth century of the Christian era. Such astounding assertions naturally induce an inquiry for the proof of their credibility.

[1] This is a very large conclusion from very slight premises. It is quite clear from the legend that the idol destroyed by the high priest was a Saxon idol, Thor or Woden, and that Coifi himself was a priest of the religion of Odin, who had adopted Christian ideas, and assisted in the conversion of his countrymen.

This proof Mr. Davies is not slow to offer. " If this be genuine British heathenism " (*i.e.* the Helio-Arkite worship and the history of Hu Gadarn), "it will be expected that vestiges of it should be discovered in the oldest Bards which are now extant; and here, in fact," says Mr. Davies, "they present themselves in horrid profusion."

It might be supposed that these views of the Rev. Edward Davies, published as long ago as 1809, had passed, under the influence of increased sources of knowledge, into oblivion; so far from this being the case, we find in a paper, published in the *Transactions of the British Association for the Advancement of Science, in* 1847, a learned philologer, Dr. Meyer, citing the Welsh Triads for the elucidation of British ethnology, and giving a metrical German and a prose English translation of a poem ascribed to Taliesin, as "one of the most ancient monuments of Welsh literature, a sacrificial hymn addressed to the god Pryd, in his character as god of the Sun."[1]

The same views are enunciated in works of even later date. Mr. Herbert, in his *Cyclops Christianus*, in 1842, the author of the *Biographical Dictionary of Eminent Welshmen*, in 1852,[2] and the Ven. Archdeacon Williams in *Gomer*, in 1854, present the same account of an ancient philosophy and mythology, to be discovered in the writings of Welsh Bards, supposed to be of the date of the sixth century, and especially in those of the celebrated Taliesin.

The ancient Druid is, in fact, the most prominent figure in British archæology. Clothed in his robe of white, "the emblem of holiness, and peculiarly of truth,"[3] with his golden sickle in his hand, he claims dominion over cairn and barrow,

---

[1] This writer also informs us that the names Ossian and Taliesin are mere mythological concentrations, and personifications of the poetical activity and influence of the interesting Siberian tribe U-sin, one of the principal tribes of the White Tartars, who are identical with the Irish, Ossian being the representative of the bards who themselves belonged to that tribe; Taliesin representing the bards of a neighbouring nation, who received from the Ua-sin the impulse of their art and inspiration.

[2] In the articles, Ceridwen, Amaethon, &c.   [3] Owen, *Essay on Bardism.*

stone-circle, cromlech and monolith, yielding an occasional but reluctant place to his almost as mysterious rival the Dane. Poet and philosopher, priest and prophet, legislator and judge, his functions are as numerous, as the religion he professed and the authority which he exercised, are doubtful and indefinable.

The true social position of the Druid, and the nature of the religious ceremonies in which he officiated as minister, are, even as to Gaul, involved in great obscurity, notwithstanding the information afforded with regard to them by the classical writers. As regards the British Druids, on the other hand, if we accept the statements of numerous modern writers on British antiquity, their social polity, their religious system, and their rites and ceremonies, are as familiarly known as the objects and transactions of any society for the propagation of learning in modern days.

" We have no reason to believe," says the Archdeacon of Cardigan, "that the heathen Druids of Gaul and Britain were, when historically known, practically less corrupt than their brethren in other nations.[1] They however, when struck down and bitterly persecuted by the Roman authorities, found a refuge in Ireland and Scotland for their persons, practices, and doctrines. Hence, when the Britons, after the confusion which immediately followed the overthrow of the Roman power in the island, had gained the ascendance, they resumed the laws, language, and traditions of their ancestors, with the important exception, that they combined with their inherited Christianity the philosophic doctrines of the Druids, which, when stripped of corruptions, represented the primitive religion of the oriental patriarchs. The chief site of the newly established religion seems to have been Gwent and Morganwg, whence it spread with comparative rapidity over all the countries then held by a Celtic population, and also over no small portion of continental Europe."

The same author professes to have given in an appendix to

---

[1] Those brethren being, according to the author, the magi of Media, the Chaldeans of Assyria, and the Brahmins of India.

2

the same work, a body of evidence from external sources which satisfy him, that long before the commencement of written history, there flourished in this island a civilized community, such as it is described by ancient writers. He adds, " nor have I any hesitation in saying, that the language of that community was the Cymraeg, and that a great portion of the lands now held by the church, were once in the possession of the priests and philosophers of that community."

This body of evidence may be shortly stated, thus : Diodorus Siculus, about the commencement of the Christian era, quotes from Hecatæus the Milesian, who lived about 500 B.C., a statement of the latter concerning the Hyperboreans. The Hyperboreans lived in an island in the ocean over against Celtica, not smaller than Sicily ; a fertile land producing two crops in the year. There Latona was born, and on that account Apollo is honoured by them above all other gods.

Among the Hyperboreans were men, priests as it were of Apollo, constantly hymning lyric songs in his praise. Also in that island was a consecrated precinct of great magnificence ; a temple of corresponding beauty, in shape spherical, adorned with numerous dedicated gifts ; also a city sacred to the god, the majority of its inhabitants harpers, who continually harping in the temple, sang lyrically hymns to the god, greatly magnifying his deeds. The Hyperboreans had a peculiar dialect, and were very friendly disposed to the Hellenes, especially the Athenians and Delians. The moon was not far distant from this island, and clearly showed certain earthly eminences.

Every nineteenth year the god descends into this island. This was the great year of the Hellenes ; when the god makes his periodical visit, he both plays the harp and dances during the night, from the vernal equinox to the rising of the Pleiades, taking great delight in his own successful efforts. A family called Boreadæ, descendants of Boreas, were the kings of this city, and superintendents of the temple, succeeding each other by birthright.

" If," says the Archdeacon, "Hecatæus derived his information on this important subject from the Phocœan merchants who frequented the court of King Arganthonius (in southern Spain), it is evident that these Hyperboreans were the occupants of Great Britain, which is so accurately described in the above passage, that even one of the earliest editors of Diodorus could not refrain in his index from writing,—'See whether this cannot be applied to Anglica!'"

Pindar, a contemporary, or nearly so, of Hecatæus, also mentions the Hyperboreans. Amongst other things, he informs us that Perseus visited them, and, having entered their hall, found them sacrificing renowned Hecatombs of Asses, wherein Apollo took incessant and most intense delight, laughing while he viewed the petulance of the restive brutes.

Various other early Greek authors mention the Hyperboreans and their Temple of Apollo. Everything would have been perfectly clear, had not Herodotus, "who was a victim to crotchets," stepped in and produced confusion, by his "wilful incredulity." He travelled far, and made every inquiry, but could hear nothing satisfactory of the Hyperboreans, as a real people, and comes to the conclusion, that they were something like the one eyed-men of the Scythians—a myth.

The pretensions of the British Druids are fairly stated, in a treatise on the Religion of Ancient Britain,[1] in terms which place them, at the least, on a level with the philosophers of Athens or Alexandria in point of science, and with the most favoured of the Biblical Patriarchs in point of religious doctrine.

It is asserted by this writer, who may be considered as giving an epitome of the generally received statements on this subject, that there existed in this island of Britain, before and at the time of its invasion by Julius Cæsar, a class or caste of persons, who, under the name of Druids, formed a powerful hierarchy; were the depositary of great and extensive learning, and the possessors of civil power; acquainted with letters, arts, and sciences; conversant in the most sublime speculations of geometry, in measuring the magnitude of the earth, and even

[1] *Religion of Ancient Britain historically considered.* London, 1846.

of the world; philosophers of a sublime and penetrating spirit, adding the study of moral philosophy, to that of physiology; skilled in mechanics, and acquainted with rhetoric and other polite arts.   The people of whom this remarkable class of gifted men were the priests, the judges, and the instructors, were, by no means, observes the same authority, a nation of wild barbarians, or " painted savages ; " but a people, " maintaining regular commercial relations with the most powerful and most polished nations of the world, who were, when they first colonized the island of Britain, possessed of considerable general information brought by them from Asia soon after the dispersion of mankind at the building of the Tower of Babel, and had not at the time of Cæsar's arrival, greatly degenerated from their original condition."

" Druidism," says another modern writer,[1] " is the term usually employed, to designate the primitive religion of our ancestors; a religion which obtained and flourished in Britain, from the time it was first colonized, down to the period of its first subjugation by the Romans, fifty-four years before the advent of Christ."

" The following epitome of the religious principles of the primitive Druids of Britain, drawn from their own memorials,[2] will show their conformity to the religion of Noah and the antediluvians; that the patriarchal religion was actually preserved in Britain under the name of Druidism; and that the British Druids, while they worshipped in groves, and under the oak like Abraham, did really adore the God of Abraham, and trust in his mercy.

" 1. They believed in one Supreme Being.[3]

" 2. In the doctrine of Divine Providence, or that God is the Governor of the universe.

---

[1] Yeowell's *Chronicles of the Ancient British Church.*   London, 1847.

[2] The author has unfortunately omitted to point out where these memorials are to be found.   He probably means the Triads; if so, it is something like citing Virgil to prove the costume of Dido.

[3] Cæsar says, that the Druids of Gaul worshipped chiefly Mercury; also Apollo, Mars, and Minerva.

" 3. In man's moral responsibility, and considered his state in this world as a state of discipline and probation.

" 4. They had a most correct view of moral good and evil.

" 5. They offered sacrifices in their religious worship.[1]

" 6. They believed in the immortality of the soul and a state of recompense after death.

" 7. They believed in a final or coming judgment.

" 8. They believed in the transmigration of the soul.[2]

" 9. They observed particular days and seasons for religious purposes.

" 10. Marriage was held sacred among them.

" This sketch is sufficient to show the identity between the religion of Noah and the antediluvians, and that of the Druids in Britain. So exact an identity of thinking and acting, by two people so far remote from each other, in the same epoch of time, cannot be satisfactorily explained, but on the supposition of the latter people having been connected with the former, and deriving their origin and their institutions from them.

" The endowment of this Druidic church, or the immunities to which the Druids as ministers of religion and teachers of the learned arts had been entitled, were, five free acres of land ; exemption from personal service in war ; permission to pass unmolested from one district to another in time of war as well as of peace ; support and maintenance wherever they went ; exemption from land-tax ; and a contribution from every plough in the district in which they were authorised teachers. These ancient privileges enjoyed by the Druids, were, upon the introduction of Christianity, legally transferred to the Christian priesthood, by King Lucius."[3]

[1] According to Cæsar, human sacrifices.

[2] Was this a patriarchal doctrine ?

[3] The Lucius here mentioned is the celebrated Llenawg ab Coel ab Cyllin, called " Lleufer Mawr," the great light, who, according to the Triads, built the first church at Llandaff, which was the first in the isle of Britain. He held a correspondence with Eleutherius, Bishop of Rome, about A.D. 180. The statement of the transference by him of the Druidic privileges to the Christian church, implies the existence in Britain of an endowed Druidic

ɔ only have the religious tenets of the ancient Druids been thus accurately ascertained, but also the particulars of the costume, ceremonial of initiation, discipline, and gradual progress through the degrees of the Druidic order, are detailed with great minuteness by many writers, and have been collected and related as though they were supposed to be true history, as lately as 1853.[1]

"The three orders of this great institution, were," says this author, " Bards, Druids, and Ovates. The Bards were poets. The Druids were priests and judges : august functions, filling to the eye of the stranger the whole field of vision ; hence the second order gave a name to the whole three. The Ovates were a mixed class, replenished from the ranks of the people. The cultivators of science and art : these occupied no mean position, though from the nature of their employments they drew to themselves less observation.

"To begin at the lowest step ; a Bardic student bore a distinctive title—Awenydd. The indispensable qualifications for a scholar, were noble birth and unimpeachable morals. On matriculation, he bound himself by oath not to reveal the mysteries into which he was about to be initiated. He was, however, seldom initiated into anything of importance, until his understanding, affections, morals, and general character, had undergone severe trials. He was closely observed when he was least aware of it ; there was an eye, to him invisible, continually fixed upon him, and from the knowledge thus obtained, an estimate was formed of his principles and abilities." "An Awennydd wore a plaid dress of the Bardic colours, blue, green, and white." "The candidate who had passed the ordeal was not immediately invested with the full privileges of the Bardic order ; he became an Inceptor, or

priesthood, in possession of recognised public rights and immunities, more than one hundred years after the proscription of the Druidic priesthood in Gaul, and the destruction of their stronghold in Anglesey by Suetonius Paulinus. This absurd fable is taken from the Welsh Triads.

[1] *Welsh Sketches*, by E. S. Appleyard, A.M. First Series. London, 1853.

Inchoate Bard, under the title Bardd-Caw, and wore for the first time the band of the order. Not till after he had presided at three Gorseddau or assemblies, was he fully qualified to exercise all the functions of the office. A full Bard could proclaim and hold a Gorsedd, admit disciples and Ovyddion, and instruct youth in the principles of religion and morality. The dress of the Bard was uni-coloured, of sky-blue, an emblem of peace and truth."

    * BON Blue.

"The Druids were the second order, but it was necessary to pass through the first to reach it. That is to say, a Druid must have been a Bard, though it was by no means required that a Bard should be a Druid." "The Druids were priests and judges; this union in their persons of the sacerdotal and judicial functions gave them great weight and authority, and caused their office to be in much request."

"The place of meeting of the Druids was called Gwyddfa, which, as the name implies, 'a place of presence,'[1] was an eminence either natural or artificial, according to the conveniency of the situation." "A white robe emblematic of truth and holiness, and also of the solar light, was the distinguishing dress of the Druids." "The judicial habit of the Arch Druid was splendid and imposing. He was clothed in a stole of virgin-white, over a closer robe of the same, fastened by a girdle, on which appeared the crystal of augury encased in gold. Round his neck was the breastplate of judgment, said to possess the salutary but uncomfortable property of squeezing the neck on the utterance of a corrupt judgment.[2] Below the breastplate was suspended the Glain Neidr, or serpent's jewel. On his head he had a tiara of gold. On each of two fingers of his right hand he wore a ring; one plain, the other, the chain ring of divination. As he stood beside the stone

---

[1] In Owen's *Dict.*, gwyddfa, a tumulus or tomb.

[2] This statement as to the breastplate of judgment, is taken from the account of the breastplate or collar of the Brehon judges of Ireland, and transferred without comment or authority to imaginary functionaries of the same kind in Britain. See Vallancey, *Collect.*

altar, his hand rested on the Elucidator, which consisted of several staves called Coelbrenan, omen sticks, on which the judicial maxims were cut; and which, being put into a frame, were turned at pleasure, so that each stave represented a triplet when formed of three sides.

"The third order was the Ovydd or Ovate, to which the candidate could be immediately admitted without being obliged to pass through the regular discipline. The requisite qualifications were, in general, an acquaintance with discoveries in science, the use of letters, medicine, language, and the like. The Ovydd could exercise all the functions of Bardism; and by some particular performance he became entitled to other degrees on the confirmation of a Gorsedd. The candidate for the order of Ovydd, was elected at a Gorsedd, on the previous recommendation of a graduated Bard of any of the three orders who might from his own knowledge, declare that he whom he proposed, was duly qualified. If the candidate were not known to a Bard, the recommendation of a judge or magistrate, or twelve respectable men, could constitute him a candidate; on which he was immediately elected by ballot. The dress of the Ovydd was green, the symbol of learning, as being the colour of the clothing of nature; and it was unmixed with any other, to show that it was uniform, like truth."

For these "historical" statements, the author in question cites as his authorities, Meyrick's *Costumes of the Ancient Britons*; Dr. Giles's *History of the Ancient Britons*; Wood's *Ancient British Church*; Owen's *Welsh Dictionary*, and certain Institutional Triads, in which the opinions and "sermons" of these orders are supposed to be preserved.

They are however, in fact, mainly derived from Dr. Owen's *Essay on Bardism*, prefixed to his translation of the poems of Llywarch Hen. That learned Welshman and scholar, appears readily to have credited the fantastic reveries of Edward Williams, otherwise called Iolo Morganwg, and the exaggerations, if not forgeries, with which he pretended to support them.

The *Essay on Bardism*, published in 1792, was drawn up

from the communications, and with the assistance of Edward Williams. The latter claimed to be a regularly graduated Bard of the Island of Britain, president of the Bardic chair of Glamorgan, and a legitimate successor to, and representative of, the ancient Druids.

We shall have occasion to inquire into the value of the assertions of Edward Williams when examining the authorities on the subject of the Druidical Metempsychosis.

All the information which can be obtained respecting the learning and condition of the Bards, and the doctrines, whether Christian or Pagan, which they may have inculcated in their writings prior to the tenth century, must, of course, be extracted from such writings, if any, as are extant of an earlier date. Fortunately for the true understanding of this question, the same materials, in the same, or even a better condition, which were at the disposal of Dr. Owen Pughe and the Rev. Edward Davies, are at command at the present day, and to these we must turn for any satisfactory elucidation of the subject.

References to British poems of the sixth century are so frequently made by writers on these subjects, that it will be well to ascertain, in the first place, what we really possess in the shape of Ancient British literature.

The most ancient manuscripts containing fragments of the Welsh language, according to Zeuss,[1] are as old as the tenth, possibly as old as the ninth century. They are not, it is true, Druidical, or even Bardic, but simply glosses written by British individuals, probably monastic persons, as marginal or interlinear interpretations or references, on manuscripts still in existence.

The oldest of these is the Oxford Codex, preserved in the Bodleian Library, which contains, among other things :—

1. A portion of the Treatise of Eutychius the grammarian, with interlinear British glosses.

---

[1] *Grammatica Celtica.* Lipsiæ, 1853.

2. A portion of Ovid's *Ars Amatoria,* also with interlinear glosses in the same tongue.

These remains of the old British language are stated by Zeuss [1] to be of equal age with the oldest Irish MSS., and to belong to the end of the eighth or the commencement of the ninth century.

3. In the same Codex are two other documents: an alphabet called the alphabet of Nemnivus,[2] a rude imitation of Runic forms, with the names of the letters attached. Also a fragment of a treatise on Weights and Measures, written partly in British, partly in Latin. These are probably as old, though not as valuable, as the former.

4. The second Oxford Codex, also in the Bodleian Library, contains a vocabulary of Latin words with British interpretations.

5. The Lichfield Codex, Llandaff Gospel, or St. Chad's Book, in which donations to the church of Llandaff are enumerated, contains many words and sentences in the British tongue, describing the boundaries of the estates given to the church, as old as the commencement of the ninth century.

6. Of the same age is a leaf found attached to the cover of a Codex in the Luxembourg Library.

" All these," says Zeuss, " are genuine ancient monuments, preserved in writing, and coeval with the older forms of the Cambric tongue." [3]

The Liber Landavensis, the ancient Chartulary or Register Book of the Cathedral of Llandaff, called also the Book of

---

[1] *Grammatica Celtica.* Lipsiæ, 1853.

[2] It is thus prefaced :—" Nemnivus invented these letters on the occasion of a certain Saxon remarking reproachfully that the Britons had no letters ; whereupon Nemnivus at once made these up out of his own invention, and so got rid of the reproach cast upon his nation."

[3] These glosses have been published by Zeuss in an Appendix to his *Grammatica Celtica.* Several of them had been previously noticed by Edward Lhuyd in his *Archæologia Britannica,* by Wanley, and Archbishop Usher ; but it was reserved for a foreigner to publish these most ancient memorials of the British language, and, after Lhuyd, the only critical examination of the Celtic dialects.

Teilo, which has been published by the Welsh MSS. Society, was, according to Zeuss and the editor of the published work, compiled in the former part of the twelfth century, but from materials of an older date. Charters contained in it relate to grants of lands to the church, professedly by personages of the sixth century.

The laws of Howel Dda, compiled in the tenth century; the oldest MS. is of the date of the twelfth century.

The oldest known manuscript containing the poetical compositions of the Welsh Bards, and the fountain of the supposed Druidic superstitions, is that known by the name of the Llyvr Du o Gaer Vyrdhin, or the Black Book of Caermarthen, in the library of the Vaughans at Hengwrt. It is a quarto of 54 leaves, the first 45 being in a different hand, and apparently older than the rest. The latter portion of the MS. contains an elegy on the death of Madog ab Meredydd, Prince of Powys in the year 1158; and in the former part is an elegy on the death of Howel, in 1104, who was great-grandson of the famous legislator of the tenth century, Howel Dda.[1]

The oldest known MS. containing poetical compositions is therefore of the twelfth century.[2] Its title of *Book of Caermarthen* is supposed to be derived from its having originally belonged to a priory in that town : a very probable account, as many of the early poems have evidently passed through a monastic laboratory.

The contents of the *Black Book of Caermarthen,* when examined by Edward Lhuyd about the close of the seventeenth century, were :—

1. The Dialogue between Myrddin and Taliesin.

---

[1] Villemarqué, *Poëmes des Bardes Bretons du 6e Siècle*, Introd. p. 8, citing the authority of Aneurin Owen. This elegy is not mentioned in the list of the contents of the Llyvr Du given by Lhuyd in the *Archæologia.*

[2] It is said in the preface to the *Mabinogion*, that there is another MS. in the Hengwrt Library containing the Graal in Welsh, also of the twelfth century; and a MS. of the Gododin, on vellum, is said by Mr. Williams ab Ithel to have been transcribed in the year 1200.

2. The Beddau Milwyr Ynys Brydain, or Graves of the Warriors of the Island of Britain.

3. The Predictions of Myrddin from his Grave.

4. The Avallenau.

5. The Hoianau, or Porcellanau.

6. The Song of Yscolan.

7. The Song of the Sons of Llywarch Hen.

8. Songs to Gwyddno Garanhir, to Maelgwn, to Gwyn ab Nudd, Gwendoleu, Gwallawg ab Llecnawg, Bran ab Gucrydh, Mcirig ab Kynele, Lhoegr ab Lhyenog, and the song " which was made when the sea overflowed the Cantref Gwaelod."

9. The names of the Sons of Llywarch Hen.

10. The Song of Geraint ab Erbin.

11. The Elegy on the Death of Madog ab Meredydd.

12. The Song to the Lord Rhys.

As far, therefore, as the evidence on this subject goes, the greater part of the poems ascribed to Taliesin had not been reduced to writing in the twelfth century. They are found in the *Red Book* of Hergest, from 100 to 150 years later.

We have also an interval of nearly six hundred years between the time at which they are supposed to have been composed, and the earliest MS. in which they are found.

There is, however, one MS. which is said to be as old as the seventh century. This is the fragment described by Edward Lhuyd in the *Archæologia Britannica*, who found it written in, as he says, a Gwyddelian hand, on the first leaf of an old copy of Juvencus. " By the writing, and by a few more words of the same language, I am certain that the book has come from Scotland, and I can also compute the age of the manuscript. I know not whether it is the language of the Strathclyde Britons, or of the Picts or old Caledonians ; it is the oldest and strangest British I have yet seen. I do not understand the aim and meaning of the lines."

The next in point of age and importance, is the Llyfr Coch o Hergest, or Red Book of Hergest, in the library of Jesus College, Oxford. It consists of a folio volume containing 721 pages, written in double columns, upon vellum. " At the end of the Llyfr Coch are some poems bearing the name of Lewis Glyn Cothi, who flourished at the close of the fifteenth century. This circumstance has given rise to the idea that the whole of the MS. (which is said to have been transcribed from one of still more ancient date) is in the handwriting of the Bard himself; but it is more probable, that, like most others of that period, it is from the hand of professed scribes, more particularly, as it bears the appearance of having been written by various persons, and at different times."[1]

According to Edward Lhuyd, it was written about the end of the fourteenth century. The poems of Taliesin and Llywarch Hen, were certainly not transcribed in the Red Book at an earlier period, as the poetry begins at the 513th page, while at the 208th page occurs " A Brief Chronology from Adam to A.D. 1318 ;" and at the 499th page, "A Chronological History of the Saxons, from their first arival to A.D. 1376."[2]

According to Taillandier, in his preface to Lepelletier's *Dictionary*, the oldest Breton (Armorican) MS. is of the date of A.D. 1450, being a collection of the predictions of a pretended prophet Gwinglaff, the same apparently as the Merddin of the Welsh.

The Bardic compositions, as they are called, certainly comprising the oldest known remains of Welsh literature, were collected and published in 1801, in a work entitled the *Myvyrian Archæology of Wales*, collected out of ancient manuscripts, edited by Owen Jones, Edward Williams, and William Owen.

This collection is in three volumes. The first volume containing, in the words of the " General Advertisement," by the editors, " so much of the ancient poetry of the Britons as fate has bequeathed to us, and comprehending all the remaining compositions from the earliest times to the beginning of the fourteenth century."

The second and third volumes are in prose, and contain the

[1] Preface to *Mabinogion*, by Lady Charlotte Guest.
[2] See *Cambro-Briton*, vol. ii. p. 107.

Triads, Collections of Proverbs, Genealogies of the Saints, the Chronicles of Tysilio and Gruffyd ab Arthur, and the Laws of Howel Dda.

The Barddoniaeth, or poetry, of the first volume of the *Myvyrian Archæology* is chronologically divided into two series. First, the works of the Cynveirdd, or earliest Bards, from the sixth to the middle of the tenth century, comprising the most celebrated names in the annals of Bardic lore. Secondly, the works of the Gogynveirdd, or later Bards, the Bards of the middle ages, from A.D. 1120 to A.D. 1380.

The Cynveirdd, or Primitive Bards, whose poems have been preserved and are contained in the *Myvyrian Archæology*, are Aneurin, Taliesin, Heinin, Llywarch Hen, Myrddin, Llevoed, Golyddan, Meigant, Elaeth, Tysilio, Cuhelyn, Gwyddno, and Gwydion ab Don, with some anonymous pieces of the earliest bards.

Of the 124 compositions comprised in this series, no less than 77, or nearly two-thirds, are attributed to Taliesin, comprehending historical, mystical, philosophical, religious, moral, and satirical pieces. These are the poems which, in conjunction with those attributed to Merlin, form the great storehouse whence the materials have been drawn, in support of the opinion that the learning and philosophy, the myths, traditions, and superstitions of the ancient Druidic hierarchy of Gaul and Britain, are to be found in compositions, none of which are pretended to be of earlier date than the commencement of the sixth century of the Christian era.

That a very considerable number of the works attributed to Taliesin by the transcribers of the MSS. and in the *Myvyrian Archæology*, could not possibly be ascribed to the sixth, or seventh, eighth, or tenth centuries, is evident on a mere inspection of their contents. The name of this celebrated Bard has, however, been a tower of strength to the majority of the Welsh archæologists, who have unhesitatingly accepted all that presented itself under this famous superscription, as evidence of the state of literature and philosophy among their countrymen in the sixth century.

The published compositions of the Welsh Bards form but a very small portion of the extant remains of their works. It appears [1] that the Myvyrian MSS. alone, now deposited in the British Museum, amount to 47 volumes of poetry of various sizes, containing about 4700 pieces of poetry, in 16,000 pages, besides about 2000 englynion or epigrammatic stanzas. There are also in the same collection, 53 volumes of prose, in about 15,300 pages, containing a great many curious documents on various subjects. Besides these, which were purchased of the widow of the celebrated Owen Jones, the editor of the *Myvyrian Archæology*, there are a vast number of collections of Welsh MSS. in London, and in the libraries of the gentry of the Principality. Notwithstanding all that has been written about the Cymry—their antiquity, learning, and the love of their native institutions—none of these have been published either by wealthy individuals, or by the numerous literary societies of Wales. It is to the liberality and public spirit of a furrier in Thames Street, that we are indebted for the means of forming an acquaintance with these early British compositions.

It would seem from Edward Lhuyd's statement in the *Archæologia Britannica*, that the possessors of Welsh MSS. in his day held the same views as "the Earl of Ashburnham, of Asburnham House, near Battle, Sussex," in 1857, who, according to Mr. Beale Poste,[2] is in possession of an inedited manuscript copy of the *History of Nennius*, but "is stated to decline his manuscripts being consulted for literary purposes." But since the publication of the *Mabinogion* by Lady Charlotte Guest, and the great interest excited by that work, in consequence of its important bearing upon the history of the Romance literature of Europe, it is to be hoped,

[1] See *Cambro-Briton*, vol. iii. p. 443.
[2] *Britannia Antiqua*, p. 46. London, 1857.

that if any literary treasures do exist among those MS. collections, they may be made available to the literary world.[1]

There being no foundation for the exaggerated and fabulous accounts of the early Welsh Bards, usually entertained, we must endeavour to ascertain their real character from more trustworthy sources, as it would be impossible to comprehend the true nature of their poems without a knowledge of the manners and customs of the age to which the minstrels who sang, and the audiences who delighted to hear these compositions, belonged.

That bards or persons gifted with some poetic and musical genius existed in Britain, as in every other country in the world at every age, may be conceded, and that among the Celtic tribes, perhaps in an especial manner, the capacity for recording in verse the deeds of warriors and the ancestry of chieftains, was held in high esteem, and the practice an honourable occupation. Strabo said, that "among the Gauls, three classes are more especially held in veneration—Bards, Ovates, and Druids.

The word "Bardd," Dr. Owen derives from "bar," a top or summit, and renders it,—"One that makes conspicuous; a priest; a philosopher or teacher; and as poetry was a principal requisite, and a vehicle for the spreading of knowledge, he was necessarily a poet." This etymology is of a piece with much contained in his truly valuable work, where the better judgment of its author has been obscured by what is perhaps a pardonable enthusiasm on behalf of Welsh antiquity. The word occurs in the Irish language with the ordinary meaning, and may probably be connected with "Cerdd," a song, an art, or a performance.

What the Bards of Wales really were in the tenth century

---

[1] We may venture to suggest to the Welsh MSS. Society, that it is not necessary to publish English translations of Welsh MSS., a process which involves a large and unnecessary expenditure of time and money. What is wanted is, to have the documents themselves in print: those who wish or are able to make use of them, can supply the translations where requisite.

we learn from an indisputable source—the laws of Howel the Good, enacted about 950.

This celebrated code of laws was compiled by a commission of thirteen of the most learned persons to be found in Wales. We may observe in passing, that there was not either a Bard or a Druid selected on this occasion. Three of them were judges, and their president was Blegwryd, Archdeacon of Llandaff, and Doctor in Civil and Canon Laws. The laws commence with the duties and privileges of the twenty-four officers of the King's Palace, sixteen of whom were attached to the service of the King, and eight to that of the Queen.

They were :—

1. Master of the household.
2. Domestic chaplain.
3. Steward of the household.
4. Judge of the palace.
5. Falconer.
6. Chief groom.
7. Chief huntsman.
8. Steward of the household to the Queen.
9. Queen's chaplain.
10. Domestic bard.
11. Crier.
12. Doorkeeper of the hall.
13. Doorkeeper of the chamber
14. Page of the chamber.
15. Chambermaid.
16. Groom of the rein.
17. Torch-bearer.
18. Butler.
19. Mead-brewer.
20. Officers of the palace.
21. Cook.
22. Foot-holder.
23. Physician.
24. Groom of the rein to the Queen.

In this series the Bard occupies the tenth place, and was one of the superior officers of the Court, since the " satisfaction for the insult and murder of the Bard, his heriot, and the rank of his daughters, was the same as that of the domestic chaplain, steward of the household, judge of the palace, falconer, chief groom, and page of the chamber. The fine, eric, or were-gild for the murder of the Bard was 909 cows with three advancements.

The functions of the Bard were confined to the exercise of his art. In these laws he is, in the tenth century, neither priest, teacher, nor philosopher; but simply a singer, and

4

most probably a composer of songs. He is to sing at the
board of the King, in the common hall, and at the desire of
the Queen. If the Queen required a song in her chamber,
the Bard was to sing three verses concerning the Battle of
Camlan—the battle in which Arthur and the Knights of the
Round Table were slain.[1]

He was to sing a song to the master of the household whenever the latter should direct, and was to pay a fine to the
judge of the palace on his appointment.

Amongst the duties of the Bard was that which was retained
among the Celtic tribes of Scotland down to the eighteenth
century—leading the clan with inspiriting music into battle.
"If there should be fighting," it is enacted by the laws of
Howel, "the Bard shall sing the 'Unbenaeth Prydain' (the
Monarchy of Britain) in front of the battle." It is to the
performance of this duty that Gwalchmai, a Bard of the
twelfth century, probably alludes in the lines—

> Mi ydwyf eurddeddf diofn yn nhrin
> Mi ydwyf llew rag llu lluch fy ngorddin,—

> I am of the golden order fearless in battle ;
> I am a lion in the front of the army ardent in my advance.

In the tenth century, then, even the Royal Bard was a poet
and minstrel, and nothing more.

His office was an honourable one, but not the most honourable. He was in an inferior position to the domestic chaplain,
and had no authority or occupation as a moral or religious
teacher.

The domestic chaplain was one of the chief officers of the
court, and of the three indispensable persons with the King;
and, with the master of the household and the judge of the
palace, was to support the honour of the court in the King's

---

[1] On the authority of the editor of the *Cambro-Briton*, vol. ii. p. 347. If
this is so, the romance of Arthur was current in Wales in the tenth century.
But it is probably an addition of later date.

absence. His satisfaction for insult and murder was higher than that of the Bard.

In the halls of the lesser chieftains the occupation of the Bard was, no doubt, of still higher importance. He was the genealogist, the herald, and to some extent the historian of the family to which he was attached, kept alive the warlike spirit of the clan or tribe, the remembrance of the old feuds or alliances, and whiled away those tedious hours of an illiterate age, which were unemployed in war or in the chase. To some extent a man of letters, he probably fulfilled the office of instructor in the family of his patron or chief.

But, besides these regularly acknowledged family or domestic Bards, there was in Wales, in the eleventh and twelfth centuries, and from thence downwards, a very numerous class of itinerant minstrels, who, like the Troubadours, Jongleurs, or Gleemen, wandered from place to place, seeking reward for the entertainment they afforded by their musical acquirements, and their recitals of songs and tales for the amusement of all classes, from the hall of the baron to the cabin of the boor.

We know little of the condition of the Welsh Bards from historical sources previous to the tenth century, though it is stated that late in the seventh century, Cadwallader sat in an Eisteddfod, assembled for the purpose of regulating the Bards, taking into consideration their productions and performances, and giving new laws to harmony. From this period no historical notices of the Welsh Bards, or of their music, occurs until the publication of the laws of Howel Dda, in the tenth century. According to the Welsh accounts, towards the close of the eleventh century, " the great Prince Gruffydd ap Cynan invited to Wales some of the best musicians of Ireland ; and, being partial to the music of that island, where he was born, and observing with displeasure the disorders and abuses of the Welsh Bards, created a body of institutes for the amendment of their manners and the correction of their arts and practices. Accordingly I find in an old MS. of Welsh music, in the library of the Welsh School, a curious account of so remarkable a revolution, beginning with these words:—'Here follow the four-and-twenty measures of instrumental music, all conformable to the laws of harmony, as they were settled in a congress by many Doctors skilful in that science, Welsh and Irish, in the reign of Gruffyd ap Cynan, and written in books by the order of both parties, princely and principally, and thence copied.'" [1]

The names of the different measures of music established by the congress of Gruffyd ap Cynan, show both the extent of Irish influence, and the previous existence, of a number of songs in the Welsh language. It appears that some part of the MSS. above alluded to was transcribed in the time of Charles I. by Robert ap Huw, of Bodwigen, in Anglesey, from William Penllyn's book. This William Penllyn is recorded among the successful candidates on the harp at an Eisteddfod at Caerwys in 1568, where he was elected one of the chief Bards and teachers of instrumental song.

Dr. Powell also was of opinion that the Welsh instrumental music came hither with Prince Gruffyd's Irish musicians, or was composed by them afterwards.

This grand reformation of the Bards consisted in dividing them into classes, and assigning to each class a distinct profession and employment. The Bards were thus divided into three grand orders—poets, heralds, and musicians; each of which again branched into subordinate distinctions.

The musicians were of three classes: performers on the harp; players on the crwth, a six-stringed or three-stringed instrument, resembling a violin; and singers whose employment was to sing to the accompaniment of the harper.

According to Mr. Stephens,[2] the division of the order made by Gruffyd was into Poets, Family Bards, and Migratory Bards. He fixed the scale of remuneration for their labours, and was the first to order the formation of Chairs for the

---

[1] Jones's *Hist. Account of the Welsh Bards.*
[2] *Literature of the Kymry,* p. 340.

victors in Bardic contests, who were ever after honourably distinguished as Chair Bards.[1]

About the same period, the patrons of literature in South Wales made an effort for the restoration of the poetic art in their portion of the principality.

But an important fact connected with this revival of the art in North Wales must not be overlooked.

About twenty years before the Eisteddfod at Caerwys, in A.D. 1100, held by Gruffyd ab Cynan, Rhys ab Tewdwr had assumed the sovereignty of South Wales. "He brought with him from Brittany," according the Welsh accounts, "the system of the Round Table, which, at home, had become quite forgotten, and he restored it as it is, with regard to minstrels and bards, as it had been at Caerlleon-upon-Usk, under the Emperor Arthur, in the time of the sovereignty of the race of the Cymry over the island of Britain and its adjacent islands."[2] "Iestyn the son of Gwrgan, took the Roll of the Round Table by force and fraud to Cardiff Castle. Cardiff was taken by Robert Fitzhamon the Norman; and Robert Earl of Gloucester, the patron of Geoffrey of Monmouth, married Mabli, daughter of Robert Fitzhamon, and received the lordship of Glamorgan in right of his wife." We here see the introduction of the Arthurian romance from Brittany preceding by nearly one generation the revival of music and poetry in North Wales.

At Christmas, A.D. 1107, Cadwgan ab Bleddyn, Prince of South Wales, held a great feast at Cardigan Castle, to which he invited the princes and chieftains of all parts of Wales, and all the best Bards, musicians, and singers in all Wales, and set chairs for them, and instituted contests between them, as was the practice at the feasts of King Arthur.[3]

At Christmas, in the year 1176, Rhys, Prince of South Wales, gave a magnificent entertainment at his castle of Car-

[1] But the Bardd Cadeiriawg, or Chair Bard, is mentioned in the laws of Howel Dda in the preceding century.

[2] Iolo MSS. page 630.   [3] Mysvyr. Arch. vol. ii. p. 536.

digan or Aberteifi, to a great number of illustrious natives and foreigners; notice of which had been given a year and a day before by proclamation through all Britain and Ireland. The musical Bards of North Wales and South Wales, who had been expressly invited to the festival and a poetical contest, were seated in chairs with much ceremony in the middle of the great hall of the castle. In the musical contest which followed, the pre-eminence in poetry was adjudged to the poetical Bards of North Wales; that in music to the domestic musical Bards of the Prince.

At this feast the Bards were confirmed by the prince's authority in the franchises and privileges granted them by former statutes. They were also recompensed with fees, settled by prescription, and proportioned to the order of their profession and the degree they had obtained in it.[1]

From this time to the death of Llywelyn ab Gruffyd, in 1282, is the brightest period of Welsh poetry. During this period, says Mr. Stephens,[2] "Wales possessed a series of great men in Gruffyd ap Cynan, Owain Gwynedd, Owain Cyveiliawg, Gruffyd ab Rhys, Rhys ab Gruffyd, Llywelyn ab Jorwerth, and Llywelyn ab Gruffyd. Of the Cambrian princes, Llywelyn ab Jorwerth deserves especial mention, as the stability of the country during his reign (from 1194 to 1240) was essentially conducive to its literary eminence. At this period a succession of great men had restored stability and order, and strengthened the regal authority; the elements of convulsion subsided, anarchy ceased, and men, conscious of personal security, could listen with pleasure to the songs of the Bards, who flourished, increased, and improved under the genial influence of regal dominion and public intelligence."

The regulations made at these congresses in the twelfth and thirteenth centuries, give us the meaning of the titles affixed to several of the pieces in the *Myvyrian Archæology*. Several of the poems ascribed to Taliesin are called Cadair; Cadair

---

[1] Jones, *Hist. Account of the Welsh Bards.*
[2] *Lit. of the Kymry*, p. 341.

Taliesin, Cadair Ceridwen, Cadair Teyrnon, &c. This is translated, The Chair of Taliesin, The Chair of Ceridwen, &c.; and such, no doubt, is its literal meaning, though a mystic sense has been attached to it by the advocates of the Bardic mysteries.

Other pieces are entitled Colofn, as the religious poem of Jonas Athraw of Menevia, entitled Awdyl Vraith, which is said in the Hanes Taliesin to be one of the Four "Colofn Cerdd," or Pillars of Song.

It appears that certain descriptions of musical composition received among the Welsh technical names as early as the twelfth century. Jones describes them as—

1. A *Cwlwm*, a congruous piece of music with words.
2. A *Colofn*, pillar or fundamental part of metrical quality.
3. A *Cydgerdd*, music in parts.
4. A *Cadair*, a masterly piece of music, as Jones conjectures, by the performance of which the Bard rose to the superior degrees, and to the chair; whence it probably took its name.
5. A *Caniad*, a tune or song.
6. A *Gosteg*, a prelude or overture.
7. A *Difr*, a measure or diverting air.
8. A *Mwchwl;* this famous piece of music, it seems, was only acquired by a Pencerdd, or Doctor of Music of the Harp.

These distinctions are said to have been invented by the commission appointed by Gruffyd ap Cynan in the eleventh century, and to form the basis of the regulations by which the *curriculum* or course of study of the candidates for degrees in music and poetry was directed. Thus a graduate probationary student of music was required to know ten *cwlwms*, one *colofn*, five *cwlwms* of *cydgerdd*, one *cadair*, and eight *caniads*. The Doctor of Music was obliged to know forty *cwlwms*, four *colofns*, twenty *cwlwms* of *cydgerdd*, four *cadairs*, thirty-two *caniads*, and four *gostegs;* to understand all the laws and modifications of harmony, especially the twenty-four measures of music, with other qualifications.

In calculating the value of these distinctions, a *cadair* was ual to five *cwlwms*, a *colofn* equal to two *cadairs*, and three noble *mwchwls* equal to the four *colofns*. The three new *mwchwls* were equal to four *cadairs*.

The same observation applies to the "*gorchan,*" which Davies translated "talisman," and which the Ven. Archdeacon of Cardigan still persists in calling a "charm and incantation," but which is nothing more than a technical term for poetic composition according to fixed rules; there being nine kinds of *gorchanau*, corresponding to the nine divisions of the *colofn*.[1] So one of the twenty-four measures of song is called "Gorchest y Beirdd," "the great achievement of the Bards."

The object of these Bardic congresses, held in the twelfth and thirteenth centuries, was not only the revival of musical and poetic literature, but also to introduce, if possible, some order among the multitude of professed idlers who, as wandering singers and minstrels, swarmed over the country. The practice of progressing from place to place, from castle to castle, and joining every occasion of festivity, was so lucrative, that the higher class of Bards were anxious to place under restraint the migratory gleemen who elbowed them out of place on such occasions. The spirit of the age would with difficulty permit chieftains of renown or persons of noble birth to refuse the demand for largess, or the boon claimed as the reward of song. The character and reputation of the knight and noble were, moreover, very much dependent on the fame which lived in the mouths of these itinerant minstrels.

In the laws of Howel we see it enacted, that when the Bard shall ask a gift from a prince he shall sing one song; when he asks a baron, let him sing three songs; should he ask a vassal, let him sing until he falls asleep. The poems of the

---

[1] It may be remarked that the term "Gorchan" is not found in Dr. J. D. Rees's elaborate account of Welsh metre, published in 1592.

Welsh Bards are full of expressions of requests for favours to be granted, or praise and gratitude for those received.

The custom of petitioning for presents by occasional poems was carried to such excess, and such respect was constantly paid to their requests, that in the time of Gruffyd ap Cynan, in the eleventh century, it became necessary to restrain them by a law which prohibited them from asking for the prince's horse, hawk, or greyhound, or any other possession beyond a certain price, or that was particularly valued by the owner, or could not be replaced. Many poems of the succeeding centuries are now extant, written to obtain a horse, a bull, a sword, a rich garment, &c.[1]

An endeavour was made to place these progresses or migrations of the Bards under some regulations, by appointing for them a regular turn once in three years, called "Clera," a name applied to the wandering minstrels themselves. It does not seem to have had much effect, since in 1403, in the reign of Henry IV., it was enacted by the "Ordinance de Gales," "that the Minstrels, Bards, Rhymers, and Questers, and other Welsh Vagabonds in North Wales, be not henceforth suffered to surcharge the land as now they do ; but that they be prohibited therefrom under pain and imprisonment for one year." These minstrels were in fact recognised by the arrangements come to at the Congress of Bleddyn ab Cynvan, under the Welsh name of Datceiniad, or those who sung the compositions of others ; and it was attempted to enforce the regular graduation of these in a kind of Bardic university. But the public taste and the spirit of the age were too strong for the higher classes of the profession, and the wandering Minstrel, and Storiawr or Reciter of tales and ballads, maintained his ground in spite of Bardic congresses, Eisteddfods, and Acts of Parliament.

The proper appellation of the strolling minstrel was Cler or Clerwr.

Dr. Owen, in his *Dictionary*, under the word *Cler*, which he

---

[1] Jones's *Bardic Relics.*

says is a plural aggregate form derived from *cy-ller*, gives as its meaning,—" The teachers or learned men of the Druidic order, who, under the primitive Bardic system, were by privilege employed in going periodical circuits to instruct the people, answering the purpose of a priesthood; but in later times, the term implied a society of wanderers; or those bards and musicians who lawfully strolled about, like the English minstrels. These wandering classes of men originated when the priesthood was made a distinct branch of the Bardic system; for the latter then ceased to have sufficient power to support its members; and as a compensation, a law was made, that such as were of this description should have regulated periodical circuits, and receive certain fees according to their degrees, and the quality of those they visited. This ended at the last in mere mendicancy."

This statement is mere imagination, entirely unfounded. The word *cler* in Welsh, as *cliar* in Irish, means a minstrel, poet, or singer. The apparent connection between the word and the Latin *clerus* is probably merely accidental. The Irish *clarsair* and *clairseoir*, a harper, from *clar* a board, the performer on a board, and *clairseach* a harp, the seven boards, or board with seven strings, appear to offer the derivation of the word. The estimation in which they came to be held, is evident, among other things, in the secondary meaning of the word *cler*, " gadflies."

A very cursory examination of the remains of Welsh poetry contained in the first part of the *Myvyrian Archæology*, that is, the poems of the Cynveirdd, suffices to assure us, that the pieces therein contained were written down from the mouths of the wandering minstrels, and that these were, as might well be expected, an exceedingly illiterate class of persons. It is this circumstance alone which explains the fact, that the poems ascribed to Taliesin in particular, are for the most part made up of allusions to local, sometimes historical events, references to the Mabinogion, or fairy and romance tales of the Welsh, scraps of geography and philosophy, phrases of monkish Latin, moral and religious sentiments, proverbs and adages, mixed together in wonderful confusion, sometimes all in the compass of one short ballad. They demonstrate most clearly, that, however ancient some of the fragments mixed up with them may be, these ballads were not reduced into writing until long after they had been handed down, by oral transmission, through the recitals of these itinerant minstrels. They furnish the best commentary on the monstrous imposture of Edward Williams and his son Taliesin Williams, and the reveries of Davies and Dr. Owen, on the subject of the *Coelbren y Beirdd*,[1] or Bardic letters employed in Britain from the most remote antiquity.

[1] The subject of the Coelbren y Beirdd will be further discussed in treating of the Historical Triads and other sources of the ancient history of Britain, in the second part of this essay.

CHAPTER II.

PERSONAL HISTORY OF TALIESIN—OF URIEN RHEGED.

BEFORE proceeding to an examination of the various compositions attributed to the celebrated Chief of Bards, Taliesin, we may offer a few observations on his history and the legends connected with his name.

If Taliesin really flourished in the sixth century, his genuine poems may be expected to contain references to historical events and personages, which will readily identify the age and locality of their author. It may also reasonably be anticipated, that, even should they fail to supply important authentic materials of history, they will at least, as Mr. Rees has observed, be interesting as records of a valiant and high-spirited people, nobly struggling against overwhelming odds, to preserve their liberties and the independence of their country.

We have before observed, that although it is now admitted by the better-informed Welsh Scholars, that the poems which constitute the " Hanes Taliesin," or romantic history of the Bard, as well as the majority of the other poems attributed to him, were composed in their present form as late as the thirteenth century, it is nevertheless contended that the ideas and traditions embodied in the romance composed by Thomas ap Einion Offeiriad, had previously existed in the form of tales and poems which had already acquired an extensive popularity and circulation, and that from these earlier fragments, the Druidism, philosophy, and superstition, of the Bards of the sixth century, are still capable of being eliminated.

Before entering upon that investigation of the poems which is necessary for deciding on the truth or falsehood of this opinion, we may endeavour to ascertain something of the personal history of Taliesin, from other sources than the romance with which he is connected.

The generally received statement on this point is, that Taliesin lived in the sixth century, and that his principal patron was Urien Rheged, a British chieftain to whose history we shall presently advert. The poems of Taliesin in honour of, or addressed to, this prince and his family, have generally been received as genuine historical documents, contemporary monuments of an age which abounded in bards and heroes of the ancient British race. Yet, upon a review of the historical poems of Taliesin, we are at a loss to discover the grounds of the great reputation which has attached to his name, as Chief Bard of the West, and the most celebrated among the poets of Wales, a reputation which had reached its height in popular estimation as early, certainly, as the middle of the twelfth century.

Taliesin is mentioned in terms of respect, and as an example of Bardic excellence by the poets of that epoch, by Cynddelw, Llywarch ab Llywelyn and Elidir Sais, and in the following century by Philip Brydydd, Davyd Benvras, and Gwilym Ddu. A fragment of a poem attributed to Taliesin, employed as evidence in support of the privileges claimed by the men of Arvon, is found in a MS. copy of the laws of Howel Dda, in a hand-writing, it is said, of the twelfth century. The contents of the historical poems of Taliesin, do not however disclose the reason for the great estimation in which this bard has been held by his countrymen. Supposing him to have flourished in the sixth century, we must adjudge him, as a poet, inferior to his contemporaries, Llywarch Hen and Aneurin, and to the Caledonian Merlin, if the compositions of this latter are also regarded as of the same epoch. The subjects of these poems, admitting them to be genuine, and written at the date of the events to which they allude, are limited in their scope, confined to the description of combats comparatively unimportant, (altogether so, in a national view) and record the deeds of only one family of British chieftains, leaving unsung, events and personages of far greater import-ance and more widely spread reputation.

It is impossible that the great celebrity of Taliesin in the twelfth century, can have been founded solely on the historical poems which have been preserved, and it would seem there-fore that Taliesin must have been the author of poetical works which have not come down to our time, but which were known to, and highly appreciated by, the Bards of the twelfth century, or that his reputation rests less upon his own compositions, than on the fame which attached to his name as a character of romance, a prophet, and magician.

To the first of these suppositions it must be objected, that had other historical poems of Taliesin been in existence in the twelfth century, had his name been employed in rendering famous the names of other chieftains than Urien and his son Owain, some notice of such compositions could not fail to have been preserved.   To the latter view two circumstances appear to give great probability.   The name Tal-iesin, " shining fore-head" is connected with the romance history of the Bard, and was given to him on his miraculous appearance at the fishing weir of Gwyddno Garanhir.   It is more probable that this significant name was invented by the writer of the romance, than that the adventure was composed to account for the origin of the name.

Llywarch ab Llewelyn in the twelfth century, mentions Taliesin in connection with the romance history of the libera-tion of Elphin :[1]—

> Cyvarchaf ym ren cyvarchuawr awen
> Cyvreu kyrridwen rwyf bartoni
> Yn dull Talyesin yn dillwng Elfin
> Yn dyllest bartrin, beirt uannyeri,—

[1] *Myv. Arch.* vol. i. p. 303.

I address my Lord, in eulogistic song,
With the treasures of Ceridwen, ruler of poets,
In the manner of Taliesin, at the liberation of Elphin,
In the fashion of the bardic lore of the leaders of the bards.

Davyd Benvras, in the thirteenth century, refers to Taliesin as a diviner, gifted with supernatural genius, and Gwilym Ddu somewhat later mentions him by his name of Gwion, by which he evidently refers to the romantic history of the bard.[1]

Da fu ffawd y wawd i Wiawn ddewin
Da Fyrddin ai lin o lwyth Meirchiawn,—

Good was the fortunate song of Gwiawn the diviner,
Good was Merddin of the line of the tribe of Meirchiawn.

It would seem from these references, that in the twelfth century, the fame of Taliesin as Chief of Bards, was chiefly connected with the romance attached to his name. It is true that Cynddelw at the same epoch, appears to refer to the Song on the Battle of Argoed Lwyfain, but without connecting the name of Taliesin with that poem. It is very probable, as Mr. Turner has shown, that the last-named poem was in existence in the twelfth century; but there is nothing more than opinion to connect its authorship with Taliesin.

We are necessarily led to the conclusion, that the romance or Mabinogi of Taliesin was in vogue in the twelfth century, and that the present form of that story was compiled from an older romance, in which the name of Taliesin had already become an object of popular admiration. But we have great difficulty in connecting the Taliesin of the romance, with the Bard of Urien Rheged. The scene of the romance is laid in North Wales and in the sixth century, the era of the most celebrated personages of Welsh history and romance. We must not forget that the writers of the Welsh romances were so discordant in their views of the era of Taliesin, that while one Mabinogi makes him a Chief Bard at the court of Arthur,

---

[1] *Myvyr. Arch.* p. 411.

and another places his adventures in the reign of Maelgwn Gwynedd, a third makes him a companion of Bran the Blessed, father of the celebrated Caractacus, who flourished in the first century of the Christian era.

But none of these romances connect the name of Taliesin with Urien Rheged, or the events in which that chieftain played a conspicuous part. This diversity of legendary statements respecting a personage so celebrated, leads to some doubts on his genuine historical character. If the position of Taliesin as the Bard of Urien Rheged was a fact well known to the Welsh, and if his genuine poems in honour of that chieftain had obtained in the eleventh or twelfth century a general acceptation, it is highly improbable that the romancers should have connected him with adventures six centuries earlier in date. But if known as Taliesin the Diviner, who claimed to have been contemporary with Alexander the Great, and to have been with Noah in the Ark, he might well find a place in companionship with the blessed Bran. These considerations lead us to hesitate in admitting the claims of Taliesin as an undoubted historical bard of the sixth century.

It must however be admitted, that the writers of the twelfth and succeeding centuries, though evidently acquainted with the romance history of Taliesin, deal with him as a historical person, and not as the mere creation of a popular fiction. We have moreover, in addition to the evidence to be derived from this general and great reputation which his name had acquired among his countrymen in the twelfth and thirteenth centuries, an independent testimony, which, though also given by a Briton, and most probably by a Briton of Wales, is of the greatest historical value, as having all the character of a legitimate and serious historical statement; though made at least four centuries after the era of Taliesin.

The compiler or transcriber of the genealogies of the Saxon kings, annexed to one copy of the *History of Nennius,* when relating the pedigree of the Deiri, and the wars of the Angles against the British chieftains of Cumbria, mentions Taliesin among the notable Bards who flourished in the time of Ida, about the middle of the sixth century.

" Ida, the son of Eoppa, possessed countries on the left-hand side of Britain, *i.e.*, of the Humbrian Sea, and reigned twelve years, and united Dinguayth Guarth-Berneich. Then Dutigirn, at that time, fought bravely against the nation of the Angles. At that time Talhaiarn Cataguen was famed for poetry, and Neirin, and Taliesin, and Bluchbard, and Cian, who is also called Guenith Guant, were all famous at the same time in British poetry."

On the other hand, we must remark, that the personage whom Geoffrey of Monmouth presents to his readers as the chief Bard and Diviner of the Cymry, is not Taliesin, but Merlin.

Whether Geoffrey were the original author of the *History of the Britons*, or, according to the opinion of the Rev. Rice Rees, the translator of an original Welsh version of the Armorican history, it seems certain that the fame of Taliesin had not, in the early part of the twelfth century, reached the ears of the Archdeacon of Monmouth, though a curious passage in the commencement of the seventh book, shows that the prophecies of Merlin had at that period attracted public attention : " I had not got thus far in my history, when the subject of public discourse happening to be concerning Merlin, I was obliged to publish his prophecies at the request of my acquaintance." It may be, however, that the reputation of Taliesin among his countrymen, was that of a Bard or poet merely, not that of a prophet ; and the public attention was directed to Merlin in the twelfth century, on account of his supposed prophecies respecting the Norman kings.

Still, if the genealogies are true which represent him as a native of South Wales, the absence of all notice by Geoffrey of so famous a character as Taliesin is represented to have been, is, at least, somewhat extraordinary.

According to the genealogies of Taliesin, which have been

published from manuscripts of which the dates are not known,[1] he was the son of Henwg the Bard, otherwise Saint Henwg, of Caerlleon-upon-Usk, and of the College of Saint Cadocus, whose pedigree, as a matter of course, ascends to Bran the Blessed, the father of Caractacus.

It is even said in one manuscript, that Taliesin, Chief of the Bards, erected the church of Llanhenwg, at Caerlleon-upon-Usk, which he dedicated to the memory of his father, called Saint Henwg, who went to Rome on a mission to Constantine the Blessed, requesting that he would send Saints Germanus and Lupus to Britain, to strengthen the faith, and renew baptism there.[2]

In the Triads,[3] Taliesin is named as one of the three baptismal Bards of the Isle of Britain ; Merddin Emrys, and Merddin son of Madoc Morvryn, being the other two ; and in the Iolo MSS., chair president of the nine impulsive stocks of the baptismal Bards of Britain. In the notes to the *History of Taliesin*,[4] it is considered probable that he was educated, or completed his education, at the school of the celebrated Cattwg, at Llanveithin, in Glamorgan. He is reported to have died in Cardiganshire, probably at Bangor Teivy, and tradition has handed down a cairn near Aberystwith as the grave of Taliesin.

Jones, in his *Historical Account of the Welsh Bards*,[5] states " that Taliesin was the master or preceptor of Myrddin ap Morvryn ; he enriched the British prosody with five new metres ; and has transmitted in his poems such vestiges, as throw new light on the history, knowledge, and manners, of the Ancient Britons and their Druids, much of whose mystical learning he imbibed."

As the romance or Mabinogi of Taliesin is supposed to

---

[1] Iolo MSS., and notes to the *Mabinogi* of Taliesin, by Lady Charlotte Guest.

[2] The name of Saint Henwg is not to be found in the lists of Welsh saints in Rees's *Essay ;* and the dedication of the church of Llanhenwg is there attributed to Saint John the Baptist.

[3] Triad, 125.   [4] *Mabinogion*, vol. iii.

[5] Published in 1784.

exhibit in great fulness the Druidical philosophy and doctrine of the metempsychosis, or transmigration of the soul, it is curious to find that a tradition exists which affects to place his early history, and some of the circumstances which have formed the ground-work of the romance, on a reasonable and historical footing.[1]

" Taliesin, Chief of the Bards, the son of Saint Henwg of Caerlleon-upon-Usk, was invited to the court of Urien Rheged, at Aberllychwr. He, with Elphin the son of Urien, being once fishing at sea in a skin coracle, an Irish pirate ship seized him and his coracle, and bore him away towards Ireland; but while the pirates were at the height of their drunken mirth, Taliesin pushed his coracle to the sea, and got into it himself, with a shield in his hand which he found in the ship, and with which he rowed the coracle until it verged the land; but the waves breaking then in wild foam, he lost his hold on the shield, so that he had no alternative but to be driven at the mercy of the sea, in which state he continued for a short time, when the coracle stuck on the point of a pole in the weir of Gwyddno, Lord of Ceredigion, in Aberdyvi; and in that position he was found, at the ebb, by Gwyddno's fishermen, by whom he was interrogated; and when it was ascertained that he was a Bard, and the tutor of Elphin the son of Urien Rheged, the son of Cynvarch, 'I too have a son named Elphin,' said Gwyddno; 'be thou a Bard and teacher to him also, and I will give thee lands in free tenure.' The terms were accepted; and for several successive years, he spent his time between the courts of Urien Rheged and Gwyddno, called Gwyddno Garanhir, Lord of the Lowland Cantred: but after the territory of Gwyddno had become overwhelmed by the sea, Taliesin was invited by the Emperor Arthur to his court at Caerlleon-upon-Usk, where he became highly celebrated for poetic genius, and useful, meritorious sciences.

" After Arthur's death, he retired to the estate given him by

[1] Iolo MSS. p. 158.

Gwyddno, taking Elphin, the son of that prince, under his protection.

"It was from this account that Thomas, the son of Einion Offeiriad,[1] descended from Gruffyd Gwyr, formed his romance of Taliesin the son of Caridwen, Elphin the son of Gwyddno, Rhun the son of Maelgwn Gwynedd, and the operations of the cauldron of Caridwen."

According to another legend, Taliesin having escaped from the ship of the Irish pirates as before described, was extricated from the weir by Elphin, the supposed son of Gwyddno. Elphin was however, in fact, "the son of Elivri, daughter of Gwyddno, but by whom was then quite unknown; it was, however, afterwards discovered that Urien, King of Gower and Aberllychwr, was his father, who introduced him to the court of Arthur at Caerlleon-upon-Usk; where his feats, learning, and endowments, were found to be so superior, that he was created a Golden-tongued Knight of the Round Table. After the death of Arthur, Taliesin became Chief Bard to Urien Rheged, at Aberllychwr in Rheged."

Another legend in the Iolo MSS. states that Talhaiarn, the father of Tangwn, presided in the chair of Urien Rheged, at Caer Gwyroswydd, after the expulsion of the Irish from Gower, Carnwyllion, Cantref Bychan, and the Cantref of Iscennen. The said chair was established at Caer Gwyroswydd, or Ystum Llwynarth, where Urien Rheged was accustomed to hold his national and royal court.

"After the death of Talhaiarn, Taliesin, Chief of the Bards, presided in three chairs: namely, the chair of Caerlleon-upon-Usk; the chair of Rheged at Bangor Teivy, under the patronage of Cedig ab Ceredig ab Cunedda Wledig; but he afterwards was invited to the territory of Gwyddnyw, the son of Gwydion in Arllechwedd, Arvon, where he had lands conferred on him, and where he resided until the time of Maelgwn Gwynedd, when he was dispossessed of that property; for which he pronounced his curses on Maelgwn, and all his pos-

---

[1] The priest.

sessions; whereupon the Vad Velen [1] came to Rhos; and whoever witnessed it became doomed to certain death. Maelgwn
saw the Vad Velen, through the keyhole in Rhos Church, and
died in consequence. Taliesin, in his old age, returned to
Caer Gwyroswydd, to Rhiwallon, the son of Urien; after
which he visited Cedig, the son of Ceredig, the son of Cunedda Wledig, where he died, and was buried with high ho-
nours, such as should always be shown to a man who ranked
among the principal wise men of the Cimbric nation; and
Taliesin, Chief of the Bards, was the highest of the most
exalted class, either in literature, wisdom, the science of vocal
song, or any other attainment, whether sacred or profane.
Thus terminates the information respecting the chief Bards
of the Chair of Caerlleon-upon-Usk, called now, the Chair of
Glamorgan."

Unfortunately, it is impossible to ascertain whether these
legends contain the foundation of the romance, or were written
after the composition of the Mabinogi of Taliesin, by persons
of a neologizing tendency. The only authority given in the
Iolo MSS. is, that the first of the two legends was copied from
Anthony Powel of Llwydarth's MS.; the second from a MS.
at Havod Uchtryd; the last is from the MSS. of Llwelyn
Sion of Llangewydd, who lived at the close of the sixteenth
century.

There is another piece of evidence of the existence of
Taliesin as a Bard in the sixth century, which has been strongly
insisted on by Mr. Sharon Turner and others. This is the
passage in the *Gododin* of Aneurin : [2]—

> Mi na vi Aneurin
> Ys gwyr talyessin
> Oveg Kywrenhin
> Neu cheing e ododin
> Kynn gwawr dyd dilin.

---

[1] A pestilence, called the Yellow Plague, represented as a serpent.
[2] Stanza 45 in edition of the Rev. J. Williams ab Ithel.

In the translation of Mr. Williams :—

> I Aneurin will sing
> What is known to Taliesin,
> Who communicates to me his thoughts
> Or a strain of Gododin
> Before the dawn of the bright day.

Whether this translation be considered correct or no,[2] the occurrence of the name of Taliesin in this, the only poem of early date not attributed to Taliesin himself in which it occurs, is a testimony of considerable weight. Still, the passage in question is not altogether above suspicion.

[2] Without offering any opinion adverse to the general correctness of this translation by a writer who evinces a very intimate acquaintance with his subject and the circle of ancient Welsh literature, we may observe that the difficulty of executing such a translation is evidenced in the stanza above quoted, in which the line

> A dan droet ronin

is translated by Mr. Williams,

> This particle shall go under foot;

that is, says the author in a note, "this treatment I despise; it is beneath my notice; I will regard it as a particle of dust under my feet." The poet is describing his lamentable condition in the earthen house or prison in which he is confined, and says,

> Under my feet is gravel,
> And my knees tied tight.

In the same way the adage, cited by Mr. Williams,

> Nid a gwaew yn ronyn,

which he translates

> Pain will not become a particle,

must be

> A spear will not go into (or pierce) a grain of corn;

importing that the means should be proportioned to the object.

The word *gronyn* is the singular of *grawn*, grains; and there are abundant instances where a singular is put with a plural meaning, and *vice versâ*, on account of the rhyme; or very probably the word may have originally been *graian*, gravel, coarse sand. Villemarqué translates "a ring" from *cron*, round, circular, which agrees very fairly with the context.

According to the view taken by Mr. Williams, the "bedin Ododin," or "troops of Gododin," were, at the battle of Cattraeth, allied with the men of Deira and Bernicia, and opposed to the British chieftains eulogized or lamented by the poet. Aneurin therefore, in the lines above quoted, gives to his poem made in honour of his countrymen, a title taken from the appellation of one, and that certainly the least important of the three hostile tribes engaged in the conflict. How, what Aneurin sung or would sing of the battle of Cattraeth, should be known to Taliesin, or why, the former should state that Taliesin communicated to him his thoughts, or thought with him, no other passage in this poem, or elsewhere, explains.

If the stanza be genuine, and the generally received translation the true one, it must bring down the date of the poem to a time when Taliesin had become sufficiently famous to be introduced with effect into a popular poem.

The difficulty lies in the true correspondence of the first line of the passage with the rest. If it belongs to and concludes the former part,

> And I am manacled
> In the earthen house,
> An iron chain
> Over my two knees;
> Yet of the mead and the horn,
> And of the men of Cattraeth,
> I Aneurin will sing,

this is the reasonable termination of the passage. The remainder will be an independent passage :—

> It is known to Taliesin
> The skilful-minded—.
> Shall there not be a song of the Gododin
> Before the dawn of the fair day?

which may well be a fragment of one of the numerous songs which we know to have been framed on the subject of the battle of Cattraeth, probably at very various dates.[1]

[1] The 93rd stanza was certainly composed after the death of Aneurin. The expression,

A somewhat similar passage occurs at the end of one of the so-called historical poems of Taliesin, the " Anrhec Urien," in which Aneurin is mentioned among the thirteen princes of the North :—

> And one of them was named Aneurin, the panegyrical poet,
> And I myself Taliesin from the banks of Llyn Ceirionydd.

The poem in which these lines occur, is, however, a composition of the twelfth century, or later, and no weight therefore can be attached to the union of the names Aneurin and Taliesin in this quotation.

If we adopt the conclusion, that a Taliesin, a bard of repute, really flourished in the middle of the sixth century, and that the halo of poetic glory which surrounded his memory, pointed him out to the romancers as a fit subject for the exercise of their art, we have still some difficulty in ascertaining the locality of the Bard, or the part of the country under the dominion of the British chieftains, in which he resided and laid the foundation of his fame.

It will be observed that all the genealogies and prose legends relating to Taliesin, describe him as a native of South Wales, and of the celebrated seat of the Arthurian Round Table, Caerlleon-upon-Usk.

Taliesin Williams, in a note on one of the above legends, observes on this, and remarks that " Taliesin's intercourse with Gower (Rheged) and its Reguli, is sufficiently decided by the several poems, addressed by him to those personages. He also wrote in the Gwentian dialect, of which district he was doubtless a native."   In proof of this latter opinion, the editor of the Iolo MSS. actually quotes two lines from the *Cad Goddeu*,—

> Er pan aeth daear ar Aneirin,—
>
> Since the time when the earth went upon Aneirin—

has reference to his death, as may be seen in the corresponding passages in the same poem.

Chwaryeis yn Llychwr
Cysgais yn mhorphor,—

I have played in Loughor;
I have slept in purple;

showing that he, at least, believed the *Cad Goddeu* to have been written by Taliesin in the sixth century. As there are but two persons to whom any poems, referred to Taliesin, are addressed—namely, Urien or Urien Rheged, and Gwallawg or Gwallawg ap Lleenawg—Taliesin Williams must, of course, refer to these.

The period at which Taliesin flourished must, if the poems addressed to Urien Rheged are genuine, be that at which this prince can be ascertained to have lived.

If it were clear that the Urien Rheged of the poems, is the Urien mentioned by the genealogist in Nennius, then the era of Taliesin must be that in which Ida the Angle was carrying on that obstinate and eventful struggle with the British chieftains of the northern and north-western portions of the island, which resulted in the establishment of the great Anglian kingdom of Northumbria.

Conspicuous among the British leaders, as well by his personal valour as by his military skill, was a chieftain named Urien, who is mentioned in the Genealogy of the Kings of the Deiri appended to one MS. of the British History of Nennius. Contemporary with this Urien were three other princes named in the same genealogy, Ryderthen, Gwallauc, and Morcant. "Theodoric, son of Ida, fought bravely, together with his sons, against that Urien."

Ida died in 560. His son Adda, according to Nennius, reigned eight years; Ethelric, son of Adda, four years; Theodoric, son of Ida, seven years. It was while besieging this Theodoric, as it is said, in the island of Lindisfarne, that Urien was treacherously slain by Morcant. This brings the death of Urien down, at the latest, to the year 579; and, as the poems which appear to have been composed by Taliesin speak of that

7

prince as living, it is probable that the Bard himself had not survived his patron.

The territories of this Urien would seem to have been situated in some portion of the Cumbrian region, or the country occupied by the Cumbrian Britons. This region, at the era of Ida's wars, extended from the vale of the Clyde on the north, to the Ribble in Lancashire on the south, having the sea for its western boundary. On the east the territories of the British chieftain had a variable boundary depending on the fortune of war, where it was conterminous with the great Saxon or Anglian kingdoms of Deira and Bernicia, of which the former extended northwards from the Humber to the Tyne, the latter from the Tyne to the Frith of Forth.

That district of the Cumbrian region called Rheged, which in the middle of the sixth century was under the sway of Urien, Sir Francis Palgrave places in the forests of the south of Scotland, " where the floating traditions of Arthur and Merlin have survived the storms of many centuries." As, however, portions of Cumberland retained their independence to a much later period, and as the friends and clansmen of Urien appear, very shortly after his death, to have taken refuge in North Wales, it seems probable that Rheged had a more southerly position. The battle of Cattraeth, the subject of the celebrated poem of Aneurin, the *Gododin*, appears to have been particularly fatal to the clans of Rheged.

In whatever part of the Cumbrian territory Rheged may have been situated, its neighbourhood would appear to have been the seat of war between those Britons with whom Taliesin was connected, and the Anglian chieftains of Deira and Bernicia. The only historical poems properly attributed to Taliesin, relate to battles in which Urien of Rheged was engaged, or refer to that prince, to his son Owain, or to his confederate chieftains.

The only Saxon chief mentioned in these poems, is one who, under the name of " Flamddwyn "—the flame-bearer or incendiary—is supposed, but apparently on no sufficient grounds, to be Ida, the Anglian King of Northumbria.

There is no mention of the personages celebrated in history or tradition as having taken part in the long-continued and obstinate struggle between the Southern, Eastern, and Midland Britons, and the tribes of Jutes and Saxons who incessantly enlarged the Saxon and contracted the British boundary in those regions. Neither Aurelius Ambrosius, nor Uther Pendragon,[1] nor the world-renowned Arthur, nor the battles of Badon, of Salisbury, or of Camlan, find any place in the Bardic eulogies of Taliesin. Yet all these personages, and all these important events, if historical, belong to the period when Taliesin is supposed to have flourished. It is evident that the sympathies of the Bard, and of the tribes with whom he was associated, were engrossed by persons and events different from those connected with the wars of the Britons against the Saxons in the central and southern portions of the island. It is indeed very probable that the Northern Britons knew little of the events occuring in the other parts of Britain.

The want of anything like unity of government, or a central authority, must have tended very greatly to isolate the several British states and prevent anything like common action against the foe. For the story of a succession of Pendragons, or Kings paramount of Britain, from Owain ap Maxen Wledig, down to Cadwallader, is a fiction invented by the compilers of the Triads, and the authors of those histories of which that of Geoffrey of Monmouth is an example. The Unbennaeth Prydain is (though there certainly was a song so called in the tenth century) as visionary as the Imperatorship of Arthur. All the historical facts, from the time of Cæsar downwards, demonstrate the falsity of the assumption.

Such are the views generally entertained of the locality of this celebrated British chieftain, and it seems to be supported by the evidence of the Saxon genealogies in Nennius. But

---

[1] The elegy of Uthyr Pendragon, falsely attributed to Taliesin, is of late date, and not historical.

a most unhappy confusion is introduced into this matter by a series of traditions,[1] which represent this same Urien as the chief of the district of Rheged, in South Wales, being the country between the Tawy and Towy, comprising the territories of Gower, Kidwely, Carnwyllion, Iscennen, and Cantref Bychan ; his royal residence being Aberllychwr,[2] in Gower, where he constructed a strong castle called the Castle of Aberllyw.[3]

According to this tradition, Urien Rheged was King of Rheged in Glamorgan, and of Moray in Scotland. " In the time of the Emperor Arthur, Glaian Ecdwr[4] and his fellow-Irishmen, came to Gower in Glamorgan, where they resided for nine months ; but Arthur sent his nephew, Urien, and 300 men, against them ; and they drove them from there : whereupon the Irish, their king, Glaian Ecdwr, being slain, went to Anglesea, where they remained with their countrymen who had settled there previously. Author bestowed Rheged (so called from the name of a Roman who was lord of that country before it was subdued by the said Glaian and his Irishmen) on Urien, as a royal conquest for his heroic achievements in war.

" Urien Rheged had a daughter named Eliwri, who became the wife of Morgan Morganwg ; and a son called Pasgen, who was a very cruel king, and a great traitor to his country, for

---

[1] Iolo MSS. p. 457.   [2] Lloughor, near Swansea.

[3] The river Llyw falls into the Llychwr near the remains of this old castle. Iolo MSS.

[4] This tradition, published in the Iolo MSS., is of some interest, as it is an instance of a legend which is found in Nennius, adapted to the history of Arthur. Nennius, after describing the colonization of Ireland by Partholanus and Nimech many centuries before the Christian era, says, " Afterwards others came from Spain (i.e. the Milesians of Irish history) and possessed themselves of various parts of Britain. Last of all came one Hoctor (called in other MSS. Damhoctor, Clamhoctor, and Elamhoctor), who continued there, and whose descendants remain there to this day. The sons of Liethali obtained the country of the Dimetæ, where is a city called Menevia, and the province Guoher and Cetgueli (Gower and Kidwelly), which they held till they were expelled from every part of Britain by Cunedda and his sons."

which he was dethroned; and the country of Rheged, because of its original position, was reunited to Glamorgan, in which state it continued to the time of Owen, the son of Howell the Good, the son of Cadell, the son of Rhodri the Great, King of all Wales."

It is difficult to suppose that a chief of North Britain, whose energies were devoted to incessant warfare with the Angles, and who lost his life while engaged in the prosecution of those wars, should, at the same time, have acquired a territory in the very extremity of South Wales. It is, however, evident that all the legends which relate to Taliesin, describe Urien Rheged as of the latter portion of the principality, and also represent his son Rhiwallon as reigning in the same district after him; but they make no mention of the assassination of Urien by Morcant in North Britain, or of the wars of the former against Ida; while the romance history of Taliesin connects him with Maelgwn Gwynedd, Prince of Gwynedd, Venedotia, or North Wales, who fell a victim to the pestilence called "Y mad felen," or the yellow plague, which devastated the principality of Wales, according to the chronology of the Red Book of Hergest, in the year 586.

The French romances of Arthur, introduce Urien, under the name of Sir Urience of Gore, that is, of Gower in Glamorganshire, agreeing in this with the legends above cited. We have, therefore, a double uncertainty introduced by these legends, both as to the person of Urien himself, and as to the situation of his territory. It is evident that the Welsh genealogists and legend-writers placed Rheged in South Wales, and were ignorant of the existence of a kingdom of the same name in Cumbria, or Northern Britain. The derivations which they offer of the word Rheged—in one instance from "rheged," a gift, because the territory was bestowed as a free gift upon Urien, in the other, from the name of a Roman so called— demonstrate the want of any genuine information on the subject in the eleventh and twelfth centuries.

Whatever doubts may rest on the individuality of the

Taliesin of these legends, there seems to be none that the name had acquired a reputation as early as the eleventh century, and that in the twelfth and succeeding centuries it became significant of all that was great and glorious in literature and song.

We have before mentioned, that no less than seventy-seven out of the 124 compositions of the Cynveirdd contained in the Myvyrian Collection, are attributed to Taliesin, and that even down to the present day, many, if not all, of these compositions are cited under this celebrated name as evidence of the learning, the civilization, and the mythology of the Welsh of the sixth century.

There have not, however, been wanting eminent Welsh scholars who have exhibited a sounder judgment on the subject of these poems. Edward Jones, as long ago as 1792,[1] asserted that many of the poems attributed to Taliesin were the productions of the thirteenth and fourteenth centuries. He says that after the dissolution of the princely government in Wales, that is, after the death of Llywelyn ap Gruffyd in 1282, " such was the tyranny exercised by the English over the conquered nation, that the Bards who were born ' since Cambria's fatal day,' might be said to rise under the influence of a baleful and malignant star. They were reduced to possess their sacred art in obscurity and sorrow, and constrained to suppress the indignation that would burst forth in the most animated strains against their ungenerous and cruel oppressors. Yet they were not silent or inactive. That their poetry might breathe with impunity the spirit of their patriotism, they became dark, prophetic, and oracular. As the monks of the Welsh Church, in their controversy with Rome, had written, to countenance their doctrines, several religious poems which they feigned to be the work of Taliesin, the Bards now ascribed many of their political writings to the same venerable author, and produced many others as the prophecies of the elder Merlin. Hence much uncertainty prevails concerning

[1] *Historical Account of the Welsh Bards,* p.21.

the genuine remains of the sixth century, great part of which have descended to us mutilated and depraved; and hence that mysterious air which pervades all the poetry of the later periods I am now describing. The forgery of those poems, which are entirely spurious, though they may have passed unquestioned even by such critics as Dr. Davies and Dr. J. D. Rhys, may, I think, be presently detected. They were written to serve a popular and a temporary purpose, and were not contrived with such sagacity and care, as to hide from the eye of a judicious and enlightened scholar, their historical mistakes, their novelty of language, and their other marks of imposture."

The critical sagacity of Sharon Turner led him, while maintaining the genuineness of the British poems in general, to speak very cautiously on the subject of the poems attributed to Taliesin. "The most important," he says, "are those which concern the battles between the Britons and the Saxons; and these are the poems for whose genuineness I argue."

The poems of Taliesin which Turner asserted to be genuine, are :—

The Poems to Urien, and on his Battles.

His Dialogues with Merddin.

The Poems on Elphin.

His Historical Elegies.

A list which, however, embraces many pieces of a much later date than the sixth century.

Dr. John Jones, a Welshman, who, in 1824, published a History of Wales, spoke very plainly on this subject. "The writings of the Welsh Bards," he says, "are numerous. The largest collection is in the first volume of the *Myvyrian Archæology;* they consist of ingenious trifles, very often on humble topics, and vested in coarse language; and do not include one epic poem. Aneurin, Llywarch Hen, and Taliesin, are said to have flourished in the sixth century; if that was the case, the Muse of Cambria fell dormant for five hundred years, and awoke again in the eleventh century. The times in which these Bards flourished have been matter of great anxiety to antiquarians, who have informed the world, that Llywarch was buried in the church of Llanfor, drawing the inconsistent conclusion, that Taliesin was buried in that church seven hundred years before the building could have been erected. The oldest Welsh MSS. do not recur further than the twelfth century. Merddin treats of the orchard, which had no existence in Wales before the Conquest; Aneurin, Llywarch Hen, Merddin, and Taliesin, make use of the English words, *frank*, *venture*, *banner*, *sorrow*, &c., and introduce the names of places not built, and the names of saints who had not been canonized, in the sixth century."

The Rev. Thomas Price, author of the *Hanes Cymru*, had pointed out some of these poems as spurious. The Rev. Rice Rees also intimates that the Bardic records contain but few authentic materials of history; and that all the poems ascribed to the sixth century are not genuine. "The number of these poems in the *Myvyrian Archæology* is upwards of a hundred; and those which are spurious may be distinguished from the rest by the modern style in which they are written." But no one has undertaken to point out and distinguish the genuine poems of Taliesin from those of a later era, falsely ascribed to that bard, except Mr. Stephens.

"It has long been suspected," says Mr. Stephens,[1] "that many of the poems attributed to Taliesin could not have been produced in the sixth century. These conjectures were undoubtedly correct; but as many of the poems may, upon most substantial grounds, be shown to be genuine, it becomes of importance to distinguish between those which are, and those which may not be, of his production, I have carefully read them; but, as a minute examination of seventy-seven poems would require a volume for itself, we shall here only present the result. The classification, in the absence of the data on which it is based, can have no strong claims to attention, apart from the weight attached to the opinion of the critic. I have, as the result of my examination, classed these poems, thus:—

[1] *Lit. of the Kymry*, p.281.

" Historical, and as old as the Sixth Century.

Gwaith Gwenystrad . . .	The Battle of Gwenystrad.
Gwaith Argoed Llwyvain . .	The Battle of Argoed Llwyvain.
Gwaith Dyffryn Gwarant . .	The Battle of Dyffryn Gwarant (part of the Dyhuddiant Elphin).
I Urien	To Urien.
I Urien	To Urien.
Canu I Urien . . .	A Song to Urien.
Yspail Taliesin . . .	The Spoils of Taliesin.
Canu I Urien Rheged . .	A Song to Urien Rheged.
Dadolwch Urien Rheged . .	Reconciliation to Urien Rheged.
I Gwallawg	To Gwallawg (the Galgacus of Tacitus).
Dadolwch i Urien . . .	Reconciliation to Urien.
Marwnad Owain ap Urien . .	The Elegy of Owain ap Urien.

Doubtful.

Cerdd i Wallawg ab Lleenawg	A Song to Gwallawg ab Lleenawg.
Marwnad Cunedda . . .	The Elegy of Cunedda.
Gwarchan Tutvwlch . .	The Incantation of Tutvwlch.
Gwarchan Adebon . . .	The Incantation of Adebon.
Gwarchan Kynvelyn . .	The Incantation of Kynvelyn.
Gwarchan Maelderw . .	The Incantation of Maelderw.
Kerdd Daronwy . . .	The Song to Daronwy.
Trawsganu Cynan Garwyn .	The Satire on Cynan Garwyn.

Romances belonging to the Twelfth and Thirteenth Centuries.

Canu Kyntaf Taliesin . .	Taliesin's First Song.
Dyhuddiant Elphin . .	The Consolation of Elphin.
Hanes Taliesin . . .	The History of Taliesin.
Canu y Medd . . .	The Mead Song.
Canu y Gwynt . . .	The Song to the Wind.
Canu y Byd Mawr . .	The Song of the Great World.
Canu y Byd Bychan . .	The Song of the Little World.
Bustl y Beirdd . . .	The Gall of the Bards.
Buarth Beirdd . . .	The Circle of the Bards.
Cad Goddeu	The Battle of the Trees.
Cadeir Taliesin . . .	The Chair of Taliesin.
Cadeir Teyrnon . . .	The Chair of the Princes.
Canu y Cwrwf . . .	The Song of the Ale.
Canu y Meirch . . .	The Song of the Horses.
Addfwyneu Taliesin . .	The Beautiful Things of Taliesin.
Angar Kyvyndawd . .	The Inimical Confederacy.
Priv Gyvarch . . .	The Primary Gratulation.

S

Dyhuddiant Elphin (2nd) . .	The Consolation of Elphin.
Arymes Dydd Brawd . . .	The Prophecy of the Day of Judgment.
Awdl Vraith	The Ode of Varieties.
Glaswawd Taliesin . . .	The Encomiums of Taliesin.
Divregwawd Taliesin . .	Poesy of Taliesin.
Mabgyvreu Taliesin . . .	Taliesin's Juvenile Accomplishments.
Awdl etto Taliesin . . .	Another Ode by Taliesin.
Kyffes Taliesin	The Confession of Taliesin.

POEMS *forming part of the* MABINOGION, *or* ROMANCE *of* TALIESIN, *composed by* THOMAS *ap* EINION *Offeiriad in the Thirteenth Century.*

Cadair Keridwen	The Chair of Keridwen.
Marwnad Uthyr Bendragon . .	The Elegy of Uther Pendragon.
Preiddeu Annwn	The Spoils of Annwn.
Marwnad Ercwlf	The Elegy of Ercwlf.
Marwnad Mad Drud ac Erov Greu-lawn	The Elegy of Madoc the Bold, and Erov the Fierce.
Marwnad Aeddon o Von . .	The Elegy of Aeddon of Mon.
Anrhyveddodau Alexander . .	The Not-wonders of Alexander.
Y Gofeisws Byd	A Sketch of the World.
Lluryg Alexander	The Lorica of Alexander,

Predictive Poems of the Twelfth and succeeding Centuries.

Ymarwar Lludd Mawr . . .	The Appeasing Lludd the Great.
Ymarwar Lludd Bychan . .	The Appeasing of Lludd the Little.
Gwawd Lludd Mawr . . .	The Praise of Lludd the Great.
Kerdd am Veib Llyr . . .	Song to the Sons of Llyr ab Brochwel.
Marwnad Corroi ab Dairy . .	The Elegy of Corroi the Son of Dairy.
Mic Dinbych (or Myg Dinbych) .	The Glory of Dinbych.
Arymes Brydain	The Prophecy of Britain.
Arymes	Prophecy.
Arymes	Prophecy.
Kywrysedd Gwynedd a Deheubarth .	The Contention of North and South
Awdl	An Ode. [Wales.
Marwnad y Milveib . . .	Elegy of the Thousand Saints.
Y Maen Gwyrth . . .	The Miraculous Stone.
Can y Gwynt	The Song of the Wind.
Anrhec Urien	The Gift of Urien.

Theological—same date.

Plaeu yr Aipht	The Plagues of Egypt.
Llath Moesen	The Rod of Moses.
Llath Voesen	The Rod of Moses.
Gwawd Gwyr Israel . . .	Eulogy of the Men of Israel."

The result of the investigation of Mr. Stephens is to assign
with certainty, to the sixth century, twelve only out of the
seventy-seven poems bearing the name of Taliesin, and to place
eight others doubtfully as belonging to the same era. It will
be seen that even this expurgated list must be still farther
curtailed.

In the Notes to the Iolo MSS.[1] the *Hanes Taliesin* is declared to be " an evidently fictitious poem, attributed until
recently to Taliesin ; and still passing current as his production, with general readers. But," says the editor of the MSS.,
Taliesin Williams, the son of Edward Williams, or Iolo Morganwg, who collected them, " to rescue the genuine fame of
the chief Bard of the West from the annihilation of such as
have lately denied the originality of his works, and would fain
even pronounce his very existence a romance, it is high time to
divest his compositions of the spurious productions commixed
with them : productions that are characterised by comparatively modern expressions and idioms, and (like other similar
deceptions) by their anachronisms, and other denouncing in-
congruities. Nor would this expurgation materially affect the
literary remains of this remote votary of the Cimbric Muse ;
for his numerous and genuine poems, being intrinsically sustained by consistency of allusions, primitive features of versification, and originality of sentiment, would still extensively
vindicate the palm so long conceded to his hoary merit. Iolo
Morganwg, in his manuscript compositions, frequently laments
the injurious effects of the counterfeit pieces ;[2] and the Rev.
Thomas Price, whose *Hanes Cymru* (History of Wales) ably
supplies the desideratum heretofore so long the object of hope,
impugns, occasionally, their originality."

[1] Eng. Transl. p. 335, *note*.

[2] When Taliesin Williams wrote this paragraph, he had forgotten that his
father, Iolo Morganwg, had stated in his essay on the Barddas, printed in the
2nd vol. of his *Poems, Lyric and Pastoral*, " that the poems of Taliesin in
the sixth century exhibit a complete system of Druidism," not hinting for a
moment that he considered any of the poems attributed to that bard to be
counterfeit or spurious.

It would have been satisfactory if Iolo Morganwg or his editor, had pointed out these numerous and genuine poems of Taliesin, and the evidences of their originality. All the evidence at present before us shows that there is not extant a single poem or metrical composition in the Welsh language, with the exception of the lines from the copy of Juvencus before mentioned, the manuscript of which is older than the twelfth century. For the proof of an earlier date of the compositions themselves, we have only such internal evidence as they may afford.

And in this statement the works of Aneurin and Llywarch Hen must be included with those of Taliesin. The materials of these compositions may have, no doubt, and in all probability did exist, perhaps for some centuries before, in the mouths of the professional minstrels and storytellers; but there is no evidence that they were reduced into writing at an earlier period than the twelfth century. Zeuss[1] is of opinion that all the extant poems have been transcribed in a modern orthography, in many instances by persons unacquainted with the meaning of the older forms, and that, in consequence, they have, in the undergoing this change of form, suffered considerable alteration and interpolation, and we have sufficient proof in the Myvyrian Collection, that poems which were written in the Llyvr Ddu, in the twelfth century, were transcribed at a later period in a more modern orthography; but we can go no farther back than the former manuscript.

That the form in which these compositions now appear in the oldest MSS. is not that in which they originally existed, if written in the sixth or seventh century, is too clear for discussion.

It is, however, supposed that these poems, though worked up and brought into their present form by writers or Bards of the twelfth and thirteenth centuries, contain materials of far more ancient date, and were, in fact, originally composed in the sixth century.

---

[1] *Grammatica Celtica*, vol. ii. p. 950.

So little importance has indeed been attached to the critical views of Mr. Stephens by his countrymen, and so little effect has his work published in 1849 produced upon this question of the antiquity and nature of the Welsh poems, that the old opinion, that they contain philosophical dogmas, and notices of Druid or Pagan superstitions of a remote origin, has been as distinctly promulgated in 1853, by the chairman of the society which adjudged the prize to Mr. Stephens's Essay in 1848, as they were by the Rev. Edward Davies in 1809. In truth, as Mr. Stephens has himself observed, any opinion on the date or character of these poems, unaccompanied by translations, has no very strong claims to attention, apart from the weight attached to the opinion of the critic.

It is somewhat remarkable, that these remains of the earliest Welsh literature, and especially the poems attributed to Taliesin, so constantly appealed to, and cited in evidence, not only for the history and condition of the Welsh, at the period during which he flourished, but also for the verification of traditions of a much earlier period, have never been translated *in extenso,* by the learned Welshmen who rely on his authority. Isolated pieces and fragments in abundance, have appeared, but a complete edition of these works in a language which would make them common property, has never been ventured.

In 1792, Dr. Owen advertised the *Works of Taliesin*, with a literal English version and notes, but the work never appeared.

The reason assigned for this apparent neglect has been, that the language in which they are written is obsolete, and that they are filled with mystical and mythological allusions which are no longer intelligible.

But the best authorities on this subject are agreed that no insuperable difficulty of this kind exists. This was asserted nearly sixty years ago by the editors of the *Myvyrian Archæology*. "These ancient poems," they state, in a *Review*

of the Present State of Welsh Manuscripts,[1] " have for ages
been secluded from the eyes of the public; and some of the
collections very difficult of access.   Very mistaken ideas of
them have for a long time circulated through every part of
Wales;   there are consequently preconceptions from which
many will too rashly criticise; but a long course of study is
absolutely necessary to understand them properly.   Facts of
which no other records remain are often alluded to; opinions
that are forgotten, manners that no longer exist, idioms and
figurative modes of expression that are obsolete and obscured
by various schemes of orthography, arising from the in-
adequacy of the Roman alphabet to represent the ancient
British one, render many passages almost unintelligible to
novices.   It is not from a supposed loss or corruption of our
language, that they are difficultly understood: they contain
very few, if any words, either radicals or derivations, that are
not at this day in common use in one part or other of Wales;
nor have any of those words materially changed their acceptation.   Our language, as some have imagined, is not altered;
it is therefore to be regretted that the Rev. Evan Evans did
not, in his *Dissertatio de Bardis,* investigate and point out the
various things which embarrassed him, instead of assigning
all the difficulties to the language.   In many of the illusions,
indeed, they are dark; mutilations are occasionally met with,
out of the question, which equally confuse in every age, the
present as well as the past, and are matters, not of language,
but of accident."

Archdeacon Williams, though he maintains that a great
orthographical change had taken place in the interval between
the eighth and twelfth century (as would necessarily be the
case), admits that " restoration and interpretation of all the
more valuable portion of the ancient poems is possible, without any further discovery, as instruments sufficient for that
purpose are within our reach."[2]

[1] *Myvyr. Archæol.* vol. i. p. xviii.   London, 1801.
[2] *Gomer,* part ii. p. 17.

Mr. Stephens, also, has recorded his opinion,[1] that as to the majority of the poems attributed to Taliesin, " though many of them contain allusions which are now unintelligible, yet a large portion of them and the intentions of the whole may be understood. They were written when the language was in an advanced state of development, as most of the words are in use at the present day; and as will be seen, cannot be supposed to have been prior to the twelfth and succeeding centuries."[2]

In fact, the result has been, as far as Taliesin is concerned, whenever any of these poems have been fairly translated, to cut down their claims to antiquity, and gradually to strip their reputed author, leaf after leaf, of the laurels assigned to him by the partial voice of his countrymen; and this may, in some degree, account for the want of any general translation of these works.

This has been eminently the case with another celebrated Bard, said to be of the sixth century—Merlin or Merddin. Translations of the most important pieces attributed to this Bard, the *Avellanau*, and the *Hoianau*, have been published by Mr. Stephens in his *Literature of the Kymry*. From these translations we are enabled to decide, not only that there is a total absence of all these mysterious allegories which have been supposed to enshroud fearful superstitions and Druidic oracles, but also that they contain allusions to personages and events belonging to the eleventh and twelfth centuries. The fourth stanza of the *Hoianau* is decisive as to the date of the

---

[1] *Literature of the Kymry.*

[2] A proposal to publish, by subscription, an English Translation of the *Myvyrian Archæology*, including those Bardic remains of the older British poets which present most interesting materials calculated to throw light upon the history, the manners, the literature, the philosophy, and the mythology of our British ancestors, was advertised by the Rev. J. Williams, Archdeacon of Cardigan, as long ago as 1840; but up to the present time it has not appeared. What such a translation would have been, may be inferred from the late publication of the Archdeacon—*Gomer; a Brief Analysis of the Language and Knowledge of the Ancient Cymry.* London, 1854.

composition being, at least, as late as the end of the twelfth
century:—

> Hear, O little pig! it was necessary to pray
> For fear of five chiefs from Normandy;
> And the fifth going across the salt sea,
> To conquer Ireland of gentle towns,
> There to create war and confusion,
> And a fighting of son against father—the country knows it;
> Also will be going the Loegrians of falling cities,
> And they will never go back to Normandy.

This stanza, Mr. Stephens observes, clearly refers to the conquest of Leinster by Richard Strongbow, who went to Ireland
A.D. 1170. He was the *fifth* Norman, having been preceded
by *four* others—Robert Fitzstephens, Maurice Fitzgerald, Hervé
de Montmarais, and David Barry. Even if this were not apparent, the two last lines could not have been written before
A.D. 1066, unless we really believe the Cambrian Bard to have
been actually gifted with the spirit of prophecy.

The other Bard of the sixth century is Aneurin. The
famous poem which passes under his name, *Y Gododin*, has
recently been carefully translated by the Rev. John Williams
ab Ithel.[1]

An excellent translation of the *Gododin*, of some of the
compositions of Llywarch Hen, and of the historical pieces
ascribed to Taliesin, was published by M. de la Villemarqué,[2]
who has paid great attention to the traditional remains of the
ancient Armorican nation still preserved among the peasantry
of Bretagne.

This celebrated poem, the *Gododin*, so unintelligible in the
tradition of Davies, and by him and Mr. Herbert supposed
to relate to the massacre of the British chiefs by Hengist at

---

[1] *Y Gododin:* a Poem of the Battle of Cattraeth, by Aneurin, a Welsh
Bard of the sixth century, with an English translation, and numerous His-
torical and Critical Notes, by the Rev. John Williams ab Ithel, M.A.
Llandovery, 1852.

[2] *Poëmes des Bardes Bretons du 6e Siècle,* par M. Hersart de la Villemarqué. Paris, 1850.

Stonehenge, is now known to describe a combat between the Strathclyde Britons and the Saxons of Deira and Bernicia, north of the Humber, the date of which Mr. Williams places at about A.D. 567. It contains no Druidism, and its author was a Christian.

> The heroes marched to Cattraeth, loquacious was the host,
> Blue mead was their liquor, and it proved their poison.
> In marshalled array they cut through the engines of war;
> And after the joyful cry, silence ensued.
> They should have gone to Churches to have performed penance;
> The inevitable strife of death was about to pierce them.[1]

Again,—

> They put to death Gelorwydd with blades.
> The Gem of Baptism was thus widely taunted;
> Better that you should ere you join your kindred
> Have a gory unction, and death far from your native home.[2]

We certainly could not, *primá facie*, expect to find any other than Christian allusions in poems of this age. For, whatever may be thought of the story of the introduction of Christianity into Britain by Bran the Blessed, the father of Caractacus, by Joseph of Arimathea, or by Aristobulus, in the first century of the Christian era, there is no doubt that in the sixth century, the period when the authors of these poems are supposed to have flourished, the Christian religion was firmly established in Wales. Saint David, apart from the monkish legends and absurd fables connected with his name, has every claim to be considered a historical character, and his era is precisely that of Taliesin. There is hardly a piece in the collection of the *Myvyrian Archæology* which does not bear direct testimony to the fact of the writer having been a Christian, and that the persons to whom these poems were addressed were Christians also. Such arguments, however, are of little weight in the opinions of those who maintain that the Druidical doctrines to be found in these poems were cherished in secret, as esoteric,

---

[1] Stanza 8. [2] Stanza 12.

and carefully hidden from the eye of the people at large, though known to and acknowledged by the select initiated among the higher classes. A little reflection will teach us that it was impossible any such doctrines could have been kept secret through a course of ages, and remain unnoticed by the Christian authorities, or by such writers as Giraldus Cambrensis, who was evidently ignorant of any such heresy existing in the bosom of the community over which he presided, unless we are to consider him, in common with every other writer, equally bound to secrecy as a member of the institution.

While on the subject of the *Gododin*, we ought not to omit to mention, that there is a still later translation of this poem, which shows it to be " an Aramitic composition which purports to have been delivered orally at a school meeting in Wilts, at some period before the Christian era," principally composed of a Treatise on the Game of Chess. At the 322nd line we have,—

> The game of chess. It rains
> Out of doors; let chess spread relaxation.

Afterwards, line 332,—

> Here's the game of chess, the game
> Of ivory troops in four squads.
> The Indian game with care consider,
> Chief game celebrated afar among the Anakim.

It is satisfactory to be informed from the *Gododin*, line 251,—

> There was a Chinese hero Sk-m-sk Kon Caph,
> First of bard chiefs, after the genius of the Britons.

and that

> The fat Chinese heroes have skill to find out little marks.

We have here also veritable Druids who have informed us what the Gododin really is; line 474,—

> " Lech " is joined. Here's " la." La is weary.
> What is " Gododin,"
> What? A trifle to Cherubim.

It may be so; but, as we are afterwards told, line 515,—

> Cast at it quickly. Give it up! Turn it over.
> Consider! Risk! Hurry on! Stand Still! Go back!
> A pleasant game of games.

We must say, we prefer giving it up.[1]

As a preliminary to the examination of these poems, we may present an example of one of these compositions, which was, no doubt, recited to delight audiences by vagrant minstrels many years before it was reduced to writing in the fourteenth century. It is certainly one of the most corrupt examples of its class, but is not singular in the mixture of topics contained in it, and enables us to appreciate the condition in which many of these pieces have come down to us.

PRIF GYFARCH TALIESIN.

Prif gyfarch gelvyd par ryleat	Y mynyd Fuaun
Puy Kyntac tyuyll ac goleuat	Yssit Gaer Gwarthawn
Neu adaf pan vu pa dyd y great	A dan don eigiawn
Neu y dan tylwet py ry Seilyat	Gorith gyvarchawr
A vo Lleion nys myn pwyllyat	Puy enw y Porthawr
Est qui peccator am nivereit	Pwy y periglawr
Collant gulad nef vy pluyf Offeirycit.	Y vab Meir mwynvawr
Boreu neb ni del	Pa vessur muynaf
Or ganon teir pel	A orug Adaf
Eingngyl gallwydel	Puy vessur Uffern
Gunaont eu ryvel	Puy tuet y llen
Pan dau nos a dyd	Puy llet y gencu
Pan vyd lluyd Eryr	Puy meint eu mein heu
Pan yw tyuyll nos	Neu vlaen gwydd ffalsum
Pan iu guyrd llinos	Py estung mor grum
Mor pan dyverwyd	Neu pet anat llon
Cud anys guelyd	Yssyd yn eu bon
Yssit teir ffynnaun	Neu leu a gwydion

[1] *Ancient Oral Records of the Cimri or Britons in Asia and Europe, recovered through a literal Aramitic Translation of the Old Welsh Bardic Relics.* By G. D. Barber, A.M., author of *Suggestions on the Ancient Britons.* London, 1855.

The same writer has translated the *Hoianau* of Merlin, and finds it to contain an account of the Institution of the Order of the Garter by the Ken or Britons, at their original site near Lake Van and the sources of the Zab, in Asia Minor, long before the Christian era.

A vuant gelvydou
Neu a rodant lyvyryou
Pan wnant
Pan dau nos a lliant
Pan vyd y diviant
Cud anos rac dyd
Pater Noster ambulo
Gentis tonans in adjuvando
Sibilem signum
Ro gentes fortium
Am gwiw gwiwam gwmyd
Am geissyant deu Gelvydd
Am Kaer Kerindau Kerindydd
Rys tyneirch *pector* Dauyd
Y mwyngant ys ewant
Ym Kaffwynt yn dirdan
Kymry yggridvan
Provater eneit
Rac Lluyth cissyflleit
Kymry prif diryeit
Rann ry goll buyeit
Gwaedd hir uehencit
As guyar honneit
Dydoent guarthvor
Gwydveirch dyarvor
Eingyl yghygvor
Guelattor aruyddion
Guynyeith ar Saesson
Claudus in Sion
O ruyvannussion
Bydaut penn Seiron
Rac ffichit lewon
Marini Brython
Ryd a roganon
A medi heon
Am Hafren Avon
Lladyr ffadyr Ken a Massuy
Ffis amala ffur ffir Sel
Dyrnedi trinet tramoed
Creaudyr oro hai——huai
Gentil divlannai gyspell
Codigni ceta gosgord mur
Gan nath ben gan Govannon
Corvu . . . . . dur

Neu bum gan vyr Kelydon
Gan Vatheu gan Govannon
Gan Eunyd gan Elestron
Ry ganhymdeith achuysson
Bluydyn yg Kaer Govannon
Wyf hen wyf neuyd wyf guion
Wyf lluyr wyf synwyr Keinyon
Dy gy vi dyheu vrython
Guydyl Kyl diaerogyon
Meddut medduon
Wyf bardd wyf ny rivaf yeillyou
Wyf llyu wyf syu amrysson
Sihei a rahei nys medry
Si ffradyr yn y ffradri
Pos Verdein bronrhein a dyvi
A ddeuont uch medlestri
A ganont gam vardoni
A geissent gyvaruys nys deubi
Heb gyvreith heb reith heb rodi
A guedy hynny dyvysgi
Brithvyt a byt dyoysei
Nac eruyn dy hedduch nyth vi
Reen nef rymavyr dy wedi
Rac y gres rym guares dy voli
Ri Rex gle am gogyvarch yn gelvyd
A ueleisty Dominus ffortis
Darogan dwfn Domini
Budyant Uffern
Hic nemor i por progenii
Ef a dyllyngys ei thuryf
Dominus virtietum
Kaeth naut Kynhulluys estis iste——est
(Est) a chyn buassun a simsei
Ruyf deruin y duu diheu
A chyn mynnuyf dervyn creu
A chyn del ewyn friw ar uyggeneu
A chyn vyg Kyvalle ar y llatheu preu
Poet ym hencit yd a Kyvadeu
Abreid om dyweit llythyr llyvreu
Kystud dygyn guedy guely aghen
Ar saul a gigleu vy mardlyfreu
Ry bryn huynt wlat Nef adef goreu
Ry prynwynt, &c.

Diwedd y Prif Gyr.

THE "FFRIF GYFARCH," OR FIRST ADDRESS OF TALIESIN.

First tell the secret you who are in the superior place,
What was before darkness and light?
Or of Adam, where was he the day he was created?
Or what could he see in the darkness?
Or was he, like a stone, without intellect?
Est qui peccator, innumerable,
The ministers of my people lose the kingdom of heaven.
In the morning let nobody come
Within three cannon balls
Of the Irish of Eingyngl
Who are making a disturbance.
Whence are night and day distinct?
Whence is the eagle grey?
Whence is the night dark?
Whence is the linnet green?
Whence is the boiling up of the sea?
Hidden and not exposed.
Is it the three fountains
In the mountain of Fuawn?
Is it Caer Gwarthawn
Under the wave of the ocean?
The illusive questioner.
What is the name of the porter?
Who is the priest?
The very kind son of Mary.
What is the greatest measure
That Adam made?
What is the measure of Hell?
How thick its covering?
How wide its jaws?
How many its stones?
Was not the measuring rod false?
What is the extent of the raging sea,
Or what kind of creatures
Are at the bottom of it?
Neither Lleu nor Gwydion,
And they were wise,
Nor do books inform
How they are made.
Whence come night and dawn,
Whither the earth is moving on slowly,
The hiding-place of night before day.

Pater noster ambulo
Gentis tonans in adjuvando
Sibilem signum
Ro gentes fortium.
To the worthy, the worthy is a companion.
They ask me two secrets
Concerning Caer Kerindydd.
Very gentle was the breast of Davyd,
In gentle song his pleasure,
They seek after thy song,
The Cymry in their grief,
It is profitable to the soul.
On account of the poverty of the land,
The chief misfortune of the Cymry,
On account of the loss of food,
Long is the cry of sorrow.
There is blood upon the spears.
The waves are bearing
Ships upon the sea.
Angles, the sea-rovers
Displaying their banners,
The false tongue of the Saxon
Claudus in Sion
From the rulers.
They shall be the chief workmen
Before twenty chiefs.
Marini Brython
Are prophesying
A reaping of the ripe crop
By the river Severn.
Slain is the father of Ken and Massuy,
Ffiis amala ffur fir sel,
It is impossible to comprehend the Trinity.
I pray to the Creator, hai—huai,
The Gentiles may be illuminated by the Gospel,
Equally worthy of the great assembly.
Have I not been with the wise Kelydon,
With Math and with Elestron,
Accompanying them with great labour
A year in Caer Govannon,
I am old, I am young, I am Gwion;
I am a soldier, I am knowing in feasts;
I am equal to the Southern Britons.
The Irish distil from a furnace

Intoxicating liquor.
I am a bard, I have an abundance of melodies ;
I am a scholar, I am constant in (musical) contests ;
In . . . . . there is none more accomplished.
Si frater in fratri.
Broad-chested rhyming bards there are,
And they prophesy over bowls of mead,
And sing evil songs,
And seek gifts which they will not get
Without law, without justice, without gifts ;
And after this there will be a tumult,
There will be quarrelling and confusion.
I am not opposed to thy peace,
Lord of Heaven, I seek thee in prayer,
Through grace it is pleasant to me to praise thee.
Ri rex . . . I am worshipping thee in secret.
Who has seen Dominus fortis ?
(Who can) relate the deep things of the Lord ?
They have been victorious over Hell.
Hic nemor i por progenii.
He hath set free its multitudes.
Dominus virtictum,
He is the protector of the assembled captives.
And before I had been . . . .
I was actively travelling in the southern parts ;
And before I cease from active motion,
And before my face becomes pale,
And before I am joined to the wooden boards,
May there be to me a good festival in my lifetime.
I have scarcely finished the letters of my book.
There will be sore affliction after the sleep of death.
And whosoever has heard my bardic books
Shall surely obtain the most blessed mansions of the land of Heaven.

End of the Prif Gyvarch.

This remarkable farrago has apparently been the property of some of the vagrant monks, with whom, previous to the Reformation, Wales swarmed almost equally with the vagrant minstrels or bards, of whom they were at once the rivals and bitter enemies. The Bardic poets abundantly repay the scorn and hatred exhibited for them by the ecclesiastics.

The poem, in its present condition, is evidently made up of several unconnected fragments, as is indeed the case with most others in the Myvyrian Collection. Though this condition of the oldest Welsh compositions may be in some measure ascribed to their having been subjects of oral recitation long before they were committed to writing, it is probable that in many instances it represents, though imperfectly, the original condition of the ballad, arising out of the customs of the Welsh minstrels.

In the great musical contests of the earlier and better age of Welsh minstrelsy, the competitors were obliged each to produce a composition of his own, and the prize was awarded to the successful candidate. According to the laws of Gruffyd ap Cynan,[1] " When the congress hath assembled, they shall choose twelve persons skilled in the Welsh language, poetry, music, and heraldry, who shall give to the Bards a subject to sing upon, in any of the twenty-four metres; but not in amœbean carols, or any such frivolous compositions. The umpires shall see that the candidates do not descend to satire or personal invective; and shall allow to each a sufficient time for composing his Englyn or Cywydd, or other task that they shall assign."

In less dignified stations, the practice of contesting by the recitation of known compositions, or the production of extempore verses, appears to have been a favourite and universal pastime.

" 'Two clerwyr" (or wandering minstrels), says Dr. Rhys,[2] " were wont to stand before the company, the one to give in rime at the other extempore, to stirre mirth and laughter with wittie quibbes," &c.

Something of the same kind also took place even on more important occasions, and in the presence of dignified personages, when a kind of saturnalia was permitted. At such

[1] Jones's *History of the Welsh Bards*, p. 16.
[2] *Cambrobrytannicæ Cymraecæve Linguæ Institutiones Accuratæ.* London, 1592.

times, and especially at the marriage of a prince, or any person of princely extraction, the higher and lower orders of Bards intermingled in the appointment of a *Cyff Cler*, a "butt" or object on whom the rest exercised their talent of ridicule. A year and a day before the celebration of the nuptials, notice was given to a Pencerdd to prepare himself to support that character. When the time came he appeared in the hall, and, a facetious subject being proposed, the inferior Bards surrounded him, and attacked him with their ridicule. In these extempore satirical effusions, they were restrained from any personal allusion or real affront. The Cyff Cler sat in a chair in the midst of them, and silently suffered them to say whatever they chose, that could tend to the diversion of the assembly. For this unpleasing service he received a considerable fee. The next day he appeared again in the hall, and answered his revilers, and provoked the laughter and gained the applause of all who were present, by exposing them in their turn, retorting all their ridicule upon themselves.

Of this custom we have a curious notice in a piece called the *Buarth Beirdd*, "the Fold or Enclosure of the Bards," in which the minstrel, among other self-commendations, says,—

Wyf bardd Neuodd wyf Kyv Kadeir,
Digonaf i feirdd llafar llestair,—

I am the Bard of the Hall, I am the Cyff of the Chair;
I am able to stop the tongues of the Bards.

In Pennant's time this species of musical contest, though the subjects of song had somewhat degenerated, was in full activity in Wales. "Even at this day," he observes, "some vein of the ancient minstrelsy survives amongst our mountains. Numbers of persons of both sexes assemble and sit around the harp, singing alternately pennillon or stanzas of ancient or modern composition. Often, like the modern *improvisatori* of Italy, they sing extempore verses, and a person conversant in this art readily produces a pennill opposite to the last that was sung."

10

"Many have their memories stored with several hundreds, perhaps thousands, of pennillion, some of which they have always ready for answers to every subject that can be proposed; or, if their recollection should ever fail them, they have invention to compose something pertinent and proper for the occasion."

This is, no doubt, the key to the condition of many of those pieces which contain apparently unconnected fragments, and to the kind of question and answer which they frequently exhibit.

An example of the somewhat hasty manner in which a remote antiquity has been ascribed to some of the compositions in the Welsh language, which have been preserved in the Red Book of Hergest or other MSS. of that age, will not be out of place here.

There is in the *Myvyrian Archæology* a piece containing the following stanzas composed in the metre called "Triban Milwr." Three of these were given by the Rev. Evan Evans, in a paper published in the *Cambro-Briton* in 1820, as the genuine production of the Druids. In 1853 the Ven. Archdeacon Williams, speaking of this same metre, says, "There is every reason to believe that this was the medium through which the instruction of the Druids was generally conveyed to the initiated. Hence we have monitory stanzas, and hints conveyed in symbols respecting the observation of secrecy, with respect to 'guid,' whether knowledge of wood or trees. It is impossible to fix the relative antiquity of such stanzas as these":—

1.

Marchwiail bedw briglas
A dyn fy nhroed o wanas
Nac addef dy rin i was

2.

Marchwiail derw mewn llwyn
A dyn fy nhroed o gadwyn
Nac addef dy rin i forwyn.

3.

Marchwiail derw deiliar
A dyn fy nhroed o garchar
Nac addef dy rin i lafar.

4.

Eurtirn ai cirn ai clwir
Oer lluric lluchedic awir
Bir diwedit blaen guit gwir.

Translation :—

1.

Saplings of the green-topped birch,
Which will draw my foot from the
    fetter.
Repeat not thy secret to a youth.

2.

Saplings of the oak in the grove,
Which will draw my foot from the
    chain,
Repeat not thy secret to a maiden.

3.

Saplings of the leafy oak,
Which will draw my foot from prison,
Repeat not thy secret to a babbler.

4.

Golden princes with their horns are
    heard,
Cold is the breastplate, full of light-
    ning the air,
Briefly it is said; true are the tree-
    sprigs.

It at once occurs, on reading these stanzas, that we have here a specimen of that triadic form of composition, so frequently met with in the productions of the Welsh, wherein of a stanza of three lines, the last is a proverbial phrase or moral maxim, having no necessary connection with the two preceding lines.

Mr. E. Davies, however, regarded them as "the oldest remains of the Welsh language, and as genuine relics of the Druidical ages." Mr. Williams, we have seen, follows in the same track.

But, on turning to the original piece in the *Myvyrian Archæology*,[1] we find that there are no less than fifty-two of these stanzas, and are at a loss to know why the Ven. Archdeacon, who refers to the *Myvyrian Archæology*, has selected the 8th, 9th, 10th, and 26th stanzas, omitting the 11th, which clearly is in the same category with the three former. It is this :—

    Marchwiail drysi a mwyar arni
    A mwyalch ar ei nyth
    A chelwyddawg ni theu byth,—

    Saplings of the thorn with berries on it,
    The blackbird is on her nest ;
    The liar will not be silent.

[1] Vol. i. page 129.

Or the next :—

> Gwlaw allan gwlychyd rhedyn
> Gwyn gro mor goron ewyn
> Tecav canwyll pwyll i dyn,—
>
> There is rain without, wetting the fern ;
> White is the sand of the sea with its crown of foam ;
> Reason is the fairest light of man.

Or the seventh, the one which precedes those selected :—

> Hir nos gorddyar morva
> Gnawd tervysg yn nghymmynva
> Ni chyvyd diriaid a da,—
>
> Long is the night, roaring the seashore :
> Usual is a disturbance in an assembly ;
> The evil with good do not agree.

Or, indeed, any other of the series.

It may be difficult to fix the age of these and similar stanzas, though not in the sense meant by the Rev. J. Williams. We find, in fact, that the editors of the *Myvyrian Archæology* ascribe these "Tribanau" to Llywarch Hen, the famous warrior Bard of the sixth century ; and Dr. Owen has given a translation of twelve of them in his *Heroic Elegies* of that Bard. They are precisely similar in form and character to the *Gorwynion*, attributed to the same poet, and may be of any age down to the time when they were written in the Red Book of Hergest. In fact, the stanzas commencing "Marchwiail," &c., are said to have been composed in the fourteenth century, or in the reign of King Edward III.

In the Iolo MSS. published by the Welsh MSS. Society in 1848, five years before the publication of *Gomer*, the following notices occur respecting these very stanzas :—

" *The Lineage of Marchwiail in Maelor.*[1]

" Llywelyn the son of Gruffyd, called Llewelyn Llogell Rhison, *who composed Englynion Marchwiail*, in the ancient style of poetry, when the great

---

[1] Near Wrexham, Denbighshire.

Eisteddvod was held there, in the time of King Edward III., under the patronage of Lord Mortimer."

Also :—

> "*The Eisteddvod of Gwern-y-Cleppa, and the Brothers of Marchwiail.*
> *Memoirs of Bards and Poets.*
>
> "In the time of King Edward III., the celebrated Eisteddvod of Gwern-y-Cleppa took place, under the patronage and gifts of Ivor Hael, and to it came the three brothers of Marchwiail in Maelor, in Powys, and Llywelyn ab Gwilym of Dôl Goch in Ceredigion. The three brothers of Marchwiail, and with them Davydd ab Gwilym, had been scholars in Bardism to Llywelyn the son of Gwilym at Gwern-y-Cleppa,—that is, the seat of Ivor Hael.
>
> "After that, an Eisteddvod was held at Dôl Goch, in Emlyn, under the patronage of Llywelyn the son of Gwilym, which was attended by John of Kent and Rhys Goch of Snowdon in Gwynedd. Upon this occasion, Llywelyn the son of Gruffyd, one of the three brothers of Marchwiail, sang the Englynion of *Marchwiail bedw briglas* in the ancient style of poetry."

Whether this story is true or false—and it is to be supposed that the Ven. Archdeacon does not give any credit to it, as he does not notice it—it is evident that the authors of this relation did not imagine that there was any Druidic mystery concealed under these triplets,—a discovery which was reserved for the nineteenth century.

The most ancient piece of British poetry extant is composed in this style of stanzas of triplets. Lhuyd was in doubt whether it was in the language of the Strathclyde Britons, or of the Pictish or old Caledonians; and Archdeacon Williams pronounces it "an unique surviving specimen of the Pictish composition in the language mentioned by Beda, as a living speech in his day, and as the representative of the language of Galgacus and his Caledonians, partially, perhaps, affected by the intercourse established between the Picts and Scots during their long-continued struggles against imperial Rome."

The composition in question, which was discovered by Lhuyd inscribed in an old copy of Juvencus, might, in his opinion, have been written in the seventh century, and may fairly be supposed to be as old as the ninth, the verbal forms being

similar to those of the glosses in the Bodleian MSS., which
Zeuss refers to about the latter date.   The Juvencus lines are
the only independent composition preserved in which those
forms appear, the MSS. of the twelfth and thirteenth centuries,
as seen in the Black Book of Caermarthen, differing only in
unimportant particulars from those of the fourteenth.

In the original MS. the lines are written continuously without division, but are evidently metrical in form, and constitute
three stanzas of three lines each.   Archdeacon Williams has
printed them in a modernized form, and gives the following
translation :—

1.

I will not sleep even an hour's sleep to-night.
My family is not formidable,
I and my Frank servant and our kettle.

2.

No bard will sing, I will not smile nor kiss to-night ;
Together ———— to the Christmas mead.
Myself and my Frank client and our kettle.

3.

Let no one partake of joy to-night,
Until my fellow-soldier arrives.
It is told to me that our lord the king will come.

"This," says the Archdeacon, " is the trifling effusion of a
young officer given to literary pursuits, who otherwise would
not have carried his Juvencus with him.   The writer of the
stanzas seems to have been on a midnight watch, at a military
outpost, whence he was not to move until a superior officer
should arrive, whom he styles a fellow-soldier.   His *callaur*,
or *padell*, was his camp-kettle.   The last line alludes to the
rumoured arrival of their common prince.   The Frank servant is evidently a Frank by birth serving with the Pictish
army—the name often occurring among the Cymric poets of
this age."

The idea of an officer of the Pictish army, in the seventh
century, carrying about with him, a Frank servant, a copy of

Juvencus, and a camp-kettle, appears a little far-fetched. We can see, however, that the words admit of a somewhat different division from that adopted by the Archdeacon, and that the lines contain what we should expect from them—the effusion of a bard desirous of obtaining a share of the feast in return for the display of his musical or poetic skill.

1.

Ni guorcosam nemheunaur henoid
Mi telun it gurmaur
Mi am franc dam an calaur.

2.

Ni can ili ni guardam ni cusam henoid
Cet iben med nouel
Mi am franc dam an patel.

3.

Na mercit nep leguenid henoid
Is discinn mi coweidid
Dou nam Riceur imguetid.

The substitution of "telun," "telyn," a harp, for "teulu," a family, or household, renders the first stanza intelligible, and gives the key to the meaning of the whole. Instead of reading the word "franc" as a proper name, a Frank, we give it the meaning ascribed to it by Dr. Owen, "a play, frolic, prank," or, as an adjective, "active, sprightly." The following translation, though not free from objections, presents a more reasonable rendering of the meaning of these antique lines, and more in accordance with the tenor and contents of those fragments of British minstrelsy with which we are, in other instances, familiar :—

1.

I shall not sleep a single hour to-night,
My harp is a very large one.
Give me for my play a taste of the kettle.

2.

I shall not sing a song nor laugh or kiss to-night,
Before drinking the Christmas mead.
Give me for my play a taste of the bowl.

3.

Let there be no sloth or sluggishness to-night,
I am very skilful in recitation.
God, King of Heaven, let my request be obtained.

We know so little of the Picts, or the dialect of the British language spoken by that people, that we cannot affirm or deny that these lines present a specimen of the Pictish dialect; the close affinity with the Cambric glosses of the Bodleian MSS. which they present, is, perhaps, no reason for denying their Pictish origin.

CHAPTER III.

THE compositions among those ascribed to Taliesin, which can lay claim to be considered historical, are few in number. In truth, if the epithet "historical" is to be restricted to poems descriptive of real events, there are only three which deserve the title, namely the *Battle of Gwenystrad*, the *Battle of Argoed Llwyfain*, and the fragment connected with the *Song of the Ale*, supposed to be descriptive of a combat in the Vale of Gwarant. There are, however, other pieces which, being addressed to or relating to historical personages, are also placed in this class, though in the majority of instances, nothing more than the name of the hero, or unconnected allusions to chiefly unknown places, can be obtained from them.

It has been observed that the pieces which may claim to be placed in the historical class, are nearly all addressed to, or connected with, the fortunes of Urien Rheged. There are, however, in the *Myvyrian Archæology*, poems relating to two other historical characters—Cunedda Wledig, and Gwallawg ab Lleenawg. The Cunedda to whom the "Elegy" refers is clearly the same as the Cunedda Wledig who lived at the close of the fourth or commencement of the fifth century, and was the founder of a line of sovereign princes in North and South Wales.

According to Mr. Williams ab Ithel,[1] the translator of the *Gododin*, "this poem is the work of one who had actually partaken of his royal munificence, who had received from him

---

[1] *Y Gododin*, Introduction, p. 1.

11

milch cows, horses, wine, oil, and a host of slaves." Mr. Williams places the death of Cunedda in A.D. 389, consequently he represents this poem as a composition of the fourth century.

Mr. Rees[1] also considers it as " perhaps the earliest specimen of Welsh poetry extant." In form, metre, grammatical construction, and orthography, it does not differ from the ordinary character of the poems ascribed to Taliesin. It is true that the name of Taliesin occurs in it, but this difficulty is overcome by assuming that " it was composed by a Taliesin older than the Bard usually known by that name."[2] A translation of it is given in Davies's *Claims of Ossian,* with which the following version can be compared.

MARWNAD CUNEDDA.

Mydwyf Taliesin derydd
Gwawd goddolaf fedydd
Bedydd rhwyf rhifeddan ciddolydd
Cyfranc allt a gallt ac Echwydd
Ergrynaw Cuneddaf ercisserydd
Ynghaer Weir a chaer Liwelydd
Ergrynawd cyfatwt cyfergyr
Cyfanwaneg tan tra myr ton
Llupawt glew i gilydd
Can cafas ei whel uch elfydd
Mal uchereid gwynt wrth onwydd
Hefynderrhyn y gwn ei gyfyl
Kyfachedwyn a choelyn cerenydd
Gwisgan feirdd cywrein canonhydd
Marw cuneddaf a gwynaf a gwynid
Cwynitor tewdor tavdun diarchar
Dychyfal dychyfun dyfnveis
Dyfyngleis dychyfun
Ymadrawdd cwddedawdd caledlwm
Caletach wrth elyn nog asgwrn
Ys cynyal Cuneddaf cyn cywys a thydwed
Ei wyneb a gadwed
Ganwaith cyn bu lleith dorglwyd

---

[1] *Essay on the Welsh Saints,* p. 114.   [2] Mr. Rees, *ubi supra.*

Duchludent wys bryneich ymmhlymnwyd
Ef caned rhag ei ofn ai arfwyd (oergerdd)
Cyn bu dayr dogyn ei dwed
Haid hafal a wydwal gwnebrwyd
Gweineu gwaith llyfredd nog addwyd
Addoed hun dimyaw a gwynaf
Am lys am grys Cuneddaf
Am ryaflaw hallt am hydyrfer mor
Am breidd aswrn a ballaf
Gwawd feirdd a ogon a ogaf
Ac eraill a refon a rifaf
Rhyfeddawr yn erflawdd a naw cant gorwydd
Cyn cymun Cunedda
Rym afei biw blith yr Haf
Rym a fei eddystrawd y gayaf
Rym a fei win gloyw ac olew
Rym a fei toraf Keith rhag untrew
Ef dyfal o gressur o gyflew gweladur
Pennadur pryd llew lludwy uedes gywlad
Rhag mab edern cyn edyrn anaclew
Ef dywal diarchar dieding
Am ryfreu angeu dychyfing
Ef goborthi aes yman ragorawl
Gwir gwrawl oedd ei unbyn
Dymhun a chyfatcun a thal gwin
Kamda difa hun o Goeling.

THE ELEGY ON CUNEDDA.

I am ardent as Taliesin.[1]
I dedicate my poem in praise of baptism.
Baptism the most valuable thing in our worship.
There was a contest on the rocks and cliffs and in the plain.
Trembling on account of Cunedda the burner,
In Caer Weir[2] and Caer Liwelydd,[3]
Trembling was the opposed league.
There was a complete sea of fire beyond the sea-wave;
The hero scattered like dust the retreat;
When shall the earth obtain a better than him?
Like the whirl of the wind (was he) against the ashen spears;
Chief of his clan, in his presence

---

[1] " I who am Taliesin, a man of the oaks."—*Davies.*
[2] Warwick, according to Williams.　　　　[3] Carlisle.

Was complete security and trust in friendship.
The garments of the Bards were skilfully wrought in conformity with the
The death of Cunedda I bitterly lament.   [Canons.
Lamented is the strong one fearless in speech ;
Accustomed to harmonious accord,
Accustomed to speak with facility,
Very severe in discourse.
Harder towards his enemies than bone.
The tribe of Cunedda is the chief in the land ;
They kept the front rank a hundred times before the fence of the door was
They challenged the men of Bryneich to battle ;   [destroyed ;
They (the Bryneich) grew pale before him through fear of his arms,
Before a portion of earth was his covering.
Like a swarm of bees swiftly moving in a thicket,
His servants did not do the work of cowards.
There was here nothing more beautiful
Than the palace and the robes of Cunedda.
From the crest of the cliff to the freely flowing sea,
None were wanting in herds of cattle.[1]
Praise of bards he obtained abundantly,
And other things in great numbers.
Wonderful was he in causing a tumult with nine hundred stately horses.
Before the encampment of Cunedda,
Thickly clustering round, were milch cows in summer,
And steeds in winter,
Bright and shining wine,
And troops of slaves before the doors.
He was diligent in showing kindness and giving a place to spectators ;
A prince with the countenance of a young lion, graceful at the banquet.
In the presence of the son of Edern chieftains were terrified ;
He displayed unrestrained boldness,
He was eminent in uplifting the shield here ;
Valiant men were his chiefs.
I respectfully request a share of the banquet, and a recompense in wine.
This has been with difficulty restored from testimony.[2]

[1] The construction of this and the preceding line is very doubtful.
[2] This last line, which Davies translates " the race of a colonial city,"
appears not to belong to the poem, but to have been a note of some transcriber.   I suppose the line may have been originally,

              " Cam daddifa hun o coeling."

Whether Coeling is a proper name or not, is unknown.

As Cunedda Wledig is represented to have died A.D. 389—
that is, twenty years before the final departure of the Romans
from Britain, and sixty years before the reputed date of the
invasion of the Saxons—we cannot admit that a poem which
speaks of contests with the men of Bernicia, and mentions
baptism in terms of such veneration, can have been composed
by a contemporary of that famous personage. It is by no
means impossible that Cunedda may have been a Christian;
but the great question on baptism, and the agitation caused
by the spread of the Pelagian doctrines, did not arise till the
commencement of the fifth century, and continued to create
trouble in the Church down to the close of the sixth. It is,
however, possible that this poem may originally have been a
production of the sixth century. There would be a reason
why one of the Bards who ministered to the pleasures of the
court of Maelgwn Gwynedd should have selected as a subject
for his muse, the praise of the renowned ancestor of that chieftain, from whom were descended the principal houses as well
of South as of North Wales.

But the line,

Gwisgan feirdd cywrein canonhydd,—

The garments of the Bards were skilfully wrought according to the canons,

must belong to a later period. Like the rest of its class, the
piece exhibits no marks of antiquity in its language or sentiments; on the contrary, it is smoother and more polished
than many other pieces in the same collection. If allowed to
have been written originally in the sixth century, it has evidently been rewritten as late as the twelfth; and, on the whole,
it is to this latter period that it ought to be referred.

We find, in fact, that Gwalchmai, a poet of the twelfth
century, addresses to his chief Owain Gwynedd a poem,[1] in
which he extols that prince as being descended from Maelgwn
Gwyned, and from Caswallon Llaw Hir and Einion Yrth, the
descendants of this Cunedda Wledig, to whom the principal

[1] *Myvyr. Arch.* vol. i. p. 198.

families of Wales traced their genealogy. Cynddelw also speaks of the same chieftain as being of the line of Einion Yrth, of Maelgwn Gwynedd and of Run. The same feeling which induced these bards to introduce the names of the sons of Cunedda Wledig into their encomiastic compositions, in all probability originated the poem under consideration, an elegy on the great founder of the race himself.

The other piece referred to, relates to a person called Gwallawg ap Lleenawg, who, it is suggested by the editors of the *Myvyrian Archæology*, is the same as the Galgacus mentioned by Tacitus, a celebrated chief of the Caledonian tribes, in the northern campaign of Agricola, about A.D. 83. From such a suggestion with respect to this poem, we can only conclude, that the editors of the *Myvyrian Archæology* did not take the trouble to read the compositions which they published, nor did they refer to other sources of information for identifying the Gwallawg ap Lleenawg whose name is prefixed to this poem. Edward Jones, "Bard to the Prince," who published, in the year 1802, a learned treatise on the Welsh Bards,[1] held the same opinion, and introduces the *Cerdd i Wallawg ap Lleenawg* as one of the most ancient poems preserved, "addressed to an illustrious character, whose name is familiar to the enlightened historian. It celebrates the battles of Galgacus, the chief of the Northern Britons, who so eminently signalized himself in opposing the Roman legions under Agricola, about A.D. 83. *Lleenog*," he says, "is a name which the father of Galgacus most likely acquired for his learning; which the word implies."

It apears, however, without going back to the first century for the subject of this poem, that Gwallawg ap Lleenawg was a warrior of the sixth century, and belonged to the same cycle of heroes with Urien, Owen, and the other chieftains who belong to the great tribe or family of Coel Godebog. A Gwallawg is mentioned in the genealogies of Nennius, as having, together

---

[1] *The Bardic Museum of Primitive British Literature, and other admirable Rarities.* London, 1802.

with Urien, Rhyderthen, and Morcant, fought against Ida in the sixth century. Gwallawg ap Lleenawg also appears in a Triad as one of the three pillars of battle, of the Isle of Britain. The Lives of the Welsh Saints, however, enable us to ascrtain the historical position of this personage.

Gwallawg ap Lleenawg was the grandson of Llyr Myrini, who, according to one pedigree, was the grandson of Cunedda Wledig, but according to another, and apparently more correct one, descended from Cenu, the son of Coel Godebog. The brothers of Gwallawg ap Lleenawg were Gwynn ap Nudd, a celebrated magician, and Caradoc Vreichvras, one of the battle-knights of Arthur. His near relations were, Iddawg Corn Prydain, who betrayed Arthur at the battle of Camlan; and Gwgan Gleddyvrudd, mentioned in the Triads as one of "the three stayers of slaughter," and one of "the three sentinels at the battle of Bangor Orchard," in the beginning of the seventh century.

Before presenting a translation of this poem to the reader, it is necessary to offer some remarks on the peculiarities which appear in it, and which it shares with a considerable number of these compositions. On commencing the translation with an idea that the poem contained matter in accordance with the title affixed to it, phrases presented themselves so unintelligible as almost to lead to the supposition that they must be full of Druidic mystery. It was not until another of these poems had been turned into English, that the mystery was solved. This was the piece entitled *Gorchan Adebon*, generally called the *Incantation of Adebon*.

" Among the most curious productions of the ancient British muse," says Mr. Davies, " we may class those little poems called *Gwarchanau, charms* or *talismans;* or else *Gorchanau, incantations*. In addition to the general lore of Druidism, these pieces bring forward certain mystical amulets, which were delivered to the patriotic warriors as infallible pledges of the protection of the gods, and which were evidently remains of the renowned magic of the Britons."

The first of these incantations is a short piece entitled *Gwar-chan Adebon*, of which Mr. Davies has given a translation which, even in his hands, presents very little of Druidic mystery. But notwithstanding his assertion, that " in this little poem the mystagogue discriminates between those probationers who duly preserved the secrets with which they were intrusted, and those who were tempted by any consideration whatever to divulge them, to which latter the talisman would be of no avail," a literal translation of the lines discloses nothing more than a string of very harmless proverbs, which from the con-cluding lines it would appear were recited before an audience by some wandering minstrel.   These lines may be compared with the conclusion of the *Elegy on the Death of Cunedda*, where the Bard prays for a share of the banquet as the reward of his song.

GORCHAN ADEBON.

Incantatio Adeboni.

Ny phel guyd aual o aual
Ny chynnyd dynal o dyual
Ny ehofn noeth yn esgal
Paub pan rydyoger yt bal
A garun y ef carei anreithgar
Ny byd marw duyveith
Nyt amsut y vut y areith
Ny cheri y gyneuin gyvieith

Emis anwychwas aneuyn
Am surn am gorn Cuhelyn
Yn adef tangdef colit
Adef let buost leu yn dyd mit
Rhudvyt ceissiessit ceissiadon
Mein uchel medel y alon
Dynen ar Uarchan Adebon.
Ac vely terunyna Goarchon Adebon.

THE SONG OF ADEBON.

The apple-tree is not far from the apple.
The industrious is not akin to the spendthrift.
No one is a hero when naked among thistles.
Every one who swears strongly fails (to perform).
Do not be the friend of one who loves injustice.
We cannot die twice.
To be dumb is not an appropriate quality for an orator.
Do not love to be foremost in conversation.
Jewels are the dainties of the feeble-minded.
Savage from hoof to horn.
Peace is lost in a mansion.

Where there is a large house there will be continual entertainments.
There is always a way for him who seeks it.
Kind gentles, victorious over the foe,[1]
Smile on the Gorchan (song) of Adebon.
And so ends the Gorchan Adebon.

Probably no literature can boast of a greater collection of proverbs than the Welsh. This concise and sententious form of presenting the "wisdom of their ancestors" appears to have been particularly congenial to the genius of the Welsh people. The third volume of the *Myvyrian Archæology* contains an extensive collection, some arranged in metrical Triads, others in the ordinary form. We need, therefore, feel no surprise at finding a collection of proverbs such as the above, though we cannot but be astonished at seeing the above poem (if we may so term it) still represented as anything else. Mr. Williams ab Ithel, the translator of Aneurin, supposes this Gorchan to be a portion of the *Gododin*. "That the Gorchanau were ' incantations' cannot be admitted; and if the word ' gorchan' or ' gwarchan' mean anything except simply ' a canon or fundamental part of song,' we should be inclined to consider it as synonymous with ' gwarthan,' and to suppose that the poems in question referred to the ' Camps of Adebon, Maelderw and Cynvelyn.' "[2]

The *Gorchanau of Maelderw and Cynvelyn* certainly contain "Cattraeth stanzas," but the *Gorchan of Adebon* as certainly does not, and we can only suppose that the learned translator of the *Gododin* has been misled by the title, and has never read the piece.

Even in the translation of Davies there is no allusion that can be made out to the battle of Cattraeth. The following version of Mr. Davies will serve to show how the Druidic mysteries have been eliminated from similar productions.

[1] Literally "reapers of the foe," a complimentary formula frequently employed.
[2] *Y Gododin*, Preface, p. 5.

12

THE TALISMAN OF ADEBON.

" The apple will not fall far distant from the tree. The sedulous cannot prosper in company with the remiss. All those who are not intrepid, when exposed naked amongst thistles, will fail when adjured.

" Should I love him who could become the friend of the spoiler? The man who cannot die twice, will govern his speech as if he were dumb. It was not thy disposition to put thy countrymen in fear.

" The fierce youth treasured up the gem of protection; yet for a trifle, for the horn of the stranger, in disclosing the word of peace, he was lost. Indirect was thy answer, and thou hast been brave in the day of battle.

" Concealed [1] was that information which the inquirer sought; the dweller amongst the high stones, the reaper of his foes, smiled upon the talisman of Adebon."

The first part of this version by Mr. Davies evidently consists of proverbs. The remainder is as mysterious as could be desired, but is certainly not a translation of the original.

We may now give the translation of the *Song of Gwallawg*, which, by the carelessness of transcribers or the ignorance of singers, has also been mixed up with proverbial maxims in a manner truly surprising. From the same cause, and perhaps also from the antiquity of the original songs, fragments of which have been thus orally preserved, both this and the following piece, which may have belonged to the same composition, are evidently very corrupt, and the translation must necessarily, in many instances, be conjectural only. It is however, on the whole, sufficiently certain to enable us to ascertain the nature of the poems, and that they contain nothing that can be construed into Bardic or Druidic mystery.

KERDD I WALLAWG AP LLEENAWG.

Yn enw gwledig nef Goludawg	Ef diffyrth addfwyn llan lleenawg
Y drefynt biefydd Gyfeil foawg	Toryd un trwch ardwyawc
Eirig ei rethren rieddawg	Hir ddychyferfyddain
Rhieu rhyfelgar gewhernawg	O Brydain gofain

---

[1] Mr. Davies's copy, taken from a MS. of Mr. Theop. Jones, has "Kudvyt,' where the *Myv. Archæol.* has " rhudvyt."

Oberth Maw ac Eiddin
Ni chymmeryn cyferbyn
Cyweith cyweithydd clydwyn
Digonwyf digones i Lynges
O beleidr o bleigheid prenwres
Prenial yw i bawb i drachwres
Anghyfrent o gadeu digones Gwallawg
Gwell gwydd fwyd nog Arthes
Cad yn Agathes o achles gwawd
Gognaw ei brod digones
Cad ymvro Vretrwyn trwy wres mawr
    tan
Meidrawl yw y trachwres
Cad ir ai cymrwy Kanhon
Cad cad crynai yn Aeron
Cad yn Ardunion ag Aeron
Eiddywed eilywed i feibion
Cat ynghoed Beid boed ron ddydd
Ni meddyliaistai dy Alon

Cad yn rhac llydawdawl a Mabon
Nid adrawdd adfrawd Achubion
Cad yn Gwensteri ag estygi Lloegr
Safwawr un a wner
Cad yn rhos terra gan wawr
Oedd hywst gwragawn egurawn
Yn nechreu ynheniad y geirawr
O rieu o ryfel ry ddiffawd
Gwyr a ddigawn goddai gwarthegawg
Haearnddur a Hyfeidd a Gwallawg
Ac Owein Mon Maelgynig ddefawd
Ac wnaw peithwyr gorweiddiawg
Ym mhen coed cleddyfein
Atfydd calanedd gwain
A brain ar ddisperawd
Ym Mhrydain yn Eiddin yn addefawg
Ynghafran yn adfan Brycheiawg
Yn ergyn yn ysgwn gaenawg
Ni wyl gwr ni welas Gwallawg

THE SONG OF GWALLAWG THE SON OF LLEENAWG.

In the name of the great Ruler of Heaven,
They who inhabit its dwellings are a glorious society.
Splendid is the princely spear
Of the warlike chief, swiftly moving,
He defended the fair enclosure of Lleenawg.
It was broken through when its defender fell.
Long were the contests
In fair Britain
On the side of Maw and Eiddin.
Do not join in dispute.
The co-operation of many is a protection.[1]
I am able to satisfy a fleet.
The sparks are because of the heat of the wood.
A coffin is for every body the end of ambition.

[1] If "Clydwyn" is a proper name, it would refer to Clydwyn, son of
Brychan, who conquered the territories in South Wales occupied by the Irish,
or Gwyddel Ffichti; and the line might be,

    Numerous is the retinue of Clydwyn.

They are quiet who are satiated with strife [Gwallawg].[1]
Better a gnat than a she bear,[2]
Fight with a she cat from a place of shelter [a mockery],[1]
Her activity is much to be feared.[3]
A battle in the country of Bretrwyn through the heat [a great fire.][1]
Ambition has its limits.
A rule (canon) of general advantage should be kept.
Battle, battle, there is trembling in Aeron.
Battle in Ardunion and Aeron.
Jealousy is a reproach upon the children.
A battle in the wood of Beid, it was a terrible day
Thou hast not been tender towards thy enemies.
A battle against Llydawdawl and Mabon.
Do not speak to the injury of thy deliverer.
A battle in Gwensteri and subduing of the Loegrian
It was gained by the spearman.
A battle in the land of Rhos in the morning
There was injury to women and men.
Flattery is the beginning of temptation.[4]
When chiefs go to war, very unfortunate
Are the men who possess huts and cattle.
Haearnddur and Hyfeidd Hir and Gwallawg,[5]

[1] The words enclosed in brackets appear to be marginal notes of some former transcriber, incorporated by a later hand into the body of the piece. The second, "a mockery," shows that the commentator was shocked at the apparent irrelevancy of this line.

[2] See Prov. xvii. 12. "Gwell i wr gyfarfod ag arthes," &c. "It is better for man to meet with a she bear," &c.

[3] Mr. Williams (ab Ithel) has given Gognaw as a proper name (though doubtfully) in the 57th line of the *Gododin*, and proposes to read the above line in this poem,

Gognaw ei brawd digones;

but there is no connection between such a reading and the rest of the piece. If Gognaw was the son of Botgad, he was not the brother of Gwallawg, and one does not see why he should be introduced here.

[4] Dr. Owen has,

Frangible was the awful arch at the first uttering of the word.

[5] One of the heroes of the *Gododin*.

Hyveid Hir shall be celebrated while there remains a minstrel.

Haearndor is mentioned in the *Elegy on Uther Pendragon*; and a person of this name is mentioned as a witness to a charter or feoffment of lands to the

And Owain of Mona, and Maelgyn of great reputation,[1]
They would prostrate the foe.
In Pen Coed there was slaughter,
Wretched white corpses,
And ravens wandering about.
In Britain, in Eiddin, it is confessed,
In Gafran[2] and amongst the strangers of Brycheiawg,[3]
In the assault, in rising up in his armour,
Never was seen a better man than Gwallawg.

There is another song relating to Gwallawg ap Llecnawg, very much of the same character as the preceding. There is nothing in it which can assist in fixing its date; the style and orthography are the same as in all the others of its class.

I WALLAWG.

Yn enw Gweledig Nef Gorchorddion
Ryganant ryghwynant y Dragon
Gwrthodes gogyfres gwelydon
Lliaws Rhun a Nudd a Nwython
Ni golychaf an gnawt Beirdd o Vry-
Ryfedd hael a sywyd Sywedydd [thon
Un lle rhygethlydd rygethlig
Ryddysyfaf rychanaf i wledig
Yn y wlad ydd oedd ergrynnig
Nim gwnel nis gwnaf ei newig
Anawdd diollwng adwloedd ni diffyg
I wledig ni omedd

O edrych awdl trwm teyrnedd
Yn ei fyw nis deubydd budd bedd
Ni ddigonont hoffedd o'i buchynt
Caletach yr artaith hael hynt
Torf pressenawl tra Phrydain
Tra phryder ry gohoyw rylycirawr
Rylycerer rytharnawr rybarnawr
Rybarn pawb y gwr banher
Ac uinat yn yngnad ac elwet
Nid y gwr dilaw ei ddaered
Gwas greid a gwrhyd gottraed
Eil eichawg Gwallawg yn llywet

church of Llandaff by the sons of Beli, in the time of Bishop Nudd, in the eighth century.

[1] Tefawg, to rhyme with Gwallawg. Mr. Williams (ab Ithel) translates this and the next line,—

> Owain of Mona of Maelgynian manner,
> Would prostrate the ravagers.—*Gododin*, p. 91, note.

[2] In a Triad, *Myv. Archæology*, vol. ii., we find, "The three losses by disappearance of the Isle of Britain. Gavran son of Aeddan, with his men, who went to sea in search of the Green Islands of the Floods, and nothing more was heard of them." In another the tribe of Gavran, the son of Aeddan, is mentioned as one of "The three loyal tribes of the Isle of Britain."

[3] Probably Brycheiniog, or Brecknockshire, which was at one time peopled by the Irish.

Hwyrweddawg gwallawg artebed
Ni ofyn i neb a wnaeth udd
Neud ym udd nac neud ych Darwerther
Tewuedd yn niwedd Haf
Nis cynnydd namyn chwech
Chweccach it gynan o hynnydd
Chedlawg trwyddedawg traeth dydd
Teyrnedd yngwedd nwys medd mad
Tebyg heul haf luenydd foned gan mwyaf
Cenhaf gan ddoeth y gan llu eiliassaf
Bint bydi derwy bryt haf pryt mab
Lleenawg lliawg hamgwrwl gwmn

Gwawl gwnn gwres tarth gwres tarth
Trangyunis yd engis heb warth
Cleda cledifa cledifarch nidd am tyri
Y lu y ledrad nid amescud i gaw ei gywlad
Tyllant tal ysgwydawr rhac taleu ei feirch
O march trwst Morial rith gar riallu
Gwynawg ry gwystlant gweiryd goludawg
O gaer Glut hyd gaer Garadawg
Ystadl tir penprys a Gwallawg
Teyrnedd tewrn tangweddawg.

TO GWALLAWG.

In the name of the Ruler of the assembly of Heaven,
They sing of and bitterly deplore the Chief.
The grave disowns any difference in rank,[1]
To the company of Rhun and Nudd and Nwython.[2]
I will not praise after the fashion of the Bards of the Britons,
Liberal of wonders and the star-knowledge of the astrologers,
In the same place singing the same cuckoo-song.
I will earnestly entreat, I will sing earnestly to the Lord.
The men of the country were afraid ;
I would not do it were I not acquainted with song.[3]
Pardon obliterating the view of our defects
The Lord will not refuse.
With looking on my poem Kings shall be sad.

[1] *Gogyfres ;* cyfres—equal rank. *Go-cyfres,* a partial equality, something less than an equality of rank.

[2] Dr. Owen, in his *Dictionary*, has given translations of many portions of this poem, which, from its supposed historical character, has attracted much attention. His translations are :—

"In the name of the governor of the high powers of heaven they shall chiefly sing, shall chiefly complain to the prince ; he who rejects the uniform column of the tribes of the numbers of Rhun and Nudd and Nwython."

The personages here mentioned are historical ; that is to say, they are named in other sources of information, and supposed to belong to the sixth century.

[3] "The station of the complete songster excellent of song I ardently desire. I will greatly sing to a sovereign, in the region where he was agitated with frailty, that he cause me not to be unable to form the lay."—OWEN, *Dict.*

In their lifetime shall not the grave be victorious?
They shall not obtain the love that they desire,
Hard-hearted, prodigal of torments.
A troop shall be hastening across Britain.
Through anxiety the most high-spirited shall be concealing themselves.[1]
He will judge all, the Supreme Sovereign,
Coming in judgment upon falsehood,
Not the man who acknowledges his obligations.
A vehement youth renowned for courage
Ruling like the lofty Gwallawg.[2]
A forbearing disposition was visible in the countenance of Gwallawg.[3]
Do not ask of any one what he has done in secret;[4]
Verily it is my secret, it is not for you to ascertain it.
Fatness comes at the end of summer.
There are only six natural qualities.
More agreeable is discourse from the old.
A talkative guest passes over the day.
In the presence of kings, grave discourse is good.[5]
Like the sun shining in summer is the highest nobility.
I will sing a wise song with the harmonious choir.
Like the oak in summer is the countenance of the son of
Lleenawg in his brown manly robe.
Light causes heat, heat causes vapour.
Death from disgrace is a deliverance.
Do not heap together (such words as) cled, cledif, and cledifarch;
The band of robbers did not mingle their lies at his feast.
They slay the warrior who pay before-hand for his harness.
Of the fierce horse of Morial[6] very noble the appearance,
Full of spirit rioting in the rich hay.
From Caer Llud to Caer Caradawg,[7]
Spread over the land are foolish and indigent persons.
Oh! King of Kings of tranquil aspect.

[1] The next line is unintelligible.

[2] Dr. Owen translates this :—"A violent youth that rejects the milky food,
like the herald of Gwallawg."

[3] Here the original poem seems to end, the remainder consisting of the
usual detached phrases in the nature of adages.

[4] "Of a forbearing aspect is the countenance of Gwallawg; he does not
inquire of any one what he has done."—OWEN.

[5] "Talkative is the privileged orator of kings in the luxuriant circle of the
good mead, like the sun, the warm animator of summer."—OWEN.

[6] See note to the *Song of the Horses*, post.

[7] From Dumbarton to Shrewsbury. In the *Biographical Dictionary of*

There are several stanzas on the death of this chieftain contained in a piece called the "Contest between Gwyddneu Garanhir and Gwyn ab Nudd," the latter being the brother of Gwallawg. They intimate that Gwallawg ab Llecnawg was slain by a stroke of a spear or arrow, which pierced the brain of the chieftain through the eye.

Boed emendigeit ir gwydd
A dynnwys y lygad yn y wydd
Gwallawc ap Lleinawc Arglwydd.

Boet emendigeit ir gwydd du
A dynnwys i lygad oed ddu
Gwallawc ap Lleinawc penn llu.

Boet emendigeit ir gwydd gwenn
A dynnwys i lygad oi benn
Gwallawc ap Lleiniawc unben.

Boet emendigeit ir gwydd glas
A dynnwys i lygad yngwas
Gwallawc ap Lleinawc urddas.

Mi a wn lle i llas Gwallawc
Mab Goholeth teithiawc
Addwod Lloegyr mab Lleynawc.

Cursed be the shaft
That pierced[1] the eye in the face
Of Gwallawg ab Lleenawg the lord.

Cursed be the black shaft
That pierced the dark eye
Of Gwallawg ab Lleenawg the chief of the host.

Cursed be the white shaft
That pierced the eye in the head
Of Gwallawg ab Lleenawg the prince.

Eminent Welshmen, it is said, that in this poem the fame of Gwallawg is represented as extending from Caer Clud or Dumbarton, to Caer Caradawg or Salisbury. This is an example of the mode in which these poems have been treated, by taking the meaning of a single line, altogether regardless of the context.

[1] Literally " pulled out, dragged out," the eye.

Cursed be the green shaft
That pierced the eye of the youth
Gwallawg ab Lleenawg the noble.

I know the place where Gwallawg was slain,
Son of the gifted Goholeth;
Mischievous to the Loegrians was the son of Lleenawg.

The remaining historical pieces are addressed to or celebrate the actions of the famous chieftain Urien Rheged, who, according to one set of traditions, was the chief patron of Taliesin. Two of these poems, the *Battle of Gwenystrad* and the *Battle of Argoed Llwyfain*, are, especially the latter, very spirited descriptions of what we can hardly doubt to have been real historical events, though it is, at the same time, quite certain that the poems themselves were not written, in their present form, in the sixth or even in the tenth century.

GWAITH GWENYSTRAD.

Arwyre gwyr Kattraeth gan dydd
Am wledig gwaith fuddig gwarthe-
    gydd
Urien hwn anwawd eineuydd
Cyfeddeily teyrnedd ai gofyn rhyfelgar
Rwysg anwar rwyf bedydd
Gwyr Prydain adwythein yn lluydd
Gwen ystrad Ystadl cad cynnygydd
Ni ddodes na maes na choedydd
Tud achles diormes pan ddyfydd
Mal tonnawr tost ei gawr tros elfydd
Gwelais wyr gwychr yn lluydd
A gwedi boregat briwgig
Gwelais i dwrf teirflin trancedig
Gwaed gohoyw gofaran gowlychid
Yn amwyn Gwenystrad y gwelid gofwr
Hag angwyr llawr lluddedig   [dion
Yn nrws rhyd gwelais i wyr lledrud-
Eirf dillwng rhag blawr gofedon

Unynt tanc gan aethant golluddion
Llaw ynghroes gryd (*ygro*) granwy-
    nion
Cyfeddwynt y gynrhein Kywyn don
Gwaneicawr gollychynt rawn y caffon
Gweleis i wyr gospeithig gospylad
A dulliaw diaflym dwys wrth gad
Cad gwortho ni buffo pan bwylled
Glyw Reged rhyfeddaf pan feiddad
Gweles i ran reodig gan Urien
Pan amwyth ai Alon yn llech wen
    Galystem
Ei wythiant oedd llafn aesawr gwyr
Goberthid wrth Angen
Awydd cad a ddiffo Euronwy
Ac yn y fallwyfi hen
Ym dygyn Angheu Anghen
Ni bydif yn dirwen
Na molwyf fi Urien.

13

THE BATTLE OF GWENYSTRAD.

Extol the men of Cattraeth who went with the dawn.
My prince is the victorious leader.
To Urien this being without praise is new.
The upholder of the kingdom and warlike in his demands,
Gentle in rule, a chief of Baptism.
The mischievous men of Britain were assembled in arms,
Constantly proposing battle in Gwenystrad.
Neither field nor wood afforded shelter to the host,
When the molestation came.
Like the fierce roar of the wave[1] is his shout across the land!
I have seen resolute men in battle array,
And after the morning of battle mangled flesh.
I have seen the violent struggling of the perishing,
Blood-wetting the active angry ones;
In defence of Gwenystrad a heap of wounded ones,
And of men severely fatigued.
In the pass of the ford I saw the blood-stained men loosening their armour
      with a cry of anguish.
They were quiet whose entrails went (out of their wounds).
With the hand on the cross, trembling on the ground the white-cheeked ones;
They are a feast for the worms rising out of the earth.
The pale birds of prey are wet with grasping the gore.
I have seen men chastising the spoiler,
With blood matted on their clothes,
And with fierce gestures earnest in fight.
Coverer of the battle, there was no retreat when he rushed on.
The hero of Rheged—wonderful was it when he desisted.
I saw the division of the spoil collected by Urien.
When his enemies were raging by the White Stone of Galystem,
His anger was like the sword of the shield-men,
Producing death.
Greedy of battle shall Euronwy be.
And till I fall into old age,
And the painful necessity of death,
May I never smile
If I praise not Urien.

To the translation appended to this poem in the *Myvyrian*

---

[1] "Mal tonnawr tost." "Like sharp thunder" would, I believe, be the true translation : "tonnawr," "tonnerre."

Archæology, a note is added :—" N.B. This battle was fought by Urien Rheged, Prince of Cymbria, against the Saxons."

The hero of the poem is undoubtedly Urien Rheged; but the poem itself is one of that cycle which goes to form the *Gododin*. The first line is a common formula in the commencement of *Gododin* stanzas. The name Gwenystrad, " the white or fair strand," affords no information as to the locality of the battle; and the battle of Cattraeth, as we learn from the *Gododin*, took place on a strand or beach of the sea or a large river.

GWAITH ARGOED LLWYFAIN.

Y Bore Dduw Sadwrn Cad fawr a fu
Or pan ddwyre Haul hyd pan gynnu
Dygrysowys fflamdwyn yn bedwarllu
Goddeu a Reged i ymddullu
Dyfwy o Argoed hyd Arfynydd
Ni cheffynt eiryoes hyd yr undydd
Atorelwis fflamdwyn fawr drybestawd
A ddodynt yngwystlon a ynt parawd
Yr attebwys Owain ddwyrain ffossawd
Nid dodynt nid ydynt nid ynt parawd
A cheneu mab Coel byddai Cymwyawg lew
Cyn attalai owystl nebawd
Atorelwis Urien Udd yr echwydd
O bydd ynghyfarfod am garennydd
Dyrchafwn eidoed odduch mynydd
Ac ymporthwn wyneb odduch emyl
A drychafwn beleidr odduch ben Gwyr
A chyrchwn fflamddwyn yn ei lluydd
A lladdwn ag ef ai gyweithydd
A rhag Gwaith Argoed Llwyfain
Bu llawer Celain
Rhuddei frain rhag rhyfel Gwyr
A gwerin a grysswys gan einewydd
Arinaf y blwyddyn nad wyf Kynnydd
Ac yn y fallwyf hen
Ym dygn angeu angen
Ni byddif ym dyrwen
No molwyf Urien.

THE BATTLE OF ARGOED LLWYFAIN.

The morning of Saturday there was a great battle,
From the rising of the sun until the setting.[1]
Fflamdwyn hastened in four divisions
With the intention of overwhelming Rheged.[2]
They reached from Argoed to Arfynyd.
They maintained their splendour only for one day.
Fflamdwyn called out very blusteringly,
"Will they give the hostages, and are they ready?"
Owain answered him rising up on the rampart,
"They will not give them; they are not nor shall be ready."
And Ceneu, son of Coel, afflicted would have been the hero
Before he would give hostages to any one.
Loudly Urien the chief proclaimed his resolution,—
"Let my kinsmen assemble,
And we will raise our banner on the hills,
And will turn our faces against the soldiers,
And will lift our spears above the heads of the men,
And will seek Fflamdwyn in his army,
And will slay both him and his troop."
And because of the battle of Argoed Llwyfain,
There were many corpses;
Red were the ravens through the strife of men.
And men hastened with the news.
And I will divine the year, that I am no longer on the increase;
And till I fall into old age,
And the painful necessity of death,
May I never smile
If I praise not Urien.

Another piece, in which the heroes of Cattraeth are mentioned, addressed to Urien, and placed by Mr. Stephens among the historical poems, as old as the sixth century, is that entitled the *Spoils of Taliesin*.

YSPEIL TALIESIN.

Canu Urien.

Yngwryd gogyfeirch yn nhrafferth gwaetwyf
A wellwyf yn Kerthwir
Gweleis i rhag neb nim gweles pob annwyl
Ef diwyl ei Neges.

---

[1] Or until midday.　　　[2] "To overwhelm Goddeu and Rheged."

Gweleis i basg am leu am lys
Gweleis i ddail o ddyfyn o dowys
Gweleis i geing gyhafal ei blodeu
Neur'r weleis udd haelaf ei ddedfau
Gweleis i lyw Catraeth tra maeau
Bid fy nar nwy lachar Cymryau
Gwerth fy nad mawr fydd ei fudd y radeu
Pen Maon milwyr amde
Preidd lydan Pren onhyt yw fy Awen gwen
Ysgawr y rhag glyw gloyw glasgwen
Glyw ryhawd glewaf un yw Urien
Nim gorseif gwarthegydd
Gorddear gorddyawg gorlassawg gorlassar goraig a gorddwyre
Pob rhai sang dilew du Merwydd y Mordei
Udd tra blawdd yn ydd el oth fodd
Vared Melynawr yn neuadd maran heddawg
Diffreidiawg yn Aeron
Mawr ei wyn ei aniant ac eilon
Mawr ddyfal ial am ei Alon
Mawr gwrnerth ystlyned i Frython
Mal rhod tanwhydin tros elfydd
Mal ton teithiawg Llwyfenydd
Mal cathl cyfluv Gwen a Gweithen
Val Mor Mwynfawr yw Urien
Yn y egin echangryd gwawr
Un yw rhieu rhwyfiadwr a Dwyawr
Un yw maon meirch mwth miledawr
Dechreu mei ymhywys byddinawr
Un yw yn deuwy pan ofwy ei werin
Eryr tir tuhir tythremyn
Addunwn i ar orwydd ffysgyolyn tud ynial
Gwerth yspeil Taliesin
Un yw gwrys gwr llawr a gorwydd
Un yw breyr benffyg y Arglwydd
Un yw hyddgre hydd yn divant
Un yw blaidd banhadlawr anchwant
Un yw gwlad fab Eginyr
Ac unwedd ac unswn cadfa cedwyr
Unswn y drwg iraven (iaeran)
A Cheneu a Nudd hael a hirwlad y Danaw
Ac os it *ytwydef* ym gwen
Ef gwneif beirdd byd yn llawen
Cyn mynhwyf meirw meib Gwyden
Gwaladr gwaed gwenwlad Urien.

THE SPOILS OF TALIESIN.

A Song to Urien.

In manliness conspicuous,
In business I am not expert,
I am better in song.
I have seen that before any one has seen all things without deception,
He is confident in his business;
I have seen the various coloured net-work of flowers,
I have seen the leaves gradually appearing of the yellow water-lily,
I have seen the branch with its blossoms of equal shape;
Have I not seen the Chief most liberal in his ordinances?
I have seen the army of Cattraeth.
My lords [1] are the two splendours of the Cymry.
My value is not great to him abounding in blessings.
Chief of the people surrounded by warriors.
The broad spoils of the spear are (given to) my fair song,
Delivered before the bright smiling hero.
The most resolute of chieftains is Urien;
No peaceful merchant is he;
Clamorous, loud-shouting, crying out with a shrill voice,[2] superior, highly
    exalted.
Every one is aware of the extermination on the side of Merwydd and Mordei.
The chief is very swift in preparing your pleasure;
When harpers are playing in hall he is of a peaceful countenance,
A protector in Aeron;
Excellent his wine, his poets, and his musicians;
Very incessant against his enemies;
The great strength of the community of the Britons;
Like a whirling fiery meteor across the earth,
Like the wave coming from Llwyfenydd,
Like the harmonious song of Gwen and Gweithen,
Like Mor the very courteous, is Urien.
In the assembly [3] of a hundred battle-heroes,
He is the director and leader of princes;
He is the chief of the people of swift-running horses.

[1] That is Urien and his son Owain.

[2] *Gorlassar* means extremely blue; but, as that does not appear a possible
reading, I suppose it to be an error for *gorlaisar*, shrill-voiced. The whole
line is an example of the alliteration so much in vogue in the twelfth and
following century.

[3] *Egin*, the crop, the blades of corn springing up.

In the beginning of May in perfect order of battle,
He is coming when his people send for him.
Eagle of the land, very keen is thy sight.
I have made a request for a mettled steed,[1]
The price of the spoils of Taliesin.[2]
One is the struggle of an ignoble man with a spirited steed,[1]
One is a baron benefiting the Lord,[3]
One is a herd of does when the stag is flying,
One is a wolf not desirous of carrion,[4]
One is a land where children sprout up like young wheat;
And of one appearance and one voice the warriors on the field of battle.
And of the same sound the fault in song.
And Ceneu and Nudd the generous, and continual mildness between them;
And perchance he may be in a smiling mood,
And he will make the Bards joyful.
Before by my will the sons of Gwyden shall be slain,
Blood shall be scattered over the fair land of Urien.

I URIEN.

Ar un blynedd	A chwaneg anaw
Un yn darwedd	Budd am li am law
Gwin a mall a medd	Wyth ugein unlliw
A gwrhyd digassedd	O loi a biw
Ac ei lewydd gorod	Biw blith ag Ychen
A haid am fereu	A pob cein amgen
Ai phen ffuneu	Ni byddwn lawen
Ai teg wyddfaeu	Bei lleas Urien
Ei bawb oi wyd	Ys eu cyn iethydd
Dyfynt ynlhymnwyd	Iais cyngryn cyngryt
Ai farch y danaw	A briger wen olched
Yngoddeu gwaith Mynaw	Ar clor ei dynged

[1] Some transcriber has added here, as a gloss apparently on the epithet *ffysgyolyn*, " tud ynial," a vigorous trotter, which spoils the rhyme, and is clearly an interpolation.

[2] The original poem appears to have ended with this line; the next seven lines are conceived in an entirely different spirit, and present a series of things which, I presume, are intended to be represented as impossibilities. " Yspeil Taliesin " is probably mistranslated " The spoils of Taliesin."

[3] *Benffyg*, apparently a corruption of " beneficus."

[4] Dr. Owen translates these two lines, —

> One is the cry of the stag in its flight,
> One is the wolf *uncovetous of the broom.*

A gran gwyarlled
Am waed gwyr gonodded
A gwr hewr bythig
A fei feddw ei wreig
Am ys gwin ffelaig
Am ysgwin mynych gyttwn
Am Sorth am porth am pen
Cym na phar cyfwyrein
Kymaran taraw
Gwas y drws gwrandaw
Py drwst ai dayar a gryn
Ai mor a ddugyn
Dy gwyawg ychyngar wrth y pedydd
Ossid uch ym mhant
Neud Urien ai gwant
Ossid uch ym mynydd
Neud Urien a orfydd

Ossid uch yn rhiw
Neud Uried ai briw
Ossid uch ynghawdd
Neut Urien a blawdd
Uch hynt uch as
Uch ymhob Kamas
Nac un tew na dau
Ni nawdd y rhag eu
Ni byddei ar newyn
A phreiddieu yn ei gylchyn
Gygoriawg gorlassawc gorlassar
Ail angeu oed ei bar
Yn lladd ei Esgar
Ac yn y vallwyf hen
Ym dygyn Angeu Angen
Ni byddif ym Dyrwen
Na molwyf Urien.

TO URIEN.

In this year
He who is the provider
Of wine and meal and mead,
And is of manliness without ferocity,
And of conquering valour,
With his swarms of spears,
And his chiefs of bands,
And his fair banners,[1]
With him all his followers
Will be in the fight;
And his horse under him,
In sustaining the battle of Mynaw.
There will be abundance, besides
Eight score of the same colour

Of calves and cows,
Milch cows and oxen,
And all good things also.
We should not be joyful
Were Urien slain;
He is beloved of his countrymen;
He terrifies the trembling Saxon,[2]
Who, with his white hair wet,
Is carried away on his bier,
And his forehead bloody;
Bloody are the feebly defended men,
And the man who was always insolent;[3]
May their wives be widows.

[1] Gwyddfaeu. *Gwyddfa* means, according to Owen, a place of presence, an elevated mound.

[2] *Iais*, in this line, must be a misprint for "Sais," the Saxon.

[3] Dr. Owen has a curious reading of these lines. His copy gives,—

> Y gwr dewr bythig
> A vei veddw ei wraig
> Am ys gwin felaig,—

"The valiant persevering one, whose wife was drunk over the wine of the chieftain."

I have wine from the chief:
To me wine is most agreeable;
It gives me impulse, aid, and head,
Before lifting up the spear
In the face-to-face conflict.
Door-keeper, listen!
What noise is that? Is it the earth
  that shakes,
Or is it the sea that swells, [feet?[1]
Rolling its white heads towards thy
Is it above the valley,
It is Urien who thrusts;
Is it above the mountain,
It is Urien who conquers;
Is it beyond the slope of the hill,
It is Urien who wounds;

Is it high in anger,
It is Urien who shouts.
Above the road, above the plain,
Above all the defiles,
Neither on one side nor two,
Is there refuge for them;
But those shall not suffer hunger
Who take spoil in his company,
The provider of sustenance.
With its long blue streamers,
The child of death was his spear,
In slaying his enemies.
And until I fall into old age,
Into the sad necessity of death,
May I never smile
If I praise not Urien.

CANU I URIEN REGED.

Urien yr Echwydd
Haelaf Dyn bedydd
Lliaws a roddydd
I ddynion elfydd
Mal y cynnullwyd
Yd wesgerydd
Llawn beirdd bedydd
Tra fo du uchydd
Ys mwy llawenydd
Gan glodfan clodrydd
Ys mwy Gogoniant
Fod Urien ai blant
Ac ef yn Arbennig
Yn oruchel wledig
Bellennig yn cyniad
Cyntau Lloegrwys ai gwyddiad
Yn Ninas Pellenig
Yn ceiniad cynteig
Lloegrwys ai gwyddant
Pan ymadroddant
Angeu a gawsant
A mynych goddiant
Losgi eu trefred

Adwyn eu lludded
Ac cimwng colledd
A mawr amgyffred
Heb gaffel gwared
Rhag Urien Reged
Rheged diffreidiad
Clod Ior angor gwlad
Fy modd y sydd arnad
O bob erglywad
Dwys dy beleidrat
Pan erglywat cad
Cad pan i cyrchud
Gweniaith a wnaud
Gweniaith a wneit
Tan ynhai cyn dydd
Rac Udd yr Echwydd
Yr echwydd teccaf
Ai dynion haelaf
Gnawd Eingl heb waessaf
Am deyrn glewaf
Glewaf Eissyllydd
Tydi goreu sydd
Or a fu ac a fydd

[1] *Cyncan,* instead of *cynghar.*

Nith oes cystedlydd
Pan dremher arnaw
Ys helaeth y braw
Gwnawd gwledd am danaw
Am deyrn gognawd
Am danaw gwyledd
A lliaws Maranhedd

Eudeyrn gogledd
Arbennig Teyrnedd
Ac yn y y vallwyf hen
Ym dygn angeu angen
Ny byddiff im dirwen
Na molwyf Urien.

SONG TO URIEN REGED.

Urien of the plain,
Most generous of baptized men ;
Much has he bestowed
On skilful men.
Like the heaping together
Of scattered corn,
Is the abundance of Christian bards.
On account of thy greatness,
There is the more rejoicing,
With exalted eulogies ;
There is the more splendour
In the abode of Urien and his children,
That he should be a sovereign,
A prince over the highest
Distant chiefs.   [is known ;
In the first place, by the Loegrians he
In distant cities,
By the principal chiefs ;
The Loegrians know him,
When they discourse of him
As the cause of death to them,
And numerous afflictions,
And the burning of their towns.
Blessed be their oppression,
And their imminent destruction,
And great their incapacity
Of obtaining deliverance
From Urien Reged,
Defender of Rheged.

Renowned Lord, sustainer of the land,
My desire shall be for thee ;
Thou art heard of by all ;
Heavy is thy spear
When the battle is heard ;
When the shock of battle comes,
He gathers in the vintage.
He fires their houses before daybreak ;
He is Lord of the plain,
The fairest plain,
And the most generous of men.
The Eingl have no hostages
From my heroic prince ;
A most valiant offspring
To thee is given.
There has not been, nor shall be,
Nor is there his equal.
When he is contemplated
There is ample proof.
He makes feasts around him ;
My glorious prince,
Around him are seen
A multitude of nobles ;
He is the King of the North,
The supreme ruler of kings.
And until I fall into old age,
And the sad necessity of death,
I shall never rejoice
If I praise not Urien.

DADOLWCH URIEN.

Lleu uydd echassaf
Mi nyw dirmygaf
Urien yd gyrchaf
Iddaw yd ganaf
Pan ddel fyngwaessaf
Cynwys a gaffaf
Or parth goreuhaf
Y dan eillassaf
Nid mawr nim dawr
Byth gweheleith a welaf
Nid af attaddynt ganthynt ni byddaf
Ni chyfarchaf fi gogledd
Ar mei teyrnedd
Cyn pei am laweredd
Y gwelwn gynghwystledd
Nid rhaid ym hoffedd
Urien nim gommedd
Llwyfenydd diredd
Ys meu eu rheufedd
Ys meu y gwyledd
Ys meu y llaredd
Ys meu y deliedeu
Ai gorefrasseu

Medd o fualeu
A da dieisicu
Gan deyrn golau
Haelaf rygigleu
Teyrnedd pob Iaith
It oll ydynt gaith
Rhagot yt gwynir ys dir dy olaith
Cydef mynnasswn
Gwey helu henwn
Nid oedd well a gerwn
Hyd ys gwybyddwn
Weithian y gwelaf
Y meint a gaffaf
Namyn y Duw uchaf
Nis dioferaf
Dy deyrn Veibon
Haelaf dynedon
Wy canan eu hysgyron
Yn nhiredd eu galon
Ac yn y vallwyf hen
Ym dygyn angen angen
Ni byddaf im dirwen
Na molwyf Urien.

URIEN'S RECONCILIATION.

Though the chief is angry,
He will not despise me.
I will seek Urien,
To him I will sing.
When he comes I will warrant,
I shall receive a summons.
I will sing a harmonious song.
Not much do I value
The tribes I continually see.
I will not go to them or be with them.
I will not seek the North
And its princes,
Though there should be to me (offered)
 abundance
Of pledges for my return.
Their love is not necessary to me,

(Since) Urien does not refuse me
The lands of Llwyfenydd.
Mine is their wealth,
Mine is the festival,
Mine is joyousness,
Mine are beautiful things,
And excellent banquets,
Mead from horns,
And a superfluity of good things,
With my splendid prince,
The most generous ever heard of.
The princes of all (other) tongues
Are all slaves,
Lamenting before thee for the desola-
 tion of their lands.
With him I should be willing

(To be until) I grow old.
There is none I could love better
As far as I know.
I have seen his actions,
I comprehend his greatness;
Except God the highest,
There is none more capable.
Thy princely sons,

The most noble of men,
The splinters of their spears resound
Through the lands of their enemies.
And until I shall become old,
And fall into the necessity of death,
I shall not rejoice
Except in praising Urien.

Owain, the son of Urien Rheged, was a warrior even more famous in popular traditions than his father. He is supposed to be one of the chief heroes of the *Gododin*, and was introduced into the Arthurian romances as one of the most noble and courteous Knights of the Court of Arthur. The following elegy on his death, treats him as a purely historical person.

MARWNAD OWAIN AP URIEN REGED.

Enaid Owain ap Urien
Gobwyllid ei Ren
    Oi Raid
Reged Udd ai cudd tromlas
Nid oed fas
    Ei gywyddeid
Isgell cerddglyd clodfawr
Esgyll gwaywawr
    Llifeid
Cany chessir cystedlydd
I Udd llewenydd
    Llathreid
Medel galon gefeilad
Eissillud y tad
    Ai taid
Pan laddawdd Owen Fflamddwyn
Nid oedd fwyn
    Og ef cysgeid

Cysgid Lloegr llydan nifer
A lleufer
    Yn eu llygaid
A rhai ni ffoynt hayaeh
A oeddynt . . ach
    No chaid
Owain ai cospas yn ddrud
Mal cnud
    Yn ymlid defeid
Gwr gwiw uch ei amliw seirch
A roddei feirch
    I eirchiaid
Cyd as cronnai mal caled
Ni ranned
    Rhag ei Enaid
Enaid Owain ap Urien, &c.

THE ELEGY ON OWAIN AP URIEN REGED.

The soul of Owain ap Urien,
May the Lord provide for
In its need.

Prince of Rheged, the heavy green
    sward conceals him;
Not shallow was his song.

A corpse is the renowned protector
   of bards;
Splintered is the sharp spear.
Where shall be sought the equal
Of the brilliant prince of the West?
Soft are the hearts of his associates,[1]
Children, sire, and grandsire.
When Fflamddwyn slew Owain,[2]
There was no advantage
From his going to rest.   [sleep
A wide number of Lloegrians went to
With the light in their eyes.[3]
And some could scarcely flee,

And they were . . . . [4]
Than slaves.
Owain valiantly chastised them
Like (the leader of) a troop of wolves
In pursuit of sheep.
He was a worthy hero, lofty his
   variegated harness.
And he would give steeds
To those who asked for them;
What he amassed of the hard coin
He shared with us.
On account of his soul,
The soul of Owain ap Urien, &c.

The following "Song to Urien" is more corrupt and less intelligible than the preceding. It contains an allusion to the clan Gododin, or the hero or fortress of that name.

CANU I URIEN.

Ardwyre Reged ryfedd Rieu
Neu ti rygostais cyn bwyf teu
Gnissynt cad lafnawr
A chad fereu gnissynt wyr
Y dan gylchwyawr
Lleeu goleu gwyn gelein
Ymathren ni mad frwydrwyd
Rhi ni mad geu
Ydd ymarmerth gwledig
Wrth Cymryau
Nis gyr neges y geissiaton
Gochawn Marchawg mwth molud gwrion
O ddreig ddylaw adnaw doethaw don
Yn i ddoeth Wlph yn dreis ar ei Alon

[1] Or "Reaper of associated foes."
[2] The ordinary construction would give

      When Owain slew Fflamdwyn.

But in an elegy on Owain the circumstances of his death are more naturally mentioned; and this reading renders the following lines more intelligible. If Fflamddwyn were Ida, the bard could hardly say there was no advantage in *his* death; but he says that, even though Owain was slain in the battle, the army of the Lloegrians was defeated.

[3] That is, "lay prostrate on their backs in death on the field of battle."
[4] The remainder of this line is wanting.

Hynny ddoeth Urien yn edydd yn Aeron
Ni bu cyfergyriad ni bu gynnwys
Talgynnawd Urien y rhac Powys
Ni hyfrwd brwd echen gynnwys
Hyfeidd a Gododin a lleu towys
Dewr yn enmynedd a thaith gyduwys
Difefl dyddwyn yngwaed gwyden
A weles llwyfenydd ufydd cyngryn
Yn eiddoedd cyhoedd yn eil mehyn
Cad yn rhyd Alclud Cad ym ynuer
Cad gellawr brewyn Cad hireurur
Cad Ymhrysg Cadleu, Cad yn Aber-ioed
Y ddygyfrang a dur breuer mawr
Cad gluduein Gwaith pen coed
Llwyth llithiawg Cunar ormant gwaed
Atveilaw gwyn goruchyr cyd mynan
Eingl eddyl gwrthryd
Lledrudd a gyfranc ag Wlph yn rhyd
Gwell ganher gwledig pyr y ganed y Udd
Prydain pen perchen broestlawn y Udd
Nid ymddug ddillad na glas na gawr
Na choch nag ehoeg uyg mawr llawr
Nid arddodes y forddwyd dros Voel Maelawr
Meirch o genedl vrych mor greidiawl
Haf y dan ayaf ag araf yn llaw
A Rhyd a Rhodwydd eu harwylaw
A gwest y dan geirdd ag ymdwyraw
Ac hyd orphen byd edrywyd Caw
Gosydin goyscub dyhawl am delw
Dilwfr am leufereu neu fi erthrycheis
Rhag hwyd Peleidr ar ysgwydd
Ysgwyd yn llaw Godeu a Rheged yn ymdulliaw
Neu fi a weleis wr yn buarthaw
Sarph sonedd firen Segidyd lawr
Neu fi gogwn Ryfel ydd argollawr
Er maint a gollwyf y argollaw
Neu fi neu ym gorwyth meddu meddlyn
Gan hyfeidd hywr hywest ddilyn
Neu fi neu ysgynhedais cysgawd gweithen
Dithrychwys fy rhieu radeu lawen
Gwasga gwlad dda wrth wruyn
Ac yn y vallwyf i hen
Ym dygn Angeu Angen
Na bydyf ym dirwen
Na molwyf Urien.

SONG TO URIEN.

Extol the glorious chiefs of Reged.
Wast not thou established before I had become strong?
They brandish the battle-spears,
Men brandish the battle-lances,
Above the bucklers.
The light shines on the pale corpses.
Trampled down are the weak combatants.
Falsehood is not good in a king.
A feast is in preparation
For the honourable.
The inquisitive man does not hasten business.
I will sing of the swift knight, praised of heroes.
Of the chiefs owned by us the wisest (was) Don.
When Wlph[1] came to spoil his foes,
When Urien came in the day in Aeron,
There was no combat in which he was not included.
He lifted up his head before Powys.
Not easily excited was the compact tribe.
Hyfeidd and Gododin, and the chief of Towys,
Bold, yet forbearing, and pledged to his oath;
Without reproach, condescending to those fallen into affliction.[2]
I have seen Llwyfenydd[3] humble and trembling,
When the banner was unfurled against the foreigner:[4]
A battle in the ford of Alcluyd, a battle in Inver—
A battle at Cellawr Brewyn,[5] a battle at Hireurur;
A battle in the thicket of Cadleu, a battle in Aber-ioed;
Loud was the noise of the combat and the steel (weapons).
A battle in Cludwein, a fight at Pencoed.
The tribe enraged,[6] the swine gorged with blood.
Decayed is the fair sovereignty of the united (tribes).[7]
The purpose of the Angles is hostile;
Slaughtering[8] and contest, and Wlph in the road.

---

[1] *Wlph* or *Gwlph.* The name seems to be Saxon; but I believe nothing is known of him.

[2] Yn gwaed gwyden.

[3] Llwyfenydd. "The Elms" was the name of the estate which the Bard hopes Urien will not take from him, in the "Dadolwch Urien."

[4] Yn ellmyn? Dr. Owen translates it "yn ail meyn" in the second place.

[5] These seem all to be names of places at which Urien had been present in battle.

[6] Llidiawg.   [7] Cydymun.   [8] Lladdrad.

Better is it for the land to contain a Chief,
The chief possessor of Britain, the harmonious Chief.
I have not worn robes neither blue nor brown,[1]
Nor red, nor green, full of pride.
Have I not ridden upon Voel Maelawr,
The fiery horses of the spotted race?
Summer and winter I moderated them with my hand,
And rapid and in circular course were their wheelings about.
And an entertainment both in disgrace and in self-exaltation.[2]
Until of the end of the world was perceived the boundary.
Whirling round a besom, was one a devil in form.
Though brave, I was afraid lest I should be torn in pieces.[3]
In front the grove of spears on the shoulders,
The shield in the hand, Godeu and Reged arranged in battle array.
Have I not seen the Lord in the cattle-shed?[4]
May I not know a battle in which the chief shall perish,
Very much should I lose by his destruction.
I shall not be displeased with the sweet mead
In company with the manly Hyfeidd of hospitable conduct.
Have I not ascended to the shelter of battle?
Fortunate is my King, full of grace?
Shelter of the country, good to the oppressed.
And until I become old,
And in the sad necessity of death,
I shall not rejoice
Except in praising Urien.

The next song addressed to Urien, breathes an entirely different spirit, and contains little allusion to the favourite themes of battle and slaughter. It is a joyous song, in which the Bard represents his condition as happy and luxurious, owing to the liberal generosity of his patron.

[1] Here begins a rhapsody which has no connection with the former part.
[2] This line seems not to belong to the rest.
[3] This part, the account of his ride on the horse Voel Maelawr to the end of the world, which has been interpolated, here ceases, and the piece returns to the subject of the former part—the actions of Urien.
[4] This is apparently a line belonging to some other piece, and refers to Christ. The next line is unintelligible.

I URIEN.

Yngorphowys
Can rychedwys
Parch a chymrwys
A medd meueddwys
Mucddwys medd
Ei orfoledd
A chain diredd
Imi yn rhyfedd
A chyfedd mawr
Ag eur ag Awr
Ac eur a ched
A chyfrifed
A chyfrifiant
A choddi chwant
A chwant oi roddi
Er fy llochi
Yd ladd yd gryg
Yd fag yd fyg
Yd fyg yd fag
Yd ladd yn rhag
Rhagwedd roddid
I feirdd y Byd
Byd yn geugant
Itti yd weddant
Wrth dy ewyllis
Duw ryth beris

Rhieu yngnis
Rhag ofn dibris
Annogiad cad
Diffreiddiad gwlad
Gnawd am danad
Lwryf pystylad
Pystylad lwrwf
Ac yfed cwrwf
Cwrwf oi yfed
A chein drefred
A chein dudded
Imi ryanllofed
Llwyfenydd fan
Ag eirch achlan
Yn un trygan
Mawr a bychan
Taliessin gan
Tidi ai diddan
Ys tidi goreu or gigleu
Ei wrdd lidau
Molaf inneu dy weithredau
Ac yn y vallwyf hen
Ym dygn angeu angen
Ni byddiff ym dirwen
Na molwyf Urien.

TO URIEN.

In tranquil retirement
I was prodigal of song,
Honour I obtained,
And I had abundance of mead,
I had abundance of mead
For praising him;
And fair lands
I had in excess,
And great feasting,
And gold and silver,
And gold and gifts,

And plenty,
And esteem,
And gifts to my desire,
And a desire of giving
In my protector;
It is a blessing, it is harsh,
It is good, it is glorious,
It is glorious, it is good,
It is a blessing in the presence,
The presence of the bestower.[1]
The Bards of the world

[1] This is one of those propositions in the nature of riddles which the Bards were constantly offering for solution.

Are certainly
Rendering homage to thee
According to thy desire.
God hath subjected to thee
The chiefs of the island,
Through fear of thy assault
Provoking battle.
Protector of the land,
Usual with thee
Is headlong activity,
And the drinking of ale,
And ale for drinking,
And fair houses,
And beautiful raiment.

On me he has bestowed
The estate of Llwyfenydd,[1]
And all my requests,
Three hundred altogether,
Great and small.
The song of Taliesin
Is a pleasure to thee,
The greatest ever heard of;
It would be a source of indignation
If I did not praise thy deeds.
And until I become old,
And in the sad necessity of death,
I shall never rejoice
Except in praising Urien.

The next poem, though it is not properly one of the historical series, is addressed to Urien Rheged, and may therefore be placed here.

ANREC URIEN.

Gogyfercheis, gogyvarchaf, gogyverchyd

Urien Reget
Duallovyet
 Y Leuenyd.

Eur ac Aryant
Mor eu divant
 Eu dihenyd.

Kyn noc y dau
Rug y duylau
 Y guesceryd,

Ieuaf a wnaeth
Coll ac alaeth
 Am feirch peunyd.

Keneu y vraut
Kynnin daervaut
 Ni by geluyd.

Urien a wnaeth
Dialynyaeth
 Y gewilyd.

Kynnin vynnu
Kyvarchuelu
 Eu dihenyd.

Deutu Aerven
Diffuys dilen
 Dydau lwyd.

Seleu delyit
Enynnyessit
 Or a dybyd.

Dybi y vaeth
A ryd alhaeth
 Oc eu herwyd.

Cochliu lavneu
Truy valch eiryeu
 Am ffruyth eu guyd.

Wy Kynnhalyant
Lle peduar cant
 Y peduar guyr.

---

[1] The estate given by Urien to the Bard, and frequently mentioned in these songs.   See the " Dadolwch Urien."

Dufyr dyvnav
Bendigwyf clav
    Ac oe herwyd,
Yr ae Kaffo
Kynvinaul vo
    Yn dragyuyd.
Dydeu collet
Or ymdiret
    Yr ardelyd.
A llau heb vaut
A llavyn ar gnaut
    A thlaut lûyd.
Oes feibionein
Nyt ymgyghein
    Ymmerueryd ;
Nyt ymganret
Nyt ymdiret
    Neb oe gylyd.
Dreic o Wyned
Diffwys dired
    Dirion drefyd.
Lloegrwys yd a
A lletaut yna
    Harchollyd.
Torrit meinueith
Yn anoleith
    Ar gyfhergyd.
Muy a gollir
Noc a geffir
    O Wyndodydd.
O gyt gyghor
Kyvrung esgor
    Mor a Mynyd.
Gotriffit Brython
Yn at poryon
    Ar antyrron gyucithyd.
Ef a dau byt
Ny byd Kerdglyt
    Ny byd Kelvyd.
Alaf gar maer
Arthauc vyd chuaer
    Wrth y gilyd.

Llad a bodi
O Eleri
    Hyt chuil fynyd.
Un gorvydyauc
Antrugarauc
    Ef a orvyd.
Bychan y lu
Yn ymchuelu
    Or Mercherdyd.
Arth or deau
Kyvyt ynteu
    Dychyfervyd.
Lloegruys lledi
Afrivedi
    O Bowysyd.
Guaith Cors Vochno
O diango
    Bydaud deduyd.
Deudeng guraged
Ac nyt ryved
    Am un gur vyd.
Oes Ieunctid
Aghyvyrdelit
    Y vaeth dybyd
Beru ymdivant
Barnauc or cant
    Nys ryuelyd.

Uryen o Reget hael ef syd ac a vyd
Ac a vu yr Adaf letaf y gled
Balch yghynted or tri Theyrn ar dec
    or gogled
A un eu enu Aneuryn guautryd
    Auenyd
A minneu Dalyesin o lann llyn
    geirionnydd
Ny dalywyf yn hen
Ym dygyn aghen
Oni Moluyf Uryen.   Amen.

Tal. Ae Dyuaul.

A GIFT TO URIEN.

I have addressed, I will address a salutation to

Urien Reged,
Who rules over
 The West.
Gold and silver
Quickly pass away,
 They have no real source.
Better than both,
In both hands,
 Covered over,
Is union and harmony.
Loss and grief
 Are my daily portion.
Children and brethren,
Foremost in contention,
 This is no falsehood.
Urien would take
Vengeance
 On deception.
First in making
Reproaches
 For their want of foundation.
On both sides of the river Dee,
Unmannered, unlearned, men
 Approaching.
Their eyes are blinded
To the flames that are
 And that shall be.
There shall be evil
And great sorrow
 Because of them.
Red are swords
Through their proud words,
 Violent their passion.
Their supporters
Are four hundred bands
 Of four men.
I am accustomed to sorrow,
I am blessed in my grief,
 And for this reason,

There is an attainment
Which will bear fruit
 In eternity.
If thou resolve
On moving forward
 In thy duty,
Hands unpolluted,
And cheerfulness of disposition,
 Lead unto happiness.
There are (some) like children,
Not agreed together
 On the greensward;
Neither pursuing
Nor moving forward,
 Nor any retreating.
The chiefs of Gwyned
Scattered in retreat
 Through the pleasant towns.
Lloegrians there are,
Armoricans there,
 Wounding.
Broken is the fair work
In the slaughtering
 Of the battle shock.
More is lost
Than is gained
 Of happiness.
By the council assembled
Between the ramparts
 Of sea and mountain,
Oppressed are Britons
By the remnants
 Of the associated enterprise.
The world is passing away;
There will be no shelter for song,
 No poetic skill.
The master covetous of wealth,
The sister churlish,
 In the corner (of the house).

There shall be a slaughter
This year
    On the slope of the hill.
One a horseman
Without mercy,
    He shall conquer.
Small the array
Which shall return
    On Wednesday.
Arth from the south,
Kyvyd with him,
    Meeting.
Slaughter of Lloegrians
Innumerable
    By the men of Powys.
From the battle of Cors Vochno
They who escape
    Will be fortunate.
Twelve women
And no marvel,
    Shall be to one man.

The period of youth
Is all graceful,
    But sorrow will come.
Shortly disappearing,
The sentence on their lusts
    Not foreseen.

Uryen of Reged, liberal he is and
    will be.
And he was the protection of Adam
    the Armorican,
Supreme in the hall of the thirteen
    kings of the North;
And one of them was named
Aneuryn the panegyrical poet.
And I also, Taliesin, from the bank of
    Llynn Ceirionydd,
May I not fall into old age
Or grievous death,
Without praising Urien.

Taliesin recited this.

This poem, addressed to Urien Rheged, is evidently of a late date. At the time it was written the English or Lloegrians were engaged in warfare with the men of Powys, and it would appear with Gwynedd also. The prophecy of the battle of Cors Vochno, also contained in a predictive poem of the pseudo-Merlin, which Mr. Stephens has shown to be a production of the twelfth century, points to the same era for the date of this poem. Gwalchmai, a bard of the twelfth century, ascribes to Owain Gwynedd the honour of having been an actor in the battle of Cors Vochno, which, from the fragment preserved, would seem to have been fought by the North Welsh against the Flemish colonists of Pembrokeshire.

Ardwyreaf hael o hil Iago
A gennys dra chas dra Chors Vochno
A gyrchws glyw Flandrys a flemychws i eu bro,—

I extol the liberal chief of the race of Iago,
Who witnessed the conflagration beyond Cors Vochno,
And assaulted the chiefs of Flanders and fired their land.

We have therefore, in the "Anrhec Urien," one instance of a poem addressed to Urien Rheged, and attributed to Taliesin, which certainly was not composed at an earlier date than the twelfth century. The latter portion has been added, either to give the piece the air of desired antiquity, and the authority of Taliesin for the prophecy, or has been accidentally transcribed with it. It contains the usual formula of the Urien ballads.

To these we might perhaps add a short fragment, which seems to have for its subject the invasion of Britain by the Romans. Its title is taken from the line referring to the story of Lludd and Llefelis, but it contains nothing of the adventures related in that tale in the *Mabinogion*.

YMARWAR LLUDD BYCHAN.

Yn enw Duw trindawd cardawd cy-
  frwys
Llwyth lliaws anuaws eu henwerys
Dy gorescynnan Prydain prif fan Ynys
Gwyr gwlad yr Asia a gwlad Gafis
Pobl pwyllad enwir eu tir ni wys
Famen gorwyreis herwydd Maris
Amlaes eu peisseu pwy ei hefelis
A phwyllad dyvyner ober efnis
Europin arafin arafanis.
Cristiawn difryt diryd dilis

Cyn ymarwar Ludd a Lefelis
Dysgogettawr perchen y wen ynys
Rac pennaeth o Rufein cain ei echrys
Nid rys nid cyfrwys ri rwyf ei araith
A rywelei a ryweleis o anghyfiaith
Dullator pedrygwern llugyrn ymdaith
Rac Rhyuonig cynran baran goddeith
Rytalas mab grat rwyf ei Areith
Cymry yn danhyal rhyfel ar geith
Pryderaf pwyllaf pwy y hymdeith
Brythonig yniwis rydderchefis.

THE RECONCILIATION OF LLUDD THE LESS.

In the name of God the Trinity, bestow charity on the skilful.
A numerous tribe hostile and vigorous
Ruled over Britain the chief island,
Men of the land of Asia and the region of Cafis,
A wise people certainly, their country is not known,
Their course was very devious on account of the sea.
Flowing their garments, who were equal to them?
And skilful diviners over their enemies.
Europin arafin arafanis.
To Christians they worked banishment and destruction,
Before the reconciliation of Lludd and Llefelis.

Agitated was the possessor of the fair island,
Because of the chief of Rome in his splendid garment.
Neither hesitating or troubled was the King, haughty his speech.
"Who has seen what I have seen of the foreigners?
The forming of a square enclosure with lanterns moving about.
There is an appearance of fire before the Roman leader."
Answered the son of Grat, haughty was his speech.
"Cymry in flames, war or captivity."
I am anxiously considering what will be the career
Of the Britons of greatly exalted energy.

Before quitting the subject of the Historical poems, we may observe, that the conclusions at which Mr. Sharon Turner arrived in the *Vindication of the Ancient British Poems* have lost much of the force which appeared to belong to them at the time of the publication of that work in 1803. The greater number of the compositions on which Mr. Turner relied as ancient, and alluding to still more ancient poems, have been found to be themselves of later date than the tenth century. The internal evidence of an antiquity as remote as the sixth century, which these compositions have been supposed to afford, had not in Mr. Turner's time been subjected to a sufficiently careful examination. The poems of Merlin the prophet, on which he placed much reliance, have been ascertained to be of modern date, attributed by their authors to the renowned magician of the sixth century; and the poems attributed to Taliesin are, as we have already stated, many of them of a like origin. The "Songs to Urien" themselves are not altogether beyond suspicion as to the genuineness of their historical character.

The poem, which of the whole series bears the most apparently genuine historical character, is that entitled "The Battle of Argoed Llwyfain." It professes to be a description of a combat by Urien, chief of Rheged, with his son Owain, and their forces, against a Saxon chief who is called Flamdwyn, and generally supposed to be the same with Ida, King of the Angles. The battle therefore would have been fought at some date between A.D. 537 and A.D. 560. But the poet has introduced as an ally or follower of Urien a person named Ceneu mab Coel. It is certainly not impossible that such a person may have flourished in the time of Urien and Ida, though no other notice of him has been met with. But Ceneu mab Coel, the son of Coel Godebog, is the great ancestor of nearly all the celebrated personages who form the subject of the Welsh romances, and constitute the splendid assembly of the Arthurian heroes. He was the great-great-grandfather of Urien himself, thus :—

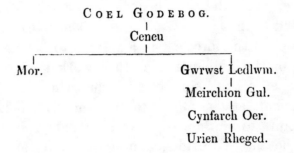

COEL GODEBOG.
|
Ceneu
|
Mor.   Gwrwst Ledlwm.
                            |
                        Meirchion Gul.
                            |
                        Cynfarch Oer.
                            |
                        Urien Rheged.

It is difficult to suppose that any other Ceneu mab Coel than the ancestor of Urien can be intended by the person of that name introduced into this poem. Yet the son of Godebog himself can hardly be imagined to have taken part in a battle at which his descendant in the fifth degree, Owain ap Urien, was a warrior; and we cannot help entertaining the inference that the song was written at a period long subsequent to the event to which it relates, and that the name of the ancestor of Urien has been introduced by a bard not intimately acquainted with the details of his genealogy. The fact that the poem is first known to us from a MS. of the twelfth or thirteenth century adds to the weight of this circumstance, in casting a doubt upon its contemporaneity with the events which its relates.

Without, therefore, venturing to decide that these "Songs to Urien" were not rewritten in the twelfth century from materials originally of the date of the sixth, and that there are no poetical remains in the Welsh language older than the twelfth century, we may nevertheless assert that the common assumption of such remains of the date of the sixth century has been made upon very unsatisfactory grounds, and without a sufficiently careful examination of the evidence on which such assumption should be founded. Writers who claim for productions actually existing only in MSS. of the twelfth an origin in the sixth century, are called upon to demonstrate the links of evidence, either internal or external, which bridge over this great intervening period of at least five hundred years. This external evidence is altogether wanting; and the internal evidence, even of the so-called " Historical Poems " themselves, is, in some instances at least, opposed to their claims to an origin in the sixth century.

CHAPTER IV.

THE MYTHOLOGICAL POEMS.

WE now come to those remains of the Welsh Bards which have been supposed to contain the mythology, superstition, and philosophy of the celebrated Druids.

The views of the Rev. Edward Davies on the subject of these poems are too well known to require recapitulation at any length. He represented the Druidic religion as a Helio-Arkite superstition, in which ceremonies commemorative of the Deluge, and certain mystical rites analogous to those of Bacchus, Ceres, and Isis, played an important part. The doctrines and ceremonies of this religion he supposed to have been preserved in songs and traditions by the inhabitants of Britain through the period of the Roman ascendancy, to have survived the introduction of Christianity into this island, and to have continued in a vital condition down to as late as the twelfth century, and produced from the writings attributed to the Bards of the sixth century abundant evidence, as he affirmed, of the truth of his positions.

In this sense he translated, or rather, mistranslated, a considerable number of the ancient Welsh poems, wresting the plainest and most obvious expressions from their simple meaning, in order to educe the mysteries which had no place save in his own imagination.

Where he met with expressions clearly indicative of Christian doctrine, as addresses to the " Merciful Trinity," " Christ the Son," " the Father," " the day of judgment," &c., which recur at every turn in these poems, he either omitted them altogether, treating them as interpolations, or gave them another and mysterious meaning, or declared them to have been introduced as a cloak, to deceive the uninitiated, and induce the outer world to believe that the Pagan Bard was in fact a good Christian.

The influence which these translations of Mr. Davies have exercised on all investigations into early British history, has been most extensive. His opinion has been widely adopted, and his translations taken as evidences of history. We have before alluded to one remarkable instance of the spread of this delusion, in the so-called translation given by Dr. Meyer of what he styles a hymn to the god Pryd in his character as god of the sun, as follows :—

"Pryd, God of Great Britain, splendid Hu, listen to me! King of Heaven, do not during my office hide thyself from me! A fair repast is spread before thee by the castle between the two lakes (a religious expression for Great Britain); the lakes surround the wall; the wall surrounds the city; the city invokes thee, King Almighty; a pure offering stands before thee, a chosen victim in its sacrificial veil; a great serpent (a common epithet of the sun, referring to its circuitous course) encircles from above the place where the sacred vases stand."[1]

This translation is hardly less absurd than that of Mr. Davies. The first two lines have no connection with the rest, but belong to the preceding piece, the *Marwnad Uther Pendragon*. They are in the same metre with those that precede, and are necessary to complete the sense.

> Fy nhafawd i draethu fy Marwnad
> Handid o meinad gwrthgloddiad byd
> Pryd Prydain hu ysgein ymwhyllad
> Gwledig Nef ynghennadeu nam doad,—

> My tongue in reciting my elegy.[2]
> Though the world should be surrounded with a wall of stone,
> Over the surface of Britain would be spreading thy memory.
> Lord of Heaven, grant oblivion for sin.

[1] *Report of the British Association for the Advancement of Science.* Oxford, 1847. P. 304.
[2] The Elegy of Uther Pendragon.

The following is the real poem, which the reader will be surprised to find, so far from being a description of these sacrificial mysteries, and the immolation of a victim in a castle between two lakes, is, in fact, neither more nor less than a Christmas carol, or song in honour of the Nativity of our Saviour :—

ARMES.

Kein gyfeddwch
Y am deulwch[1] lluch omplaid
Pleid am gaer
Caer yn chaer ry yscrifiad
Virain fo rhagddaw
Ar llen[2] caw mwyedig Vein
Dreig amgyffreu
Odd uch lleeu llestreu llad
Llad yn eurgyrn
Eurgyrn yn llaw
Llaw yn ysci
Ysci ymodrydaf
Fur itti iolaf
Buddyg Veli
A Manhogan
Rhi rhygeidwei deithi
Ynys fel Feli
Teithiawg oedd iddi

Pump pennaeth dimbi
O wyddyl ffichti
O bechadur cadeithi
O genedl ysgi
Pump eraill dymbi
O Norddmyn mandi
Wheched ryfeddri
O hen hyd fedi
Seithfed o heni
I weryd tros li
Wythfed lin o Ddyfi
Nyd llwydded escori
Gynt gwaedd Venni
Galwawr Eryri
Anhawdd y deui
Iolwn Eloi
Pan yn bo gan Geli
Addef Nef dimbi.

A FRAGMENT, ENTITLED "A PROPHECY."

A splendid feast
For the reconciliation of contending parties.
Contention in the city,
Hateful violence.
Beautiful was his presence,
In linen swaddling clothes extremely delicate.
The chiefs around
Place on high the gift-vessels,

Gifts of golden goblets.
The goblet in the hand
Full of liquor,
The liquor of the beehive.
I adore thy wisdom.
The victorious Beli,
Son of Manogan
The King, who was the chief guardian
Of the Island of Britain,[3]
Was journeying to thee.

[1] Dadolwch.   [2] Lleng.

[3] Ynys Feli, the Honey Island, said in the Triads to be one of the names of Britain. It has a very suspicious resemblance to Inis-fail, the old name of Ireland.

This is the termination of the Christian hymn, for such it is evident that it is. The poet speaks of the gifts brought by the chiefs, the wise men from the East, and says that Beli the son of Manogan, one of the kings of Britain who reigned before the time of Julius Cæsar, was also present. The rest of the piece is of a predictive character, which evidently did not originally belong to the former part. The mention of the chiefs from Normandy is sufficient to show its date.

Five chieftains there shall be
Of the Gwyddel Fichti,
Incorrigible sinners
Of a headlong race.
Five others there shall be
From Normandy,
The sixth a wondrous king
From his birth to his grave.
The seventh of these

From the country beyond the sea.
The eighth of the line of Ddyfi,
Not fortunate his enemies.
Before the shout of Menni
Calling upon Eryri (Snowdon),
Not easily shalt thou come.
Let us adore Eloi,
When, in being with Christ,
Our dwelling shall be in heaven.

This astounding fallacy of a hymn to the god Pryd in the Welsh language, being preserved among the works of the Cynveirdd, has been, together with the equally fantastic notion that "Ossian and Taliesin, *i.e.*, Ua-sin and Tal-ua-sin, are mere mythological concentrations and personifications of the poetical activity and influence of the tribe of the Fena," reprinted by M. Bunsen in his *Outlines of the Philosophy of Universal History*,[1] in the "Last Results of the Celtic Researches." Dr. Meyer, however, in preparing his Report for M. Bunsen's work, has omitted the remarkable and amusing statement in that report, as published in 1847, concerning "that interesting Siberian tribe U-sin, one of the principal tribes of the White Tartars, blue-eyed and fair-haired, as they are described by the Chinese chroniclers (who mention them, together with the Yueti, *i.e.* Goths), and the same, as I believe, with the Irish (or Fenish) Ua-sin, *i.e. light fair* tribe, celebrated in Irish legends for its cultivation of the arts alike of war and

[1] Vol. i. pp. 143—171. London, 1854.

peace, and for the number of bards as well as heroes it has produced."

But M. Bunsen has embalmed in his work, for European circulation, Dr. Meyer's opinion, that "the Irish poem of *Oigidh Llainne Uisnech* (the death of the sons of Uasin)[1] contains, in a mythological and symbolical form, the story of the final destruction of this interesting Siberian tribe of White Tartars in the northern part of Ireland, in consequence of a long series of combats against the Picti or Cruithne."

We are not at present concerned with the story of Ossian or the Fingalian heroes; but we may remark, that as the sons of Uisneach were slain by Conchobar Mac Nessa, King of Ulster, the tribe of White Tartars must have been revived to fight the battle of Gabhra with Cairbre son of Art, son of Conn of the Hundred Battles, more than two centuries later, according to all Irish tradition and chronology. Such statements as these of Dr. Meyer, published with such apparent authority, are real obstacles to all progress in investigating the true history and relations of the two great branches of the Celtic race. They have not even the merit of novelty to recommend them; for Strahlenberg in 1730, and Bochat in his *Memoires Critiques sur l'Ancienne Suisse*, derive the Keltæ from the Siberian Tungusi, the most powerful tribe of the Sabatzi Tungusi being the Keltakæ, that is the Keltai or Celts —an opinion which received the approbation of Vallancey, in his *Irish Grammar*.

Another song of Taliesin, called the *Elegy of Aeddon*, is one of Davies's most prominent examples of Druidic lore.

Aeddon, on whose death the song is written, means, according to Mr. Davies, "Lord of the Din, a title of the Helio-Arkite god, which title is here transferred to his priest."

Archaeddon, who according to the poem is certainly represented as an apostle or messenger surrounded by angels, means

---

[1] Called *Uisneach* in the original Irish. The poem itself is called *Oidhe Chloinne Uisneach.*

"the Ark of Aeddon." He translates the succeeding stanzas of the first portion of the poem :—

"When Aeddon came from the land of Gwydion into Seon of the Strong Door, a pure poison diffused itself for four successive nights, whilst the season was yet serene. His contemporaries fell. The woods afforded them no shelter, when the winds arose in their skirts. Then Math and Eunydd, masters of the magic wand, set the elements at large; but in the living Gwydion and Amaethon, there was a resource of counsel to impress the front of his shield with a prevalent form—a form irresistible. Thus the mighty combination of his chosen rank was not overwhelmed by the sea: and in every seat of presidency, the will of his mighty representations in the feast will be obeyed. The dear leader of the course; whilst my life continues he shall be commemorated."

"We have here," says Mr. Davies, "much Arkite mythology."

"1. The patriarch came from the land of Hermes (Gwydion being Hermes in the Arkite system) or the old world.

"2. He entered the enclosure of Seon, or of the nine sacred damsels, which was guarded by a strong door or barrier. This enclosure was the ark.

"3. When he was shut up in this sanctuary, the Great Supreme sent forth a poisonous vapour to destroy the wicked world. But the messenger of death entered not the enclosure of Seon.

"4. By this pestilential vapour, which filled the whole atmosphere, the patriarch's wicked contemporaries were destroyed. But the earth was still polluted.

"5. Then the great magicians, with their magic wands, set free the purifying elements; one of the effects of which, as described in the Triads, was the dreadful tempest of fire, which split the earth to the great deep, and consumed the greatest part of all that lived. Upon this, the waters of Llyn Llion, or the abyss, burst forth.

"6. These powerful agents would have destroyed the patriarch and his family in Caer Seon, had not Hermes counselled him to impress a mystical form, or to strike a peculiar signal on his shield. This, I suppose, had the same effect as the horrid din with which the heathens pretended to save the moon at the hour of her eclipse.

"7. This device, together with the integrity of the just ones, preserved them from being overwhelmed by the deluge.

"8. Hence, an imitation of these adventures became a sacred institution, which was duly observed in the mysteries, and conducted by the presiding priest."

A more unfortunate selection could scarcely have been made from the whole series of the poems attributed to Taliesin, for the purpose of exhibiting an example of Arkite or any other mysteries. The portion of the poem which is so evidently Christian, Mr. Davies has, however, altogether ignored, and has not included in his translation. This he has done in accordance with his system, as explained in the Preface to his *Mythology*.

"I must here endeavour," he says,[1] "to obviate another objection. In the British poems which treat of heathenish superstitions, a sentence is often inserted containing the name of Christ, or some allusion to his religion, and having no connection with the matter which precedes or follows. Some of these sentences I have omitted, for obvious reasons. I have been not a little puzzled to account for their admission into the text; but, as all our remaining poems were composed or altered subsequent to the first introduction of Christianity, it is probable that St. Augustine supplies us with the true reason of such admixture—'that those who endeavour to mislead by charms, incantations, or other devices of the enemy, insert the name of Christ in their incantations, adding, as it were, a portion of honey to their poisonous draught, so that its bitter may be concealed by that which is sweet, and may be quaffed to the destruction of those who drink it.'"

In this instance, however, if the title "Archaeddon" means in the fifth stanza, "the Ark of Aeddon, Lord of the Din," it must receive the same translation in the seventeenth, and should not have been omitted by Mr. Davies.

There can be no doubt that the poem is of modern date, written by a Christian poet, probably a monk of the island of Anglesey. Mr. Stephens, misled probably by the names of Math and Eunydd, two celebrated magicians of Welsh romance, supposes this poem to form a part of the *Mabinogi*, or history of Taliesin, composed by Thomas ap Einion Offeiriad. It is a genuine production of a religious, probably of the

---

[1] Page vii.

thirteenth or fourteenth century, who, acquainted with the current romance of the day, has introduced allusions to the stories in vogue into his elegy upon his friend the Archdeacon of Anglesey, as Mr. Davies's "Lord of the Din" undoubtedly was.

MARWNAD AEDDON O FON.

Echrys Ynyt gwawd hu Ynys gwrys
    gwobretor
    Mon Mad gogei
    Gwrhyd erfei
      Menai ei dor
    Lleweis wirawd
    Gwin a bragawd
      Gan frawd esgor
    Teyrn wofrwy
    Diwedd pob rhwy
      Rhwyf rewintor.
    Tristlawn ddeon
    Yr Archaeddon
      Can rychior
    Nid fu nid fi
    Ynghemelrhi
      Ei gyfeissor
    Pan ddoeth Aeddon
    O wlad Gwydion
      Seon tewdor
    Gwenwyn pur ddoeth
    Pedair peunoeth
      Meinoeth tymhor
    Cwyddynt gytoed
    Ni bu clyd coed
      Gwynt yngoror
    Math ag Eunydd
    Hudwyd gelfydd
      Rydd elfinor
    Ym myw [1] Gwydion
    Ac Amaethon
      Atoedd cyngbor

    Twll tal y rodawg
    Ffyrf ffodiawg
      Ffyrf ddiachor
    Cadarn gyfedd
    Ymhob gorsedd
      Gwnelid ei fodd
    Cu cynaethwy
    Hyd tra fwy fyw
      Crybwylletor
    Cadarn gyngres
    Ei faranres
      Ni bu werthfor
    Am bwyf gan Grist
    Hyd na bwyf trist
      Pan ebostol
    Hael Archaeddon
    Gan Engylion
      Cynwyssetter
    Echrys ynys
    Gwawd hwynys
      Gwrys gochymma
    Y rhag buddwas
    Cymry ddinas
      Aros ara
    Draganawl ben
    Priodawr perchen
      Ym Mretonia
    Difa gwledig
    Or bendefig
      Ae tu terra
    Pedeir morwyn
    Wedy eu cwyn
      Dygnawd eu tra

[1] Mwy.

Erddygnawd wir
Ar fwr heb dir
   Hir eu trefra
Oi wironyn
Na ddigonyn
   Dim gofetra
Ceryddus wyf
Na chrybwyllwyf
   Am rywnel da
I lwrw lywy
Pwy gwaharddwy
   Pwy attrefna

I lwrw Aeddon
Pwy gyneil Mon
   Mwyn gywala
Am bwyf gan Grist
Hyd na bwyf trist
   O ddrwg o dda
Rhan trugaredd
I wlad rhiedd
   Buchedd gyfa.

Taliesin.

AN ELEGY ON AEDDON OF MONA.

Disturbed is the island,
Lamenting is the island,
   For its zealous ruler.
Fair Mona is shaken,
Agitated is the deep
   Of Menai its defence.
I have drunk the liquor,
The wine and the bragget,
   With the brethren of the convent.
Pervading Lord,
There is an end of all superfluity,
   Now the ruler is fallen.[1]
Sorrowful is the Dean
For the Archdeacon,
   The gifted in song ;

There has not been, nor will be,
In time of trouble,
   His equal.
When Aeddon came[2]
From the land of Gwydion,
   The strong Seon,[3]
Pure damsels came,[4]
Four every night,
   Serene was the season.
The joined roofs fell in,
Nor was there shelter in the wood
   When the wind was on the coast.
Math and Eunydd,
Skilful in sorcery,
   Let loose the elements.

[1] Under the word "gwofrwy," Dr. Owen gives as the translation of this stanza,

     The universal tyrant ends every energy ;
     Sovereign of destruction ;

but under the word "rhewintor" he gives,

     The end of every leader is to be falling.

[2] Whether Aeddon was the name of the Archdeacon, or whether, as Arch-aeddon means Archdeacon, Aeddon means Deacon, I cannot decide. The latter is most probable.

[3] Caernarvon, Caer Sciont. The land of Gwydion, son of Don, was in Gwyned.

[4] Gwenwyn. This word is translated by Dr. Owen "poison," being evi-

Better than Gwydion
And Amaethon
   Was he in counsel.
Pierced is the front of the shield
Of the strong, the fortunate,
   The firm inflexible one.
Supporter of festivity,
In every Gorsedd
   His will was performed.
Beloved of his family,
While I am in life
   He shall be commemorated.

The supporter of mutual hospitality,
To him, rank
   Was not precious.

May I be with Christ,
So that I may not be sorrowful,
   When as an apostle

The bountiful Archdeacon,
With angels,
   Shall summon me.

The remainder of this poem, as printed in the *Myvyrian Archæology*, is most probably a distinct composition on the same subject, the death of the Archdeacon of Anglesey, written either by the same hand, or in imitation of the preceding.

Disturbed is the island,
Lamenting is the island,
   For its zealous ruler.
On account of the useful servant
Of the city of Wales
   And Ross-hir.[1]
A leading chief,
An hereditary proprietor
   In Britain.
Passing away is the prince,
And of the nobles
   Thou art in the earth.
Four damsels
Are uttering lamentations,
   Great was their affliction.
Very grievous in truth,
Going away without any certainty,
   How distant their abode.

In their helplessness
They could do nothing,
   On account of their grief.
I should be rebuked
If I did not commemorate,
   My benefactor.
In the place of Llywy,
Who shall make regulations,
   Who shall keep order?
In the place of Aeddon,
Who shall sustain Mona
   With equal courtesy?
May I be with Christ,
So that I may not be sorrowful
   For evil or good.
May I obtain mercy
In the land of the Lord
   Of perfect life.

dently a corruption of the Latin *Venenum;* but it cannot have that meaning here any more than where it occurs in the names of individuals, as Gwen-wynwyn. Gwen is a common component in the names both of males and females. The other stanza lower down, beginning " Pedeir morwyn," shows the true meaning here to be that which I have given above.

  [1] *Rosshir* or *Rhosyr*, one of the three cantrefs or hundreds of Mon, or Anglesey.

Upon the strength of the occurrence of the word "hu" in the first line of this poem, a great deal has been said by Mr. Davies and others about the worship of Hu, a supposed solar deity. But these writers have omitted to notice, that where this line is repeated in the 18th stanza, at which a second version of the poem commences, instead of "gwawd hu ynys," it is printed "gwawd hwynys." There is therefore an error of transcription in one of the two. This has not troubled Mr. Davies, who has printed both alike, and given "hu" a capital letter. The whole tenor of the poem shows us that Hu would be quite out of place in company with the Dean, Archdeacon, and Angels; and the "hu" or "hw" is most probably a mistake for "yw." I have altered the word *gwawd*, "praise," to *gwaedd*, "crying out," which, though more in accordance with the sense of the preceding epithet, is not a necessary substitution.

With regard to the 5th stanza, there can be no doubt that the rendering I have given of the word "Deon" is the correct one :—

> Sorrowful is the Dean.

In Richards's *Welsh Dictionary*, 4to ed. 1839, we have the meaning, *Deon*, a "Dean." Dr. Owen gives for it, "the distributor or divider; the giver; he that sets aright; an epithet often applied to the Deity by the ancients; also as a plural: visitors, strangers, foreigners." The word has, no doubt, the meaning of "giver or distributor of gifts" in many instances; in others, apparently that of leader or ruler, as in the following lines from *Cynddelw* :—

> Golchynt eu deurut dewr weissyon o cad
> Gwastad gymynad gymynogyon
> Can etyw an llyw llew teyrnon
> Teyrnet ohen dreic benn dragon
> Canys dir hepcor dewrder deon
> Deus Dominus duw boed gwiryon,—
>
> Wet are their cheeks, the bold warriors,
> The steady-striking battleaxe-men,

Because our chief, the princely lion, has departed.
The example of princes, the head chief of chiefs,
Because the bold leader has left the earth.
Deus Dominus God, may he be faultless (before thee).

Cynddelw Marwnad Cadwallawn mab Madawc.

There is here no question of a distributor of gifts, but of a dead chieftain; though it must be admitted that the quality of " bestower of gifts" was inseparable, in the state of society which these poems refer to, from the condition of chieftain.

A curious triplet has been preserved by Dr. Owen, which contains this epithet. It is an incantation or charm to remove a disease of the tongue in cattle :—

Llawer aer llawes eon
Y triwyr duon a'r tri deon
A noror davawdwst ar yr eidion.

The first line Dr. Owen translates

The many bold grasping conflicts—

a strange beginning for a rustic charm. The line is, no doubt, corrupt, and was probably

Lloer air llawer seon;

and the whole incantation,

Bright moon, many stars,
The three black men and the three Deon,
May they break the tongue blister on the cattle.

But in the stanza of this elegy on Aeddon, where the word *Deon* occurs, its connection with the word *Archaeddon,* " an Archdeacon," in the next line, clearly justifies the rendering it " Dean," as it certainly had that meaning, among others.

As Davies has taken his version of many passages from Owen's *Dictionary*, he must have laboured under a strong delusion when he translated Archaeddon, the ark of Aeddon; for Dr. Owen gives the true version under the word :—

The generous Archdeacon, may he be received by angels.

It is quite clear that there is no Druidism in this "Elegy upon Aeddon," and we must pass on in search of it to other poems attributed to Taliesin.

One main and essential doctrine of the Druidic superstition has been said to be that of the metempsychosis, or transmigration of the soul, in other corporeal forms, through a succession of periods.

That the Druids of Gaul, and therefore probably of Britain, professed a belief in a future state of existence, appears to be sufficiently established by the testimony of the classical writers, but that this was a belief in the transmigration of the soul in the supposed Pythagorean sense, is very doubtful.

The words of Cæsar, " In primis hoc volunt persuadere, non interire animas, sed ab aliis post mortem transire ad alios," certainly seem to give credit to the idea that they believed in actual transmigration. Diodorus Siculus, also, expressly refers to the doctrine of Pythagoras on that subject, and says, that the same belief obtained among the Druids. But some of the customs of the Gauls, related by the historians, rather point to the belief common to almost all known peoples, of a life after death in another and a better world, than to a return to this world in another form. Pomponius Mela relates, that the settlement of accounts and the payment of debts were sometimes adjourned to take place in the next world—in the words of Lucan, " orbe alio." The same is mentioned by Valerius Maximus. And Diodorus relates a custom of throwing letters written by the relations of the deceased on the funeral pile, which might be read by the defunct, thus conveying to him in the next world the latest intelligence from his " own correspondent." These customs are inconsistent with the notion of a metempsychosis, and return to earth in a different form, whether human or animal. The belief was more probably similar to that of the Scandinavian nations—an existence after death in another world, in which the pleasures and the business of life, such as they had been accustomed to, were to be more fully and constantly enjoyed.

This seems to be the meaning of Pomponius Mela, "æternas esse animas, vitamque alteram ad manes." The Elysium of the Celts was no cold lifeless Hades like that of the Greeks, with its pale shadows that parted before the attempted embrace of the human form; but a real living life, with its bowls of mead, its songs, its bloody combats, stone circles, and human sacrifices.

> Vobis auctoribus, umbræ
> Non tacitas Erebi sedes Ditisque profundi
> Pallida regna petunt; regit idem spiritus artus
> Orbe alio; canitis si cognita, vitæ
> Mors media est.[1]

In this other world, too, it is clear that friend and foe, debtor and creditor, expected to meet again, to recognise and be recognised as upon the present earth. This, however, is a very different thing from a belief in the transmigration of the soul through a variety of forms, human and animal, upon this earth itself. As far as the evidence on this subject goes, we know nothing of the pretended cycles of transmigration, and find no trace of belief that the soul passed into an animal form after death. On the contrary, the reason which Cæsar and Lucan give for the inculcation of this belief is, that it made its votaries the more bold, causing them to have no fear of death.

> Felices errore suo, quos ille, timorum
> Maximus haud urget lethi metus. Inde ruendi
> In ferrum mens prona viris, animæque capaces
> Mortis; et ignavum redituræ parcere vitæ.[2]

The warrior, however, who might look forward without regret to a renewal of his earthly life, or a continued festival in some Celtic Valhalla, would scarcely have contemplated

---

[1] Lucan, *Pharsalia*, l. v. 454.　　　　[2] Ibid. 459.

with pleasure the return to existence in the form of a beast of burden, a bird, or a worm.

We ought also to find, if the doctrine of transmigration through animal forms were a part of the Druidical tenets, some trace of an indisposition to destroy animal life—a tenderness in dealing with creatures which might possibly be the temporary habitations of the souls of ancestors or kinsmen. Of this feeling also, which in other creeds accompanies the belief in transmigration, we find no trace, either in the historians or in the manners and customs of the Celtic race.

It has, however, been so repeatedly asserted that evidence of these doctrines is still extant, that the subject demands some further investigation.

We have already mentioned that the learned author of the *Welsh Dictionary* derived his statements respecting the Bardic polity and mythology from Edward Williams. This remarkable man has played an important part in the history of Welsh literature.

In his *Poems, Lyric and Pastoral,* published in 1794, he presented to the public the following

"ADVERTISEMENT.

"The patriarchal religion of Ancient Britain called Druidism, but by the Welsh most commonly *Barddas,* Bardism, though they also term it *Derwyddoniaeth,* Druidism, is no more inimical to Christianity than the religion of Noah, Job, or Abraham ; it has never, as some imagine, been quite extinct in Britain ; the Welsh Bards have, through all ages *down to the present,* kept it alive. There is in my possession a manuscript synopsis of it by Llewelyn Sion, a Bard, written about the year 1560 : its truth and accuracy are corroborated by innumerable notices and allusions in our Bardic manuscripts of every age up to Taliesin in the sixth century, whose poems exhibit a complete system of Druidism. By these (undoubtedly authentic) writings it will appear, that the Ancient British Christianity was strongly tinctured with Druidism."

"The old Welsh Bards kept up a perpetual war with the Church of Rome, and from it experienced much persecution. Narrow understandings may conceive that they were the less Christians for having been Druids. The doctrine of the metempsychosis is that which, of all others, most clearly

Vindicates the ways of God to man.

"It is sufficiently countenanced by many passages in the New Testament, and was believed by many of the primitive Christians and the Essenes among the Jews." [1]

Upon this point we may observe, that one of the doctrines of the Barddas is, "that a state of eternal punishment is in itself impossible; and the infliction of such punishment is the only thing which the Deity cannot do."

The Bardic doctrine of the transmigration of the soul, supposed, on the authority of Edward Williams, to have been thus preserved, has attracted the attention of several learned writers who have not very strictly inquired after the proofs of its existence. Mr. Turner, in his celebrated work on these Welsh poems, thus noticed the doctrines of the Barddas :[2]—

"Among the Welsh remains is a MS. of poetical triads. The MS. has been entitled 'Barddas, or the Book of Bardism, or Cyvrinach Beirdd Ynys Prydain.' The triads were collected together at different periods. Some of them state the Bardic doctrines about the Metempsychosis. These triads, of course, only prove that the bards of the middle ages had these notions; but it is highly probable, that what they believed on this point they derived from their ancestors; and, as we know that the Druids believed in transmigration, we may consider them as the source of the opinions.

"They mention three circles of existence :—1. The Cylch y Ceugant, or all-enclosing circle, which contains the Deity alone. 2. The circle of Gwynvydd or Felicity, the abode of good men who have passed through their terrestrial changes. 3. The circle of Abred or Evil, that in which mankind pass through their various stages of existence before being qualified to enter the circle of felicity.

"All animated beings have three states of existence to pass through—the state of *Abred* or evil, in *Annwn* or the Great Deep; the state of freedom in the human form; and the state

---

[1] *Poems, Lyric and Pastoral*, vol. ii. p. 194.
[2] *Vindication of the Ancient British Poems*, page 226.

18

of love, which is happiness in the *Nef* or heaven.   All beings but God must undergo three *angen* or necessities : they must have a beginning in *Annwn* or the great deep ; a progression in *Abred* or the state of evil ; and a completion in the circle of felicity in heaven.

" In passing through the changes of being, attached to the state of Abred, it is possible for man by misconduct to fall retrograde into the lowest state from which he had emerged. There are three things which will inevitably plunge him back into the changes of Abred—1. Pride ; for this he will fall to Annwn, which is the lowest point at which existence begins. 2. Falsehood, which will replunge him in Obryn, or a transmigration into some degrading form.   3. Cruelty, which will consign him to Cydvil, or a transmigration into some ferocious beast.   From these he must proceed again in due course, through changes of being, up to humanity.

"Humanity was the limit of degrading transmigrations ; all the changes above humanity were felicitating, and they were to be perpetual, with ever-increasing acquisitions of knowledge and happiness."

When we ask for the authority for these statements, and the proofs of these doctrines of cycles of transmigration, through the circles of Ceugant, Gwynvydd, and Abred, having ever been held by any bard, Druid, or philosopher, at any time or in any place, we can get no farther back than the MSS. of Llywelyn Sion of Llangewyd, who died in A.D. 1616, though his MSS. are said to have been copied from others about a century older.

But even for this moderate antiquity of the commencement of the sixteenth century, the sources of information fail us.

The extracts which Sharon Turner supposed, on the authority of Edward Williams, to be contained in the *Cyfrinach Beirdd,* were taken by the former from the *Lyric Poems,* published by the latter in 1794.

The MS. of Llywelyn Sion was, according to the statement of Dr. Owen Pughe, last transcribed and revised by Edward

Davydd of Margam, who died in 1690. The latter says, in his preface, that he compiled it from the books of bards and learned teachers, lest the materials should become lost; and more particularly from the books of Meyrig Davydd, Davydd Llwyd Mathew, Davydd Benwyn, and Llewellyn Sion, who were Bardic presidents of the Glamorgan chair from 1560 to 1580.

Llewellyn Sion, who died in 1616, says, that the authors, teachers, and judges, who sanctioned this system and code, were the Druids and Bards after they had come to the faith in Christ.

"The original manuscript of Edward Davydd is" (says Mr. Turner in 1803) "yet extant in the library of Llan Haran, in Glamorganshire; but there is nothing else to connect this remarkable system of psychology with the sixth century, unless it is to be found in the works of the ancient bards themselves." Mr. Turner thought, and such has been the general opinion, that this doctrine of transmigration is exhibited in many passages of Taliesin.

The *Hanes Taliesin*, which we shall presently give, is, according to this view, "a recital of his pretended transmigrations; and when we read in his other poems that he has been in various animal shapes—as a serpent, a wild sow, a buck, a crane, and such like—we must call to mind that those scenes of existence in Abred which were between Annwn and humanity were the changes of being in the bodies of different animals."

Dr. Owen, in his *Welsh Dictionary*, quotes passages from the "Barddas"; but he does not cite it as authority for his statements in the *Sketch of British Bardism*. On the contrary, he gives a reason for not producing his authorities which is simply ludicrous. "The first thing," he says, "taught to disciples were the Bardic Institutes, which were retained only by tradition in aphorisms, poems, and adages of a peculiar cast. It is from those traditions that the present sketch of Bardism is formed, wherein is given the general scope of them. With respect to the traditions themselves, *as one of the order*, I feel a propensity (a pardonable one, I hope), in common with a few remaining members, to preserve amongst ourselves undisclosed, except at a Gorsedd, those very curious remains, as an incitement to preserve the system." [1]

The only document, in fact, on this subject which Dr. Owen produces, is a proclamation dated in the year 1792 :—

"When it was the year of our Lord one thousand seven hundred and ninety-two, and the sun in the point of the vernal equinox, a summons and invitation was given, in the hearing of the country and prince, under the period of a year and a day, with protection for all such as might seek for privilege and graduation appertaining to science and Bardism, to repair to the top of Pumlumon in Powys, at the expiration of the year and the day, in the hours of noon, when there will not be a naked weapon against them; and then in the presence of Iolo Morganwg, Bard according to the privilege of the Bards of the Isle of Britain; and with him W. Mecain, Hywel Eryri, and D. Ddu Eryri; and they being all graduated Bards under the privilege and custom of the Bards of Britain, for the purposes of pronouncing the judgment of a Gorsedd, in the eye of the sun and face of the light, on all, with respect to genius and moral conduct, who may seek for presidency and privilege, according to the privilege and custom of the Bards of the Isle of Britain. 'Y Gwir yn Erbyn y Byd.' —'The truth against the world.'"

Whether Dr. Owen or any one else repaired to the top of Plinlimmon at the vernal equinox in 1793, in obedience to this summons, we are not informed; but the venerable society of Bards had shortly before that time fallen to so low an ebb, as to consist only of Edward Williams and the Rev. Edward Evans of Aberdare.

Mr. Turner, it will be observed, knew nothing of these Bardic Triads except from the publication of a portion of

[1] Llywarch Hen, Preface, p. xxxiv.

them by Edward Williams in the *Lyric Poems*. Unfortunately for the interests of Welsh literature, the same publication has been taken as a foundation for a learned commentary on the Druidical theology, by a writer whose reputation will give authority to assertions which have not been supported by any evidence.[1]   As this is a matter of the first importance for the true understanding of the early Welsh poetry, being no less than a question of the independent existence of testimony to the transmission and preservation of these curious doctrines from a remote antiquity to the time of the seventeenth century, we must endeavour to trace the history of this supposed MS. a little further.

The *Poems, Lyric and Pastoral*, by Edward Williams, which contained the account of the cycles of transmigration and the other Druidic doctrines, were published in 1794.   In 1822, Edward Williams published and circulated prospectuses in English and Welsh in the following terms :—

"In the press, and speedily will be published, in the Welsh language, the *Esoteric Literature of the Ancient British Bards*, under the heads of—

"1. Canons of the poetical criticism of the Bards.

"2. Laws of Welsh versification, in all its varieties and singular peculiarities, from the remotest periods to the close of the sixteenth century.

"3. Laws, polity, and discipline of the ancient Bards.

"4. The esoteric mythology, and theology of the ancient British Bards or Druids.   Compiled from ancient and authentic MS. documents, and from the Bardic voice conventional, or guarded oral tradition of the ancient British Bards, still from time immemorial retained in the *Chair* so termed, or Bardic Presidiality of Glamorgan, by Llywelyn Sion, about the year 1600, with augmentations by Edward Davyd about the year 1680, both Institutional Bards of the

---

[1] *La Mystère des Bardes de l'Ile de Bretagne, ou la Doctrine des Bardes Gallois du Moyen Age, sur Dieu, la Vie Future et la Transmigration des Ames.* Par Adolphe Pictét.   Génève, 1856.

Chair of Glamorgan.   With Explanatory Notes, and an Historical and Critical Introduction by the Editor."

Edward Williams died in 1826, not having brought out the work advertised.

In 1821, a selection from the Triads of Bardism had been published in the *Cambro-Briton*,[1] but they were confessedly taken from Edward Williams's poems, and the editor had never seen them in the original MS.   Only twenty-four out of the forty-six published by Edward Williams were given in the *Cambro-Briton*, "the remainder being so involved in metaphysical obscurity as to be for the most part unintelligible." From this circumstance, and from their occasional reference to the doctrines of Christianity, the editor of the *Cambro-Briton* concludes that "they are not to be regarded throughout as genuine memorials of the primitive institution of Bardism, although they may in some degree be impregnated with its singular tenets."

The Institutional Triads also were published in the *Cambro-Briton*, with the remark that they were copied from the *Lyric Poems*.   The editor observes, that "Mr. Williams gives the originals also, but does not state on what authority.   It may be presumed, however, that he would not have ventured to make them public without being convinced of their genuineness as memorials of the singular system of Bardism, or, as it is more generally called, Druidism, which anciently prevailed in this island."

In 1829, the *Cyfrinach Beirdd Ynys Prydain* was published by Taliesin Williams, son of Iolo Morganwg, in the Welsh language, and from the MS. of Llywelyn Sion.

But here, to our great surprise, we derive no information whatever on the subject of the Druidic doctrine of transmigration.

In fact, the doctrines represented by Iolo Morganwg to be contained in the Barddas are not to be found in the published work.   It does indeed mention the "Ofydd" as one of the three kinds of singers (cerddor); and the editor has added a

---

[1] Vol. ii. page 339.

note stating that in Meyryg Dafydd's MS. the Druid is mentioned among them. We are still therefore in the dark as to the source whence Iolo Morganwg at the close of the eighteenth century obtained the doctrines of the Bards and Druids of the sixth, and in doubt as to whether there ever were any documents in existence of the kind referred to by him. This doubt is not lessened by the fact that there is another copy of the *Cyfrinach* in the Hengwrt Library, and that it does not contain the esoteric mythology and theology of the Bards or Druids.

In 1848, the Welsh MSS. Society published a selection of the MSS. left behind him by Edward Williams, among which we find, the *Voice Conventional of the Bards of Britain*, from the MS. of Llywelyn Sion, one of the authorities noticed by Edward Williams in his Prospectus. But the *Esoteric Mythology and Theology of the Ancient Bards or Druids* has not made its appearance.

The Welsh MSS. Society comprehends among its members the most learned Welsh scholars of the age. It is much to be lamented, that in making a selection from the Iolo MSS. of Edward Williams, they should have neglected, when publishing the *Voice Conventional of the Bards of Britain*, which forms part of the work advertised in 1822, to give to the world a document so interesting and important to European literature in general, and to the history of Britain and Welsh archæology in particular, as the *Esoteric Mythology and Theology of the Ancient Bards or Druids*, giving an account of the Bardic views of the transmigration of the soul, and of a future state of rewards and punishments unknown to the Christian Church.[1] Until such a MS. shall be published, we may be

---

[1] It is to be presumed that the editors of the Welsh MSS. Society satisfied themselves of the genuineness of the MS. called the *Voice Conventional of the Bards of Britain* before publication; but it is remarkable, that neither in the body of the work of Dr. J. D. Rhys, published in 1592, in which the works of the earlier Bards are frequently cited, nor in the dedication, or the preface by Humphrey Prichard, is there any mention of Druids or of the tissue of absurdities contained in the *Voice Conventional*.

justified in reserving our belief as to its genuineness, if not as to its existence.

The author of the *Mythology and Rites of the Ancient Druids* did not hesitate to assert that "a slight inquiry into the credentials of the society (the Chair of Glamorgan, of which Edward Williams pretended to be the regularly inducted president) will discover some marks of gross misrepresentation, if not of absolute forgery, and consequently suggest the necessity of great caution in admitting its traditions."[1]   One of the doctrines of Edward Williams's *Bardism*, as given by Dr. Owen, was, that one man cannot assume authority over another; for if he may over one, by the same reason he may rule over a million or over a world.   All men are necessarily equal; the four elements in their natural state, or everything not manufactured by art, is the common property of all. "The principles here announced," says Davies, "seem to go rather beyond the levellers of the seventeenth century, and to savour strongly of a Druidism which originated in Gaul, and was then transplanted into some corners of Britain, not many ages before the year 1792, when the *Memorials of Bardism* made its appearance.   It is not the Druidism of history or of the British Bards."[2]

This Gallic origin, in the eighteenth century, of the pretended Druidic institutes of Edward Williams, hinted at by Davies, is, we believe, the true one.

As the *Cyfrinach Beirdd Ynys Prydain* has never been translated into English, and probably, from the peculiar and special nature of its contents, never will be, it may be useful to state what it really contains, in order to prevent future historians from citing it as a repertory of the Druidical philosophy and superstitions, and an evidence of the persistence of this philosophy and learning down to the seventeenth century of the Christian era.   The *Cyfrinach Beirdd* is, in fact, a learned and copious Essay on poetical composition and the art of framing the Welsh metres, which are extremely

---

[1] Page 33.   [2] Page 57.

numerous and complicated in their nature. It commences with a history of the nature and origin of the Welsh language, and the nine qualities appertaining to song.

It informs us,[1] that there have been three languages: "the first, that which Adam spoke in Paradise, and which he lost when he ate the apple through the deceit of the devil; the second was that of the prophet Moses when he passed through the Red Sea, and this tongue is that used by the prophets for 3000 years; the third language is that of the Cymry, which was that of Enos, son of Seth, son of Adam, who was the first man born after the expulsion of Adam from Paradise. It came to the Cymry through Japhet the son of Noah, whose descendants brought it from the ends of the world when the confusion of tongues took place among those who built the Castle of Babel, which was a town of prodigious size, and displeasing to the Holy Spirit; whence came to pass the corruption and imperfection of all tongues in the world except that of the Welsh. Of the three primeval tongues, the one is used in heaven, by God, the saints, and the angels; the second in the Holy Scriptures; and the third is the Cymraeg or Welsh, and is used at this day, in its genuine form and condition, by the Cymry of the Island of Britain. All other languages are imperfect, ignoble, and half-witted; and neither song nor poetry can be properly composed in them, because they were taught by the devil at the Tower of Babel. The consequence is, that the *Awen*, or poetical inspiration of the Welsh, is a divine inspiration proceeding from God; the poetry of the Saxon, English, and other corrupt tongues, is an inspiration of the devil, which was obtained from him at the Tower of Babel. The true or divine Awen was possessed by Adam in Paradise, but lost at the fall; again possessed by Enos the son of Seth after the expulsion from Paradise; it was enjoyed by the Hebrew prophets, and was brought by the Cymry to Britain, where it was used by the Bards and Druids in praising God, and in all good and wise things. In the course of time it

[1] *Cyfrinach*, page 29.

was lost through the wickedness of men, who accepted an evil
Awen or inspiration of the devil in its place, until the coming
of Christ, when it was restored to the apostles, as Saint Paul
tells us, as the Holy Spirit or divine inspiration; and this
divine inspiration remains with us to the present day."

The remainder of the work consists of an account of the
different kinds of poetical composition; of the proper arrangement of topics in poems, in praise of the Deity, of ministers
of religion, of learned persons, kings, queens, nobles, judges,
young men, married men, married women, invisible things
such as angels, every kind of animals or creatures, and all
inanimate things. Lastly, the Canons of Song and Metre,
which occupy the great bulk of the work, consisting of an
elaborate exposition of the complex and difficult subject of
Welsh metre.

Of the Druids and their mythology and philosophy, of
Bardic religious mysteries, and psychological speculations, the
" Cyfrinach Beirdd " has not a word. The only Triads con-
tained in it are called the " Triads of Song," which describe
the nature, qualities, and qualifications of poetry and poets.
The *Cyfrinach Beirdd Ynys Prydain*, published by Taliesin
Williams, is not therefore the MS. referred to by his father
Edward Williams as containing a synopsis of the Bardic or
Druidic religion, written by Llywelyn Sion, and in his (Edward
Williams's) possession in the year 1792; and the manuscript
of the " Barddas " is still a desideratum.

It was, of course, impossible to suppose that such doctrines
as those of the Barddas should have been held by the Welsh
Bards, without having left behind, evidence of its existence in
their writings. Accordingly Mr. Edward Williams adduces
an instance, among others, from the poems of Taliesin. " I
have," he says, " in one passage mentioned a qualified sense
in which the Christian Bards and Druids believed the metempsychosis; this was, that the depraved soul of man passes
in a state beyond the grave into progressive modes of existence corresponding with the natures of earthly worms and

brutes, into whom, in the literal sense, the aboriginal or patriarchal Druids believed it passed. Taliesin places this probationary, divestigating, or purifying metempsychosis in the
Hell of Christianity, whence the soul gradually rises again to
Felicity, the way for it having been opened by Jesus Christ;
for this is his obvious meaning when he says—

> Nifer a fuant yn anghyffred
> Uffern oer gwaredred
> Hyd bumoes byd
> Hyd pan ddillyngwys Crist gaethiwed
> O ddyfnfais affwys Abred
> Maint dyddwg Duw trwy nodded :

i. e., multitudes were, ignorant of their state in Hell, in the
miserable progression of deliverance, during the world's five
ages, until released by Christ from the captivities of the im-
mense deep of the abyss of Abred : all those has God taken
into his possession."

This is not quite a literal interpretation of the passage,
which runs thus :—

> Numbers there were incomprehensible
> Kept in a *cold* hell,[1]
> Until the fifth age of the world.
> Until Christ should release the captives
> From the profound depths of evil ;
> Many God took under his protection.

Even if this passage stood alone, we should not see in it
anything more than the views of a Christian writer of the
middle ages, on the subject of the state of those who had
lived and died, previous to the coming of Christ in the fifth
age of the world. These souls, he says, were retained in a
hell or place of ward, but not one of fiery punishment, until
the coming of the Saviour broke the bonds of their captivity.
We certainly may allow that a Christian may have entertained

---

[1] Mr. E. Williams does not translate the word *oer* "cold" in his version,
though the whole sense of the passage depends on it.

such opinions in the twelfth or thirteenth century, without having recourse to the phantom of a Druidical theology. The condition of the souls of those who had not heard the tidings of the Gospel, was a subject discussed by many writers who certainly were not acquainted with the Druidical philosophy.

But when we turn to the original piece from which the above extract was taken, we can only feel surprise that any writer with honest intentions should have quoted it as a work of Taliesin without further comment. It is entitled *Marwnad y Milveib*, or an Elegy on the Thousand Children or Saints; and in the *Myvyrian Archæology* there is appended to the title, " Taliesin ai cant, e ddywedir "—" Taliesin sung it as it is said;" for, like the great majority of the Welsh poetical remains, it has been ascribed to that Bard. The following is a literal version of the commencement of the poem :—

THE ELEGY ON THE THOUSAND SAINTS.

I address a prayer to the Trinity,
May inspiration be given me in thy praise.
In the passing present state perilous is their condition
Who, by disobedience, are incurring wrath;
Very great truly is the society of the Saints.
King of Heaven, I will be eloquent in asserting,
Before my soul is separated from my flesh,
Before are made known my good deeds and my sins,
My entreaty before the paternal Lord,
That I may have mercy from the Trinity.
I revere, I earnestly long for, the elements of the blood![1]
There are nine ranks of the mystic troops of heaven,
And the tenth of the saints prepared for the seventh age.

* * * * *

Apostles and martyrs,
Youths of glorious appearance,
And Solomon served God,
Pure in speech, pure in walk, thy nature,

---

[1] The cup, which was withheld from the laity. If this is the true meaning of the passage, it marks it as of the thirteenth century at the earliest.

And in virtue shall be an example to me,[1]
As long as I shall retain my faculties.
Numbers there have been of a holy disposition,
Steps of the golden pillars of the church.
By many authors it is declared,
From the very profitable books of the wise,
For those who love not thy service there is a precipice,
May my soul be protected from it.
Numbers there were incomprehensible
Kept in a cold hell,
Until the fifth age of the world,
Until Christ should release the captives
From the profound depths of evil,
Many God took under his protection,
Two thousand sons of the children of Elia.
Abimatu et infra.

*　　　*　　　*　　　*　　　*

There shall be at Jerusalem
Many saints of Armorica,
And many of the rule of Tours,
Who broke through the city of Rome,
Apoli and Alexandria,
And Garanwys and Judæa,
Tres partes Divitia
Asia, Affrica, Europa;
Many saints of Capharnaum, Maritnen, and Nain,
And Zebulon, and Cisen, and Nineveh, and Neptalim,
In Dubriatus and Zorim,
According to the prophecy of Christ, son of Mary, daughter of
　　　Joachim,
Upon the pinnacle of the Temple.

*　　　*　　　*　　　*　　　*

Many saints of Sicomorialis
And the island of Defrophani.

*　　　*　　　*　　　*　　　*

Many saints of other regions,
Effectus re inferior,
A superare superioræ
And Armonim and Thysor,
And the vales of Enor and Segor,
And Carthage the greater and less,

---

[1] Yn dawn glas. The word "glas" is here the English word "glass," a
mirror.

And the green island at the border of the sea.
Many saints of the island of Britain
And Ireland, a blessed portion.
Many saints Oriento,
And the united people of Judah.
Language of Greek and Hebrew
And Latin, men will be speaking,
Seven score seven thousand saints,
And seven thousand and seven times ten score.

    *   *   *   *   *

Twelve thousand in one assembly
Believed through the word of John,
I pray they may receive their recompense.
In the heavens is no displeasure.
Nine thousand saints have received
Baptism, faith, and confession.
After death the punishment of the multitude is fire;
A cold hell is their refuge,[1]
Created by the Lord,
Through the chief (of the saints) Peter prepared for the destitute.
Qui venerunt Angeli
In natali Domini
Media nocte in laudem
Cum pastoribus in Bethlehem
Nivem Angeli de Cœlo
Cum Michaelo Archangelo
Qui præcedunt præcelio
Erga animas in mundo.

    *   *   *   *   *

Quando fuit Christus crucifixus ut sibi
Ipse placuisset venissent ibi in auxilium
Plusquam duodecim legiones angelorum
Toto orbe terrarum
Jesus Christus videntem in agonia in muordo
Ut sint nostri auxilium
Duodecim millia millium
Anti tribunal stantium
Qui laudantie laudantium
Tues mores Rex Regum

    *   *   *   *   *

---

[1] We have here the explanation of the former passage cited by Mr. Williams, and can see that it is connected with the doctrine of purgatory.

The poem concludes with these lines :—

> When I fall into a sinful word,
> May neither you nor others hear me.

Such is the supposed repository of a qualified doctrine of the Druidical metempsychosis, preserved from the time of Julius Cæsar, and taught by the Christians of the sixth century. It seems probable, from other writings of Iolo Morganwg (Edward Williams), that he really believed this and other pieces of the same stamp to have been written by Taliesin in the sixth century.

As, however, the work in which the Bardic Triads were published was a collection of poems in the English language, the author might very reasonably speculate on the ignorance of English readers on the subject of the Welsh poems, and almost equally so on that of his countrymen in general, since the *Myvyrian Archæology* was not published at the time "The Lyric Poems" issued from the press. Had the Myvyrian collection been then in print, it seems hardly possible that the above example of "evidence" in support of the "Barddas" should have been allowed to pass unnoticed.

Discarding altogether the pretended authority of the Barddas, the principal, if not the only source, from whence the notion that this doctrine of transmigration is to be found in the Welsh poems, is drawn, is the *Romance of the History of Taliesin,* and the pieces connected with it. In its present form, it has already been observed, this tale is not older than the thirteenth century; but it is evident that it was composed of materials which had previously existed in the shape of tales and traditions, and must have been current in popular fiction long before Thomas ap Einion reduced them to a consistent form.

The copy of this tale contained in the Red Book of Hergest, has been published with an excellent English translation, in the collection of *Mabinogion,* or Tales of the Welsh, by

Lady Charlotte Guest, a work which marks an era in the history of Welsh literature.

The prose portion of the following translation is abridged from that work; in the poetical part the versions of Lady Guest and of Mr. Stephens have also been partly made use of.

THE HISTORY OF TALIESIN.

In times past there lived in Penllyn a man of gentle lineage named Tegid Voel, and his dwelling was in the midst of the lake Tegid, and his wife was called Caridwen. And there was born to him of his wife a son named Morvran ab Tegid, and also a daughter, Creirwy, the fairest maiden in the world was she; and they had a brother the most ill-favoured man in the world, Avagddu. Now, Caridwen his mother thought that he was not likely to be admitted among men of noble birth, by reason of his ugliness, unless he had some exalted merits or knowledge.

For it was in the beginning of Arthur's time and the Round Table. So she resolved, according to the arts of the books of the Fferyllt, to boil a cauldron of Inspiration and Science for her son, that his reception might be honourable because of his knowledge of the mysteries of the future state of the world. Then she began to boil the cauldron, which from the beginning of its boiling might not cease to boil for a year and a day, until three blessed drops were obtained of the grace of inspiration. And she put Gwion Bach the son of Gwreang of Llanfair in Powys to stir the cauldron, and a blind man named Morda to kindle the fire beneath it, and she charged them that they should not suffer it to cease boiling for the space of a year and a day. And she herself, according to the books of the astronomers, and in planetary hours, gathered every day of all charm-bearing herbs. And one day towards the end of the year, as Caridwen was culling plants and making incantations, it chanced that three drops of the charmed liquor flew out of the cauldron and fell upon the finger of Gwion Bach. And by reason of their great heat he put his finger to his mouth, and the instant he put those marvel-working drops into his mouth, he foresaw everything that was to come, and perceived that his chief care must be to guard against the wiles of Caridwen, for vast was her skill. And in very great fear he fled towards his own land. And the cauldron burst in two, because all the liquor within it, except the three charm-bearing drops, was poisonous, so that the horses of Gwyddno Garanhir were poisoned by the water of the stream into which the liquor of the cauldron ran; and the confluence of that stream was called the Poison of the Horses of Gwyddno, from that time forth.

Thereupon came in Caridwen, and saw all the toil of the whole year lost.

And she seized a billet of wood, and struck the blind Morda on the head until one of his eyes fell out upon his cheek. And he said, "Wrongfully hast thou disfigured me, for I am innocent. Thy loss was not because of me." "Thou speakest truth," said Caridwen; "it was Gwion Bach who robbed me." And she went forth after him running. And he saw her, and changed himself into a hare and fled. But she changed herself into a greyhound and turned him. And he ran towards a river and became a fish. And she, in the form of an otter bitch, chased him under the water, until he was fain to turn himself into a bird of the air. Then she, as a hawk, followed him, and gave him no rest in the sky. And just as she was about to stoop upon him and he was in fear of death, he espied a heap of winnowed wheat on the floor of a barn, and he dropped amongst the wheat and turned himself into one of the grains. Then she transformed herself into a high-crested black hen, and went to the wheat and scratched it with her feet, and found him out and swallowed him. And, as the story says, she bore him nine months, and when she was delivered of him, she could not find it in her heart to kill him by reason of his beauty. So she wrapped him in a leathern bag, and cast him into the sea to the mercy of God, on the twenty-ninth day of April. And at that time the weir of Gwyddno was on the strand between Dyvi and Aberystwith, near to his own castle, and the value of an hundred pounds was taken in that weir every May eve. And in those days Gwyddno had an only son named Elphin, the most hapless of youths, and the most needy. And it grieved his father sore, for he thought that he was born in an evil hour. And by the advice of his council, his father had granted him the drawing of the weir that year, to see if good luck would ever befal him, and to give him something wherewith to begin the world. And the next day, when Elphin went to look, there was nothing in the weir. But as he turned back he perceived the leathern bag upon a pole of the weir. Then said one of the weir-wards unto Elphin, "Thou wast never unlucky until to-night, and now thou hast destroyed the virtues of the weir, which always yielded the value of an hundred pounds every May eve, and to-night there is nothing but this leathern skin within it." "How now," said Elphin; "there may be therein the value of an hundred pounds." Well! they took up the leathern bag, and he who opened it saw the forehead of the boy, and said to Elphin, "Behold a radiant brow!" "Taliesin be he called," said Elphin. And he lifted the boy in his arms, and, lamenting his mischance, he placed him sorrowfully behind him. And he made his horse amble gently, that before had been trotting, and he carried him as softly as if he had been sitting in the easiest chair in the world. And presently the boy made a "Consolation and praise to Elphin," and foretold honour to Elphin; and this consolation was as you may see :—

20

DYHUDDIANT ELPHIN.

Elphin deg taw a'th wylo
Na chabled neb yr eiddo
Ni wna les drwg obeithio.
Ni wyl dyn dim ai portho
Ni bydd coeg gweddi Cynllo
Ni thyr Duw a'r addawo
Ni chaed yn ngored Wyddno
Erioed cystal a heno.
Elphin deg sych dy ddeurudd
Ni weryd vod yn rhybrudd
Cyd tybiaist na chevaist vudd
Ni wna les gormodd cystudd
Nag ammau wyrthiau Dovydd
Cyd bwyv bychan wyv gelvydd
O voroedd ac o vynydd
Ac o eigiawn avonydd
Y daw Duw a da i ddedwydd

Elphin gynneddvau diddan
Anwraidd yw dy amcan
Nid rhaid it ddirvawr gwynvan
Gwell Duw na drwg ddarogan
Cyd bwyv eiddil a bychan
Ar gorverw mor dylan
Mi a wnav yn nydd cyvran
It well no thrichan maran

Elphin gynneddvau hynod
Na for er dy gafaelod
Cyd bwyv wan ar lawr vy nghod
Mae rhinwedd ar vy nhavod
Tra bwyv vi i'th gyvragod
Nid rhaid it ddirvawr ovnod
Drwy gofa henwau'r Drindod
Ni ddichon neb dy orvod.

THE CONSOLATION OF ELPHIN.

Fair Elphin, cease to lament!
Let no one be dissatisfied with his own,
To despair will bring no advantage.
No man sees what supports him;
The prayer of Cynllo will not be in vain,
God will not violate his promise.
Never in Gwyddno's weir
Was there such good luck as this night.
Fair Elphin, dry thy cheeks!
Being too sad will not avail,
Although thou thinkest thou hast no gain.
Too much grief will bring thee no good;
Nor doubt the miracles of the Almighty;
Although I am but little, I am highly gifted;
From seas and from mountains,
And from the depths of rivers,
God brings wealth to the fortunate man.
Elphin of lively qualities,
Thy resolution is unmanly;
Thou must not be over sorrowful:
Better to trust in God than to forbode ill.
Weak and small as I am,

On the foaming beach of the ocean,
In the day of trouble, I shall be
Of more service to thee than 300 salmon.
Elphin of notable qualities,
Be not displeased at thy misfortune;
Although reclined thus weak in my bag,
There lies a virtue in my tongue.
While I continue thy protector
Thou hast not much to fear;
Remembering the names of the Trinity,
None shall be able to harm thee.

And this was the first poem that Taliesin ever sang, being to console Elphin in his grief for that the produce of the weir was lost, and, what was worse, that all the world would consider that it was through his fault and ill luck. And then Elphin asked him what he was, whether man or spirit. Whereupon he sang this tale, and said :—

HANES TALIESIN.

Knytaf im lluniwyd ar lyn dyn glwys
Yn llys Caridwen em penydiwys
Cyd bawn bach o'm gwlled gwyl fy
    nghynnwys
Oeddwn fawr uwch llawr llann am
    tywys
Prid fum parwyden per awen Parwys
Ag ynghyfraith heb iaith am rhydd
    rylliwys
Hen widdon ddulon pan lidiwys
Anghuriawl ei hawl pan hwyliwys
    Ffoes yn gadarn
    Ffoes yn llyffan
    Ffoes yn rhith bran
        Braidd orphwys
    Ffoes yn derwyn
    Ffoes yn gadwyn
    Ffoes yn Iyrchwyn
        Mewn llwyn llychwys
    Ffoes yn fleiddyn
    Ffoes bleiddawr
        Yn niffaeth
    Ffoes yn fronfraith
        Cyfiaith Coelwys

    Ffoes yn gadno
    Cyd naid ystumau
    Ffoes yn Felau
        Fal na thycciwys
Ffoes yn wiwair ni chynnydd celwys
Ffoes yn Gern Hydd rhudd im
    rhwyfwys
Ffoes yn haearn mewn tan towys
Ffoes yn ben gwayw gwae ai puchwys
Ffoes yn Darw taer ymladdwys
Ffoes yn faedd Gwrych mewn rhych
    rhithiwys
Ffoes yn ronyn gwyn Gwenith lwys
Ar ael llen carthen im carfaglwys
Cymmaint oedd ei gweled a chyfeb
    rhewys
A fai yn llenwi fal llong ar ddyfrwys
Mewn boly tywyll im tywalldwys
Mewn mor dylan im dychwelwys
Bu goelfain im pan im cain fygwys
Duw Arglwydd yn rhydd am rhyd-
    dhawys.
        Tal. ae cant.

THE HISTORY OF TALIESIN.

Before I was formed into the form of a handsome man,
I did penance in the hall of Caridwen.
Though small in appearance, a festival was my reception.
I was (placed) high above the floor of the hall of my chief;
My ransom was set apart by reason of my sweet song;
And by law without speech I was set at liberty.
The old hag, black her appearance when irritated;
Dreadful were her screams when pursuing me.
I fled with vigour, I fled as a frog;
I fled in the semblance of a raven, scarcely finding rest;
I fled vehemently, I fled as a chain;
I fled as a roe into an entangled thicket;
I fled as a wolf cub, I fled as a wolf in a wilderness;
I fled as a thrush, the interpreter of omens;
I fled as a fox, leaping and turning;
I fled as a marten, which did not avail;
I fled as a squirrel, that vainly hides;
I fled as an antlered stag of free course;
I fled as iron in a glowing fire;
I fled as a spear-head, woe to him who desires it;
I fled as a bull fierce in fighting;
I fled as a bristly boar seen in a ravine;
I fled as a white grain of pure wheat,
On the skirt of a hempen sheet entangled,
.   .   .   .[1]
That seemed of the size of a mare's foal,
.   .   .   .   .[1]
That was flowing in like a ship on the waters.
.   .   .   .   .[1]
Into a dark leather bag was I thrown,
And on a boundless sea was I set adrift.
It was good tidings to me when I was entangled in the branch.[2]
And God the Lord set me at liberty.

Then came Elphin to the house of Gwyddno his father, and Taliesin with him. And Gwyddno asked him if he had had a good haul at the weir; and

---

[1] It is evident from the story that several lines are wanting in these places, describing the black-crested hen, her swallowing him, &c.

[2] The branch of the pole of the weir, "im cainge faglwys," which is consistent with the story. Stephens reads,

> Which was to me an omen of being tenderly nursed.

he told him that he had got that which was better than fish. "What was that?" said Gwyddno. "A Bard," answered Elphin. Then said Gwyddno, "Alas! what will he profit thee?" And Taliesin himself replied and said, "He will profit him more than the weir ever profited thee." Asked Gwyddno, "Art thou able to speak, and thou so little?" And Taliesin answered him, "I am better able to speak than thou to question me." "Let me hear what thou canst say," quoth Gwyddno. Then Taliesin sang:[1]—

> Ar dwr mae cyflwr can fendigaw
> Ar Duw mae iawnaf iawn synwyraw
> Ar Duw mae cyfiawn gweddiaw'n brudd
>   Can ny ellir lludd cael budd iwrthaw.
>
> Teirgwaith i'm ganed gwn fyfyriaw
> Truan oedd i ddyn na ddoe geisiaw
> Holl gelfyddydau byd sy'n byddinaw i'm bru
>   Canys gwn a fu ac a fydd rhagllaw.
>
> Cyfarch i'm naf nawdd i'm ganthaw
> Cyfarchwel i'm del dawn oi eiddaw
> A'm crair Mab Mair mawr arnaw vy mryd
>   Canys delir y byd bob awr iwrthaw.
>
> Bu Duw i'm dyscu a'm disgwyllaw
> Gwir greawdyr nef nawd i'm gantaw
> Cywraint yw i'r saint weddiaw beunydd
>   Canys Duw Dofydd a'u dwg attaw.

     *   *   *   *   *   *

TRANSLATION.[2]

In water there is a quality endowed with a blessing.
On God it is most just to meditate aright.
To God it is proper to supplicate with seriousness,
Since no obstacle can there be to obtain a reward from him.
Three times have I been born, I know by meditation;
It were miserable for a person not to come and obtain
All the sciences in the world collected together in my breast.
For I know what has been, what in future will occur.
I will supplicate the Lord that I get refuge in him.
A regard I may obtain in his grace.

---

[1] This is printed in the *Myvyrian Archæology*, p. 76, with the title *Canu Cyntaf Taliesin*—"The First Song of Taliesin."
[2] From the *Mabinogion*, vol. iii. p. 363.

The Son of Mary is my trust, great in him is my delight ;
For in him is the world continually upholden.
God has been to instruct me and to raise my expectation,
The true Creator of Heaven who affords me protection.
It is rightly intended that the saints should daily pray,
For God the renovator, will bring them to him.

* * * * * * *

Elphin, the protector of Taliesin, having been thrown into prison by
Maelgwn Gwynedd, Taliesin undertook to procure his release ; and in answer
to the inquiry of the wife of Elphin, as to how he would bring this about, he
sang the following :—

Pedestrie a wnaf
Ac ir porth mi a ddeuaf
Ar neuadd a gyrchaf
Am cerdd a ganaf
Am gwawd a draethaf
A Beirdd y Brenhin awaharddaf
Ger bronn y pennaf
Gogyfarch a wnaf
Ac arnyn mi dorraf
Ac Elphin yn rydd mi ollyngaf
A phan ddel yr Amryson
Yngwydd y Teyrnon
A gwys i'r beirddion
Am y gerdd gywir gysson
A gwyddbwyll Dewinion
A doethder Derwyddon
Yn Llys meibion Deiion
Mae rhai a ymrhithiason
O gyfrwys ddichellion
Ac ystrywgar foddion
Yngofidian gloesion
Am gamweddu ar y Gwirion.
Tawon ynfydion.
Mal pan fu waith Faddon

Arthur Benhaelion
Ei lafnau'n hir gochion
O waith gwyr gofwynion
Gwaith Rhi ar ei alon.
Gwae hwynt yn ynfydion
Pan ai del ddialon
Mi Daliesin ben Beirddion
A doeth Eirian Derwyddion
A ollwng Elphin dirion
O garchar y trabeilch trawsion.
Ei gofwynion gwaed aredd
O waith Gorwydd rhyfedd
O feith bellder Gogledd
Hwn a wna ei diwedd
Na bo rad na gwedd
Ar Faelgwn Gwynedd
Am drais a chamwedd
A dirfawr gyfrwysedd grculonedd
Dialedig ddiwedd
Ar Rhun ei etifedd
Poed fyrr fo 'i fuchedd
Poed diffaith ei diredd
Poed hir ddifroedd
Ar Faelgwn Gwynedd.

TRANSLATION.

A journey will I perform,
And to the gate will I come,
Into the hall will I enter,
And my song I will sing;

My speech I will pronounce,
And I will silence the Bards of the King.
In the presence of the Chief
I will make a supplication,
And the chain [1] will I break,
And Elphin will I set free.
And when the contention shall arise
In the presence of the King,
And the Bards shall be summoned
For a truly harmonious song,
With the craft of the magicians,
And the wisdom of the Druids,
In the hall of the sons of Deiion
There shall be some who shall appear
With cunning tricks
And subtle devices,
In grief and pain,
On account of the wronging of the innocent ;
They shall be silent like fools.[2]
As when was in the battle of Badon,
Arthur, chief of liberal ones,
His blades on the tall red ones,[3]
For the purpose of assisting their memory,[4]
The work of a King to his enemies.
Woe to them on account of their playing the fool,
When his vengeance comes.
I Taliesin, chief of Bards,
Who know the words of the Druids,
I will release fair Elphin
From the prison of the overproud unjust ones.

[1] "Upon them will I break."—LADY C. G. Break what ? If it is written " Ac arnyn," in mistake for " A caduyn," this makes the passage consistent with the story.

[2] As the story goes on to relate what Taliesin afterwards did to the Bards of Maelgwn, it is evident that his promises in this song to the wife of Elphin must correspond with his subsequent acts. The translation in the *Mabinogion* destroys this necessary connection.

[3] *i. e.* the Bards of Maelgwn. It appears to mean that Maelgwn shall be as fierce with his Bards as Arthur was in the battle of Badon against his enemies; and so it happened, only that Heinin the bard was struck with a broomstick instead of a sword. Maelgwn did not hold bards in much respect.

[4] " Cofweinion," instead of " cofwynion."

To him there shall be remembrance of the crime of blood.
By means of a wonderful steed,
Which shall appear from the distant North,
The same shall bring him to an end.
There shall be neither grace nor favour
To Maelgwn Gwynedd.
For this oppression and iniquity,
And very great subtle cruelty,
Fearful shall be the end
Of Rhun his son.
May his life be short,
May his lands be wasted ;
Long may be the banishment
Of Maelgwn Gwynedd.

On arriving at the court of Maelgwn, Taliesin cast a spell upon the Bards, so that on appearing before the king, instead of reciting verses in his praise, they could only pout out their lips, make mouths at him, and play " Blerwm, blerwm," on their lips with their fingers as they had seen Taliesin do. Maelgwn, imagining them to be drunk with many liquors, " ordered one of his squires to give a blow to the chief of them named Heinin Vardd; and the squire took a broom and struck him on the head, so that he fell back in his seat."[1] This seems to have broken the spell, for the chief Bard thereupon explains to Maelgwn that they were affected not by strong drink, but by the influence of a spirit sitting in the corner of the hall, in the form of a child. " Forthwith the king commanded the squire to fetch him; and he went to the nook where Taliesin sat, and brought him before the king, who asked him what he was and whence he came; and he answered the king in verse."

[1] Perhaps it was on this occasion that Heinin composed the verse attributed to him in the " Sayings of the Wise Men."

> A glywaist ti chwedl Heinin
> Fardd o Nangor Llanfeithin
> Gwrawl ni fydd disgethrin.

> Hast thou heard the saying of Heinin,
> The Bard of the College of Llanveithin?
> The brave is never cruel!

There is a prophetic poem preserved in the *Myvyrian Archæology* attributed to this Bard.

HANES TALIESIN.

Prifard cyffredin
Wy fi i Elphin
Am gwlad gynhefin
Iw bro Gerubin

Joannes Dewin
Am gelwis i Merdin
Bellach pob Brenin
Am geilw Taliesin.

Mi a fum nawmis hayach
Yn mol Gridwen wrach
Mi a fum gynt Wion bach
Taliesin ydwy bellach

Mi a fum gyda'm ner
Yn y goruwchelder
Pan gwympiod Luciffer
I Uffern dyfnder

My a fum yn dwyn banner
O flaen Alecsander
Mi a wn enwau'r ser
Or gogledd hyd Awster

Mi a fum ynghaer Bedion
Tetragrammaton
Mi a dygum Heon
I lawr glyn Ebron

Mi a fum yn y Ganon
Pan las Absalon
Mi fum yn y Llyd don
Cyn geni Gwdion

Mi a fum bedrenog
I Eli ag Enog
Mi a fum ar fan erog
Mab Duw Trugarog

Mi a fum ben ceidwod
Ar wneuthur Twr Nimrod
Mi a fum dri chyferod
Ynghaer Eirianrhod

Mi a fum in Arca
Gyda Noe ag Alpha
Mi a weleis difa
Sodoma a Gomorra

Mi a fum yn Affrica
Cym adeilad Roma
Mi a ddoethym yma
Ar wedillion Troia

Mi fum gyda'm Rhen
In mhresob yr asen
Mi a nerthais Foesen
Trwy dwr Urdonen

Mi a fum ar yr Wybren
Gyda Mair Fadlen
Mi a gefais awen
O bair Gridwen

Mi a fum fardd telyn
I Theon Lychlyn
Mi a gefais newyn
Am fab y forwyn

Mi a fum yn y Gwynfryn
Yn llys Cynfelyn
Mewn cyff a gefyn
Undydd a blwyddyn

Mi a fum am Logawd
Yngwlad Drindawd
Ni wyddis beth yw y cnawd
Ai cig ai pysgawd

Mi a fum dysgawd
Ir holl fydysawd
Mi a fyda hyd dyd brawd
Ar wyneb daiarawd

Mi a fum ynghadair flin
Uwch Caer Sidin
A honno yn troi fydd
Rhwng tri alfyd
Pand rhyfedd in byd
Nas argenydd.

21

THE HISTORY OF TALIESIN.

An impartial Chief Bard
Am I to Elphin ;
My accustomed country
Is the land of the Cherubim.

Johannes the Diviner
I was called by Merddin,[1]
At length every king
Will call me Taliesin.

I was nine months almost
In the belly of the hag Ceridwen ;
I was at first little Gwion,
At length I am Taliesin.

I was with my Lord
In the highest sphere,
When Lucifer fell
Into the depths of Hell.

I carried the banner
Before Alexander ;
I know the names of the stars
From the North to the South.

I was in Caer Bedion
Tetragrammaton ;
I conveyed Heon [2]
Down to the vale of Ebron.

I was in Canaan
When Absalom was slain ;

I was in the Hall of Don
Before Gwydion was born.[3]
I was on the horse's crupper[4]
Of Eli and Enoch ;
I was on the high cross
Of the merciful Son of God.

I was the chief overseer   [rod ;
At the building of the tower of Nim-
I have been three times resident
In the castle of Arianrhod.[5]

I was in the Ark
With Noah and Alpha ;
I saw the destruction
Of Sodom and Gomorra.

I was in Africa
Before the building of Rome ;
I am now come here
To the remnants of Troia.

I was with my King
In the manger of the ass ;
I supported Moses
Through the waters of Jordan.

I was at the Cross
With Mary Magdalen ; [6]
I obtained my inspiration
From the cauldron of Ceridwen.

[1] "Idno and Heinin called me Merddin."—*Mabinogion.*

[2] "The divine Spirit."—*Mabinogion.* This may be the meaning ; but it is not a Welsh word, and ought not to be translated, as by so doing the peculiar jargon of these poems is lost, and an air of unnecessary mysticism given to them.

[3] The famous necromancer. See the tale of "Math ab Mathmwy."

[4] Both of whom were taken up to heaven in a chariot.

[5] The constellation called the Northern Crown, according to Dr. Owen ; but there can be no doubt that there is here an allusion to the romances relating to Arianrhod.

[6] "Wybren," the sky or firmament ; as the line stands, therefore, it ought to be translated,

> I was in the firmament
> With Mary Magdalen ;

I was Bard of the harp
To Deon of Llychlyn ;
I have suffered hunger
With the Son of the Virgin.

I was in the White Hill [1]
In the hall of Cynvelyn,
In stocks and fetters,
A year and a half.

I have been in the buttery
In the land of the Trinity ;
It is not known what is the nature
Of its meat and its fish.

I have been instructed
In the whole system of the universe ;
I shall be till the day of judgment
On the face of the earth.

I have been in an uneasy chair
Above Caer Sidin,
And the whirling round without motion
Between three elements.

Is it not the wonder of the world
That cannot be discovered.

And when the king and his nobles had heard this song, they wondered much, for they had never heard the like from a boy so young as he. And when the king knew that he was the Bard of Elphin, he bade Heinin, his first and wisest Bard, to answer Taliesin, and to strive with him. But when he came he could do no other, but play "Blerwm" on his lips ; and when he sent for the others of the four-and-twenty Bards, they all did likewise, and could do no other. And Maelgwn asked the boy Taliesin what was his errand, and he answered him in song :—

Cul Fardd ceisiaw ir wyf [2]
Cadw'r gamp nis gallwyf
Darogan dywettwyf
A rygeissio ir wyf
Y golled a gafwyf
Cwbl geissyd coelwyf
Elphin ynghystwy
O Gaer Deganwy,
Arnaw na ddoded rhwy,
Hual o Aerwy,

Cadair Caer Deganwyf
Eilchwyl a archwyf,
Cadr fy ngorawen wyf
Cadarn ym a geiswyf,
Trichan cerdd a mwyf
Yw'r gerddwawd a ganwyf,
Ni ddyly saw y lle ydd wyf
Na maen na modrwyf
Na bydd im Cylchwy
Un Bardd nis Gwypwyi

---

which is nonsense ; but if the line was originally, " Mi a fum ar y bren," the meaning corresponds with the rest of the allusions.

[1] The Tower of London, where the head of Bran was buried.

[2] This song is not contained in the *Myvyrian Archæology*, but is taken from the " Hanes Taliesin" in the *Mabinogion* of Lady Guest. It is probable that the songs sung by the minstrels in the course of the relation of this celebrated story varied a good deal in details, retaining the general idea of the contest of Taliesin with the Bards of Maelgwn, their signal discomfiture, and the ultimate release of Elphin from prison by the agency of the Bard.

Elphin ap Gwyddno
Y sydd dan anrhaithdro
Dan dri ar ddeg clo
Am ganmawl ei athro.

A minnen iw Taliesin
Pen Beirdd y Gorllewin
A ollwng Elphin
O'r hual goreurin.

Puny Bards, I am trying
To secure the prize, if I can;
I am uttering a prophecy,
And I am earnestly seeking
That which is lost, and am obtaining
The whole of my quest, I believe.
Elphin is in punishment
In Caer Deganwy;
On him let there not be laid
Too many chains and fetters;
The Chair of Caer Deganwy
Again I will demand.
Strong am I in my powerful ley,
Strong am I who demand.
Three hundred songs and more
Are in the song which I sing.[1]
There shall not hold him in the place where I am
Neither stone nor ring;[2]
Nor shall there be in my circles
One Bard upon whom I cannot cast a spell.
Elphin the son of Gwyddno
Is in an evil turn,
Under thirteen locks,
For praising his instructor;
And I am myself Taliesin,
Chief of the Bards of the West,
Who shall deliver Elphin
From the golden fetter.

After this another composition is introduced into the tale as given in the *Mabinogion*, which forms part of a poem published in the *Myvyrian Archæology*, under the same title as

---

[1] This is probably an allusion to the great Bardic test of excellence, the capability of singing the three hundred and sixty-three stanzas in which the heroes of the Gododin were enumerated, or the Gorchan, which was equivalent to them, and which every Bard was required to know who pretended to enter into a musical contest.

[2] That is, Elphin. Lady Guest translates these four lines,

> There ought not to stand where I am
> Neither stone, neither ring;
> And there ought not to be about me
> Any bard who may not know
> That Elphin, &c.

According to the story, Taliesin had cast a spell on the Bards of Maelgwn; and the word *gwypwyf* evidently refers, in its grammatical form, as well as by reference to the preceding lines, where the bard is speaking in the first person, to something doing or to be done by Taliesin.

one before given, "The Consolation of Elphin," in which some transcriber has mixed together, as did most probably the Bard, so called, who sung it, portions of the Romance of Taliesin, with lines relating to Cynan and Cadwallader, and parts of a Gorchan, or song concerning the warriors who figured at the battle of Cattraeth. It illustrates, though even less forcibly than the "Prif Gyvarch" and some other productions hereafter to be mentioned, the lamentable state into which the Welsh Manuscripts had fallen as early as the fourteenth century. The romance collected by Thomas ap Einion, was, no doubt, written down. This was in the thirteenth century, and yet at the date of the collection made in the *Red Book of Hergest*, in the fourteenth or beginning of the fifteenth century, we find the component parts of the romance in this corrupt state. Possibly the Clerwr and Storiawr varied the songs very much at pleasure, according to the powers of memory in each individual. Lady Guest has omitted the first part of this piece down to the line " Y mae pryf atcas "; but it is desirable to give these pieces in their entirety, as otherwise a false idea of the character of this literature is presented.

DYHUDDIANT ELPHIN.

Gognawd gyrru
A gwawd dyfyrru
A thraethawd gedu
Pa fyd a ddyfu
Pwy a wyr canu
Gar bron yr Iessu
Yngwydd y tri llu
Pan foe'r yn barnu
Pa gerddor a gan
Pan alwer Cynan
I ddyfyn gader
Ger hron Cadwaladr
Pan fo'r dranc enaiar
Ar Cynan ap Bran
Os ywch brif feirddion
Crwyf celfyddon

Treuthwch oruchuddion
Or Mundi Maon
Y mae pryf atcas
Oi Kaer Satanas
A o esgynas
Rhwng dwfn a bas
Cyfled yw ei enau
A mynydd Mynnau
Nys gorfydd angeu
Na llaw na llafneu
Mae llwyth naw can maen
Yn rhawn dwy bawen
Un llygad yn ei ben
Gwyrdd fal glas iaen
Tair fynnon y sydd
Yn ei wegorlydd

Mor fryched arnaw
A nofiant trwyddaw
Bu laith bualawn
Deifr ddonwy dyfr ddawn
Henwa'r tair ffynnawn
O ganawl Eigiawn
Un llwydd heli
Pan fo yn corini
I edryd lliant
Dros Moroedd difant
Yr ail yn ddinam
A ddigwydd arnam
Pan fo'r glaw allan
Drwy awyr dylan
Y drydedd a ddawedd
Trwy wythi Mynyddedd
Fal callestig wledd
O waith Rex Rexedd
Ydywch bosfeirdd
Mewn rhwyf ofeiliant
Ny wyddoch ddychanu
Teyrnas y Brytannaec
Minneu yw Taliesin
Ben beirdd y Gorllewin
A ollwng Elphin
Oi hual Lurin
Aryf ag cynnil [1]
Ag cyman dull
Twryf yn agweud
Erac menwed
Erac maryed
Pan ysteyrn gwern
Eam gamgyrn eam gamled
Y voli rhi alar peithiu racwed
Yd y gweles
Arhul tres Turdei galed
Dygochuiaur a chloi a phor
A pherth a pher
Arud morua
Ac ymorua
Ac Eivionyd

A Gwynheidyd
Cein edryssed
Trybedaut raut
Rac y Defaut
Eil dal rossed
Taryannen ban amdal henfan [2]
Bu edryssed
Bleid y vynyt
Oedd bleidyat rhyd
Yn y deuredd
Pubal Peleidyr
Penyr pryd neidyr
O luch nadredd
Velyd yt wyd
Gwelydon rhuyt
Riein gared
Carut vreidun
Carun dyvuyn
Vur heyured
Cam hurauc daru
Cuynaf dy varu
Carut dyhed
Baran mor y goryf guyt
Y am Gatpul yn man bran ygcynnyt
Tardei don gyu cyngon gouytawr byt
Aesawr yn uellt a llavyn yguallt dri o
      betror
Ur guylyas
O gyrn glas
Med meitin
Bre eych tutuulch baran ret tost ben
      guaed gwin
Yr med a fauryf yd aethan aury dros
      eu heufin
Guyar van vaith
Er cadu cynrheith
Bu cynyeuin
Cynan cenon
Teithugir o Von
Ar vreint Goelin
Tutuulch cyuulch

---

[1] Cynnull.   [2] Heulan.

A goreu vulch
Ar van caercu
Gad vynydauc
Bu atveilyauc
Eu gwirodeu
Blwydyn hiraeth
Er gwyr Gattraeth
Am maeth yt meu

Eu llafneu dur
Eu med eu bur
Eu hualeu
Aryf ag cynnul
Ag cyman dul
Turyf nis cigleu

   Ac vely tervyna.

THE CONSOLATION OF ELPHIN.

Pursue your custom,
Shorten your praises,
And give a discourse,
On what will come to pass.
What was it the men sang
In the presence of Jesus,
In the presence of three armies?
When shall he come in judgment?
What singer has sung,
When Cynan shall be called
By the strong summons
Into the presence of Cadwallader?
When shall the earth be loosened,
Upon Cynan ap Bran?[1]
If ye are chief bards,
Strong in the sciences,
Relate the supreme powers
Of the inhabited world.
There is an odious worm

From the stronghold of Satan,
And he rules
Between the deep and the shallow.
His jaws are as wide
As the mountains of Mynnau,
Death shall not overcome him,
Nor hand nor blade.
He is as heavy as nine hundred stones,
His two paws are covered with bristles,
One eye is in his head
As green as the green ice.
There are three fountains
In the back of his neck.
The sea was stained by him,
And, swimming through it,
Was the destruction of cattle.
Deifr, Donwy, Dyfrdawn,
The names of the three fountains,
From the midst of the sea.[2]

[1] Cynan and Cadwallader, like Arthur, were to return and expel the Saxons from Britain.

[2] Lady Guest's translation of this passage is,—

  Three springs arise
  In the nape of his neck,
  Sea roughs thereon
  Swim through it.
  There was the dissolution of the oxen
  Of Deifrdonwy the water-gifted.
  The names of the three springs
  From the midst of the ocean,

One is of the pale brine
Where it is breeding.
The sources of the floods
Dispersed through the seas.
The second certainly
Falls upon us,
When there is rain without,
Water coming through the air.
The third is gliding
Through the veins of the mountains,

Like liquid flint,[1]
Of the work of the King of Kings.
Are you questioning bards?
With all your excessive care
You do not know how to celebrate[2]
The kingdom of the Britons.
I am Taliesin,
Chief of the Bards of the West;
And I will deliver Elphin
From the golden fetter.

The remainder of this piece consists of a portion of the song called " Gorchan Tutvwlch,[2] commencing with the lines which occur in the 23rd stanza of the *Gododin*,[3]—

> Aryf ag cynnul
> Ag cyman dull, &c.

The twenty-four bards of Maelgwn appear to have had nothing to say in reply, and Taliesin proceeds with an objurgatory address, which, in the *Myvyrian Archæology*, is appended to the song called *Fustl y Beirdd*.

> Tewch chwi Bosfeirddion ffeilsion anhylwydd
> Ni wyddoch i farnu rhwng gwira chelwydd
> Odych bryfeirdd ffydd o waith Duw ofydd
> Dywedwch i'ch Brenin beth fydd ei dramgwydd
> Myfi fydd Dewin a phrif Fardd cyffredin
> A wyr bob gorfin yngwlad eich Brenin
> Mi a rhyddaf Elphin o fol twr meinin

> One generated brine,
> Which is from the Corina,
> To replenish the flood, &c.

But this does not furnish the names of the three fountains; and Deifrdowny and his oxen are altogether a novelty. In Owen's *Dictionary*, Dyvrdonwy is said to mean " the virtue-giving water "—one of the names of the river Dee, not the name of a person.

[1] *Gwlaidd*—flowing gently, moist.
[2] It is printed " dychanu," to revile or lampoon, in the *Myvyr. Arch.*
[3] Rev. J. Williams ab Ithel's arrangement.

Ag a dywedda i'ch Brenin bethe i gyffrin
Fe ddaw pryf rhyfedd iar Forfa Rhianedd
I ddial anwiredd ar Faelgwn Gwynedd
Ai flew ai ddanedd ai lyged yn eurwedd
A hwnnw a wna ddial ar Faelgwn Gwynedd.

Another copy of the latter part of the same address, with some slight variations, is appended to the "Prif Cyfarch Taliesin."

Myfi sydd Ddewin
  A Phrifardd cyffredin
Mi adwaen bob corfin
  Yn gogof gorthewin
My a ryddhaf Elphin
  O fol y Twr Meinin
Mi a fynagaf ich Brenin
  Ac hir bobl gyffredin

I ddaw pryf rhyfedd
  O Forfa rhianedd
I ddial enwiredd
  Ar Faelgwn Gwynedd
Ai flew ai ddanedd
  Ai lygaid yn euredd
A hun a una ddiwedd
  Ai Faelgwn Gwynedd.

Be silent, unlucky, mistaken, catechising Bards,[1]
Ye know not how to judge between truth and falsehood.
If ye are chief bards of the work of the Lord,
Tell your king what will be his fate.
I am a diviner and an impartial chief Bard,
And I know every doorpost in the land of your king.[2]
I will liberate Elphin from the cavern of the tower of stone,
And I will tell to your king something that will trouble him.
There shall come a wonderful worm from the sea-marsh of Rhianedd,
To take vengeance for iniquity upon Maelgwn Gwynedd.
His hair, his teeth, his eyes of a golden form,
And he shall take vengeance on Maelgwn Gwynedd.

---

[1] *Posfeirddion*—according to Dr. Owen, "teaching bards, preceptors;" in the *Mabinogion*, translated "rhyming bards"; but the word is derived from *porian*, "to question," and refers to the practice of the bards of putting questions to their audience on a variety of subjects, of which numerous instances appear in these poems. It is here, though not always, used in a taunting sense.

[2] In the copy appended to the "Prif Cyfarch Taliesin" it is,

"I know every doorpost in the cave of the great diviner."

22

This threat on the part of the Bard, not being accompanied by any overt act, produced no effect on Maelgwn.

Taliesin then appears to have left the hall, and standing at the gate, to have uttered an invocation to the wind, which was followed by a miraculous or magical intervention in his favour. The note in the *Myvyrian Archæology* states that Taliesin made the song at the door of Castle Teganwy, praying the Almighty that he might obtain a wind which should break open the prison of Elphin.

I'R GWYNT.

Dychymic di pwy yw
Creadur cadarn eyn dilyw
Heb gig heb asgwrn heb wythen heb
Heb peu a heb draet   [wacd
Ni bydd hyn ni byd iau
Nog yn y dechreu
Er ofn nag ny ddifoes eisiau
Gan greaduriau
Mawr Dduw mor wynneu
Ban ddaw o ddechreu
Mawr ei fretheiriau
Pan ddel or dehau
Mawr ei ferthidau
Y gur gan goreu
Ef yn maes ef ynghoet
Heb law ac heb droet
Heb henaint heb hoet
Ac ef yn gyfoed
A phumoes pymhoed
A hefyd y sydd hyn
Pet pemwnt flwyddyn
Ag ef in gyfled
Ag wyneb tudwed
Ag ef in anet
Ag ef in weled
Ef a nona gythrudd
Lle mynno Dofydd
Ef ar for ef ar dir
Ni wyl ni welir
Ag ef yn anghywir

Ni ddaw pan fynnir
Ef ar dir ef ar for
Ef yn anhepcor
Ef yn diesor
Ef yn beteiror
Ef yn ddi achor
Ef yn ddieisor
Ef o bedeiror
Ni bydd wrth gyngor
Ni fydd heb gyngor
Ef cychwyn agor
O dduch maen mynor
Ef yn llafar ef yn fud
Ef yn fynud
Ef yn wrdd ef yn ddrut
Pan drenyn drosdud
Ef myd ef llafar
Ef yn orddear
Mwyaf y amar
Ar wyneb daear
Ef yn dda ef yn ddrwg
Ef yn orddwc
Ef yn anamlwc
Cannis gwyl golwc
Ef yn ddrwg ef yn dda
Ef hwnt ef yma
Ef a anrhefna
Ni ddiwg a wna
Ni ddwg a wnech
Ec ef yn ddibech

Ef yn wlyb ef yn sych
Ef a ddaw 'n fynych
O wres haul ac oerfel
Lloer yn hanhel
Lloer yn anlles
Handid llai ei gwres
Un gwr ai goreu
Yr holl greadwrieu
Drwy ddirfawr awel
I wneuthur dialedd
    Ar Faelgwn Gwynedd.

Drwg y gwr goreu
Greaduriau
Ef biau dechreu
A diwedd diheu
Yr hwn a roddes
Yr oerfel ar gwres
Yr huan ar tes
Ar Lloer llwyr achles
Nyd cerddor celfydd
Ny molwy Ddofydd
Nyd cywir ceinad
Ni molwy y Tad
Ny nawd fydd arad
Heb heyrn heb had
Ny bu oleuad
Cyn Celi cread

Ny bydd offeiriad
Na bendicco afrllad
Ny wybydd anygnad
Y saith lafanad
Dengwlat darmarthad
Yn yngylaw wlad
Degvet digarad
Digarwys eu tad
Digaru cawat
Yn rhwy rhewiniat
Llucuffer Llygrad
Eisor eisyf wlad
Saith seren y sydd
O seithnawn Dofydd
Seon a Sywedydd
A wyr eu defnydd
Marca mercedus
Ola olumis
Luna lafurus
Jupiter Venerus
O Haul o hyd yrfer
Hyd gylch lloer leufer
Nyt cof yn ofer
Nyt crog ny chreter
Ein Tad ein pater
An car an cymer
An tad an Rhen nin rhaner
Gan hu Lucuffer.

TO THE WIND.

Discover thou what it is,
The strong creature from before the
   flood,
Without flesh, without bone,
Without head, without feet;
It will neither be older nor younger
Than at the begnining.
It has no fear nor the rude wants
Of created things.
Great God! how the sea whitens
When first it comes!
Great are its gusts,
When it comes from the south;

Great is the exhaustion
Of man from its rapid motion.
It is in the field, it is in the wood,
Without hand and without foot,
Without age, without season;
And it is always of the same age
With the five ages of ages,
And likewise it is old,
Some ages of years;
And it is of equal breadth
With the surface of the earth,
And it was not born,
And is not seen.

It is making a perturbation
In the place where God wills.
On the sea, on the land,
It sees not nor is seen.
And it is not fickle,
It does not come when desired.
On land, on sea,
It is indispensable,
It is unequalled.
It is in the four quarters,
It is fierce,
It is unequalled.
It is from the four quarters,
It will not be advised to the contrary;
It sets out to the cave,
Above the marble rock;
It is noisy, it is dumb,
It is mild,
It is strong, it is bold,
When it glances over the land.
It is dumb, it is noisy,
It is the most active thing

On the face of the earth.
It is good, it is bad,
It is a great oppressor,
It is not manifest,
For the eye cannot see it.
It is bad, it is good,
It is there, it is here;
It is in innumerable places.
It has no form,
It bears no burden,
For it is void of sin.
It is wet, it is dry,
And it frequently came
With the heat of the sun and the cold.
Proceeding from the moon,
The moon void of benefit,
Less is her heat.
There is one God, and he rules
Over all creatures.
By a dreadful blast
Vengeance shall be wreaked
    On Maelgwn Gwynedd.

The copy of this poem, as printed in the *Hanes Taliesin*, concludes with these lines, and the story proceeds to say, that " while he was thus singing his verse near the door, there arose a mighty storm of wind, so that the King and all his nobles thought that the castle would fall upon their heads. And the King caused them to fetch Elphin in haste from his dungeon, and placed him before Taliesin. ·And it is said, that immediately he sang a verse, so that the chains opened from about his feet."

In the *Myvyrian Archæology*, however, the poem to the wind is continued.

God has created
Evil creatures.
He appoints the beginning of life,
And a certain end.
He himself has given
The cold and the heat,

The sun for warmth,
And the protecting moon.
There is no skilful singer
Who does not praise the Lord.
There is none truly wise
Who does not praise the Father.

It would not be easy to plough
Without iron and without seed.
Nor was there light
Before the creation of heaven.
There was no priest
Nor blessed wafer,
Nor witnessing before the judge.
The seven senses.[1]
God appointed a region
In the country of the angels.
The tenth part were forsaken.
Ceasing to love their Father,
The discarded ones were shut up
In utter destruction,
With Lucifer the spoiler,
Like his progeny.

There are seven stars,
The seven gifts of the Lord,
Wise men and astronomers
Know of what they are made.
Marca mercedus,
Ola olumis,
Luna lafurus,
Jupiter Venerus.
From the sun it is a vast length
To the circle of the shining moon.
Do not call to mind useless things.
No cross, no faith,
One Father, one Pater.
Let not friend nor companion,
Nor father, nor king, have the lot
To be with Lucifer.

The song given in the *Mabinogion*, as that which caused the fetters of Elphin to fall from around him, is the "Mead Song," one of the most poetic and most elegant of the series.

KANU Y MEDD.

Golychaf wledig pendefig pob wa
Gwr a gynneil y Nef Arglwydd pob tra
Gwr a wnaeth y dwfr i bawb yn dda
Gwr a wnaeth pob llad ac ai llwydda
Meddwer Maelgwn Mon ag an meddwa
Ai feddgorn ewyn gwerlyn gwymha
As gynnull gwenyn ac nis mwynha
Med hidleid moleid molud i bob tra
Lleaws Creadur a fag terra
A wnaeth Duw i ddyn er ei ddonha
Rhai drud rhai mud ef ai mwynha
Rhai gwyllt rhai dof Dofydd ai gwna
Yn dillig iddynt yn ddillad ydd a
Yn fwyd yn ddiawd hyd frawd yd barha
Golychaf y wledig pendefig gwlad hedd
I ddillwng Elphin o alltudded
Y gwr am rhoddes y gwin ar cwrwf ar medd
Ar meirch mawr modur mirein eu gwedd

---

[1] This line is wrongly inserted.

Am rothwy etwa mal diwedd
Trwy fodd Duw y rhydd trwy enrhydedd
Pump pemhwnt calan yughaman hedd
Elffinawg farchawg medd hwyr dy Ogledd.

THE MEAD SONG.

I pray the Lord, the ruler of every place,
He who sustains the heavens, the Lord over all,
He who made the waters and all things good,
He who bestows every gift and all prosperity.
A giver of mead is Maelgwn of Mona, and at his mead-board
His mead-horns circulate wine of the right colour.
The bee has collected it and has not used it.
For the distilling of the luscious mead,[1] praised be it above all
The numerous creatures the earth has produced.
God made it as a gift to man.
The wise and the foolish enjoy it.
Some wild, some tame, God has made them,
They produce good clothing.
I entreat the prince, the chief of a peaceful land,
For the release of Elphin from banishment.
He who has given me wine and ale and mead,
And large powerful horses of beautiful shape,
And would give me anything at my request,
By the will of God, if set free through respect
(There shall be) five times five hundred festivals in perfect peace,
Should Elphin the keen warrior possess thy confidence.[2]

And afterwards he sang the ode which is called "Gorchestion y Beirdd,"
The great Achievements of the Bards.

Pa ddyn gyntaf   Pa fwyd pa ddiod
A oruc Duw naf   Pa do ei wasgod
Para weniaith deccaf   Pa cyntaf annod
A drefnodd Jeuaf   Ei brif fy fyrdod

[1] *Moleid,* "concrete, full of particles," alluding to the appearance of
honey.
[2] This last line has been translated,

"Elphin, knight of mead, late be thy dissolution."—*Mabinog.*
And

"Elphinian knight of mead! Thou'lt yet be free."—STEPHENS.

Pwy ddocthai ddillad
Pwy a ddug ymwad
O ystryw gwlad
Yn y dechreuad
Paham i mae caled maen
Paham i mae blaenllym draen
Pwy sydd galed fal Malen
Pwy yn hallt fal halen

Pwy yn felus fal mel
Pwy a ferchyg yr awel
Paham i mae cefnog y trwyn
Paham y mae cronn yr olwyn
Paham y traeth y tafawd
Amgen nag arall aclawd
O medri di a'th feirdd Henin
Atteb attebant i mi Daliesin.

THE EXCELLENCE OF THE BARDS.

Who was the first man
Whom the God of Heaven made?
What was the fairest flattering speech
Which was prepared by Jeuaf?[1]
What meat, what drink,
What roof his covering,
What his first shelter?[2]
With what did he first board it?[3]
Who taught him his clothing?
Whose the design of a roof
For the habitations of the land
In the commencement?[3]
Why is a stone hard?

Why is a thorn sharp-pointed?
What is as hard as steel?
What is as salt as brine?
What is as sweet as honey?
Who rides on the gale?
Why is the nose ridged?
Why is a wheel round?
Why is speech (given to) the tongue
Different from every other gift?
If you and your bards are able, O
    Heinin,
Let them give an answer to me,
    Taliesin.

Neither Heinin or his bards replied to this invitation to answer the above comprehensive series of riddles, upon which Taliesin proceeds finally to overwhelm the unfortunate Heinin in the following address :—

---

[1] This and the five following lines refer to some unknown story, if we are to read Jeuaf (the youngest). Most probably it should be Adaf—Adam, which renders the whole intelligible.

[2] Ei nodd.

[3] Translated in the *Mabinogion*.

> What the first impression
> Of his primary thinking?
> What became his clothing,
> Who carried on a design
> Owing to the wiles of the country
> In the beginning?

" And after that he sang the address which is called

CYSTWY'R BEIRDD.

Os Ydwyt di Fardd cyfrisgin
O awen ddisgethrin
Na fydd yn ddiscethrin
Yn Llys dy frenhin
Oni wyppir dy henw rimin
Gorthaw di Henin
A henw rimiad
A henw ramiad
A henw dy hendad
Cyn ei fedyddiad
A henw dy furment
A henw yr element
A henw dy iaith
A henw'r dalaith.
Gosco feirdd uchod [1]

Gosco feirdd isod
Fy anwyl i sydd isod
Dan hual arianrhod
Ni wyddoch chwi ynddiau
Ddeall y gan y min mau
Na dosparth diau
Rhwng y gwir ar gau
Beirddion bychain ei bro
Paham nad ewch chwi ar ffo
Y Bardd nim gostecco
Gostec nis caffo
Oni ei mewn gortho
Dan raian a gro
Y sawl ym gwrandawo
Gwrandewid Duw fo.

THE REPROOF OF THE BARDS.

If thou art a bard capable of striving,[2]
Imbued with the mysteries of the muse,
Be not ungentle
In the hall of thy King.
Unless thou art acquainted with the powerful name,
Be thou silent, Heinin,
As to the powerful name,
And the lofty name,
And the name of thy grandsire,
Before he was baptised ;
And the name of the firmament,
And the name of the elements,
And the name of the [3] languages,
And the name of the headband.[4]

[1] The fragment in the *Myvyrian Archæology*, p. 47, belongs to this place, but differs considerably from the above. I have adopted this from the *Mabinogion*, with Lady C. Guest's translation.

[2] " Cyvrys "—contention.

[3] " Thy," as printed, but the context shows that this is an error.

[4] This was one of the famous questions of the " Questioners":—" They know not the bridled ox with the thick headband."—*Preidden Annwn*.

Avaunt, ye bards above,
Avaunt, ye bards below;
My friend is below
In the fetter of Arianrhod.
You know not, certainly,
The meaning of the song in my mouth;
Nor can you distinguish clearly
Between the true and the false.
Bards of little repute in the land,
Why do you not take flight?
A bard who will not pay attention to me
Shall not obtain attention
Until he is under the covering
Of gravel and pebbles.
Whosoever shall listen to me,
May God listen to him.

" Then he sung the piece called

FUSTL Y BEIRDD.[1]

Cler o gam arfer a ymarferant
Cathlau aneddfol fydd eu moliant
Clod orwas ddiflas a ddatcanant
Celwydd bob amser a ymarferant
Gorchmynau deddfau Duw a dorant
Gwragedd priodol wrth ei moliant
Drwy feddwl drygbwyll a fawr dwyllant
Morwynion gwynion mair a lygrant
A goelio iddynt a gwilyddiant
A gwirion ddynion a ddyfalant
Ai hoes ai hamser yn ofer y treuliant
Y nos y meddwant y dydd y cysgant
Segur heb lafur yr ymborthiant
Yr Eglwys a gashantar Dafarn a gyrchant
A lladron ffeilsion y cydsyniant
Llysoedd a gwleddoedd a ymofynant
Pob parabl dibwyll a grybwyllant
Pob pechod marwol a ganmolant
Pob pentre pob tre pob tir a dreiglant

---

[1] This piece, from the *Myvyrian Archæology*, differs considerably from that published in the *Mabinogion*.

Pob salwedd ofer a ymarferant
Gorchmynau y Drindod a ddifrodant
Gwiliau na suliau nis addolant
Am ddydiau angau nis gofalant
A phob glothineb nis arbedant
Gormod o fwyddyd i diodydd a fynant
Degwm ag Offrwm teulwng nis talant
Deddfolion ddynion a ddyfalant
Adar a hedant gwenyn a felant
Pysgod a nofiant pryfed a'mlysgant
Pob beth a ymdaith i gynull i borthiant
Ond cler ag Oedion a lladron diswyniant
Ni chabla i'ch mysg dysg na cherdwriaeth
Can's Duw ai rhoes gloes ar gyllaeth
Ond sawl syn arfer o gam arfaeth
Am watwar Jesu ai wasanaeth.

THE SPITE OF THE BARDS.[1]

Strolling minstrels are addicted to evil habits.
Immoral songs are their delight.
In a tasteless manner they rehearse the praises of heroes.
Falsehood at all times they use.
The commandments and ordinances of God they break.
Married women they lay hold of.
With evil intentions, they are very deceiving.
The fair virgins of Mary they corrupt.
Those who put trust in them they bring to shame,
And true men they laugh to scorn,
And times and seasons they spend in vanities.
At night they get drunk, by day they sleep.
In ease without work they support themselves.
The church they hate, the tavern they frequent.
With false thieves they associate.
Halls and banquets they seek after.
All kinds of senseless stories they relate.
All kinds of mortal sins they praise.
Through every village, town, and country, they stroll.
All filthy vanities they indulge in.
The ordinances of the Trinity they deny;
Neither on holidays or on Sundays do they worship.

[1] More properly, " The Flail of the Bards."

Of the day of death they think not.
From all kinds of gluttony they do not refrain.
Fond of excess in eating and drinking.
Tithes and household offerings they do not pay.
Legally appointed persons they mock at.
Birds fly, and bees collect honey;
Fish swim, and worms crawl:
All creatures are journeying after food,
Except minstrels and idle fellows, and manifest thieves.
Do not disparage mixed learning or minstrelsy;
For God has given us (enough of) pain and sorrow;
But those who put them to a bad use,
In blaspheming Jesus and his service.

It is astonishing that this piece should ever have been considered to be a composition of the sixth century. It is an attack upon the *Cler* or strolling minstrels, for whose better regulation, as we have before mentioned, so many ordinances were enacted, as well by the Welsh princes as by the English sovereigns, from the twelfth to the fifteenth centuries. The whole style of the piece is of the fourteenth century; and it is now recognised as the production of Jonas Athraw, or Doctor, a monk of St. David's, who, according to the *Biographical Dictionary of Eminent Welshmen*, flourished in the tenth, but must most undoubtedly (if the author of the pieces attributed to him) have lived in the thirteenth or fourteenth century. The remaining composition, included in the *Mabinogi* of Taliesin, is also the production of this same Jonas Athraw. It is entitled "Awdyl Vraith," and has no proper connection with the story. It will be given under the religious poems attributed to Taliesin.

The tale itself concludes with an account of a horserace, in which Elphin, the patron of the bard, contends against the twenty-four horses of Maelgwn. Through the magic assistance of Taliesin, Elphin was victorious; and the bard not only thus assists his patron, but also enables him to discover upon the site of the racecourse a large cauldron full of gold.

It is very probable that the "Canu y Meirch," or Song of

the Horses, which will be given hereafter, belongs to this place, and was originally sung as part of the *Mabinogi* of Taliesin.

Reverting to the doctrine of the Metempsychosis, which has been supposed to be contained in this story, we see that there are two sets of statements ascribed to Taliesin. The first relates his change of form into various shapes while endeavouring to escape the pursuit of the enraged sorceress Ceridwen.

In the other he asserts his having been in various places at remote periods of time.

With regard to the former of these, it seems quite clear that the supporters of that theory have not made a distinction between transmigration and transformation.

We cannot agree with Mr. Stephens,[1] that "it is very possible that the changes said to have been undergone by the Taliesin of the tale, may have reference to the doctrine of transmigration, though we have here the romance of the metempsychosis, and not an exposition of the doctrine itself." It is, on the contrary, abundantly evident, on reference to the *Mabinogion*, which are but a remnant of an abundant romance literature which belonged to the Welsh, that we have here nothing to do with the doctrine of a transmigration of the soul after death. In these tales we find a machinery of necromancers and magic, such as has probably been possessed by all people in all ages, more or less abundantly. Math, the son of Mathonwy, was a necromancer of power, and with his magic wand he changed Gwydion ap Don, himself a skilful enchanter, and Gilvaethwy ap Don, into the forms of deer, of swine, and of wolves successively.

Gwydion ap Don was the most celebrated of the magicians introduced into these tales, and his name frequently appears in the poems attributed to Taliesin. In the deception which he practised upon Pryderi, in the matter of the swine of Annwn, he proceeded in a way familiar to every reader of fairy tales.

---

[1] *Literature of the Kymry*, p. 188.

"Then he betook himself to his arts, and began to work a charm. And he caused twelve chargers to appear, and twelve black greyhounds, each of them white-breasted, and having upon them twelve collars and twelve leashes, such as no one that saw them could know to be other than gold. And upon the horses twelve saddles; and every part which should have been of iron was entirely of gold, and the bridles were of the same workmanship. Now these he had formed of fungus."

With these fairy productions he deceived Pryderi into an exchange for the swine.

"Then Gwydion and his men took their leave and began to journey forth with the pigs. 'Ah, my comrades,' said Gwydion, 'it is needful that we journey with speed. The illusion will not last but from the one hour to the same to-morrow.'"

On another occasion Gwydion went to walk on the sea-shore,—

"And there he saw some sedges and seaweed, and he turned them into a boat. And out of dry sticks and sedges he made some cordovan leather," which afterwards returned again into seaweed and sedges. He changes the form of himself and Llew Llaw Gyffes, produces illusory spectacles, and creates a woman out of flowers, all by the aid of the art magic:—

"In the early twilight Gwydion arose, and he called unto him his magic and his power. And by the time the day dawned, there was resounded through the land uproar and trumpets and shouts."

"He took the blossoms of the oak, and the blossoms of the broom, and the blossoms of the meadow-sweet, and produced from them a maiden the fairest and most graceful that man ever saw. And they baptized her and gave her the name of Blodeuwedd."

The conduct of Blodeuwedd not proving satisfactory, Gwydion, by way of punishment, turned her into an owl, while Llew Llaw Gyffes was changed into an eagle.

Kai, the steward and companion of Arthur, could render himself when he pleased as tall as the highest tree in the forest. Menw, the son of Teirgwaedd, could cast a charm and illusion so as to render himself and his companions invisible.

The tale of Kilhwch and Olwen, or the Twrch Trwyth, luxuriates in magical and supernatural wonders.

In the story of Manawydden, the son of Llyr, we have an enchanted castle into which Pryderi is tempted to enter.

> "In the centre of the castle floor he beheld a fountain with marble-work around it, and on the margin of the fountain a golden bowl upon a marble slab, and chains hanging from the air, to which he saw no end. And he was greatly pleased with the beauty of the gold, and with the rich workmanship of the bowl. And he went up to the bowl and laid hold of it; and when he had taken hold of it, his hands stuck to the bowl, and his feet to the slab on which the bowl was placed, and all his joyousness forsook him, so that he could not utter a word. And thus he stood."

His wife Rhiannon followed him, with the same consequences :—

> "And with that, as it became night, lo! there came thunder upon them, and a fall of mist, and thereupon the castle vanished, and they with it."

The enchanter who performed this feat, Llwyd, the son of Kilcoed, transformed his whole household into mice, for the purpose of destroying Manawydden's corn, and himself appeared before him in various forms. It is needless to multiply instances to show that the exercise of supernatural power in the transforming of human beings into the shape of animals, was as favourite a component part of these tales as of those of Oriental origin.

There is no perceptible difference between the supernatural power, the necromancy or magic, represented as being exerted in these tales, and the same power ascribed to the magicians and sorcerers in the *Arabian Nights*. The belief in such a power appears to have existed in all communities, and the relation of its wonders to satisfy a natural craving in the human mind for the marvellous. It will be scarcely contended that the Arab storytellers derived their machinery from the Welsh; and certainly we shall not look for a Druidic origin for the tale of the Princess and the Genie, which, in the transformations the parties undergo in their mortal combat, has some curious coincidences with the transformations of Taliesin.[1]

There is no more necessity for seeking for a hidden meaning in the tale of Taliesin than in that of Cinderella. Tales of the same kind are found in the popular traditions or ballads of all nations. In the Eddaic poems, Loki changes himself into a salmon to avoid the wrath of the Asi, and his son Narfi is changed into a wolf.

How little meaning was attached to these relations of the forms pretended to have been assumed, may be seen from another piece, of the same style and age as all the rest, in which the bard, instead of saying that he had been, declares that he is, a variety of strange things :—

> I am water, I am a wren ;
> I am a workman, I am a star ;
> I am a serpent ;
> I am a cell, I am a chink ;
> I am a depositary of song, I am a learned person, &c.[2]

The Irish tales are even more prodigal of necromancy and magic transformations than the Welsh, and are more full and connected in their details.

There may be a remote foundation of these stories in the natural and universal belief, in all climes and in all ages, in the existence of supernatural beings—the denizens of the air, the forest, or the lake, sometimes hostile, sometimes friendly to man ; but we must not distort the wonders added by the genius of the poet into evidences of a lost philosophy or theology. The Ousel of Cilgwri, the Stag of Redynore, and the Salmon of Llyn Llyw, may be allowed the gift of human speech and to hold converse with Bedwyr and the blessed Kai, without furnishing themes for a treatise on the Druidic belief. How similar are the creations of the human mind in times and

---

[1] In the tale of "Branwen the Daughter of Llyr," there is an adventure most curiously similar to one in the story of "Ali Baba and the Forty Thieves."

[2] Buarth Beirdd, *Myr. Arch.* p. 27.

places the most remote, may be seen in the remarkable similarity of these Celtic stories with an Egyptian tale, which, if known to the Welsh antiquarians, would have furnished a theme for unbounded comment. We see in it only an evidence of the existence of a common stock of ideas, variously developed according to the formative pressure of external circumstances.

Thus, amongst the tales recited by the Irish Bards, we have the story of Tuan Mac Coireall,[1] who was first a man, then lived three hundred years in the shape of a deer, three hundred years as a wild boar, three hundred in the shape of a bird, and three hundred more in the shape of a salmon, which, being caught by a fisherman, was presented to the Queen of Ireland, who, immediately when she tasted it, conceived and brought forth the noted Tuan Mac Coireall, who narrated the history of the antediluvian colonization of Ireland by Ceasair and her people.

Another remarkable Irish legend connected with this subject is given in the "Tale of Festivities at the House of Conan," in which the history and adventures of the celebrated Fionn or Fingal are collected and related in the form of a dialogue.

" 'Tell me,' says Conan to Fionn, 'who among the Fenian heroes is he who leaps over his own gravestone every day, whose own daughter is his mother, and who is demanding *eric* and reparation from the man who killed him, though he is himself alive?'

" 'I will tell you about that,' says Fionn. 'Two Fenian chiefs of my people, namely, Oscur the son of Criomthann, and Daolgas son of Cairrill Cas, one day quarrelled about a fight that occurred between two dogs, and Daolgas was slain upon that occasion. The beautiful marriageable daughter of Daolgas came over him, and having stooped down to kiss him, a red spark of fire flew from his mouth into hers, and she became pregnant in consequence, and brought forth a broad-crowned son in due time; and, since no other name was found for him, he was called by the name of his father. He was nurtured in a fitting manner until his seventh year; and the first feat of youthful folly that he performed was to leap over his own gravestone; and he is now demanding *eric* from Oscur, son of Criomthann.' "[2]

[1] In the book of Lecane, *Trans. of Ossianic Society*, vol. i. 1853.
[2] *Transactions of Ossianic Society*, vol. ii. 1854.

How very similar were the tales of wonder which delighted the dwellers on the banks of the Nile, 1600 years before the Christian era, may be seen in a genuine Egyptian romance, translated by M. De Rougé from a Hieratic papyrus of that date. In this story the hero successively takes the form of a flower, a bull, and a Persea tree. The latter being cut down, a splinter from it enters the mouth of a princess. She becomes pregnant, and ultimately is delivered of a son, in whom the hero again assumes the human form.

The assertions of Taliesin, that he was present with Noah in the ark, at the Tower of Babel, and with Alexander of Macedon, we may fairly ascribe to the poetic fancy of the Christian priest of the thirteenth century, who brought this romance into its present form. We may compare these statements of the universal presence of the wonder-working magician with those of the gleeman who recites the Anglo-Saxon metrical tale called, the "Traveller's Song."[1] After exhausting the names of every possible tribe and kingdom which he had visited, he says :—

I have been with the Israelites and with the Exsyringi,
With the Hebrews and with the Indians and with the Egyptians.
I have been with the Medes and with the Persians and with the Myrgings.

The object is the same in both—to excite wonder by the recital of marvels, and thereby to enhance the pleasure to be derived from the entertainment.

The address of Glewlwyd Gavaelvawr to Arthur, in the tale of "Kilhwch and Olwen," is of the same character.

"Then Glewlwyd went into the hall. And Arthur said to him, 'Hast thou news from the gate?'—'Half my life is passed, and half of thine. I was heretofore in Kaer Se and Asse, in Sach and Salach, in Lotor and Fotor; and I have been in India the Great and India the Lesser; and I was in the battle of Dau Ynyr, when the twelve hostages were brought from Llychlyn. And I have also been in Europe and in Africa, and in the Islands of Corsica, and in Caer Brythwych and Brythach and Verthach; and I was present when

[1] *Rev. Archæol.* vol. ix. p. 385.

24

formerly thou didst slay the family of Clis the son of Merin, and when thou didst slay Mil Du, the son of Ducum, and when thou didst conquer Greece in the East. And I have been in Caer Oeth and Annoeth, and in Caer Nevenhyr; nine supreme sovereigns, handsome men, saw we there, but never did I behold a man of equal dignity with him who is now at the door of the portal."

The gleeman here, as in the "Traveller's Song," evidently exhausts his store of localities; and it is very probable that the names of the places differed in recitals by different persons.

We must hold the same opinion of Ceridwen as of the fictitious Taliesin. She is a creation of the fancy, a sorceress, or enchantress, and nothing more.

According to the author of the *Biographical Dictionary of Eminent Welshmen*, published so lately as 1852, Ceridwen was a British goddess, and a well-known personage in the Druidical Pantheon.

" *Ceridwen,*" the author says, " is a celebrated character in Druidical mythology whose attributes were, in many respects, similar to those of *Ceres.* Davies, in his *Mythology of the British Druids*, has collected much information respecting her from the earliest Welsh poets. In them we find her described as a fury, a botanist, the first of womankind, a giantess, the goddess of corn, the modeller of youth, the moon, a mystic goddess, the ruler of Bardism, a sailing-vessel, and as transforming herself into a bird. He has also advanced arguments to prove that she was worshipped, as late as the twelfth century, conjointly with the moon.

" Pair Ceridwen, 'the cauldron of Ceridwen,' is frequently alluded to by the ancient poets. In a poem of Taliesin, we find the goddess Ceridwen preparing the water of this sacred vessel, which contained a decoction of potent herbs, collected with due observation of the planetary hours. So efficacious was the medicated water, that no sooner had three drops of it touched the lips of the bard, than all futurity was displayed to his view. Her temple was at Caergyvylchi, in Caernarvonshire."

This statement, that the goddess Ceridwen had a temple at Caergyvylchi in Caernarvonshire, is made with all the historical seriousness with which we might affirm that there was a temple of Diana at Ephesus, or of Jupiter at Rome. It is, nevertheless, destitute of the slightest foundation, and affords another example of the modern manufacture of the Druidical mythology. The editor of the *Biographical Dictionary* has, however, persisted in adopting the absurdities enunciated by Davies on the subject of two short poems by Howel ab Owain[1] in the twelfth century, though Mr. Stephens[2] had conclusively shown that the whole of the supposed mythological allusions in those poems to Ceridwen and her temple, had no existence except in the imagination of Mr. Davies. The name "Ceridwen" does not, in fact, appear in the poems in question, Mr. Davies having converted the word *Cecidwen*, "white-necked"—an epithet applied by the bard to the fair object of his affections—into "Ceridwen," and founded on this correction his statement, "that the proud-wrought enclosure of the Cyvylchir, in the desert of Arvon near Snowdon, and towards the shore, was the Caer, or sanctuary of the mystical goddess, and the chosen place of her daughter Llywy, or the British Proserpine."

Nothing, in fact, can be more clear, on a perusal of these pieces, than that the princely bard, the son of Owain Gwynedd, sovereign of North Wales, is speaking of an earthly fair one, whose charms he celebrates in elegant and appropriate language, without the remotest allusion to pagan goddesses of any description whatsoever.

The lines are :[3]—

> I love the fort of proud workmanship in the Cyvylchi,
> Where my own assuming form is wont to intrude ;
> The high of renown eagerly seek admittance there,

---

[1] *Myvyr. Archæol.* vol. i. pp. 275, 278.
[2] *Literature of the Kymry*, p. 120.
[3] Dr. Owen Pughe's translation. *Literature of the Kymry*, p. 120.

And near it speaks the mad resounding wave.
It is the chosen place of a luminary of splendid qualities, and fair.
Glorious her rising from the verge of the torrent,
And the fair one shines on the now progressing year,
In the wilds of Arvon, among the Snowdonian hills.
The tent does not attract, the glossy silk is not looked on
By her I love with passing tenderness.
If her conquest could be wrought by the muse's aid,
Ere the coming night I should next to her be found.

I love the time of summer when the steed
Of the exulting chief prances in the presence of a gallant lord,
When the nimbly moving wave is covered with foam,
When the apple-tree wears another aspect,
And when the white shield is borne upon my shoulders in the conflict.
I have loved ardently, but unsuccessfully,
A tall and white-necked fair of slowly languid gait;
Her complexion vies with the mild light of the evening hour,
Bright, slightly formed, feebly bending, white-hued knowing one.
In stepping over a rush she would nearly fall,
The small and delicate one of feeble step;
But though small she is older than a ten-year old youth;
And though child-like in appearance is full of propriety.
From her childhood she has learned to give freely;
And the virgin would rather impede her own prosperity
Than utter one sentence of unseemly import.
I will be a pilgrim worshipper at the place of meeting.
How long shall I worship thee?   Stop and think of thine office.
If I am unskilful through the dotage of love,
Jesus the well-informed will not rebuke me."

The lady celebrated in these lines presents an appearance
so different from that of the " black screaming hag" who pursued Gwion and brought forth Taliesin, that Mr. Davies remarks, "If we may judge from Howel's description, Ceridwen
had greatly improved in her person and manners since the
sixth century; but still, she is the same object of idolatrous
veneration; she still communicates her mystical laws to the
devoted aspirant."

A poem in the *Myvyrian Archæology*, entitled " Cadair Ceridwen," is supposed to contain evidence of the mythological character of this enchantress.

KADEIR KERRIDWEN.

Rhen rym awyr titheu
Cerreifant on correddeu
Yn Newaint yn mhlygeieu
Llewychawd yn lleufereu
Mynawg hoedl Minawg ap Lleu
A welais i yma gynneu
Diwedd yn llechwedd Lleu
Bu gurdd ei hurdd ynghadeu
Afagddu fy mab inneu
Dedwydd Dofydd rhwy goreu
Ynghyfamryson Kerddeu
Oedd gwell ei Synwyr no'r fau
Celfyddaf gwr a gigleu
Gwydion ap Don dygnferthau
A hudwys gwraig a Flodeu
A dyddwg Moch o Ddeheu
Can ni bu iddaw disgoreu
Drud ymyd a gwryd pletheu
A rithwys gorwyddawd y ar plagawd
   lys
Ac enwerys cyfrwyau
Pan farner y Cadeiriau

Arbennig uddun y fau
Fynghadair am pair am deddfon
Am Araith drwyadl gadair gysson
Rym gelwir gyfrwys yn llys Don
Mi ag Euronwy ag Euron
Gweleis ymladd taer yn Nant ffrancon
Duw sul pryd pylgeint
Rhwng wythaint a Gwydion
Dyfieu yn geugant ydd aethan Von
I geissaw yscut a hudolion
Aran rhod drem clot a gwawr hinon
Mwyaf gwarth y marth o barth Bry-
   thon
Dybrys am ei Lys Enfys Afon
Afon ai hechrys gurys gwrth terra
Gwenwyn ei chynbyd cylch byd eda
Nid wydywaid geu llyfrau Breda
Cadair gedwiddedd yssyd yma
A hyd frawd parawd yn Europa
An rothwy y drindawt
Trugaredd Dyddbrawd
Cein gardawd gan wyrda.

THE CHAIR OF KERRIDWEN.

Lord, I especially seek of thee
Forgiveness of my sins,
At midnight and at early dawn,
And in the brightness of the light.
Courteous in his lifetime was Minawg, the son of Llew;
And I saw him here a short time since,
At the finishing of the grave mounds of Llew.
Strong was his assault in battle.
Afagddu my son,
Blessed of the most powerful God,
In the competitions of the Bards,
There was no wiser man in the land.
The most skilful man ever heard of

(Was) Gwydion ap Don, a hard toiler,
Who made by enchantment, a woman from flowers,
And brought the swine out of the South;
For it was not difficult to him.
A strong enclosure (he made) out of plaited twigs,
And the appearance of a troop of horses out of the buds of flowers,
And such-like wonders.
If a judgment should be given on the chairs,[1]
He was the chief magician in the land.
For my chair, my cauldron, and my ordinances,
And the active rule of my harmonious Cadair,
It is mine to be called skilful in the Court of Don,
I and Euronwy and Euron.
I saw a fierce fight in Nant Ffrancon,
On Sunday at the dawn of day,
Between Gwythaint and Gwydion;
On Thursday, truly, they went to Mona,
Seeking charms[2] and illusions.
Arianrhod of beautiful aspect.[3]
Not falsely is it related in the books of Breda.[4]
The guardian of the chair is here,
And until the day of judgment, it shall continue in Europe.
May the Trinity give me
Mercy in the day of judgment.
A handsome donation from the gentry.

With reference to the last three lines of this song, Davies says:—"This poem was evidently intended to be sung or recited in the ceremonies of a heathen solemnity, by a priest or priestess who personated Ceridwen; but some paltry and

[1] This must mean, "If we may judge from the Cadairs, *i.e.* the poetry so called, which has been written on these subjects, Gwydion was the greatest of magicians."

[2] *Yscut,* "darkness," "shadow,"—perhaps the mist which the enchantress, such as Menw ab Tairgwaedd, used to render himself invisible.

[3] The next four lines I cannot understand. If Brython is put by mistake for Gwydion, they may relate to the story of the appearance of Dylan Ail Ton, and Llew Llaw Gyffes, in the romance of "Math ab Mathonwy," to which the preceding portion relates.

"Great was the scandal made evident on the part of Gwydion."

[4] Or, according to one version, Beda.

mendicant minstrel, who only chanted it as an old song, has tacked on three lines in a style and measure totally different from the preceding verses." The publication of the *Mabinogion* has, however, furnished the true key to all these supposed mysteries. The story of Gwydion and the Swine of Pryderi, of Llew Llaw Gyffes, Arianrhod and Blodeuwedd, must have been well known to the audience before whom this ballad was recited, and the allusions in it well understood. It must necessarily have been composed long after these tales had been current among the people.

The " books of Breda," mentioned in this song, do not give us any information as to its date. The same name occurs in the "Song of the Months," attributed to Aneurin, though written partly in the fourteenth and partly in the fifteenth century.[1] In reference to this latter poem, Mr. Stephens says :—" There is no saint of the name of Breda; this must, therefore, be either Brenda or Beda." Saint Brenda was the son of Helig Voel, son of Glanog ab Gwgan Gleddyv Rhudd, or Gwgan Redsword, who was one of the three sentinels at the battle of Bangor Iscoed in A.D. 607. This Brenda is not, however, a person of any celebrity; and probably, therefore, the proper reading is Beda, the venerable Bede of the eighth century.

The Cauldron of Ceridwen, and a number of allusions to the romances, are also found in a poem entitled " A Song concerning the Sons of Llyr, Son of Brochwael Powys." By the latter is generally understood Brochwael Ysgythrog, Prince of Powys, who commanded at the battle of Bangor in A.D. 607. It is not known whether he had a son named Llyr, and it would seem that the title has been taken from the names found in the poem, and was originally, perhaps, " Cerdd am Veib Llyr a Brochwael Powys "—a song concerning the sons of Llyr and Brochwael Powys. The sons of Llyr are, no doubt, the brethren of Bran the Blessed, four of whom, according to the Irish romances, were changed into swans by their stepmother.

---

[1] *Literature of the Kymri*, p. 298.

This poem has no further reference to them than the mention of a battle against them.

KERDD AM VEIB LLYR AB BRYCHWEL POWYS.

Golychaf i gulwydd Arglwydd pob echen
Arbennig torfoedd ynhyoedd am Ordden
Ceint yn yspyddawd uch gwirawd aflawen
Ceint rac meibon Llyr ym ebyr Henfelen
Gweleis treis trydar ac afar ac anghen
Yd lethrynt lafnawr ar bennawr disgywen
Ceint rhag udd clodeu yn noleu Hafren
Rhag Brochwel Powys a garwys fy Awen
Ceint yn addfwyn rodle ym more rhag Urien
Yn ewydd am antraed gwaed ar ddien
Neud amug ynghadeir o beir Ceridwen
Handid rydd fy nhafawd
Yn addawd gwawd Ogyrwen
Gwawd Ogyrwen Uferen rwy ddigones arnunt
A llefrith a gwlith a mes
Ystyriem yn llwyr cyn clwyr cyffes
Dyfod yn ddiheu angeu neses
Ac am diredd Enlli dyvi dylles
Dyrchawr llongawr ar glawr aches
A galwn ar y gwr andigones
An nothwy rhag gwyth llwyth Anghes
Pan alwer ynys Von tirion vaes
Gwyn eu byd hwy gwleiddon Saesson artres
Doddwyf Deganhwy i amrysson
Ellyngais fy Aglwydd yngwydd Deon
A Maelgwn fwyaf ei Achwysson
Elphin pendefig ry hodigion
Yssid imi deir Cadeir cyweir cysson
Ac yd vrawd parhawd gan Gerddorion
Bum ynghat Goddeu gan Llew a Gwydion
Wy a rithwys gwydd Elfydd ac Elestron
Bum i gan Vran yn Iwerddon
Gwleis pan lladdwyd morddwyd tyllon
Cigleu gyfarfod am gerddorion
A gwyddyl diefyl diferogion
O Benryn wleth hyd Luch Reon
Cymru yn unfryd gerhyd Wrion
Gwret dy Cymry yghymeiri
Teir cenedl gwythlawn o iawn deithi

Gwyddyl a Brython a Rhomani
A wahan dyhedd a Dyuysgi
Ac am derfyn Prydein cein ei threfi
Ceint rhag Teyrnedd uch medd lestri
Yngheinion Deon im ai dyroddi
An dwy ben sywed . . . . ced ryferthi
Ys cyweir fy nghadeir ynghaer Sidi
Nis plawdd haint a henaint a fo yndi
Ys gwyr Manawyd a Phryderi
Tair Orian y am dan a gan rhegddi
Ac am ei bannau ffrydieu gweilgi
Ar ffynnawn ffrwythlawn yssyd odduchti
Ys whegach nor gwin gwyn y llyn indi
Ac wedi ath iolaf Oruchaf cyn gweryd
    Gorod cymmod a thi.

SONG CONCERNING THE SONS OF LLYR AB BROCHWEL POWYS.

I adore the love-diffusing Lord of all nations.
Lord of Hosts, may he delay my appointed time.
There was a battle at the banquet over the joyless beverage ;
A battle against the sons of Llyr, on the banks of Hen Felen.
I saw the fierce tumult and wrath and calamity,
The falchions gleaming on the bright helmets.
There was a battle against the renowned chief in the vales of Severn,
Against Brochwel Powys, who loved my song.
A battle in the pleasant meadow, in the morning against Urien,
Fresh around the feet was the blood of the slain.
Not inglorious is my Chair of the Cauldron of Ceridwen.
My tongue shall be free,
In declaring the praise of Ogyrwen.[1]
For praising Ogyrwen, the water of the brook will suffice,
And new milk, dew, and acorns.
Let us ponder deeply before our last confession is heard,
Death is certainly approaching nearer and nearer.

---

[1] These lines are corrupt, as appears by the incongruity of the terminations of the lines, and the change of rhythm. It seems probable that the words "Gwawd Ogyrwen" have been repeated from the last line, and "arnunt" inserted, owing to a confusion in the MS., as the sense of the passage refers to the fare of a hermit or religious, and the whole of this stanza breathes the complaining prophetic spirit so common in these productions.

And on the shores of Enlli there shall be an overwhelming,
Ships shall be riding on the water.
Let us call upon the Lord who can aid us,
Our refuge against the violence of the stranger tribes.
When the Island of Mon shall be called a pleasant field,
Happy shall they be who are under the yoke of the gentle Saxons.[1]
I am come to Teganwy to contend
With Maelgwn, the greatest of criminals.
I have liberated my Lord in the presence of Deon,
Elphin the prince, king of magicians.[2]
I have three Cadeirs, in right tune harmonious.
And until the day of judgment they shall remain with the singers.
I was in the Cad Goddeu with Llew and Gwydion.
He who changed the form of trees, earth, and plants.
I was with Bran in Ireland.
I saw when Morddwydtyllon was slain.
I heard the meeting of the singers,
With the Irish, furious devils,[3]
From Penrhyn Bleth to Loch Reon,
Were the Cymry of one mind, there would be a multitude of heroes.
Deliver thy Cymry from the oppression
Of three tribes of truly cruel nature,
Irish, and Britons, and Romans,
Who make disturbance and confusion.
And around the borders of Britain, with its fair dwellings,
Brawling in the presence of princes over the cups of mead,
At the feast of the chieftains who have bestowed gifts on me,
And loaded with gifts the two chief astrologers.
Tuneful is my Cadeir in Caer Sidi,
Neither disease nor old age affects those who are there.
It is known to Manawyd, and Pryderi.
Three utterances around the fire shall be sung before it ;
And around its borders are the streams of the ocean ;
And sweet is its fruitful fountain,
Sweeter than the bright wine is the liquor therein,
And after I have worshipped thee,
O Most High, before I am covered with the sod,
Grant I may be in covenant with thee.

[1] That is, I presume, never ; it is a sarcasm.
[2] " The sovereign of those who carry ears of corn."—DAVIES.
[3] Perhaps alluding to the Eisteddfod held by Gruffydd ab Kynan in 1100, at which the Irish and Welsh Bards and Musicians assembled to frame laws for the regulation of their craft.

It is not clear what is meant by Ogyrwen. Dr. Owen translates it, "an angelic form, a personified idea." It seems to be another name for Ceridwen, as is seen in the "Cadeir Teyrnon," and to mean "a giantess." Gogyrfan Gawr, the giant, belongs to the Arthurian romance. The word seems to have descended to our nursery tales, as the ogre or giant of the Cornish stories.

In the "Angar Cyvyndawd" it is said, "There are seven score Ogyrfen in Awen,"—that is, apparently, seven score sources of poetic inspiration, or Muses.

The recovery of more of the *Mabinogion*, or Fairy Tales of the Welsh, can alone furnish an explanation of this and numerous other allusions of a similar character.

It is evident that in the original story, the cauldron of Ceridwen is a true witch's cauldron, the magical contents of which are compounded according to the directions given in the books of the Feryllt, or wise men, just as in all other stories of a similar character. The magic liquor intended for Afaggdu, but drunk by Gwion, bestows upon the latter magical powers, not only gifting him with extraordinary knowledge, but enabling him to transform himself into a variety of shapes at pleasure. These transformations of Gwion have no connection with the passage of the soul liberated by death from one body to another, but are voluntary changes of form assumed to escape the pursuit of a magician of greater power than himself. The details of these supernatural events, and the number and variety of these transformations, varied with the ingenuity and imagination of the minstrels. In the "Angar Cyvyndawd," the "Song of the Horses," and the "Battle of the Trees," they differ from those related in the *Hanes Taliesin*.

This magic cauldron, and the story of its miraculous gifts, was adopted by the later bards as a representation of the Greek Helicon, or fountain of the Muses, the source and well of poetic inspiration. This is clearly shown in the "Preiddeu Annwn," where the cauldron is said to be warmed by the breath of nine damsels, a detail unknown to the original and genuine tale, and which exhibits the workmanship of a very different class of persons from the minstrels who framed the original story. The later bards constantly speak of the cauldron of inspiration, and of the Awen or inspiration itself, which in the seventeenth century we have seen Llywelyn Sion in the " Cyfrinach Beirdd" represents as derived from the Holy Ghost itself. The Christian bards of the thirteenth and fourteenth centuries, indeed, repeatedly refer to the Virgin Mary herself, as the cauldron or source of inspiration, to which they were led, as it seems, partly by a play on the word " pair," a cauldron, and the secondary form of that word, on assuming the soft form of its initial " mair," which also means Mary. Mary was " Mair," the mother of Christ, the mystical receptacle of the Holy Spirit, and " Pair," the cauldron or receptacle and fountain of Christian inspiration. Thus we have in a poem of Davyd Benvras, in the thirteenth century,

> Crist mab Mair am Pair pur vonhedd,—
> Christ, son of Mary, my cauldron of pure descent.

But all this is Christian, and not Druidic mysticism, and an adaptation of popular ideas, which forms another phase in the employment of this symbol. The terms " cauldron of Ceridwen," " cauldron of the muse, of song, or of poetic inspiration," were convertible, and the same image was adopted to express the fount of holiness and the source of religious inspiration, or the gift to be employed in praise of God.

In some cases " Awen " means simply a song, poesy, and nothing more, as in the " Cerdd am Veib Llyr":—

> Ceint rhag udd clodeu yn noleu Hafren
> Rhag Brochwel Powys a garwys fy Awen,—
>
> I have sung before the glorious chief in the dales of Severn,
> Before Brochwel Powys who loved my song.

It is impossible to read this romance of the History of

Taliesin, and his transactions with Maelgwn, without observing a strong resemblance between this story and that told by Nennius and Geoffrey of Monmouth, of Merlin Emmrys and Vortigern.

In both instances, the magician, prophet, and bard, is one born without a father. As the boy Merlin puts to the wise men or magicians of Vortigern, questions which they are unable to answer, " but were ashamed, and made no reply," so the child Taliesin casts a spell on the twenty-four bards of Maelgwn, overwhelms them with questions, and convicts them of ignorance. Merlin foretells to Vortigern the coming of the sons of Constantine to revenge the murder of their father, and Taliesin prophesies the destruction of Maelgwn by means of the sea-serpent from the Morva Rhianedd.

This mystery of a child born without a father, appears to have been a favourite theme of Welsh romance, both secular and ecclesiastical.

Merlin the wizard was born of a nun. " His mother was daughter to the King of Demetia, and she lived in Saint Peter's Church among the nuns of the city of Caermarthen."[1] Saint David, the greatest of the Welsh saints, was born of a nun, violated by Sandde Bryd Angel, one of the heroes of the Battle of Camlan; in other respects his birth was miraculous; in fact, his birth had been foretold to Sandde thirty years before, by an angel. His mother was, both before and after this occurrence, a most chaste person, both in mind and body.

Saint Dubricius, almost the equal of Saint David in saintly reputation, had no visible father.[2] His mother, Eurddil, was the daughter of Pebiau, King of the region of Ergyng (Archenfield), and being discovered by her father to be pregnant, was by his command placed alive upon a funeral pile. Unhurt by the flames, she gave birth to Dubricius, who instantly com-

---

[1] Geoffrey's *British History*, ch. 17.
[2] *Life of Saint Dubricius in Liber Landav.* p. 323.

menced the performance of various miracles, and became a most pious and saintly bishop.

Dylan Ail Ton, and Llew Llaw Gyffes, were also born in a mysterious manner, and without any visible father. We should be tempted to assign the introduction of this quality of " son of a virgin " to the influence of Christian ideas, though a similar mysterious origin has, no doubt, been ascribed to their heroes by other nations, before the date of the Christian era.

The coincidence between the story of Taliesin and that of Merlin is the more worthy of observation, since there has evidently been some confusion between those two personages.

Taliesin himself, in the copy of the romance published by Lady Guest, says,

> Idno and Heidin called me Merddin,
> At length every king will call me Taliesin.

The story in Nennius and Geoffrey is older by some centuries than the version of Thomas ab Einion. But neither the original Nennius nor Geoffrey mention Taliesin, nor does his name occur in the *Brut y Tysilio*, which some will have to be the original of Geoffrey. His fame as a hero of romance, and Chief Bard of the West, cannot, it would seem, have arisen before the eleventh century at the earliest. In the tale of Bronwen the Daughter of Llyr he is mentioned by name, in a casual way, as one of the seven who returned from the Irish expedition, and is certainly very much out of place in company with Bran, his son Caractacus, and Caswallon, the Cassibelaunus of Cæsar. In the Arthurian romance however, as developed by the bards of South Wales in the eleventh and twelfth centuries, after the introduction of the History of the Round Table from Britanny by Rhys ab Tewdur, Taliesin plays a far more important part. In the tale of Kilhwch and Olwen Taliesin is called the Chief of the Bards of Arthur's Court, and the legends which remain of him all connect him with the Arthurian heroes. It seems, therefore, that if a Taliesin the

Bard of Urien Rheged lived in the sixth century, the Taliesin of the romance of Thomas ab Einion is altogether a poetic fiction unknown to the traditional or historical literature of the country before the eleventh century at the earliest, and that his name must have been sufficiently in repute as a bard to have been selected, in preference to any other, as the Chief Bard of Arthur, and that it was this reputation, derived from this source, that caused him to be made the hero of those ballads afterwards worked up into the History of Taliesin, such as we find in the collection of the *Mabinogion.*

We have already observed, that there are many songs in the Myvyrian collection which were probably printed as part of the History of Taliesin, though not found in the copy in the Red Book of Hergest. These are so similar in character to those before given, that there can be no doubt of their belonging to the same series. Such is the "Song of the Ale," a portion of which was probably made in imitation of the "Song of the Mead," and the so-called Chairs, the "Cadair Teyrnon," and "Cadair Taliesin."

KANU Y KWRWF.

Teithi edmynt
Gwr a gadwynt gwynt
Pan del ei rihudd
Gorfloeddawg Elfydd
Menhyd yn dragywydd
Ys tydi a fedydd
Dylif deweint a dydd
Oedd ym amogawr
Nos yn Orphowyssawr
Maswedd a folhawr
Y wrth wledig mawr
Mawr Dduw digones
Heul haf ai rywres
Ag ef digones
Budd Coed a Maes
Galwettawr Yraches

Ar eilig anghymes
Gallwellawr pob neges
Deus dymgwares
Achyn dybyddyn
Llwyth byd i'r unbryn
Ni ellynt ronyn
Heb gyfoeth Mechdeyrn
Ef ai tawdd yn llyn
Hyn y vo Eginyn
Ef ai tawdd waith arall
Hyn y fo yn fall
Drehawg dydderfydd
Dysgofag yr Elfydd
Golchettawr ei lestri
Bid gloyw ei frecci
A phan fo anawell

Dyddyccawr o gell
Dyddyccawr rhag rhieu
Ynghein gyfeddeu
Nis gwrthryn pob dau
Y mel ai goreu
Duw edwynt ynof
Ydd fydd yn ei fodd
Llaryaf yw trindawd
Gorwyth meddw meddwhawd
O fynud pysgawd meint y godrefi
Grayan mor heli y dan dywawd
Am cudd y ar teithiawg
Mi hun am gwarawd
Ni ddigonir nebawd
Heb gyfoeth y Drindawd
Teithi edmygant
Yn Nyffryn Garant
Gallawg gallwgyd anchwant
Sybwll symudant
Ban erddefel tant
Neu nos cwdd dyfydd
Cwdd dirgel rhag dydd
A wyr cerdd Gelfydd
Py gel Kallofydd
Am dyro amde
Or porth pan ddwyre
Py ddyddug llyw gayaf
Py gyd ddechreu lle [1]
Yn dewis eichiawg
Ffus ffons ffodiawg [2]
Ef dyhun hunawg
Ef gobryn Carawg
Cymry Caerneddawg
Ytat Garadawg
Dear menciuon
Dear Mynawg Mon
Mawr erch anudon

Gwenhwys gwallthirion
Am Gaer Wyrangon
Pwy a dal y Ceinon
Ai Maelgwn o Von
Ai dyfydd o Aeron
Ai Coel ai Canawon
Ai gwrweddw ai feibion
Nid anchwardd ei Alon
O Ynyr Wystlon
Ef cyrch cerddorion
Se Syberw Seon
Neu'r dierfeis i rin
Ymordei Uffin
Ymhorroedd Gododin
Ys geirfrith cyfrenhin
Bran bore ddewin
Wyf carddenhin hen
Wyf cyfreu llawen
Athaw y dygen
Meu molawd Urien
Eirian eirioes
Llyminawg llumoes
Rhuddfedel afwys
Rhuddyn ai llynwys
Cad yn Harddnenwys
Ynyr ai briwys
Cant calan cynnwys
Can car amyuwys
Gweleis wyr gorfawr
A ddygyrchynt awr
Gweleis waed ar llawr
Rhag ruthr cleddyfawr
Glessynt esgyll gwawr
Esgorynt yn waeywawr
Trychant calan cyman clodfawr
Ynyr ar dir yn wir Cochawr.

---

[1] " Llef," in Jones's copy.
[2] " Ffysg ffons ffodiaws," id.

THE SONG OF THE ALE.

He was a quick traveller,
The man who harnessed the wind;
How much did he soar above
The noisy earth.
Eternal happiness [1]
Is for thee who art baptized.
Passing is the night, and the day
Has been opening.
The night is for taking rest.
Vain discourse and folly
Are unpleasing to the Almighty.
The great God made
The summer sun and its great heat,
And he made
The fruits of the wood and the field.
He is the efficient cause of the river
Abundantly flowing;
He is the efficient cause of all things:
The redeeming God.
And before he caused to grow,
All the inhabitants of the earth were in famine,
They could not procure a single grain
Without the power of the Lord.
He shall steep it in the lake [2]
Until it shall have sprouted.
He shall steep it again
Until it shall have become soft;
After a time it will be accomplished,
The juice which is the delight of the earth. [3]
Let his vessels be washed clean;
Let his wort be bright;
And when there shall be song,
Bring it from the cellar,
Bring it before kings
In brilliant festivals.

---

[1] *Menwyd,* "happiness." It is written *menhyd,* which would be "There is a place in eternity for thee," &c.

[2] Here commences the part which relates to the Ale, the subject, according to the title, of the song.

[3] That is, if it may be permitted to alter the words to "Dws gorffawg yr Elfydd."

26

Without dispute of all good things,
It is by far the best.
God has given it to us.
It will be in his pleasure.
Most beneficent is the Trinity,
But very wrathful with the drunkard.[1]
Of the manners of fishes and the size of their habitations,
The sand of the salt sea is in the recital.[2]
Of my secret for journeying to them
I myself am the guardian.
No one shall be possessed of it
Without the assistance of the Trinity.
They commend the journey
In Dyffryn Garant.
The mighty ones careless of prudence,
They dash through the pools
When the lash is used.
Will not the night be a shelter,
A secret retreat for them
Who know the secrets of song?
What is the retreat of the Callofydd,
Wrapped up in his robe
When he rises in the gate?
Who took the falsest oath?
Who commenced the tumult
In the noisy election?
Fortunate was his hasty flight.
He will awake the sleeper.
He will redeem the wild boar[3]
Of Wales spread over with cities,[4]
At the coming again of Caradawg.[5]

[1] Here the "Song of the Ale" properly terminates. The next seven lines belong to some other ballad, and the following form what is sometimes called the "Battle of Dyffryn Garant."

[2] As numerous as the sands of the sea.

[3] The tale of the Boar's Head, which Caradawg alone was able to carve, is probably alluded to. See the note to stanza 30, in the Rev. J. Williams's translation of the *Gododin*.

[4] In some copies it would appear that this epithet is written *Carneddawg,* "stone-piled," or "abounding with stones"; but in the *Myvyrian Archæology* it is "Caerneddawg."

[5] Dr. Owen's translation of these lines, beginning with "A wyr cerdd gelfydd," is as follows :—

Sad are the men of Menevia,
Sad is fair Mona.
Very dreadful the perjury
Of the long-haired men of Gwent.
For Caer Wyrangon,[1]
Who will pay the ransom?[2]
Is it Maelgwn of Mona?
Is it Dyfydd of Aeron?
Is it Coel, is it Cenau?
Is it Gwrweddw and his sons?
Not unlaughable his foes,
The hostages from Ynyr.[3]
He is the resort of minstrels,
The star of proud Seon.[4]
Have I not proclaimed the secret
On the seashore of Uffin,
By the waters of Gododin?
He is a true diviner,
The raven prophesying in the morning.
I am an old wanderer,
I am a promoter of joyousness,
And I am silent through anger,
That there is no praise of Urien.
Beautifully splendid,
Keenly sharp,

"That knows the ingenious art that is concealed by the discreet Ovate will give me a splendid garment when he ascends from the gate.—Caradawg will purchase Wales abounding with heaps of stones."

[1] Worcester.

[2] Perhaps it should be "ccinion." Then,

> At Caer Wyrangon,
> Who will give the first drink at the feast.

[3] The tale to which this passage relates is noticed in the *Mabinogion* of Kilhwch and Olwen. Glewlwyd Gavaelwawr says, "I was in the battle of Dau Ynyr when the twelve hostages were brought from Llychlyn." If we had a complete collection of the romances of the Welsh, we should have no difficulty in understanding the greater part of the allusions in these poems, which are so obscure, but which must have been perfectly intelligible to those before whom they were recited.

[4] Seon. Caer Seiont, near Caernarvon, the Segontium of the Romans, once the most famous city in North Wales.

A fierce blood-reaper,
Like heart of oak his body.
At the battle of Harddnenwys [1]
He wounded Ynyr. [2]
Admitted to a hundred festivals,
Sought after by a hundred friends.
I saw the mighty ones
Approaching at the shout.
I saw blood on the ground,
From the onset of the swordsmen.
The splinters caused anguish to the warrior,
Scattered about like lances.
In three hundred perfect festivals shall be celebrated,
Ynyr, who is in truth the reddener of the earth. [3]

[1] The men of Harddnen, the beautiful roof—probably a castle so called.
[2] Or shattered the land of Ynyr.
[3] These lines have been very differently translated by Edward Jones, whose version has for the most part been followed by Mr. Stephens.   It is :—

> I saw the warriors of dread appearance
> Rushing together to the shout of war;
> I saw the ground strewed with blood
> From the conflict of the men of swords.
> *They tinged with blue the wings of the morning,*
> *When they poured forth their ashen messengers of pain.*
> In three hundred festivals will be sung the high fame
> Of Ynyr, whose feats are seen on the crimson-tinted earth.

The lines in italics are certainly poetic, but they cannot be accepted as a translation of the original.   The word *esgyll*, no doubt, generally means *wings*, being the plural of *asgell*, a wing; but it has also a technical meaning in these descriptions of battle scenes.   The root of the word, according to Owen, is *asg*, " a piece split off," " a splinter"; and in this sense it is used in a passage of Llywarch Hen, and another of Taliesin.

In the poem of Llywarch Hen on the loss of his sons, he says of Pyll,

> Dychonad ystavell o esgyll ysgwydawr
> Tra vydded yn sevyll
> A vriwed ar angad Pyll.

> A room might be formed from the *wings* of shields,
> Which would hold one standing upright,
> That were broken in the grasp of Pyll.

In this instance *esgyll*, the wings, must be taken to mean some portion of

KADEIR TALIESIN.

Mydwyf Merwerydd
Molawd Duw dofydd
Llwrw cyfranc cywydd
Cyfreu dyfynwedydd
Bardd bron Sywedydd
Pan atleferydd
Awen cud echwydd
Ar feinoeth feinydd
Beirdd llafar lluc de
Eu gwawd nym gre
Ar ystrawd ar ystre
Ystryw mawr mire
Ac mi wyf cerdd fud
Gogyfarch feirdd tud
Ryd ebrwyddaf drud
Ry talmaf ehud
Ryddy hunaf dremud
Teyrn terwyn wolud
Nid mi wyf cerdd fas
Gogyfarch feirdd tras
Bath vadawl idas
Dofn eigiawn addas
Pwy am lenwis cas
Camp ymhob noethas
Pan yw dien gwlith
A lladd gwenith
A gwlid Gwenyn
A glud ac ystor
Ac elyw tramor

Ac aur bib lleu
A llon ariant gwiw
A rhudd em a grawn
Ac ewyn eigiawn
I'y ddyfrys fynnawn
Berwr byryrddawn
Py gysswllt gwerin
Brecci bonedd llynn
A llwyth lloer wehyn
Lledaf lloned verbyn
A synion synhwyr
A sewyd am loer
A gofrwy gwedd gwyr
Gwrth awel awyr
A mall a merin
A gwadawl tra merin
A chorwg gwydrin
Ar llaw pererin
A phybyr a phyg
Ag urddawl segyrffyg
A llyseu Meddyg
Lle allwyr Venffyg
A Beirdd a blodeu
A guddig bertheu
A briallu a briwddail
A blaen gwydd goddeu
A mall ameuedd
A mynych adneuedd
A gwin tal cibedd

---

a shield; but the context shows that broken shields are meant, and the line should be,

A room might be formed with the splinters (broken pieces) of shields.

The other instance is in the Elegy on Owain ap Urien :—

> Isgell cerddglyd clodfawr
> Esgyll gwaywawr
> Llifeid.—

A corpse is the renowned protector of song.
In splinters is his sharpened spear.

Where the rendering "wings" is evidently impossible.

O Rufein hyd Rossedd
A dwfnddwfr echwydd
Dawn ei lif Dofydd
Neu pren purawr fydd
Ffrwythlon ei gynnydd
Rei ias berwidydd
Oedd uch pair pumwydd

A gwiawn afon
A gofwy hinon
A mel a meillion
A meddgyrn meddwon
Addwyn i Ddragon
Ddawn y Dderwyddon.

THE CADEIR TALIESIN.

I am apt in composing
Praise of God the Creator.
On account of my contests in song,
Shining with jewels [1]
Is the breast of the bard gifted with a knowledge of the stars;
When is recited
The song in the evening,
Or in the fine night of a fine day.
Bards of rapid utterance,
Your encomiums are not pleasing to me,
Passing from point to point
With a great appearance of skill.
I am not a mute bard. [2]
Conspicuous among the bards of the land,
I hasten on the course of the bold;
I rouse the heedless,
I keep sleep from the eyes
In praising valiant princes.
I am not a shallow artist,
Conspicuous among my kindred bards.
My emblem is the subtle snake,
Fitted for the deep waters of the ocean.
Who is there can fill me with envy,
Contesting in every science?
Whence is the deadly dew
That kills the wheat?
And the moisture of the bee,
And the paste which it stores up,
And its abundant provision, [3]

---

[1] Tywynedig—resplendent.
[2] " Mi" must be wrongly written here for " ni."
[3] " And frankincense and myrrh, and transmarine aloes."—OWEN's *Dict.*

And the colour of the golden herb,[1]
And the proper form of silver,
And the ruby berries,
And the foam of the sea?
What hastens the (course of) the spring,
Producing the watercresses?
How can men procure
Wort of a noble liquor?
What burthen is it that is separate from the moon
Against its crescent form?
And the reason of the appearances
Of the stars scattered around the moon,
And the universal nature of men?
Of the opposing currents of air,
And plague and famine?
And what is deposited by rain,
And the glass vessel,
In the hand of the pilgrim?
And of valour and honour,
And nobility and false nobility,
And medicinal plants,
And a place entirely poisonous,
And bards and flowers,
And the secret qualities
Of primroses and small herbs,
And the shoots of trees and shrubs?
And the evils of idleness,
And of frequent pledging?
And wine overflowing the brim,
From Rome to Rossed;
And the deep still water,
Its stream is the gift of God.
Is there not a tree of pure gold,
Fruitful its nature;
Very hot is its boiling,
In the sweet cauldron of the five trees,
Of the water of Gwion.
And what sends fine weather,
And honey and trefoils,

---

[1] No doubt the Herbe d'or, alluded to in the Breton poems as a herb of great medicinal power. Villemarqué says it is the Selago. See *Barzaz Breiz*, t. i. page 62.

And the mead-horns of the mead-drinkers?
Blessed to the chief,
If the gift of the Druids.[1]

KADEIR TEYRNON.

Areit awdl eglur
Awen tra messur
Am gwr deu awdwr
O echen aladwr
Ai ffonsai ai ffwr
Ai reon rechdur
Ai ri rhwyfiadur
Ai rif ysgrythwr
Ai goch gochlesswr
Ai ergyr dros fwr
Ai Kadair gymmesswr
Ymlith gosgordd mur
Neus dug o gawrmwr
Meirch gwelw gostrodwr
Teyrnon henwr
Heilyn pasgadwr
Treded dofn doethur
I fendigaw Arthur
Arthur fendigad
Ar gerdd gyfaenad
Arwyneb ynghad
Arnaw bystylad
Pwy y try chynweissad
A werchedwis gwlad
Pwy y tri chyfarwydd
A gedwis Arwydd
A ddaw wrth awydd
Erbyn eu Harglwydd
Ban rinwedd rotwydd
Ban sydd hyn hoywedd
Ban corn cerddetrwyd
Ban biw wrth echwydd
Ban guir pan ddisglair

Bannach pan lefair
Ban pan ddoeth o bair
Ogyrwen Awen teir
Bum Mynawg mynweir
Ynghorn im neddair
Yy ddyly cadeir
Ni gatwo fy ngair
Cadeir gennyf glaer
Awen hyawdl daer
Pwy yw enw y teircaer
Rhwng lliant a llaer
Nis gwyr ni fo taer
Eissillut eu Maer
Pedair caer yssydd
Ym Mrydain powyssedd
Rhieu Merwerydd
Am nid fo nid fydd
Nid fydd am nid fo
Llynghessawr a fo
Tohid Gwaneg tra gro
Tir dylyn dirbo
Nag Aillt nag *ado*
Na bryn na thyno
Na rhynnawd godo
Rhag gwynt pan sorho
Cadeira Teyrnon
Celfydd rwy catwo
Ceissitor yngno
Ceissitor Cedig
Cedwyr colledig
Tebygaf ddull dig
O ddifa Pendefig
O ddull difynnig

[1] I have translated the word Derwyddon "Druids," in deference to general usage, though it will be seen that it had no other meaning in these compositions than philosopher, sage, or magician, and is quite unconnected with any mythological notions.

O Leon luryg
Dyrchafawd Gwledig
Am derwyn hen enwig
Breuhawd bragawd brig
Breuhawl eissorig
Orig a Merin
Am derfyn chwefrin

Ieithoedd eddein
Aches ffysgiolin
Mordwyaid Merin
O blan Seraphin
Dogyn dwfa diwerin
Dyllyngein Elphin.

THE ROYAL CADEIR.

Sing a brilliant song
Of boundless inspiration,
Concerning the Man who is to come[1]
To destroy the nations,
And his staff and his intrenchment,
And his swift devastations,
And his ruling leadership,
And his written number,
And his red purple robes,
And his assault against the rampart,
And his appropriate seat
Amid the great assembly.
Has he not brought from hell
The horses of the pale burden-bearer,
The princely old man,
The cupbearing feeder?
The third deeply wise one,
Is the blessed Arthur.
Arthur the blessed,
Renowned in song,
In the front of the battle,
He was full of activity.
Who were the three chief ministers

Who guarded the land?
Who were the three skilful ones
Who preserved the token,
And came with eagerness
To receive their Lord?
Great is the mystery of the circular
    course.[2]
Conspicuous is the gaiety of the old.
Loud is the horn of the traveller.
Loud the cattle towards evening.
Conspicuous is truth when it appears,
More so when spoken.
Conspicuous when came from the
    cauldron
The three inspirations of Ogyrwen.
I have been Mynawg wearing the
    collar,[3]
With a horn in my hand.
He does not merit the chair,
Who does not preserve my word.
Mine is the splendid chair,
The inspiration of my ardent song.
What are the names of the three cities

---

[1] Gwr deu awdwr. Davies and Herbert translate it "the man of two authors," which they say is a great mystery. This part is certainly very obscure: it may relate to Christ, or to the anticipated return of Arthur. It is a question whether the word in the fourth line is "lladwr," a blesser, or "lladdwr," a destroyer. I have given it the latter sense, because there seems a reference to the number of the destroyers in the Revelation. After all, it may be a reference to some lost romance of Arthur.

[2] Here begins a different subject altogether.

[3] Or the courteous Mynweir; that is, Rhiannon. See the "Tale of Manawyddan ab Llyr."

Between the sea and the land?
No one knows who is not earnest,
The offspring of their lord.
There are four cities
In peaceful Britain.
Tumultuous chiefs
Have not been nor shall be,
Shall not be nor have been.[1]
There shall be a conductor of fleets.
The billows shall cover the strand,
Overwhelming the land;
Nor rock nor roof,
Nor hill nor dale,
Nor the least shelter
From the wind when it shall rage.
The Cadeir Teyrnon,
Skilful is he who keeps it.
Is there here one who is inquiring,
A bounteous inquirer,
For the lost warriors?[2]
I think with wrathful gesture
Of the destroyed Chieftain,
Of the lacerated form
Of the corslet-wearing Leon.[3]
Exalted be the Lord,
To the end be his name celebrated.
Brittle are the young shoots of the tree,
Frail like them,
A little while and we melt away;
At the end of our toil,
Languages shall pass away.
The ardent soul
Shall be voyaging through the clouds
With the children of the Seraphim,
Gliding on shall be thy people,
To the liberation of Elphin.[4]

One of the most interesting and instructive pieces in this collection, and one which gives us a complete clew to the nature of most of the compositions, is that entitled "Preiddeu Annwn,"—the Victims of Annwn, or the Spoils of Hell, as it has been called. It has generally been considered to overflow with mythology and Druidic lore. Mr. Davies declared the subject of the poem to be "the mythology of the Deluge, and the mysteries which were celebrated in commemoration of it."

[1] "'As for what may not be, it will not be; it will not be because it may not be,'—a curious specimen of Druidical logic," says Mr. Davies.

Dr. Owen, connecting the next line, makes it,

> He will not be on account that he shall not be an admiral.

[2] "Seeking would be there, seeking the munificent departed warriors."— Owen, *Dict.*

[3] Dr. Owen gives these lines as a quotation from Lewis Glyn Cothi. If this is not a mere accidental error, it would be a curious circumstance, as that bard lived in the end of the fifteenth century. They seem out of place here.

[4] It is probable that some mystical sense is involved here. Dr. Owen translates it,—

"The briskly moving plain of the water voyagers" (of the children of the Seraphim), "pure and profound the spell to liberate Elphin."

Turner declared it to be utterly incomprehensible, and even Mr. Stephens says, that "it is one of the least intelligible of the mythological poems;" and Lady Charlotte Guest calls it "a mystical poem which appears to be full of allusions to traditions now no longer intelligible." The following translation is taken from Mr. Stephens, with some few alterations :—

PREIDDEU ANNWN.

Golych wledig pendefig gwad ri
Pe ledas y pennaeth tros draeth Mundi
Bu cywair carchar Gwair ynghaer Sidi
Trwy ebostol Pwyll a Phryderi
Neb cyn nog ef nid aeth iddi
Yr gadwyn dromlas cywirwas ai cedwi
A rhac Preiddieu Annwn tost yt geni
Ac yd frawd parahawd yn barddweddi
Tri lloneid prydwen ydd aetham ni iddi
Nam saith ni dyrraith o Gaer Sidi.

Neud wyf glod geymyn cerdd o chlywir
Ynghaer Pedryfan pedyr y chwelyd
Ynghynueir or pair pan leferid
O anadl naw morwyn gochynnessid
Neu pair pen annwfn pwy vynud
Gwrym am ei oror a Mererid
Ni beirw bwyd llwrf ni rydyngid
Kleddyf lluch lleawc iddaw rhyddychid
Ac yn llaw Lleminawg ydd edewid
A rhag drws porth Uffern llugyrn lloscid
A phan aetham ni gan Arthur trafferth llethrid
Namyn saith ni ddyrraith o Gaer Vediuid.

Neud wyf glod geimyn cerdd glywanawr
Ynghaer Pedryfan Ynys Pybyrddor
Echwydd a muchydd cymysgettor
Gwyn gloyw eu gwirawd rhag ei gosgordd
Tri lloneid Prydwen ydd aetham ni ar for
Namyn saith ni ddyrraith o Gaer Rigor.

Ni obrynaf lawyr llen llywiadur
Tra chaer wydr ni welsynt wrhyd Arthur

Tri ugeint canhwr a sefi ar y mur
Oedd anawdd ymadrawdd ai gwiliadur
Tri lloneid Prydwen ydd aeth gan Arthur
Namyn saith ni ddyrraith a Gaer Goludd.

Ni obrynaf i lawyr llaes eu cylchwy
Ni wyddant hwy py ddydd peridydd pwy
Py awr ym meinddydd y ganed Cwy
Pwy gwnaeth ar nid aeth dolau Defwy
Ny wyddant hwy yr ych brych bras ei benrhwy
Seith ugein cygwn yn ei aerwy
A phan aetham ni gan Arthur afrddwl gofwy
Namyn saith ni ddyrraith o Gaer Vandwy.

Ni obrynaf lawyr llaes ei gehen
Ni wddant py ddydd peridydd pen
Py awr ym meinddydd y ganed perchen
Py fil a gatwant ariant y pen
Pan aetham ni gan Arthur afrddwl gynhen
Namyn saith ni dyrraith a Gaer Ochren.

Mynaich dychnud fal cunin cor
O gyfranc uddydd ai Gwiddanhor
Ai un hynt gwynt ai un dwfr mor
Ai un ufel tan twrwf diachor
Myneich dychnud fab bleiddawr
O gyfranc uddydd ai gwyddyanhawr
Ni wddant pan ysgar deweint a gwawr
Neu wynt pwy hynt pwy ei rynnawd
Py va ddifa py dir a plawdd
Bed Sant yn ddifant o bet allawr
Golychaf i wledig pendefig mawr
Na bwyf trist Crist am gwaddawl.

THE SPOILS OF ANNWN.

Praise to the Lord, Supreme Ruler of the high region,
Who hath extended his dominion to the shores of the world.
Complete was the prison of Gwair in Caer Sidi ;
Through the permission of Pwyll and Pryderi,
No one before him went to it.
A heavy blue chain firmly held the youth ;
And for the spoils of Annwn gloomily he sings,
And till doom shall continue his lay.

Thrice the fulness of Prydwen we went into it.
Except seven, none returned from Caer Sidi.

Am I not a candidate for fame to be heard in the song,
In Caer Pedryvan four times revolving?
The first word from the cauldron, when was it spoken?
By the breath of nine damsels gently warmed.
Is it not the cauldron of the Chief of Annwn which is social?
With a ridge round its edge of pearls,
It will not boil the food of a coward nor of one excommunicated.
A sword bright flashing to him will be brought,
And left in the hand of Llyminawg.
And before the door of the porch of hell a lantern is burning.
And when we went with Arthur in his splendid labours,
Except seven, none returned from Caer Vendiwid.

Am I not a candidate for fame, to be heard in song?
In Caer Pedryfan, the island of Pybyrdor,
Twilight and darkness meet together.
Bright wine was their drink in their assembly.
Thrice the burden of Prydwen we went on the sea.
Except seven, none returned from Caer Rigor.

I will not allow great merit to the directors of learning.
Beyond Caer Wydr they have not beheld the prowess of Arthur.
Three score hundred men were placed upon the wall;
It was difficult to converse with the sentinel.
Thrice the fulness of Prydwen we went with Arthur.
Except seven, none returned from Caer Golur.

I will not allow merit to the multitude trailing on the circuit;[1]
They know not on what day or who caused it,
Nor what hour in the splendid day Cwy was born,
Nor who prevented him from going to the vales of Deowy.
They know not the brindled ox, with this thick headband,
And seven score knobs in his collar.
And when we went with Arthur of mournful memory,
Except seven, none returned from Caer Vandwy.

---

[1] "Trailing shields," Mr. Stephens gives. But it is clear that the persons who did not know these things were not warriors with shields, but bards, apparently Clerwr, who are said to be unacquainted with the songs and recitations in which these circumstances were mentioned.

I will not allow merit to the multitude with their weak effusions ;
They know not what day the head was made,
Nor what hour in the fine day the owner was born.
What animal they guard with a silver head.
When we went with Arthur of mournful contention,
Except seven, none returned fron Caer Ochren.

This is the end of this poem.   The remaining lines consist merely of the ordinary abuse of the monks, and have evidently been added by a very inferior hand, and at a later date.

Monks pack together like dogs in the choir,
From their meetings with their witches.
Is there but one course to the wind, one to the water of the sea ?
Is there but one spark to the fire of unbounded tumult ?
Monks pack together like wolves,
From their meetings with their witches.
They know not when the twilight and dawn divide,
Nor what the course of the wind, nor who agitates it ;
In what place it dies, on what region it roars.
The grave of the Saint is vanishing from the foot of the altar.
I pray to the Lord the Great Supreme,
That I may not be wretched ; may Christ be my portion.

All the difficulty which has arisen in comprehending the meaning of this poem, lies in the error of not distinguishing between tradition and what we may, for want of a better term, call romance. The allusions in this song are not to traditions, but to works of fiction, stories or tales of adventure, many of which were, no doubt, purely works of imagination ; in others, if originally founded on tradition, the thread of tradition had been altogether lost in the materials with which it had been worked up.

We may, in the first place, observe, that this is a song with a *burden* that is not uncommon with many old English ballads. The singer commences with the story of Gwair, who was confined in Annwn, and continually sings the lay which forms the burden of the song. The story of Gwair we do not possess, though it appears to be alluded to in one of the triads. Gweir

Gwrhyd Vawr was one of the knights who accompanied Geraint into Cornwall. After an allusion to the Pair Ceridwen, or fountain of Bardic inspiration, the singer intimates his superiority to the most learned who are not acquainted with the further adventures of Arthur, after his entry into Caer Wydr, or Glastonbury; that is, no doubt, after his removal to the Isle of Avallon, to be cured of the wounds received at the battle of Camlan. As to the mass of bards and minstrels, he asserts that they are not acquainted with a number of tales which he mentions. One relates to the brindled bull, who is probably the one mentioned in the tale of Kilhwch and Olwen. Indeed it is only necessary to read this latter tale, to see what a multitude of stories there must have been, which are now lost. The allusions in the " Preiddeu Annwn " are to romances sung or recited by the minstrels, and not to either mythology or traditions, as such.

We can give an example which will make this perfectly clear. Let us suppose there had been this line in the "Preiddeu Annwn,"—

> They know not who it was that divided the apples,

which would be in perfect keeping with those of the two last stanzas.

In such a line, imaginative persons might easily see a reference to Greek mythology,—the apple of Paris, or the fruit of the Hesperides. But we should be able to point out the source of the allusion, though we could not explain its meaning. It is in the story of " Peredur mab Evrauc."

" And one day they saw three knights coming along the horse-road on the borders of the forest. And the three knights were Gwalchmai the son of Gwyar, and Geneir Gwystyl, and Owain the son of Urien. And Owain kept on the track of the knight who had divided the apples in Arthur's court, whom they were in pursuit of."

The story of the Knight who divided the Apples is lost, like many others; but we see at once that there is no reference to mythology, but to some romantic adventure of the heroes of

Arthur and the Round Table. It is precisely the same with the story of the Cwy, of the Brindled Ox, and of the Animal with the Silver Head. There were once extant stories relating to them which were well known when the "Preiddeu Annwn" was composed, though it was not every minstrel that was capable of reciting them. The singer in this ballad boasts that he was acquainted with them. When we come to examine the prose Triads, we shall find abundant evidence of the former existence of a host of similar inventions, which have unfortunately perished.

There is a poem, more elegantly written and better preserved than most of these pieces, to which the unmeaning title of "Mic Dinbych" has been given—the Prospect or Glory of Tenby. According to Archdeacon Williams, "Notices continually recur in the older Bards, of a mystic city situated on and among the waters, to which worshippers went in procession on great festivals with sacred songs and hymns." The following poem the Archdeacon supposes to have been "a long hymn, which was evidently to be sung as a 'Prosodos' on approaching the holy spot in procession. As we know from other sources that the great temple on Salisbury Plain was supposed to be surrounded by a boundless sea, we may easily suppose that this 'Prosodos' might have been sung by the Bards and Druids, when leading the band of worshippers along the spacious avenues to Abury and Stonehenge." As, in order to support this view, the learned writer gives only two or three lines out of each stanza, we must see what the entire poem contains, to appreciate the value of the Druidical character assigned to it.

MIC DINBYCH.

1.

Archaf y wen i Dduw plwyf esgori
Perchen nef a llawr pwyll fawr wofri
Addfwyn Gaer y sydd ar Glawr gweilgi
Bid lawen Ynghalan eirian yri

Ac amser pan wna mor maw wrhydri
Ys gnawd gorun beirdd uch medd lestri
Dyddybydd gwaneg ar frys dybrys iddi
Addaw hwynt y werlas o Glas Ffichti
Ac am bwyf o Ddews dros fy ngweddi
Pan gattwyf ammod cymod athi.

2.

Addfwyn Gaer y sydd ar lydan Lynn
Dinas diachor mor ai cylchyn
Gogyfarch ty Prydain cwdd gyngein hyn
Blaen Llyn ap Erbin boed teu voyn
Bu gosgordd a bu cerdd yn eil mehyn
Ac eryr uch wybr a llwybr granwyn
Rhag udd ffelyg nag esgar gychwyn
Clod wasgar a Gwanar ydd ymdullyn.

3.

Addfwyn Gaer y sydd ar don nawfed
Addfwyn ei gwerin yn ymwared
Ni wnant eu dwyn cyt trwy festhaëd
Nid ef eu defawd bod yn galed
. Ni lefaraf au ar fy nhrwydded
Nog eillon deudraeth gwell caeth Dyfet
Cyweithydd o rydd wledd waredied
Cynnwys rhwng pob ddau goreu ciwed.

4.

Addfwyn Gaer y sydd ai gwna cyman
Meddut a Molut ac adar ban
Llyfn ei cherddau yn ei chalan
Am arglwydd hywydd hewr eiran
Cyn ei fyned yn ei adwyd yn derfyn llan
Ef am rhoddes medd a gwin o wydrin ban.

5.

Addfwyn Gaer y sydd yn yr eglan
Addfwyn y rhoddir i bawb ei ran
Adwen yn Ninbych gorwen gwylan
Cyweithydd wleiddydd udd erlyssan

Oedd ef fy nefawd i Nos Galan
Lleddfawd y gan ri ryfel eiran
A llen lliw ehoëg a meddu prain
Hyn y fwyaf tafawd ar feirdd Prydain.

6.

Addfwyn Gaer y sydd ai cyffrwy cedau
Oedd mew ei rhydan a ddewisswn
Ni lafaraf i daith rhaith rysgattwn
Ni ddyly celennig ni wpo hwn
Ysgrifen Brydain bryder briffwn
Yn yd wna tonneu eu hamgyffryn
Pereit hyd bell y Gell attreidwn.

7.

Addfwyn Gaer y sydd yn arddwyrein
Gochawn y meddut y molut gyfrein
Addfwyn ar ei hor esgor gynrhein
Godde gwrych dymbi hir ei hadain
Dychyrch bar carreg creg ei hadnein
Llid ymywn tynged treidded troth mein
A bleiddud gorllwyd goreu affein
Dimpyner o dduch pwy llad cofein
Bendith culwydd Nef gydlef afein
Arnyn gunel yn frowyr gorwyr Owein.

8.

Addfwyn Gaer ysydd ar llan lliant
Addfwyn yd roddir i bawb i chwant
Gogyfarch ti fyned boed teu fwyant
Gwaywawr ryn rein a dderllyssant
Duw Merchyr gweleis wyr ynghyfnofant
Dyfieu bu gwarthau a amugant
Ac ydd oedd friger coch ac och ardant
Oedd lludwed fyned dydd y doethant
Ac am gefn llech Vaelwy cylchwy friwant
Cwyddyn y gan gefn llu o garant.

The last stanza of this poem is found in the Black Book of Caermarthen. It affords a good specimen of the orthography

of that MS. and of the changes which the poems have undergone at the hands of subsequent transcribers.

Adwin caer yssit an llan llyant.   Adwin yd rotir
y pawb y chwant.   Gogywarch de gwinet boed tev wy-
ant.   Gwaewaur rrin.   Rei adarwant Dyv merch
ir. gneleisse guir yg cvinowant. Dyv iev bv. ir
guarth. itadcorssant.   Ad oet bryger coch ac och
ardant.   Oet llutedic guir guinet.   Dit ydeuthant.
Ac am kewin llech vaelwy kylchwy wriwant
Cuytin y can keiwin llu ocarant.

THE MICH DINBYCH, OR GLORY OF TENBY.

1.

I pray to the Son of God to deliver the people;
Lord of heaven and earth, in intelligence so wise.
There is a pleasant city on the surface of the sea,
Joyous its festival, beautiful its king.
And in the time when the sea is very tumultuous,
Customary is the noise of bards over their cups of mead.
The day is passing on in haste, there is hastening to thee;
Promised to them are the drinking-cups of painted glass.
And may I be of the elect through my supplication,
Since I keep the covenant entered on with thee.

2.

There is a pleasant city by the broad lake,
A fortress without a boundary, very great its circuit;
Formerly Llyn ap Erbin was its courteous chief.
There was a concourse and songs in their turn;
Like an eagle in the sky was his shining path.
Before the ruling chief no enemy was stirring;
It is my duty to spread the praise of the ruler.

3.

There is a pleasant city by the ninth wave;
Courteous are its people in their diversions.
They are not accustomed to suffer disgrace;

They do not employ their tongues with severity;
I will not say a falsehood on my admission.
Better than other shores is captivity in Dyfed.[1]
Fellowship is preserved by liberal festivities.
Admission given to all brings a great multitude.

4.

There is a pleasant city, it is made complete
(With) mead and songs and white birds.
Smooth are its songs in its festival.
My intelligent lord, the splendid chief,
Before he came to his grave within the bounds of the enclosure,
He gave me mead and wine from the glass goblet.

5.

There is a pleasant city upon the shore of the gulf,
Pleasant things there are given to every one his share.
I know in Dinbych the white sea-mew;
Courteous the assembly, beneficent[2] the chief.
It was my custom on the eve of the festival,
To soothe with song the king brilliant in war;
And to have a robe of green colour, and mead in the palace,
That is the greatest privilege of the Bards of Britain.

6.

There is a pleasant city, and its blessings I know,
Mine were its gifts, whatever I might choose.
I will not tell the journey (to it), it is just that I retain it.
He who knows not this does not merit the festival.
The writings of Britain are my primitive care;
And lest the waves should be agitated around them,
Long has it been commanded that I should penetrate to their repository.[3]

---

[1] This very natural and patriotic remark has been supposed to contain some allusion to the eminence of Dyfed as a chief seat of the Druidical worship.

[2] Erlyssan.   Dr. Owen makes this a proper name.

[3] "If necessary to the centre I would penetrate the chamber."—OWEN.

7.

There is a pleasant city greatly exalted,
I speak scornfully of its mead and its mutual praise.
Pleasant on its border the separation of kindred.
There shall be a cormorant, long his wings,
Resorting to the summit of the rock, hoarse his screams.
The wrath destined (for it) penetrates its walls;
And the wolf is prospering successful in conflicts,
And no covering above him who is asking a blessing.
Blessed love-prospering heaven, there is a united cry,
Give us for our leader the grandson of Owain.

8.

There is a pleasant city on the banks of the stream.
Pleasantly is given to each his desire.
I salute thy coming, mayest thou be prosperous.[1]
Spearmen with vibrating spears are spreading about.
On Wednesday I saw them mutually enjoying themselves.
On Thursday there was disgrace, and they were dishonoured,
Red (with blood) were their hair and their teeth.
Their coming was opposed on the day they came,
And shields were broken at the back of the stone of Maelwy.
Fallen upon their backs was the army of Geraint.

All that appears mysterious in this poem may be reasonably attributed to the imagery employed by a poetic fancy, and the ordinary scope which must be allowed for a play of the imagination in such compositions in any age or country.

It seems probable that these stanzas are the production of different authors, and have been framed by minstrels singing in turn (after the fashion mentioned by Camden) upon a given theme, viz. "There is a pleasant city." The last stanza is very inferior to the rest. The bard had partaken of the Awen of the cauldron of Ceridwen in so slight a degree that his ima-

---

[1] Mr. Davies's note on these lines is truly remarkable. He says :—"After the Bard had received the omen from the cormorant and concealed his memorials, he still persists in celebrating his holy sanctuary, till he is interrupted by a repeated message from some bird of augury, protecting spirit, or brother Druid, who seems to speak to the end of the stanza."

gination failed him, and he was obliged to fall back on the old model of the *Gododin* stanza. Both in the second and last stanza the family of Erbin are mentioned, and perhaps also in the second, Gwanar is a proper name, as Mr. Williams ab Ithel supposes it to be in the *Gododin*.

It is possible that a careful examination of Welsh history would enable us to ascertain the individuals alluded to in these stanzas. The "grandson of Owain," mentioned in the 7th stanza, is probably Cadwaladr, second son of Gruffyd ab Cynan, who in the twelfth century distinguished himself by a series of brilliant victories over the Norman invaders of the principality, but was afterwards compelled to fly at one time to Ireland, at another to England. He was grandson of Owain ab Edwyn.

Another poem ascribed to Taliesin, and supposed to be full of mystic lore, is the " Cad Goddeu," or " Battle of the Trees." It is unnecessary to say that in Mr. Davies's commentary upon this piece, we have the wildest notions of a Helio-Arkite super-stition, the metempsychosis of a Chief Druid, and a symbolical account of the Deluge. Even Lady Charlotte Guest describes it as " a long mystical poem by Taliesin." It is, I believe, one of the very latest of these productions, very inferior in style and spirit to the compositions worked up by Thomas ab Einion. Like most others, the subject from which it takes its title forms but a small portion of the whole piece, which is made up of several unconnected fragments.

There was, it appears, a story or romance on a subject called " Cad Goddeu," or " Battle of the Trees," of which only a fragment has been preserved in the *Myvyrian Archæology*. This real Cad Goddeu must not be confounded with the Cad Goddeu ascribed to Taliesin, which, though often represented as treating of the same subject, has, in fact, not the slightest connection with it. The fragment in the Myvyrian collection is entitled " Englynion, or Verses on the Cad Goddeu," and is thus prefaced :—

" These are the Englyns that were sung at the Cad Goddeu,

or, as others call it, the Battle of Achren, which was on account of a white roebuck, and a whelp; and they came from Annwn, and Amathaon ap Don brought them. And therefore Amathaon ap Don and Arawn King of Annwn fought. And there was a man in that battle, unless his name were known, he could not be overcome; and there was on the other side a woman called Achren, and unless her name were known, her party could not be overcome. And Gwydion ap Don guessed the name of the man, and sang the two Englyns following:"—

> Carngraf vy march rhagotoyw
> Benn Olgen gwera ar yasfoyw
> Bran ith elwir briger loyw
> *Ac fal hyn.*

> Carngraff dy farch yn y dydd cad
> Bann blaen gwern ar dy angad
> Bran lorgric ai vrig arnad
> Y gorfu Amathaon mad.

Translation :[1]—

> Sure-hoofed is my steed before the spur;
> The high sprigs of alder are on thy shield;
> Bran art thou called of the glittering branches.

And thus :—

> Sure-hoofed is thy steed in the day of battle;
> The high sprigs of alder are in thy hand,
> Bran with the coat of mail and the branches with thee,
> Amathaon the good has prevailed.

This battle is styled in the Triads one of the three frivolous battles of the Island of Britain, and is said to have been on account of a bitch, a hind, and a lapwing; and it is added that it cost the lives of seventy-one-thousand men.

---

[1] From the *Mabinogion*, vol. ii. notes, p. 348. The translation of the two first lines is certainly not satisfactory.

We have here all that remains of a lost romance, belonging to that earlier series in which Arthur and the Knights of the Round Table are not introduced, and which are full of magic and necromancy. Probably it was the sequel to the stories of Pwyll, Prince of Dyved, and Math ab Mathonwy.

Pwyll Prince of Dyved was the sworn friend of Arawn King of Annwn, one of the combatants in this Cad Goddeu; and Pryderi the son of Pwyll had received from Arawn some remarkable swine of a breed theretofore unknown. Gwydion the son of Don, brother of the Amathaon here mentioned, by magic art, obtained these swine from Pryderi, and in a battle which ensued, Pryderi was slain by Gwydion, owing to the magical devices employed by his adversary. In the "Cad Goddeu," Amathaon appears to have carried away, probably by fraud and sorcery, a white roebuck and a whelp from the same Annwn whence the swine of Pryderi were obtained, and in the contest which ensues he prevails over Arawn by the aid of his brother Gwydion, who was the most celebrated of the many magicians known to the Welsh circle of romance.

The more modern piece, which has taken the name of "Cad Goddeu," is as follows :—

KAD GODDEU.

Bum yn lliaws rhith
Cyn bum dysgyfrith
Bum cleddyl culfrith
Credaf pan urith
Bum deigr yn awyr
Bum *serwaw* syr
Bum geir yn llythyr
Bum llyfr ym mhrifder
Bum llugyrn lleufer
Blwyddyn a hanner
Bum pont ar trigar
Ar drugain Haber
Bum hynt am Eryr
Bum corwg emyr
Bum darwedd yn llad

Bum das ynghawad
Bum cleddyf yn angad
Bum Ysgwyd ynghad
Bum tant yn nhelyn
Lledrithiawg blwyddyn
Yn nwfr yn Ewyn
Bum yspwng yn nhan
Bum gwydd ynguarthan
Nid mi wyf ni gan
Ceint er yn fychan
Keint ynghad godeu brig
Rhag Prydein wledig
Gweint feirch canholig
Llynghessoed menedig
Gweint mil mawrem

Arnaw ydd oedd canpenn
A chad er ddy gnawd
Dan fon y tafawd
A chad arall y sydd
Yn ei wegilydd
Llyffan du gaflaw
Cantewin arnaw
Neidr fraith gribawg
Cant enaid trwy bechawd
Bum ynghaer Fefenydd
Yt gryssynt wellt y gwydd
Cenynt Gerddorion
Eryssynt cad faon
Dadwyrain i Frythron
A oreu gwydion
Gelwyssid ar Neifon
Ar Grist o achwysson
Hyd pan y gwarettai
Y rhen rwy digonesai
Os attebwy Dofydd
Trwy ieith ag elfydd
Rhithwch rhieddawg wydd
Gantaw yn llwydd
A rhwystraw peblig
Cad ar llaw annefig
Pan swynhwyd godeu
Y gobeith an goddeu
Dygottoroynt godeu
O bedryddant danheu
Cwyddynt am aereu
Brychwn trym ddieu
Dyar gardei bun
Buddiant buch anhun
Blaen llin blaen bum
Tarddei am at gun
Nim gwnei amellun
Gwaed gwyr hyd an clun
Mwyaf tair argyfryd
A chweris ymmyd
Ac un a dderyw
O ystyr dilyw
A Christ y croccaw
A ddydd brawd rhag llaw
Gwern blaen lin

A wnaent gyssevin
Helyg a cherddin
Buant hwyr ir fyddin
Eirinwydd ys prin
Auchwant o *dynin*
Keri cywrenhin
Gurthrychiad gurthrin
Ffaonwydd eithyt
Ertwyn llu o Gewryt
Afanwydd gwneithyt
Ni goreu emwyt
Er amgelwch bywyd
Rhyswydd a Gwydd-fyd
Ac eiddo ar ei bryd
Mor eithin ir gryd
Sirian senyssid
Bedw er ei fawr fryd
Bu hwyr gwisgyssid
Nid er ei lyfrder
Namyn er ei fawredd
Auron delis bryd
Allmyr uch allfryd
Ffeinidwydd ynghyntedd
Cadeir gyngwrysedd
Omi goreu arddyrchedd
Ger bron teyrnedd
Llwyf ar ei farannedd
Nid osgoes troedfedd
Ef laddei a pherfedd
Ac eithaf a diwedd
Collwydd barnyssid
Eiryf dy argyfryd
Gwyros gwyn ei fyd
Tarw trin teyrn byd
Morawg a moryd
Ffawydd ffyniessyd
Celyn glessysid
Bu ef y gwrhyd
Yspyddad amnad
Heint *ech* i angad
Gwiwydd gorthorrad
Gorthorryssid ynghad
Rhedyn anrcithad
Banadl rhag bragad

29

Eithin ni bu fad
Er hynny gwerinad
Grug bu ddydd amnad
Dy werin swynad
Hyd gwyr erlyniad
Derw buanawr
Rhagddaw cryneu nef a llawr
Gelyn glew dryssiawr
Ei enw ym peullawr
Clafuswydd cymgres
Cymnaw a roddes
Gwrthodi gwrthodes
Ereill o tylles
Per goreu gormes
Yn mhlymnwyd maes
Gorwythawg Cywydd
Aches feilon wydd
Castan cywilydd
Gwrthriad ffenwydd
Handud du muchudd
Handid crum Mynydd
Handid kyl Koetdydd
Handid cynt myr mawr
Er pan gigleu'r awr
An deilas blaen bedw
An datrith an datedw
An maglas blaen derw
O warchan mael derw
Wherthiniawg tu creig
Ner[1] nid Ystereig
Nid o Fam a Thad
Pan ymddigonad
Am creu am cread
O nawrhith llafanad
O ffrwyth o ffrwytheu
O ffrwyth Duw dechreu
O Friallu blodeu bre
O Flawd gwydd a Goddeu
O bridd o briddredd
Pan ym digoned
O Flawd danet
O ddwfr ton nawfed

Am swynwysei Math
Kyn bum diaered
Am swynwys i Wydion
Mawrnwr o Brython
O Eurwys o Eurwn
O Euron o Fedron
O bump pumhwnt Celfyddon
Athrawon ail Math
Pan ymdygaid
Am swynwys i wledig
Pan fu led losgedig
Am swynwys sywydd
Sywydon cyn byd
Pan fei gennyf fi *vot*
Pan fei faint byd
Hardd bardd budd an gnawd
Ar gwawd y tueddaf a draetho tafawd
Gwaryeis yn Llychwr
Cysgais ym mhorphor
Neu bum yn ysgor
Gan ddylan ail mor
Ynghylchedd ymherfedd
Rhevng deulin teyrnedd
Yn deu wayw anchwant
O nef pan ddoethant
Yn annwfn llifeiriant
Wrth frwydin dybyddant
Peduar ugein Kant
A Gweint ar eu chuant
Nid ynt hyn nid ynt iau
No mi ym eu banau
Arial cannwr a geni pawb o naw cant
Oedd gennyf inneu
Ynghledyf brith gwaed
Bri am darwedd
O Ddofydd o *Golo* lle ydd oedd
O dof hyd las baedd
Ef gwrith ef datwrith
Ef gwrith ieithoedd
Llachar ei enw Llawffer
Lluch llywei Nifer
Ys gein ynt yn ufel

[1] According to Dr. Owen, "Per."

O dof yn uchel
Bum neidr fraith ym mryn
Bum gwiber yn llyn
Bum ser gam gymbyn
Bum bwysfer hyn
Fy ughassul am Cawg
Armaaf nid yn ddrwg
Peduar ugeint mwg
Ar bawb a ddyddwg
Pum pemhwnt angell
A ymdal am cyllell
Whech March Melynell
Canwaith y sydd well
Fy March melyngan
Cyfred a gwylan
Mi hun nid Eban
Cyfrwng mor a glan
Neu gorwyf gwaed lan
Arnaw cant cynrhan
Rhudd em fy nghylchwy
Eur fy ysgwydrwy
Ni ganed yn adwy
A vu im gowy

Namyn Goronwy
O Ddolen Edrywy
Hirwyn fy myssawr
Pell na bum heussawr
Treiglais y mewn llawr
Cyn bum lleenawr
Treiglais cylchyneis
Kysgeis Cant Ynys
Cant Kaer a thrugys
Derwyddon doethur
Darogenwch i Arthur
Yssid y sydd gynt
Neu'r mi ergenhynt
A Christ y Crocaw
A dydd brawd rhagllaw
Ac am un a dderyw
O ystyr dilyw
Eurem yn euryll
Mi hydwyf berthyll
Ac ydwyf drythyll
O ormes fferyll.

Taliesin.

THE BATTLE OF THE TREES.

I have been in many shapes,
Before I attained a congenial form.
I have been a narrow blade of a sword.
I will believe when it appears.[1]
I have been a drop in the air.
I have been a shining star.
I have been a word in a book.
I have been a book originally.
I have been a light in a lantern
A year and a half.
I have been a bridge for passing over
Three score rivers.
I have journeyed as an eagle.
I have been a boat on the sea.
I have been a director in battle.
I have been the string of a child's swaddling clout.

[1] This line is evidently an interpolation.

I have been a sword in the hand.
I have been a shield in fight.
I have been the string of a harp,
Enchanted for a year
In the foam of water.
I have been a poker in the fire.
I have been a tree in a covert.
There is nothing in which I have not been.
I have fought, though small,
In the Battle of Godeu Brig,
Before the ruler of Britain,
Abounding in fleets.
Indifferent bards pretend,[1]
They pretend a monstrous beast,
With a hundred heads,
And a grievous combat
At the root of his tongue.
And another fight there is
At the back of his head.
A toad having on his thighs
A hundred claws,
A spotted crested snake,
For punishing in their flesh
A hundred souls on account of their sins.
I was in Caer Fefenydd,
Thither were hastening grass and tree.
Wayfarers perceive them,
Warriors are astonished
At a renewal of the conflicts
Such as Gwydion made.
There is calling on Heaven,
And on Christ that he would effect
Their deliverance,
The all-powerful Lord.
If the Lord had answered,
Through charms and magic skill,

[1] In *Gomer*, part ii. p. 74, this is translated :—

>   Before the ruler of Britain
>   There hastily passed midland horses,
>   Fleets full of wealth.

But the lines are evidently wrongly placed, and "feirch" has been written for "feirdd." The above restoration renders the passage intelligible.

Assume the forms of the principal trees,
With you in array
Restrain the people
Inexperienced in battle.
When the trees were enchanted
There was hope for the trees,
That they should frustrate the intention
Of the surrounding fires.

The eight following lines, commencing

The chiefs are falling,

and ending with

Blood of men up to the hips,

though the intermediate lines appear unintelligible, belong, as it seems to me, to some of the *Gododin* Gorchans.   The poem then continues :—

Better are three in unison,
And enjoying themselves in a circle,
And one of them relating
The story of the deluge,
And of the cross of Christ,
And of the day of judgment near at hand.
The alder-trees in the first line,[1]
They made the commencement.
Willow and quicken tree,
They were slow in their array.
The plum is a tree
Not beloved of men ;
The medlar of a like nature,
Overcoming severe toil.
The bean bearing in its shade
An army of phantoms.
The raspberry makes
Not the best of food.
In shelter live,
The privet and the woodbine,
And the ivy in its season.
Great is the gorse in battle.
The cherry-tree had been reproached.

[1] The subject of the enchanted trees here commences again.

The birch, though very magnanimous,
Was late in arraying himself;
It was not through cowardice,
But on account of his great size.
The appearance of the   .   .
Is that of a foreigner and a savage.
The pine-tree in the court,
Strong in battle,
By me greatly exalted
In the presence of kings,
The elm-trees are his subjects.
He turns not aside the measure of a foot,
But strikes right in the middle,
And at the farthest end.
The hazel is the judge,
His berries are thy dowry.
The privet is blessed.
Strong chiefs in war
Are the   .   .   and the mulberry.
Prosperous the beech-tree.
The holly dark green,
He was very courageous:
Defended with spikes on every side,
Wounding the hands.
The long-enduring poplars [1]
Very much broken in fight.
The plundered fern;
The brooms with their offspring:
The furze was not well behaved
Until he was tamed.
The heath was giving consolation,
Comforting the people.
The black cherry-tree was pursuing.
The oak-tree swiftly moving,
Before him tremble heaven and earth,
Stout doorkeeper against the foe
Is his name in all lands.
The corn-cockle [2] bound together,
Was given to be burnt. [3]

[1] The light wood of the poplar was used in making shields.

[2] Clafuswydd —the sick or diseased wood. Dr. Owen translates it "the cyanus, or blue corn-cockle."

[3] Or cut down.

Others were rejected
On account of the holes made
By great violence
In the field of battle.
Very wrathful the   .   .   .
Cruel the gloomy ash.
Bashful the chestnut-tree,
Retreating from happiness.
There shall be a black darkness,[1]
There shall be a shaking of the mountain,
There shall be a purifying furnace,
There shall first be a great wave,
And when the shout shall be heard—
Putting forth new leaves are the tops of the beech,
Changing form and being renewed from a withered state;
Entangled are the tops of the oak.
From the Gorchan of Maelderw.
Smiling at the side of the rock
(Was) the pear-tree not of an ardent nature.[2]
Neither of mother or father,
When I was made,
Was my blood or body;
Of nine kinds of faculties,
Of fruit of fruits,
Of fruit God made me,
Of the blossoms of the mountain primrose,

---

[1] It appears to me that the lines beginning "There shall be," &c. belong to that part of this piece which mentions the discourse concerning the Deluge and the Day of Judgment; that the line "O gwarchan Maelderw" was originally a marginal note to the lines beginning "Cwyddynt a maereu;" and that the three lines

> An deilas blaen bedw
> An datrith an datedw
> An maglas blaen derw,

belong to the following fragment, which is an imitation of the creation of the woman from flowers by the enchanter Gwydion.

When we see that the two following lines have clearly been displaced from the list of the trees, this suggestion, which clears away many of the difficulties hitherto met with in the explanation of this piece, will appear to be well founded.

[2] Dr. Owen's copy gives "per," a pear-tree, instead of "ner," a lord, as in the *Myvyrian Archæology*, which renders the line intelligible.

Of the buds of trees and shrubs,
Of earth of earthly kind.
When I was made
Of the blossoms of the nettle,
Of the water of the ninth wave,
I was spell-bound by Math
Before I became immortal.[1]
I was spell-bound by Gwydion,
Great enchanter of the Britons,
Of Eurys, of Eurwn,
Of Euron, of Medron,
In myriads of secrets,
I am as learned as Math.
I know about the Emperor
When he was half burnt.
I know the star-knowledge
Of stars before the earth (was made),
Whence I was born,
How many worlds there are.
It is the custom of accomplished bards
To recite the praise of their country.
I have played in Lloughor,[2]
I have slept in purple.
Was I not in the enclosure
With Dylan Ail Mor,
In the centre of the enclosure,
Between the two knees of the prince
Upon two blunt spears ? [3]
When from heaven came
The torrents into the deep,
Rushing with violent impulse.
(I know) four score songs,
For administering to their pleasure.
There is neither old nor young,
Except me as to their poems,
Any other singer who knows the whole of the nine hundred
Which are known to me,
Concerning the blood-spotted sword.[4]

[1] Owen, *Dictionary.*
[2] The castle of Urien Rheged at Aber Llychwr.
[3] The story of Dylan Ail Mor, or Ail Ton, is lost.   A very short notice of him is given in the tale of Math ab Mathonwy.
[4] Perhaps the blood-dropping lance in the tale of Peredur mab Evrauc.

Honour is my guide.
Profitable learning is from the Lord.
(I know) of the slaying of the boar,
Its appearing, its disappearing,
Its knowledge of languages.[1]
(I know) the light whose name is Splendour,
And the number of the ruling lights
That scatter rays of fire
High above the deep.
I have been a spotted snake upon a hill;
I have been a viper in a lake;
I have been an evil star formerly.
I have been a weight (in a mill. (?)
My cassock is red all over.[2]
I prophesy no evil.
Four score puffs of smoke
To every one who will carry them away;
And a million of angels,
On the point of my knife.[3]
Handsome is the yellow steed,[4]
But a hundred times better
Is my cream-coloured horse,
Swift as the sea-mew,
Which cannot pass me
Between the sea and the shore.
Am I not pre-eminent in the field of blood?
I have a hundred shares of the spoil.
My wreath is of red jewels,

---

[1] This refers to the Twrch Trwyth in the tale of Kilhwch and Olwen.

[2] Mr. Stephens quotes two lines from Cynddelw to show that a red robe was the most honourable dress among the Welsh (p. 32). This explains the assertion of the minstrel in this line.

[3] This was one of the questions entertained by the middle-age controversialists—how many legions of angels could stand on the point of a knife?

[4] Dr. Owen translates this,

Six steeds of yellow hue;

but "march" is in the singular, and the first word is falsely written for *Gwach*, "brave, fine."

These lines are in the same style as the "Song of the Horses," and perhaps belonged to them. The horse-race of Elphin and Maelgwn is probably the subject.

Of gold is the border of my shield.
There has not been born one so good as me,
Or ever known,
Except Goronwy,
From the dales of Edrywy.
Long and white are my fingers,
It is long since I was a herdsman.
I travelled over the earth
Before I became a learned person.
I have travelled, I have made a circuit;
I have slept in a hundred islands;
I have dwelt in a hundred cities.
Learned Druids,
Prophesy ye of Arthur?
Or is it me they celebrate,
And the Crucifixion of Christ,
And the Day of Judgment near at hand,
And one relating
The history of the Deluge?
With a golden jewel set in gold
I am enriched;
And I am indulging in pleasure
Out of the oppressive toil of the goldsmith.

Dr. Owen Pughe translates the last three lines :—

"I am splendid, I am wanton from the oppression of the chemist."

The Rev. E. Davies gives :—

"With my precious golden device upon my piece of gold, lo! I am that splendid one who sportively comes from the invading host of the Fferyll."

It is quite evident that the mystery and Druidism of this passage is in the translation, and not in the original. Fferyll is a worker in metals, a metallurgist, or artist in general, and, as the subject here is a golden jewel, may very fairly be translated " goldsmith."

We cannot see in that portion of this poem which relates to the personification of the trees, any reference to the employment of sprigs or branches of trees, in the formation of a symbolical alphabet. We cannot here go at length into the question of the origin of the written characters employed by the Welsh Bards, but may assert that there is no evidence that they ever possessed any other alphabet than that of the Roman form called the "set Saxon," or that they had, like the Irish, an alphabet in which the names of the letters were derived from those of trees. We have already mentioned the Alphabet of Nemnivus, the history of which speaks for itself, and does not pretend to be older than the ninth century at the earliest. We need say no more about the Coelbren y Beirdd of Edward and Taliesin Williams, than that if Triads can be kept in a private repository, to be produced for the first time in the nineteenth century, to prove the existence and employment of a Bardic alphabet any number of centuries earlier, there can be no difficulty in proving anything which may be deemed desirable.

This later "Battle of the Trees" appears to be a very unimaginative work of fiction, which probably, in its original state, terminated with some moral application of the allegory which it was intended to relate.

That the story of the real Cad Goddeu was known to the minstrels, is shown by the allusion in the "Cerdd am Veib Llyr."

> I was in the Cad Goddeu with Llew and Gwydion,
> He who changed the form of wood, earth, and plants.
> I was with Bran in Ireland;
> I saw when Mordwydtyllon was slain, &c.

Archdeacon Williams has entertained the idea that the word *Derwydd*, "a Druid," is compounded of *derw*, "an oak," and *gwydd*, "knowledge." We do not, however, know the form of the word earlier than the twelfth century. But the Archdeacon connects the word through *dar*, "an oak," with *taran*, "a thunderbolt," and supposes *daron* and *daronwy* to be synonymous with *taranon* and *taranwr*, "the thunderer." He says, that in the "Song of Daronwy" we have ample proof that the thunderer is identified with the oak. This identification is derived from two lines in this song :—

> Py pren a vo mwy
> Nog ef Daronwy,

the literal translation of which is—

> What tree has been greater
> Than he, Daronwy?

But, on reading the whole song, we can see no reason for the introduction of the word *pren*, " a tree," into these lines. Daronwy was, according to the Triads, one of the three plagues of Anglesey. According to one legend, he was the son of Urnach the Irishman, and grandfather of Don, King of Lochlin and Dublin. As the song goes on to speak of the magic wand of Mathonwy, and of Goronwy, there can be no doubt that the Daronwy here mentioned is a man and not a tree—Daronwy of the family of the great necromancers of North Wales, Don and Gwydion. The word *pren*, " a tree," is therefore most probably an error of transcription for *pen*, " a chief," and as such we restore it in the translation.

KERDD DARONWY.

Duw differ Nefwy
Rhag llanw lled ofrwy
Cyntaf attarwy
Atreis tros fordwy
Py pren a fo mwy
Nog ef Daronwy
Nid wy am noddwy
Am gylch balch nefwy
Yssid rin y sydd fwy
Gwawr gwyr Goronwy
Odid ai gwypwy
Hutlath Fathonwy
Ynghoed pan dyfwy
Ffrwytheu mwy cymrwy
Ar lan Gwillionwy
Kynon ai kaffwy
Pryd pan wledychwy
Dyddenant et waeth
Tros drei a thros draeth

Pedair prif Bennaeth
Ar pummed nid gwaeth
Gwyr gwrdd chelaeth
Ar Brydain arfaeth
Gwragedd a fu ffraeth
Eillon a fi caeth
Ryferthwy hiraeth
Medd a marchogaeth
Dyddeu dwy rain
Gweddw a gwriog fain
Heyrn eu hadain
Ar wyr yn goriein
Dyddeu cynrain
O am dir Rhufain
Eu cerdd a gyngein
Eu gwawd a ysgain
Anan derw a drain
Ar Gerdd yn gyngain
Ki i dynnu

March i rynniaw
Eidion a wân
Hwch i dyrvu
Pymhed llwyn gwyn a wnaeth Iesu
O wisg Adaf i ymtrau
Gwydded coed cain eu syllu
Hyd yd fuant a hyd yd fu
Pan wnel Cymry camfalhau
Ceir arall fro pwy caro fu

Llemais i lâm o lam eglwg
Hewssit da nir gaho drwg
Mygedorth Run ys ef a ddiwg
Rhwng caer Rian a chaer Rywg
Rhwng Dineiddyn a Dineiddwg
Eglur dremynt a wyl golwg
Rhag rhynnawd tan dychyffrwymwg
Ar rheu Duw ann ry amwg.

THE SONG OF DARONWY.

O God, protect the sanctuary
From the widely spreading flood .
First, in driving back
The oppression across the sea.
What chief has been greater
Than he, Daronwy?
He is not my protection
Around the lofty sanctuary.
Is there a mystery which is greater
Than the darting of the spear of Goronwy?[1]
Wonderful its magic lore.
The magic wand of Mathonwy,
When it came into the wood,
Caused an abundance of fruit (to appear)
On the banks of Gwillionwy.
Kynon obtained it
At the time when he ruled.[2]
There are coming again,
Over tide, over strand,
Four chief rulers,
The fifth, not inferior,
A hero strong and mighty,
Nourished in Britain.
Women shall be eloquent (about him).

[1] That is, supposing "gwawr gwyr" to be an error for "gwaewawr." The present reading, "the light of the men of Goronwy," affords no sensible meaning; but that proposed is quite clear, and is found in the tale of "Math ab Mathonwy," where the assassination of Llew Llaw Gyffes is detailed.

[2] The subject here breaks off to enter upon a prophecy of the expected prince of British descent, probably Owen Gwynedd or Llewellyn ap Iorwerth.

To others in captivity (shall come)
The long-desired abundance
Of mead and horsemanship.
There shall come two queens,
A widow and a fair bride,
With iron wings,
To rule over men.
There shall come a race
From the land of Rome,
Their songs and chants,
Their hymns and sprinklings,
Under oak and thorn,
With their songs in tune.
A dog to pull,
A horse to run,
A steer to gore,
A hog to burrow.
The fifth fair form he made was Jesus,[1]
Of the clothing of Adam originally,
The foliage of trees, fair their appearance;
An apt covering they were and have been.
When the Cymry shall be unjustly driven out,
Another land shall be obtained where they shall be loved.
I have leaped, leap by leap, over the crag.
A boot is good lest hurt be taken.
The funeral pile of Rhun is, by his desire,
Between Caer Rian and Caer Rywg,
Between Din Eiddyn and Din Eiddwg.
They see clearly who see its appearance.
From a very little fire there is a great production of smoke.
In the eternal God is my great defence.

[1] This extraordinary collocation of lines must be the result of the same
kind of errors in transcription which have so frequently occurred in these
pieces. It is a striking instance of the mutilated condition in which they
have come down to us.

CHAPTER V.

OF NEO-DRUIDISM AND THE DRUIDICAL PHILOSOPHY.

THE difficulty of maintaining the proposition, that the Welsh Bards of the sixth century had preserved, and were in the practice of proclaiming and celebrating in the midst of a Christian community, the doctrines and traditions of an ancient and apparently extinct superstition, induced the learned author of *Britannia after the Romans*, to present a new theory to account for such a remarkable phenomenon.

"The separation of the British province from the Empire,"[1] says Mr. Herbert, "was not merely the case of an effete civilization giving way to irrumpent bardism, such as its other provinces exhibit. But, it was attended by an abandonment of established Christianity, and the rise of a strange and awful apostatic heresy; of which the historical vestiges are rare, but the internal evidences numerous and strong. Symptoms of that change have tinged British history and literature from the separation downwards, to an indefinitely modern point of time. But it had its paroxysms; its times of greater ascendancy and power than others; times of greater publicity and more unreserved avowal. The long and great paroxysm of this mania was the period extending from the revolt against the Gwynethian King-Insular, Gwrtheyrn of the Untoward Mouth, down to the conflict (called) of the Field-of-Iniquity, or Cam-Lan. Its point of extreme exacerbation was from the establishment of that power (known by the name of Arthur)

---

[1] *Britannia after the Romans*, part ii. p. 1.

which fell in the Cam-Lan, unto its downfall in that revolution. After which event, the aforesaid power or principle was removed out of sight by the two chief Bards of Britain, and kept alive, from thenceforward, indefinitely in the secrecy of a charmed and magical asylum."

The period adopted by Mr. Herbert as that in which this substitution of Paganism for Christianity prevailed in Britain, comprises, if taken from the date of the arrival of the Saxons in A.D. 449, to the commonly received date of the battle of Camlan, A.D. 542, about one hundred years.

According to Mr. Herbert's view, "the history of that period is a mere compound of romantic and mythologic imposture. Emrys Wledig, otherwise Ann ap Lleian, Uthyr Pendragon, and Arthur, by whom that poem was filled, were not real persons; but terms expressive of the long rule of fanaticism and of the three sub-periods in which it presented varying aspects; while a number of real men of inferior glory (Nathan Loed, Caradoc, Cawrdav, Maelgwn, &c.) were those that actually performed the brawlings and ruinations of that dismal time."

The nature and history of this strange and awful apostatic heresy is further developed by Mr. Herbert in a later work upon this subject.[1]

" Paulinus and Agrippa, by the conquest of Mona, the slaughter of the Druids in that island, and the ' cutting down of the groves that were sacred to their cruel superstitions,' struck a fatal blow to their craft. The three centuries and upwards that intervened between Vespasian and Honorius consigned to silence the Druidical system in the Roman provinces of Gaul and Britain—the religion of Rome first, and then that of Christ, being established in them, and the Latin language extensively prevalent. But in the very height of their Roman civilization, when the vicious empire was tottering, a pagan apostasy crept into Gaul and Britain, which ended in establishing in the latter country that Neo-Druidism to which the fables of Ambrosius and Arthur relate. A sort of magical association had grown up in the eastern parts of the Roman dominions, founded upon the doctrines and mysteries of the Persian magi. These were the Mithriacs, followers of the ineffable orgies of Mithras. Very early in the Christian era this pagan sect began in a

---

[1] *Essay on the Neo-Druidic Heresy in Britannia.* 1838.

measure to play the part of heretics, and, under their name of Mithriacs, imitated and parodied the rites of Christianity. They worshipped the sun by his Persian title of Mithras, but pretended that it was Christ they worshipped, and that Christ was the spirit of the sun.

"These doctrines were introduced into Britain, a rich and well-civilized island, in which Christianity had been some time established, and Roman manners still longer. We therefore meet with a frequent dissimulation of that heathenism to which the authors of the system were addicted—a disinclination to call the demons of polytheism by their ancient and known titles, or to give them the rank of gods, and a feeble attempt to conciliate their mysteries with the Christian. Manes, whose followers were a very similar class to the Neo-Druids, pursued the same course and honoured the name of Christ, but meant the sun by that name. No more can be understood by the Christ Gwledig of the bards. Their Trindawd is the triad of the Pythagorean cabalism, or theological arithmetic, and should be rendered Supreme Trias, and not Trinity, to express the mind of the primary bards. Some have carelessly, some affectedly, confounded together the Druidism of the times before the Romans with this modified revival of it in an heretical form. I have studied to keep them distinct by terming the professors of the latter Druidists and Neo-Druids.

"The College of Druids was not re-established by name. The votaries of Belenus in Gaul referred to the Druids as to an extinct race, from whom some of them affected on uncertain grounds to be descendants. In Britain, that order which was lowest and least important, and which alone was either tolerable to the Romans or compatible with Christianity, viz. the order of Bards, was the only one that flourished. Everything was referred to Bardism; and all the functions of priest, prophet, and magician, all the learning of the country and the right of teaching it and inventing it, was claimed by that order of minstrels."

The great deity of the Neo-Druidists was Beli:—

"The Beli who presided over Neo-Druidic Bardism is the god of bloodshed and slaughter, the deified sword of Scythia and the Arthur of Britain."

Instead of attempting to enter upon any farther investigation of this marvellous history, which would lead us beyond the scope of this essay, we will content ourselves with inquiring into the evidence upon which it rests.

This would seem to be a matter of some difficulty, since the Neo-Druids, "like their pagan predecessors, were bound to strict secrecy. Their doctrine was imparted to the aspirant amidst horrific and intimidating orgies, and under the sanction of a self-imprecated curse binding him to silence." "They had barbarous usages to conceal from the eye of civilization, and impious follies from that of Holy Church."

It is supposed, however, that the remaining works of the Welsh bards contain sufficient indications of these mysterious proceedings enveloped in a kind of technical jargon from which it is yet possible to eliminate the genuine hidden meaning.

The evidence which is to support and give credit to these statements, must necessarily be sought in what remains to us of the writings of the learned, of the period when these doctrines are supposed to have flourished; and, in fact, it is to the works of the Cynveirdd, that is, Taliesin, Aneurin, and Merlin, that Mr. Herbert has recourse for the proof of the theory which he enunciates. The romance of Taliesin, and the song of the "Battle of Gododin," are the main sources upon which Mr. Herbert draws for the support of his views, without any apparent suspicion of the real date of the former composition, and with a most mistaken notion of the real character and contents of the latter. We have seen that the ballads of which the former are composed contain nothing more mysterious than the ordinary wonders of faëry and magic. We shall now present a ballad which, according to Mr. Herbert, contains the secret doctrines of the worship of the Sun and Fire symbolized under the form of the Horse.

" The Neo-Platonists, or Syncretists," says Mr. Herbert, referring to this poem,[1] the " Can y Meirch, or Song of the Horses," "who in a manner revived the Pythagorical union, were of equal date with the Neo-Magi of Artaxares the Sassanide. Then the Mithriac heresy took its grand start, and struck roots which have never been extirpated, and probably never will be till all hidden things are brought forth to judg-

---

[1] *Neo-Druidism*, page 105.

ment. The Sun displacing Mercury from his old superiority over Apollo, became the Gwledig or national Deity of renascent Druidism. Mithras (Melyn) was the son of Oromazdes (Cynvelyn) or the ether, 'sublimè candens,' quintessentia, or super-elemental fire. The Polyhistor of Solinus, mentions perpetual fires in the temples of Minerva in Britain. Hector Boethius informs us that the fire of dignity was carried before the chief priest of Gael, when their college was established in Man; and though that statement bears a fabulous date, it is really illustrative of the times subsequent to the Roman Conquest, if not to the departure of the Romans. Fire-worship was of the essence of Neo-Druidism; and in it, as in Magianism and Neo-Magianism, a horse was the symbol of that sublime substance. Avaon, son of Taliesin, wrote a " Song of Horses," from the remains of which it is apparent that the horses are mystical or allegorical, and connected with Pyrolatry."

Mr. Davies[1] also considered the horses of this poem to be mythological; and naturally enough, according to the views he entertained on these subjects, concluded that the song contains a specimen of Druidical fire-worship, and pertains to the Helio-Arkite superstition.

When, however, we ascertain for ourselves what this poem really contains, we cannot but conclude that all the learning displayed by Mr. Herbert on this subject has been altogether thrown away; for the song, when fairly translated, turns out to be a ballad in which the celebrated horses of personages well known in the Arthurian romances are enumerated. The minstrel commences with the praise of his own horse or that of his patron, Llyr, and compares him with the most famous horses of the story, of whom he declares him to be the equal.

---

[1] *Mythology of the British Druids*, page 533. See the " Remarks upon the Ancient British Coins," appended to that work.

CAN Y MEIRCH.

Torrid Anuynudawl
Tuthiawl dan Yogawl
Ef iolen o dduch lawr
Tan tan hwstin gwawr
Uch awen uchel
Uch no pob nyfel
Mawr ei anyfel
Ni thrig yngofel no neithiawr Llyr
Llyr llwybyr y tebyr
Dy far ynghynebyr
Gwawr gwen gwrth uchyr
Wrth wawr wrth wrys
Wrth bob heuelis
Wrth heuelis nwython
Wrth Pedyr Afaon
Arddyreafi a farn gwrys
Cadarn trydar dwfn ei gas
Nid mi gwr llwfr llwyd
Crwybr wrth clwyd
Hud fy nau garant
Deu dich far dichwant
Om llaw ith llaw *dyt dwp dim*
Trithri nodded
Atcor ar hened
A march mayawg
Cymrwy teithiawg
A march gwythur
A march gwarddur
A march Arthur
Ehofn roddi eur
A march Taliesin
A march lleu lledfegin
A Phebyr llai llwynin
A Grei march Cunin

Cornan cynneifawg
Awydd awyddawg
Ar tri carn aflawg
Nid ant hynt hiliaw
Cethin march Ceidaw
Corn avarn arnaw
Ysgwyddfrith Ysgodig
Gorwydd llemenig
March Rydderch ryddig
Llwyd lliw elleig
A llamrai llawn elwig
A ffrocnfoll gwyrennig
March Sadyrnin
A March Custennin
Ac eraill in rhin
Rhag tir all gwin
Henwn Mad dyddug
Cychwedl o Hiraddug
Bwm swch bum bwch
Bym syw bum swch
Bum ban bum banhwch
Bum gawr yn rhythwch
Bum llif yn eirth
Bum ton yn engweirth
Bum ysgof ysgeiniad dilyw
Bum cath benfrith ar driphren
Bum pell bum pen
Gafr ar ysgaw bren
Bum garan gwala gweled golwg
Tragwres miled morial
Cadwent cenedl dda
Or y sydd is awyr gwedi caffolwir
Nid byw ormodd maint am gwyr

THE SONG OF THE HORSES.

Bursting his collar,
Trotting actively,
His hoofs high above the ground,
Scatter fire even in the daytime.
High he lifts his rein;
Above all comparison
He is the greatest of animals.
There is none more perfect
Bears the saddle than Llyr.
Swift is the course of Llyr,
Unequalled in swiftness
From break of day till evening,
In play or in strife,
In all alike,
Spirited in all;
In the four quarters of the world
I extol and adjudge him to be the most worthy,
Strong in battle, deep his hatred;
A sluggish one is not agreeable to me
With his haunch (leaning) on the gate.
I will prove by nine warranties,
Or twelve if desired,
My hand to thy hand,
Of the most celebrated
He is equal in birth.
The horse of Mayawg,
Expeditious in travelling;
The horse of Gwythur,
The horse of Gwarddur,
The horse of Arthur,
The bold knight-errant;[1]
The horse of Taliesin,
The horse of Lleu Lledfegin
And the quick-stepping dun horse of Pebyr,
And Crei, the horse of Cunin,
Cornan[2] inured (to toil).
The ardent Awyddawc,[3]

[1] Or, "gold-giver."
[2] He was the horse of the sons of Elifer Gosgorddfawr, and carried Gwrgi, Peredur, Dunawt, and Chynfelyn Drwscyl to the battle of Arderydd.
[3] The horse of Cyhoret eil Cynan.

And the three cloven-hoofed horses
They have left no issue.
Cethin, the horse of Ceidaw,
With the cloven hoof,[1]
Ysgwyddfrith[2] Ysgodig,
The stately steed of Llemenig,
The bay horse of Rydderch
Of the colour of a stag,
And Llamrai of perfect shape,[3]
And Ffroenfoll[4] the lively
Horse of Sadyrnin,
And the horse of Constantine,
And others in the poem,
From the land of Germany,
Which of old Mad brought,
The story of Hiraddug.

This is the true termination of the "Song of the Horses," which, as we have before stated, was not improbably sung in the course of the recital of the history of Taliesin, at that part where the race between the horses of Elphin and Maelgwn is mentioned. Of the fifteen additional lines, thirteen have no connection with the preceding, but are merely a variation of the common formula repeated in so many of the pieces in the *Myvyrian Archæology*. They are evidently founded on the reputed changes of form of Gwion before being born of Ceridwen, which appear to have been a favourite subject with the minstrels, and also, no doubt, with the audiences to whom they sung. In this piece the lines run thus:—

I have been a hog, I have been a cow;
I have been clean, I have been a hog;
I have been a woman, I have been a sow;
I have been a gaping giant;
I have been the flood of a cataract;
I have been a wave on the beach;

[1] Cethin was a *carn aflawg*, "cloven-footed" horse; perhaps, therefore, "corn avarn" should be read "carn aflawg." Suetonius relates that the hoofs of Cæsar's horse were divided like toes.

[2] Spotted shouldered.   [3] The mare of Arthur.   [4] Wide-nostrilled.

I remember the sprinkling of the Deluge.
I have been a spotted-headed cat on a forked tree;
I have been a ball, I have been a head
Of a goat on an elder-tree;
I have been a crane on a wall, a wonderful sight.
Very fierce was the beast of Morial,
Of a good race in the battle-field.[1]
Great is the firmament when it is reached.
The life of man is not over long.

Mr. Herbert commences his translation—

Inimitably bursts forth
The vehement fast-spreading fire.
Him we worship above the earth.
The fire! the fire! fierce his dawning.
High above the bard's inspiration,
Higher than every element,
The great one is unequal to him.

The first word of the second line, however, is *tuthiawl,*
"trotting"; and Mr. Herbert has felt compelled to add in a
note that the word he has translated "fast-spreading" is
literally "fast-trotting," an epithet which, allowing for any
extent of bardic fancy, is very inappropriate to fire. There
can, however, be no doubt as to the nature of the poem, which
is far more interesting in its real form than when translated
into an unintelligible mass of mysterious absurdity.

Another and still more portentous example of the length to
which Mr. Herbert has pushed his views on the Neo-Druidical
Heresy in Britain, and of the mode of translation and interpretation of the Welsh poetry by which he procures evidence
to support his opinions, is to be seen in his observations on
the piece entitled "Gofeisws Byd," *i. e.* "A Sketch or Memo-
randum of the World," but which he calls "The Devised or

---

[1] These two lines seem to belong to the "Song of the Horses." The
horse of Morial is mentioned in the "Song to Gwallawg," *ante.* Morial
is one of the heroes of the *Gododin,* according to the Rev. J. Williams's
translation, and is mentioned by Llywarch Hen and in the Englynion y
Beddau.

Contrived World." This poem is, without doubt, a genuine production of some storiawr or minstrel of the thirteenth or fourteenth century, on a subject which was always one of much interest in the middle ages, the wars and adventures of Alexander the Great. These formed the subject of a romance similar in kind to those of Arthur and Charlemagne, with this difference, that in the romance of Alexander that hero himself appears in the character of a magician, and performs some of the feats attributed by the *trouvères* of Britanny to the enchanter Merlin.

Two other short pieces, one relating to the Macedonian conqueror, the other, having his name prefixed as its title, are contained in the Myvyrian collection.

The piece in question commences abruptly without the usual religious exordium, adopted in similar productions, and is therefore probably only a fragment of the original poem.

Y GOFEISWS BYD.

Bu den teg ar wlad gwledychyssid
Bu haelaf berthaf or Rhianedd
Bu terwyn gwenyn gwae ei gywlad
Ef torres ar Ddar teirgwaith ynghad
Ac ef ni fydd corgwydd i wlad dar plufawr
Pebyr pell athrecwys coed gyrth y godiwawd
Alexander yn hual eurin gwac a garcharer
Ni phell garcharwyd angeu dybu ac lle
Ei cafas ergyr o lu neb cynnog ef ni
Ddarchawd myued bed berthrwydd or addwyndawd
Hael Alexander ai cymmerth yna
Gwlad Syr a Siriol a gwlad Syria
A gwlad Dinifdra a gwlad Dinitra
Gwlad Pers a Mers a gwlad y Cana
Ag Ynyssed Pleth a Pletheppa
A chiwdawd Babilon ag Agascia mawr
A gwlad Galldarus bychan y da
Hyd ydd ymddug y tir tywarch yna
Ac yd wnahon eu bryd wrth eu helya
Y weddont gwystlon i Europa
Ac anrheithio gwladoedd gwissioedd terra

Gwythyr gwcnynt gwragedd gorddynt yma
Bron losgedigion gwyledd gwastra
O gadeu afor pan adroddet
Digonynt brein gwneint pen brithred
Y milwyr mageidawr pan atrodded
Neu wlad ith weisson ti pan ddiffyded
Ny bydd ith esgor esgor lludded
Rhag gofal yr hual ai Agaled
Milcant rhiallu a fu farw rhag syched
Eu geu gogwilleu ar eu miled
As gwenwynnwys ei was cyn noi drefred
Cyn no hyn bri gwell digoned
Inn harglwydd gwladlwyd gwlad gogoned
Un wlad Ior oror goreu ystlyned
Diwyccwyf digonwyf poed genyt dy gyffred
Ar sawl am clyw poed meu eu huned
Digonwynt hwy fodd Duw cyn gwisg tudwed.

The following is the translation which Mr. Herbert gives of this simple piece, and nothing can more forcibly exhibit the extraordinary fallacies on which his theory of the history of Britain in the fifth and sixth centuries is founded. He gives it the title of

THE DEVISED OR CONTRIVED WORLD.

There were twelve by whom the land was ruled.
There was the most generous and fairest of ladies :
A woe of the ardency of bees was her border;
It burst out upon the oak-trees thrice in battle;
And it shall be our wood-circle of feathered oak-trees from the land.
Widely the Mighty One vanquished the wood of overtaking thrust.[1]
In golden fetters of woe is Alexander imprisoned;

[1] Mr. Herbert's comments upon his translation are as follows :—" This country (says the poet) was subject to the College of Saint Greal, twelve in number. Ceridwen, the constant theme of the bards, was its patron goddess. Her fanatical votaries, hived within the periphery of her awful circle, came forth like stinging bees whenever their hive was assailed; thrice did they thus burst forth victorious upon the Maes Beli; and the stone pillars that form her border are the sacred oaks in the Neo-Druidic grove, as the green trees were in the Druidic."

Nor was he imprisoned afar: death was near the place.
He sustained an onslaught from the host, none of us being answerable.
The oak enclosed goes to his grave, fair and free by his blessedness.[1]
Generous was Alexander with his fair possessions yonder.[2]
The land of stars and the cheerful, and the land of Syria,
And the land of Dinivdra, and the land of liberation;
The land of Persia and Mersia, and the land of Cana;
And the isles of plaiting, and of the plaiting of the Ape;
And the nation of Babylon, and Agascia the Great;
And the land of the might of Darius, of little avail
Till he brought himself into the sod of the earth there.
And they did their pleasure in their hunting.
They subjected hostages to Europa,
And the plunder of the countries, the raiment of the earth.
Grimly smiled the women that urged them on,[3]
With seared bosoms, casting away modesty.
With battles on the sea in the hour of retribution,
They satiated ravens; they brought confusion on the head
Of the soldiers of the Chief of Multitudes in the hour of retribution.
Truly, oh land! when thou art stript of thy young men,
There can be to thee no riddance, no riddance of oppression,
With the anxiety of the fetters and their hardship,
An army of 100,000 died of thirst.

[1] "This passage shows us the Crist Celi, confined, and about to undergo his mysterious death. The oak-enclosed, the dweller of the sanctuary is about to depart. But they who would remove him do not as yet appear as poisoners. They are an open assailing host. Neither are they foreign enemies."

[2] "The Bard proceeds to recount the glories of his empire, mixing the eastern provinces of Alexander, and the Holy Land of the Lord's miracles, with other strange titles belonging to this country in the days of her madness. Din-ivdra, whatever it may mean, is such. But the islands of plaiting, braiding, or interweaving, are none other than our great Ambrosian sanctuaries of the megalithic architecture, and are so called either from something originally observable in their actual structure, or from their being wood-circles representing the entangled shade of the 'feathered oak-trees of the land.' The island of the plaiting or braided texture of Eppa (the Ape) is that one most famous to which, above all others, Emmrys bequeathed his own name: it is his *cor*, his *gwaith*, his *dewys vynydd* or mount of election, and the *go-vur byd* in which the sacred Henvonva and the sacred Eppa were supposed to be."

[3] "Here we find the fall of Ambrosius mainly ascribed to the fanatical women of the sect."

Vagabondish were their arts in pursuing their prey.
The plain poisoned the youth ere he ran to his homestead,[1]
Ere he could become more sufficiently old.
For our land-prospering Lord a land of glory,
Our land of Eternity of excellent communion,
I will adorn, I will prepare.   Be with thee the plenitude,
And of whoso hear me be granted to me the repose.
They will make God their happiness ere they put on the earth.[2]

According to Mr. Herbert, this poem exhibits the Crist Celi, or man-god of the mysteries, in his form of Alexander Mawr (the Great), in which, as well as in Ercwlf Mawr (Hercules the Great), his miraculous conception by the Dragon Jove is signified.   It likewise introduces the Judaism of those mysteries by identifying the twelve Knights of the Round Table with the twelve tribes of Israel, and these countries with the Holy Land, to which the occupation of Syria and Palestine by Alexander lent a handle.

It must be admitted that, if Mr. Herbert's translation of the "Gofeisws Byd" is somewhat mysterious, his comments and explanations are far more so.   In fact they are, when taken in connection with the plain meaning of the poem, perfectly incomprehensible.   All this mystery of the Crist Celi, the *Cor* of Ambrosius, the Ape of the sanctuary, and the awful crimes

---

[1] " We find him poisoned on the great plain in which his *cor*, the ' ynys pleth Eppa,' stood.   And, moreover, we obtain the almost conclusive admission that he was cut off not only *upon* but *by* the plain which called him its own ; that is to say, by the spiritual iniquities there enthroned and enshrined. ' As gwenwynwys ei was.'   The Ape of this sanctuary, to whom great sanctity, together with foul crime, deception, and treachery, is ascribed, must signify the mercurial principle, that strange and unexplained disgrace of Paganism.   Gwion Gwd, or Gwydion ap Don, into whose knaveries and villanies all that is most sacred and awful in Neo-Druidism seems to resolve itself, must be the Eppa."

[2] "These lines, in which the bard glorifies the object of his poem, and promises to devote himself to preparing the precious communion of the sacred place, do not require any explanation at present.   They are general expressions, including in their purport all the terrible and hidden things of Bardism. He concludes with a blessing on his congregation."

and iniquities imputed to them, are the merest fancies of a disordered imagination. This famous Ape, who has been specially created by Mr. Davies, and antiquaries of his school, performs a great part in Mr. Herbert's Neo-Druidism. He is supposed to be commemorated in a passage in the " Gwawd Lludd of Mawr, or Praise of Lludd the Great," a poem attributed to Taliesin, which we will presently examine. In the first place, the following is the literal translation of the " Gofeisws Byd," in which none of the mysteries or hidden doctrines of the Bards or Neo-Druidists have any possible place, and exist only in Mr. Herbert's and Mr. Davies's translations.

SKETCH OF THE WORLD.

He was strong and handsome by whom the country was ruled;
He was the most bountiful and most beautiful of princes;
Strong was the poison, woe to his countrymen;
He vanquished Darius three times in battle.
But he will not remain supreme in the land of the plume-bearing Darius;
Fever, a farther reaching vanquisher than the thrust of the spear, overtook
     him.
Alexander in golden fetters—alas! for the prisoner,
Not remote his imprisonment; death came to the place,
And took away the impulse of the army; no one can be a debtor to him.
Covered up he goes to his grave enriched with glittering ornaments.
Generous Alexander obtained there,
The land of Syr and Siriol, and the land of Syria;
And the land of Dinifdra, and the land of Dinitra;
The land of Persia and Mersia, and the land of Cana;
And the islands of Pleth and Phletheppa;
And the city of Babylon, and Agascia the Great;
And the land of Galldarus, of little worth,
Until much toil is employed on the sod of the earth there.
And they performed their purpose according to their intention,
And subjected hostages in Europe,
And took the spoils of all the known countries of the earth.
Wrathful, lustful, lecherous, they pour over here;
Breasts are burning at beholding their devastation.
Of the battles of Porus when it shall be told,
Satiated were ravens, their heads were spotted (with blood).

Of the soldiers of the Magician [1] when it shall be told,
Will not thy country be inquiring of thee how it was devastated?
Will there not be to thee a deliverance from the extreme fatigue?
Through anxiety and toil and hardships
A hundred thousand millions perished with thirst.
Vainly were they searching after their soldiers.
Poisoned was the hero before he could reach his habitation.
Rather than this, it were better he had been contented.
To us there is a beneficent Lord of a glorious land,
The land of Eternity, the region of a great community,
I am content if thou be included in it;
And whoever shall hear me may his sleep be the better.
They do enough who please God before they are clothed with earth.

This piece speaks for itself, and needs no farther comment. The other fragment relating to Alexander the Great mentions his adventure in the ship of glass, a marvel which belongs to the romance of Merlin the Magician, but was ascribed to Alexander by a Spanish romance of the middle of the thirteenth century, and is, according to Southey, found in a German legend of St. Anna, written at the close of the year 1100. The title given to this fragment by some transcriber is, "The Not-Wonders of Alexander," displaying that unbelieving and practical turn of mind which has militated against the preservation of similar documents.

ANRHYFEDDODAU ALEXANDER.

Rhyfeddaf na chiawr
Addef nef i lawr
O ddyfod rhwyf gawr
Alexander mawr
Alexander Magidawr
Hewys hayarnddawn
Cleddyfal enwogawn
Aeth dan eigiawn
Dan eigiawn eithyd
I geisiaw celfyddyd
Bid o iewin ei fryd

Eithyd odduch gwynt
Rwng deu grifft ar hynt
I weled dremynt
Dremynt ni weles
Present ni chymhes
Gweles rhyfeddawd
Gorllin gan bysgawd
A eiddunwys yn ei fryd
A gafas or byd
A hefyd o'r ddiwedd
Gan Dduw drugaredd.

[1] Mageidawr. Alexander is called by this name in the next piece given. Mr. Stephens translates it "the nourisher."

THE NOT-WONDERS OF ALEXANDER.

I wonder there is no acknowledgment.
From heaven to earth
Of the coming of the giant Emperor,
Alexander the Great.
Alexander the Magician,
Passionate, iron-gifted,
Renowned for sword-strokes.
He went beneath the sea,
Beneath the sea he went,
In search of mysteries.
In seeking for mysteries,
Very clamorous his desire.
He went above the wind,

Between two griffins on his journey,
To see sights.
If he did not see sights,
The present state was not sufficient
    for him.
He saw great wonders,
Creatures of superior lineage among
    the fish.
That which his mind desired,
He obtained in this world;
And also in the end,
Mercy from God.

The other piece is called,

LURYG ALEXANDER.

Ar glawr elfydd
Ei gystedlydd
Ni ryaned
Teir person Dew
Un mab addwyn
Terwyn trinded
Mab ir Dwydid
Mab ir dyndid
Un mab rhyfedd
Mab Duw dinas
Mab gwen Mairgwas
Mab gwas gwledig
Mawr ei ordden

Mawr Dduw Reen
Ran gogened
O Hil Adda
Ac Abraha yn ryaned
O hil Dofydd
Dogn ddyfnwedydd
Llu ryaned
Dyddug o eir
Deill a byddeir
O bob aeled
Rac pob anuaus
Pob yn ddilis
Dinas diffred.

THE BREASTPLATE OF ALEXANDER.

On the surface of the earth
He was afflicted.
Does not God comprehend
Three persons,
One the blessed son?

Glorious the Trinity.
Son of God he is.
Son of man he is.
One son wonderful,
Son of the bountiful God.[1]

---

[1] Duw dinas. *Qu.* " daionus."

Son of the Virgin Mary.
Son, servant, Lord.
Great his destiny,
In part begotten
Of the race of Adam
And Abraham,
Of the line of David,
The skilful speaker,

Variously he sung.
He took away by his word
From the blind and deaf
All their sadness.
For all the weak,
For all, it is certain,
A city of refuge.

The title of "Breastplate of Alexander" affixed to this song is evidently an accidental mistake, the real piece to which that title belongs having been lost. This song, it is unnecessary to say, relates to Christ, and ought to be placed under the head of the "Religious Poetry."

We now return to the "Ape of the Sanctuary," as exhibited in the song entitled "Gwawd Lludd y Mawr, or the Praise of Lludd the Great." It is probably, however, called "the Great" to distinguish it from another piece with a similar title called "the Less," as it has no reference to Lludd, or any praise of that personage. This poem, which has given rise to a great deal of misconception, is a collection of fragments which it is very difficult to disentangle. A portion has been represented as pure Hebrew, and the translations given of it most unintelligible. It is, however, a fragment commencing with lines which are intended to satirize and ridicule the monks, the hereditary enemies and rivals of the strolling singers, with whose vocation they interfered, and whose emoluments they intercepted. It commences abruptly and without any exordium, only a portion of it having been preserved.

GWAWD LUDD Y MAWR.

Kathl gereu gognant
Wyth nifer nodant
Duw llun dybyddant
Peithiawg ydd ant
Duw mawrth yd rannant
Gwyth yn ysgarant
Duw merchyr medant
Ryodres rychwant

Duw Ieu escorant
Ei ddiolydd anchwant
Duw gwener dydd gormant
Yngwaed gwyr gonesant
Duw Sadurn . . . .
Duw sul yn geugant
Dieu dybyddant
Pum llong a phum caut

Oranant oniant
O brithi brithoi
Nuoes nuedi
Brithi brithanai
Sychedi edi euroi
Eil coed cogni
Antaredd dymbi
Pawb i adonai
Ar weryd pwmpai
Darofyn darogan
Gwaed hir rhag gorman
Hir cyhoedd cynhyn
Cadwaladr a chynan
Byd buddydd bychan
Difa gwres huan
Dysgogan derfydd
A un anudyd
Wybr geiryonydd
Cerdd awn y genhyd
Wylhawd eil echwydd
Yn nhorroedd Llynydd
Ben beu llawn hyd
Brython ar gynghyr
I Vrython dymbi
Gwred gwneddri
Gwedy eur ag eurynni
Diffaith Moni a Lleini
Ac ergri anhedd ynddi
Dysgogan perffaith
Anhedd ym diffaith
Cymry pedeiriaith
Symudant ei haraith
Yn y vi y uuch y vuch freith
   A wnaho gwynieith
Meinddydd brefawd
Meinhoeth berwhawd
Ar dir berwhodawr
Yn llonyd yssadawr
Cathl gwae canhator
Cylch Prydain amgor
Deddeuant un gyngor
I wrthod gwarthmor
Boet gwir venryt
Dragwynawl byd

Dolwys dolhwy kyd
Dolaethwy eithyd
Cynran llawn yt
Gyvarch cynud
Heb eppa
Heb henfonfa heb ofur byd
Byd a fydd diffeith dyraid cogeu
   tynghettor
Hoywedd trwy groywedd
Gwyr bychain bron otwyllyd
Toruenawl tuth iolydd
Hwedydd ar fedydd
Ni wan cyllellawr cleddyfawr meiwyr
Nid oedd uddu y puchasswn
Maw angerddawl trefddyn
Ac i wyr caredd creuddyn
Cymry Eingl Gwyddyl Prydyn
Cymry cyfred ag asgen
Dygedawr gwyddfeirch ar llynn
Gogledd a wennwynwyd o hermyn
O echlur caslur caslun
O echen Addaf henyn
Dygedawr trydw i gychwyn branes o
   gosgordd
Gwyrein merydd miled seithin
Ar for angor ar cristin
Uch o for uch o mynydd
Uch for ynial erbyn
Coed maes tyno a bryn
Pob arawd
Heb erglywaw nebawd
O vynhawg o bob mehyn
Yd fi brithed
A lliaws gynnired
A gofud am wehyn
Dialeu trwy hoywgredeu breswylo
Goddi creawdr cyvoethawg Dduw
   Urddin
Pell amser cyn dydd brawd
Y daw diwarnawd
A dwyrein darlleawd
Terwyn tirion tir Iwerddon
I Brydain yna y daw dadwyrain
Brython o fonedd Rhufain

Ambi barnodydd o anhyngres dien
Dysgogyn sywedyddion
Yngwlad colledigion
Dysgogan Derwyddon
Tra mor tra Brython
Haf ni bydd hinon
Bythawd breu breyron
Ai deubydd o gwanfed

Tra merin tra ced
Mil ym brawd Brydain Urddin
Ac vam gyffwn kyffin
Na chwyaf yngolud gwern
Gwerin gwaelodwedd Uffern
Ergrynaf cyllestrig Caen
Gan wledig gwlad anorphen.

THE PANEGYRIC ON LLUDD THE GREAT.

They make harsh songs;
They note eight numbers.
On Monday they will be
Prying about.
On Tuesday they separate
Angry with their adversaries.
On Wednesday they drink,
Enjoying themselves ostentatiously.
On Thursday they are in the choir;
Their poverty is disagreeable.
Friday is a day of abundance,
The men are swimming in pleasures.

On Saturday . . . .
On Sunday certainly,
Five legions and five hundred of them,
They pray, they make exclamations,
" O brithi brithoi
Nuoes nuedi
Brithi brithanai
Sychedi edi euroi."
Like wood-cuckoos
In noise they will be,
Every one of the idiots
Banging on the ground.

These lines were thus translated by the Rev. E. Davies :—

" A song of dark import was composed by the distinguished Ogdoad, who assembled on the day of the Moon, and went in open procession. On the day of Mars they allotted wrath to their adversaries; on the day of Mercury they enjoyed their full pomp; on the day of Jove they were delivered from the detested usurpers; on the day of Venus, the day of the great influx, they swam in the blood of men; on the day of Saturn . . . . . .; on the day of the Sun there truly assemble five ships and five hundred of those who make supplication, ' O Brithi, Brithoi, &c.—O son of the compacted wood, the shock overtakes me! we all attend on Adonai, on the area of Pwmpai.' "

Where the area of Pwmpai may be we are not informed, but Mr. Davies transforms the lines, " O Brithi, brithoi," &c. into Hebrew characters, under the impression that they may be vestiges of sacred hymns in the Phœnician language. It is clear that they are meant in mockery of the chants used by

33

the monks at prayers.   Another writer[1] has also lately given these lines as Hebrew, with the following interpretation :—

> " Rise ! woe to ye, and woe to ye,
>   Briton, Briton, alas !
> Thou'rt wanderer of wanderings,
>   Britons ! Britons, alas !
> Wake misery and nakedness,
>   Know yourselves naked."

As this author, however, conceives the Welsh language to be Hebrew, and explains all names of places and rivers—Oxford, Bucks, Thames, Spithead, &c.—out of the latter language, we may be excused from entering further into an investigation of his theory.

The next part of this poem is a prophecy respecting Cadwalader and Cynan, and therefore not earlier than the twelfth century.

I make a prophecy;
Blood (shall be) in abundance,
Long the public contention
Of Cadwalader and Cynan.
The world shall profit little,
The heat of the sun vanishing.
There is a prophecy,
And one not obscure,
Of subtle words;
I sung it for thee.
The overflowing of another land
From the bursting of the waters
When full to the top.
Britons in council
With Britons shall be,
Men striving greatly
After gold and trinkets.
The devastation of Mon and Leini,

And trembling and loss of tranquillity there.
The Cymry of four languages
Shall change their speech,
Until shall come the cow, the spotted cow,
Who shall bring a blessing,
On a fine day lowing,
On a fine night boiling;
In the land of the boiler
The timid shall be in tranquillity.[1]
A song of woe is singing
Round the circle of Britain.
They are assembling in council
To ward off a great disgrace.
May the blessed One
Be their director !

[1] *Suggestions on the Ancient Britons*, part i. p. 60.   London, 1852.

[2] These lines, though unintelligible, are not more so than the prophecies of Merlin in Geoffrey of Monmouth, or those of Thomas the Rhymer.

The two next lines are obscure, and then follows the passage in which mention is made of the "Ape of the Sanctuary." The whole passage of four lines,

> Heb eppa
> Heb henfonfa, heb ofur byd.
> Bydd a fydd diffaith dyraid cogeu tynghettor
> Hoywedd trwy groywedd,

was translated by Davies,

"Without the ape, without the stall of the cow, without the mundane rampart, the world will become desolate, not requiring the cuckoos to convene the appointed dance over the green."

The first part of this translation is adopted by Mr. Herbert, and was originally that of Dr. Owen. But in his *Dictionary* (ed. 1832) the latter gives a different interpretation. Under the word *henfonfa*, he gives as the meaning, "the stall of the cow of transmigration;" and for the passage in question,

"Without a monkey, without a milch-cow stall, without a luxury in the world;"

whence it would appear that a monkey was among the luxuries indulged in by the ancient Druids. In this interpretation "luxury" is substituted for "rampart," and the whole sense of the passage altered.

But we have very good reason for believing that *henfon* is not "the cow of transmigration," but simply a cow, an old cow. There are two adages preserved in which the word *henfon* occurs, where the cow of transmigration cannot very well have a place :—

> Pieufo yr henfon
> Aed yn ei chynffon.
>
> Whoso owns the old cow,
> Let him go at her tail.

and

> Pawb yn llosgwrn ei henfon.
> Every man at the tail of his cow.

In which cases Dr. Owen translates "the cow of proceeding,

and the cow of procession." But when once we get rid of the "cow of transmigration," we can see a very reasonable interpretation of the line,

> Heb henfonfa heb ofur byd.

> Without the cow-stall there would be no dung-heap.[1]

This line, then, is an adage introduced, as we have before seen in other instances, similar adages introduced into these fragments; and the line, "Heb eppa" belongs to the preceding clause of the passage, in which two other adages or proverbs are contained. We therefore translate it :—

> The first share is the full one.
> Politeness is natural,
> Says the ape.[2]
> Without the cow-stall there would be no dung-heap ;
> The world would be barren,
> Vain the call of the cuckoo,
> Lively and clear sounding.
> The man of little heart is a deceiver,
> Very smiling, trotting along,
> Talking about baptism.
> The knifeman cannot stab the sword-bearing warrior.
> It was not with them that I should have desired (to be).
> Very violent is the townsman,
> And the man who lusts after bloodshed.
> Cymry, Angles, Irish, and Britons ;
> Cymry running together to ruin,
> Carrying their boats to the lake.
> The North harassed by the foreigners,
> Of pale hateful appearance and hateful form,
> Of the race of old Adam.
> Carrying them a three days' journey.[3]
> The raven soaring above the assembly
> Of the sluggish brutes of Seithin.[4]

[1] *Gofwr*, a heap or mound.

[2] *Cyfarch*, "mutual salutation;" and *cynedd*, a natural quality.

[3] This line is evidently misplaced. It should come after the line,

> Carrying their boats to the lake.

[4] Perhaps for Saisin, *i. e.*, Saxons.

On the sea the anchor of the Christian,
Over the sea, over the mountain,
Over the sea to take vengeance,
Wood, field, dale, and hill.
To every discourse,
Every one paying attention,
To reports on every side.
Corn shall be mixed (with rye),
And multitudes wandering about,
In inexhaustible misery.
Prepare through ready belief against the vengeance
Intended by the Creator, the powerful Supreme Lord,
A long time before the day of judgment.
The day will come,
It is shown in the reading.[1]
The most violent of lands is the land of Ireland.
To Britain thence shall come an exaltation,
Britons of the stock of Rome.
May I be judged by the merciful God.
Astronomers are predicting
Misfortunes in the land.
Druids are prophesying,
Beyond the sea, beyond Britain,
That the summer shall not be fair.
The nobles shall be broken;
It shall be through want of faith.[2]
And lest I should fall among the lost multitude,
The miserable inhabitants of hell,
I greatly dread the stone covering.
With the Lord, there is a country at the last.

It is unnecessary to make any comment on this collection of fragments, further than to observe on the strange fatality by which so many of these worthless pieces have been preserved, while the more valuable compositions of the flourishing period of Welsh literature, which must have existed in the twelfth and thirteenth centuries, have been almost entirely lost.

There are in the Myvyrian collection some pieces which are evidently framed upon the events recorded in the Old Testa-

[1] *i. e.*, the Scriptures.
[2] The next three lines are omitted as unintelligible.

ment—the " Plagues of Egypt," the " Rod of Moses," and the " Praise of the Men of Israel." Even in these a mystery has been found, and a store of hidden allusions to heretic or mythological doctrines.

The extraordinary application which Mr. Herbert has made of his theory to these poems, is best exhibited in the view he takes of the meaning of the poem entitled the " Plagues of Egypt," a piece attributed to Taliesin.

" The British apostasy," says Mr. Herbert, " was so deeply tinctured with Judaism that it required an Easter more conformable to the Passover of the Jews; and that was furnished by the scheme of Sulpicius. For, according to that scheme, Easter Sunday would fall upon the 14th day of the first month, or strict legal Passover, upon a general average of once in seven years ; whereas by the Catholic scheme, which they rejected, it could never fall upon the 14th day. To this difference the British owed the appellation of Quarto-decimans, and St. Adhelm's imputation of Judaism. Without possessing any evidence of the fact, I cannot but think that the recurrence of those Paschals in which the Levitical and the Dominical feasts were coincident, must have been an especial festival of the sect.

" But the Passover kept by the true Jews and, anciently, by the Asiatic churches, would have suited their purpose even less than it did the generality of Christians. For their Judaism was that of the Emperor Julian, and those unreal Jews (of the Satanic synagogues) with whom Julian was concerned. Their Jehovah was Oromazdes, and their Moses and Christ were forms of Mithras. Therefore it was a great point with them, that the hidden things of their Pascha should fall upon that day which, in the new Hermetic week, was dedicated to the Sun.

" The affairs of the new British Easter, whatever they were, doubtless were kept very decent by a Germanus, a Lupus, an Iltutus, and churchmen of that leaven. But when these matters passed out of the hands of false-hearted priests into those of the College of the Bards of Beli (as they did, in a great measure during the Ambrosian, Uthyrian, and Arthurian eras), discretion gave way to frenzy, indiscreet and self-betraying, in the midst of its avowed and boasted cryptography. Those days gave voice to the ' Song of the Pass-over,' as we might better entitle that of the ' *Plagues of Egypt.*' *It is probably among the most ancient British songs that have come down to us.* It announces the approach of the great annual feast of the Jews. And it leads us to suppose that cruelties of several sorts, imitating the ten plagues of Egypt, so far as they were susceptible of imitation, were then inflicted by these raving fanatics on their victims. One of them however, *the third*, was no imitation of the acts of Moses, but a new and interpolated plague, to find room for which, the third and fourth plagues of Moses were thrown into one, and placed fourth in the list. The remembrance of that mixing up of two plagues was never lost; and the fourth plague is called *the mixed plague* to this day, even in the authorized Welsh version of Exodus. That important circumstance fixes the *Post-Roman* British Church with the whole length of the Neo-Druidical heresy, and prevents her advocates from throwing off the blame upon idle minstrels and private secretaries. The lice and flies were *mixed together* (cymmysg) solely to make place for the Gwyddvedd. Therefore by adopting, so fully as she must have done, the idea of crasis or commixture in the fourth, she virtually recognized the intrusive third plague. That third plague is the awful secret of secrets."

In his preface to the second volume of *Britannia after the Romans,* Mr. Herbert states that he has made progress towards the illustration of the Neo-Druidic Heresy in its several branches, among which are "the great mysteries of the Gwyddvedd, and of the Saint Greal or Cauldron of Ceridwen." In the absence of such illustrations, we may reasonably be excused from withholding our belief in the existence of any such mystery as the Gwynvedd, and in the connection between the Saint Greal of the middle-age romance-writers and the Pair Ceridwen, or fountain of poetic inspiration (the Welsh Helicon), of the same era.

The piece on which Mr. Herbert relies as containing the evidence of these statements is the following :—

PLAEU YR AIPHT.

Efrei edwyl ar feib Israel	Tai a threfnau
Uchel enfryd	A thyleeu
Cyd rif dilyn	A chelleu bwyd
Ry dynesseyn	Trydedd gwyddbed
Ry gadwys dduw ddial	Gwychr gonoged gwaladwyd
Ar blwyf Pharaowys	Pedwar *icewr*
Deg pla poeni	Cwr am ystyr edynogion
Cyn eu boddi	Ail cygnoës
Ym môr aphwys	Ffrwyth coed a Maes
Cyssefinbla pyscawd ddifa	Cnwd cylion
Dignawd annwyd	Pumed bwystnon
Eilbla llyffeint lluossawg	Ar holl Vibnon
Llewyssynt Aronoed	Egypeion

Belsid miled

O drum aeled

Deritolion

Chwechad heb au

Chwyssig crugau

Creithiau *morion*

Seithfed tarian

Cynllysg a than

A glaw cynwyd

Gwynt gorddiberth

Ar ddeil a gwydd

Wythfed Locust

Llydan eu clust

Blodeu cyfys

Nawfed Aruthr

Diwedlawg uthr

Doniawg nofys

Du dywyllwg

Drem eneglwg Egiptuis

Deg veinoeth

Mwyaf gwyniaith

Ar blwyf cynrain

Christ Jesu Christioni grein

Hyd ynt clydwr

Chwechant milwr

Miled Efrei.

The mystery in this poem is supposed to exist in the lines which relate to the third and fourth plagues. Mr. Herbert's translation of the passage is—

"Thirdly the GWYDDVEDD

Bold in its precious elevation was prepared.

The fourth to the Devil.

The circumscription of his knowledge

Of winged insects,

And another such that gnawed

The fruit from trees and from fields,

The harvest of flies."

This is not the true reading of the passage. The poem reads as follows :—

THE PLAGUES OF EGYPT.

Joyous the festival of the children of Israel,

Exalted in courage,

With the number of their followers

Drawing near their deliverance.

God inflicted punishment

On the people of Pharaoh,

Ten plagues of punishment

Before their drowning

In the abyss of the sea.

[1] *Britannia after the Romans*, vol. ii. p. 66.

The first plague, the destruction of the fish
With unaccustomed coldness.
The second plague, an abundance of frogs;
Numerous were they in the kneading troughs,
Houses and utensils,
And cupboards,
And provision closets (larders).
The third (plague) gnats,
Both troublesome and grievous.
The fourth, the affliction,
In my opinion,
Of winged insects
And others gnawing
The fruit of wood and field,
A swarm of flies.
The fifth, the murrain
On all the children
Of the Egyptians:
Destruction it is to the animals,
From the heavy disease.
The sixth, in truth,
Blister pustules,
(Like) swellings made by emmets.
The seventh, thunder,
And fire, and flame,
And rain therewith,
And a blasting wind
On leaves and trees.
The eighth, locusts,
Broad their ears,
Devouring the blossoms.
The ninth, wonderful,
An unaccustomed marvel—
Overspreading the heavens is
Black darkness;
The countenance not merciful
Of the Egyptians.
The tenth, the night
Very painful
To the people of the family.
Christ Jesu, Christians are (prostrate with fear)
Until they are in safety,
The six hundred thousand men,
Of the Hebrew soldiers.

34

There can be no doubt that this, in common with the other religious compositions contained in the *Myvyrian Archæology*, is of the date of the thirteenth or fourteenth century; but even if it could be shown to have been written in the sixth century, a very slight examination of its contents would suffice to demonstrate, that so far from there being any mystery, Druidical or Mithraic, in this poem, it is simply what it purports to be— a metrical version of the Plagues of Egypt, as they are represented in the Hebrew Scriptures.

The third plague described in this poem is not a new and interpolated plague, by which, under the name of "gwydd-bed," some fearful mystery is concealed; nor is the fourth plague, or *cymmysg-bla*, the mixed plague, made up by the consolidation of the third and fourth plagues of the Mosaic history, for the purpose of admitting the insertion of the supposed mysterious *gwyddbed*.

In our English version of the Bible the third plague is interpreted the plague of lice. "And the Lord said unto Moses, Say unto Aaron, Stretch out thy rod, and smite the dust of the land, that it may become *lice* throughout all the land of Egypt."

"And they did so; for Aaron stretched out his hand with his rod, and smote the dust of the earth, and it became *lice* in man and in beast; all the dust of the land became *lice* throughout all the land of Egypt."[1]

The Hebrew word thus translated lice is *kinim*, which, in the Septuagint, is rendered σκνίφες, or σκνίπαι. On the true meaning of the word *kinim* commentators are not agreed, but the better opinion seems to be that it would be best translated by *gnats*. Philo, in his first book *De Vita Mosis*, and Origen, describe the σκνιφες as winged creatures. Augustine, or the author of the work entitled *De convenientia decem preceptorum et decem Plagarum*, describes them as "muscæ minutissimæ, inquietissimæ et inordinate volantes." This is also the opinion of Gesenius, who translates "gnats," though the Jews and

[1] Exodus viii. 17.

Josephus interpret the word *lice*. The Talmudists also use the word *kinah* in the singular for *a louse*.

In the Welsh translation of the Bible which was made from the original Hebrew in the reign of Elizabeth, the same reading as in our English version has been followed in this instance, *kinim* being translated *llau*, "lice." But the author of the poem under consideration has adopted the interpretation *gnats* for the Hebrew *kinim* and the Greek σκνίφες. His meaning is perfectly clear,—"The third plague was that of ' gnats,' *gwyddbed*," in which statement there is nothing heretical or mysterious.

But if with Mr. Herbert, in opposition to the plain meaning of the word, we interpret *gwyddbed* (not *gwyddvedd*, as he writes it) to mean " wood sepulchre," or " sepulchral wood," then indeed it is necessary to find a place for a plague altogether unknown to the writer of the Hebrew Pentateuch, and all interpreters of and commentators on the same.

The author of the poem makes the fourth plague to consist of two kinds of insects : one of winged insects, " edenogion "; the other he probably intends to represent, as without wings, creatures that gnawed the produce of trees and fields.

In the Welsh version of the Bible this fourth plague is called *cymmysgbla*, " the mixed plague."

" A dywedodd yr Arglwydd wrth Moses, Cyfod yn fore, a saf ger bron Pharaoh; wele efe a ddaw allan i'r dwfr; yna dywed wrtho, Fel hyn y dywedodd yr Arglwydd; Gollwng ymaith fy mhobl, fel y'm gwasanaethont;

" O herwydd os ti ni ollyngi fy mhobl, wele fi yn gollwng arnat ti, ac ar dy weision, ac ar dy bobl ac yth dai, gymmysgbla; a thai yr Aiphtiaid a lenwir o'r gymmysgbla; a'r ddaear hefyd yr hon y maent arni."

" A'r Arglwydd a wnaeth felly; a daeth cymmysgbla drom i dy Pharaoh, ac i dai ei weision ac i holl wlad yr Aipht; a llygrwyd y wlad gan y gymmysgbla."

In the authorized English version :—

" And the Lord said unto Moses, Rise up early in the morning, and stand before Pharaoh; lo, he cometh forth to the water; and say unto him, Thus saith the Lord; Let my people go that they may serve me.

" Else, if thou wilt not let my people go, behold, I will send swarms *of flies* upon thee, and upon thy servants, and upon thy people, and into thy houses; and the houses of the Egyptians shall be full of swarms *of flies*, and also the ground whereon they are."

"And the Lord did so; and there came a grievous swarm *of flies* into the house of Pharaoh, and into his servants' houses, and into all the land of Egypt: the land was corrupted by reason of the swarm *of flies*."[1]

The marginal reading of the English version gives, as a substitute for "swarm of flies," a "mixture of noisome beasts," which is, in fact, the rendering adopted in the Welsh version, and which appears to be a more exact interpretation of the Hebrew than that which has been adopted in the English translation.

The Hebrew word is ערוב, *arob,* which the Septuagint translates κυνόμυια, the dogfly, and the English version "a swarm of flies." Almost all the Hebrew interpreters understand it to be a *collection* of noxious beasts, as if a miscellaneous swarm (from *arob* in the signification of *mixing*[2]). Thus, Rabbi Selomo calls *arob,* "every kind of poisonous animals, such as serpents and scorpions." Aben Ezra believes the word to signify "all kinds of hurtful beasts mixed together—lions, wolves, bears, and leopards." Jonathan and Josephus equally adopt the signification of "*a mixture* of wild beasts," which has been also employed by the Arabic interpreters of the Pentateuch. All these interpretations are founded on the primary meaning of the root *arb,* "mix." There seems to be no authority for the Greek translation, "dog-fly," though the text requires that the word *arob* should mean some particular creature. Aquila combined the notion of a mixed collection with that of the specific fly-like nature of the plague, and translated the word πάμμυια, "every kind of fly"; and in this he was followed by St. Jerome and the Vulgate, which latter has "omne genus muscarum."

The origin of the appellation *cymmysgbla,* "the mixed plague," given in the Welsh version of the Pentateuch, to the fourth plague, is therefore clearly made out; and though the compound

---

[1] Exodus viii. 20, 21, 24.   [2] Gesenius, *Hebrew Dict. in voce.*

phrase *cymmysg-bla* may not be a completely satisfactory interpretation of the Hebrew word *arob*, it is evident that it is
meant to be such, and that the term is not derived from any
mixing up of two plagues (the third and fourth) into one, for
the mysterious purpose of making room for some heretical interpolation. The whole theory of the "mystery of the *gwyddvedd*," which has been shown to be simply the Welsh (and
most probably the true) reading of the third plague as "gnats,"
and of the participation of the Post-Roman British Church in
the supposed heresy with which that mystery was connected,
is the merest fantasy without any kind of real foundation.[1]

A similar misapprehension has led Mr. Herbert to suppose
that in the religious poem called the "Wand of Moses," which
is a kind of compendium of Scripture history, "Hu or the Sun
is identified with Christ, Herod with Pharaoh, and Christ with
Moses; that the Judaism of the 'Wand of Moses,' the Christianity of the Christ Celi, and Neo-Druidism, all resolve themselves into one spiritual energy, viz. the art magic; and what
that is or was seems to be very ill concealed."

The "Wand of Moses," a very long piece, which it is unnecessary to translate at length, commences as a fragment—

> At every return[2]
> The crowd of brethren
> Meeting together,
> Shall be acknowledging
> To Christ the Lord
> The appropriate praise.
> The bright Lord sits
> In the lap of Mary, like unto her.
> Way of truth,
> Perfect Ruler,
> Pattern of saints,
> Stem of Jesse,
> Thy people Judah
> Bring together.

[1] The only remarkable point in this poem is, that in the description of the
first plague there is no mention of the waters having been turned into blood.
The destruction of the fish only is noticed.

[2] Perhaps of some festival previously mentioned.

Then follow the lines,

> Hu gelwir lleu
> O luch a letro
> Er eu pechawd ;

which Mr. Herbert translates,

> He is called Hu, the lion,
> Of radiance imperfectly given
> By reason of their sins ;

by which it is supposed that Hu, who is represented to be the Solar deity, is intended. But it is impossible that such an exordium can be followed by such an abrupt and uncalled-for piece of heathenism as we are here presented with, and we must suppose that the orthography is corrupt. We see that the rhyme requires the word " lleu " to sound with " letro," and this at once furnishes us with the true reading: " llo," a calf, instead of " lleu " a lion.

> They called upon the calf
> In adoration, and turned back
> To their sins :

alluding, of course, to the golden calf, an allusion which is in accordance with the whole of the poem, the substance of which relates to the birth of Christ, with references of various kinds to the children of Israel.

The " Gwawd Gwyr Israel " is another piece of the same kind, of which Mr. Herbert says, that the twelve men of Israel were the twelve knights of the Saint Greal seated at the Arthurian table around the seat Perilous. The reader may judge for himself :—

GWAWD GWYR ISRAEL.

Trindawd tragywydd
A oreu elfydd
A gwedy elfydd
Addaf yn gelfydd
A gwedy Addaf
Da y goreu Efa
Yr Israel bendigaid

A oreu Murgreid
Gwrdd ei grybwylleid
Glan ei gyweddeid
Deudeg tref yr Israel
Dwyrein gywychel
Deuddeg veib Israel
A oreu Duw hael

Deuddeg tra dinam
Teir Mam ai maeth
Un gwr ai crewys
Creawdr ai gwnaeth
Mal y gwna a fynho a fo Pennaeth
Deuddy Mab Israel a wnaeth culwydd
Mal y gwna a fynho a fo Arglwydd
Deuddeg meib Israel dymgofu
O ganhad Iesu

Ac untan ai bu a their Mam uddu
O naddu y doeth rhad
Ag eissydyd mad
A mair mad gread
A Christ fy nerthiad
Arglwydd pob gwenwlad
A alwaf a eilw pob rhydd
Ha bo fynghynydd
Genhyd gerennydd.

THE PRAISE OF THE MEN OF ISRAEL.

It was the Merciful Trinity
That made the earth ;
And after the earth,
Adam very skilfully ;
And after Adam,
Made the good Eve.
And the blessed Israel,
He made of mighty spirit,
Strong his intellect,
Handsome his appearance.
The twelve tribes of Israel
Rise up equally great.
The twelve sons of Israel
Also the bountiful God made,
The twelve very blameless ;
Three mothers nourished them,
One man begat them,
The Creator made them,
As the Supreme makes all that has been and shall be.
The loving God made the twelve sons of Israel,
As the Lord makes all that has been and shall be.
Remember the twelve tribes of Israel,
Of them was born Jesus.
And there was one father to them and three mothers ;
Of them came grace
And a good progeny.
And (of them) the good Mary was created ;
And Christ our strength,
Lord of all fair regions.
And I will call on, and sing of thee every day ;
For it has been my desire
To be in friendship with thee.

It is certainly not necessary to go farther than the Old and New Testament in search of the origin of all the allusions contained in this piece.

Having examined the evidence on which the Neo-Druidic theory of Mr. Herbert, so far as it is derived from the Welsh poems, is founded, we turn to the latest views propounded on on the subject of the mystic lore supposed to be contained in these poems; and here a new surprise awaits us. As though the Druidism, pure and simple, of Mr. Davies, and the Neo-Druidism of Mr. Herbert, were not sufficiently startling when eliminated from works of Christian writers, even if so early a date could be ascribed to them as the sixth century of the Christian era, we are introduced by the Venerable Archdeacon Williams, in a work published in 1854, to a specimen of Egyptian mythology discovered in these same poems.

After stating that the poems in question contain examples of Druidical doctrines blended with the worship of many of the Pagan idols of Greece and Rome, " We also," says Mr. Williams,[1] " find *Apis* under the suggestive form of Ap-is, the son of Isis; and I may remark here, that the traditions of Egypt, especially as connected with the worship of the elements, are still traceable among us. In the following passages from an unknown author, the son of Isis and of Mair is singularly confounded with the material sun :—

> Cyvoethawg Duw dovydd
> Ap-is Lleuver Llawenydd
> Hael (" undeb ") Haul undydd
> Eil canwyll cristion
> A lewych uch eigion
> Lloer viloed vilenyd.

" Translation :—

> Powerful and civilizing God,
> Ap-is is the light of gladness.
> Liberal " unity " the one day sun.
> The second lamp of the Christian (is she),
> The moon for thousands of years.

[1] *Gomer*, part i. p. 9.

"And lower down we have the following expression :—

> Duw vab mair, Ap-is nev ac elvydd.
>
> God the son of Mary, Apis of heaven and the elements."

If this interpretation of the passages in question be the true one, any attempt to investigate the religious notions contained in the old British poems must be abandoned in despair. The combination of Egyptian traditions and Druidic paganism with Christianity in the sixth century would offer a formidable complication of difficulties, having regard to the scanty materials in our possession. Fortunately there is not a particle of truth in the supposition that the Egyptian form of Osiris under the figure of a bull, or other Egyptian deity whatsoever, is mentioned in any Welsh poem, Druidic or otherwise. Indeed Mr. Williams has not been at the trouble to explain how the word Ap-is, if it mean the son (Ap) of Isis, can also mean Apis, a form of Osiris, the sacred bull of Egypt. The word Apis in the mouth of an Egyptian, or on an Egyptian monument, or in the writings of any Greek author, never meant "the son of Isis." Even if this *ignis fatuus* of Apis be rejected, and the word taken as a purely Celtic one—Ap Is, the son of Isis—there is no pretence for asserting its existence with that meaning in the passages above quoted.

The fragment from which these lines are taken is the last in the Myvyrian collection, and is from the oldest known MS. the Black Book of Caermarthen, transcribed, as the editors inform us, letter for letter. The orthography differs somewhat from that of the pieces in the Red Book of Hergest, but presents no difficulty in translation. It is entitled "Awdyl," a song (properly a particular kind of metre), and is here given exactly as in the original, except that here the lines are arranged not continuously, but according to the rhyme.

AWDYL.

Bendith y wenwas ir dec diyrnas
Breisc ton bron ehalaeth
Duw y env in nufin impop ieith
Dyllit enweir meir rymaeth
Mad devthoste yg corffolaeth
Llyva mab gowri gobeith
Adylivas idas y leith
Bu divivewil athuyllvriaeth
In hudaul gvar guassanaeth
Yargluit bu hywit ac nybu doeth
Ac hid vraud ny vn yarvaeth
Kyffei bart pridit
Ar yssit in eluit
Ar hallt ar echuit
Ar graean ar mir ar sir syweditiaeth
Beirnad rodiad llara llau fraeth
Mui y dinwas sune gunaune eddwaeth
Kyuoethev ri nifrdraeth
Maur duv hetiv moli dyvrdaaeth
Bendith nautoryw new
Ir keluit creaudir kyvothauc duw

Douit ap'is lleuver lleuenit
Hael vynver heul indit
Eill kanuill cristaun
A leuich uch eigaun
Lloer vilioet vilenhit
Athrydit ryvet
Yn merwerit mor
Cv threia cud echwit
Cuda cvdymda
Cv treigil cvthrewna
Pa hid a nev cud vit
Y pen yseith mlinet
Y duc ren y risset
Ydad wet ynyduit
Iolune ara beir
Kyvoethauc duu vab meir
Ap'is new ac eluit
Pan deuthoste y passe diwedit
Ovffern awn ran iti bv rit
Ren new ryphrinomne digerenhit.

TRANSLATION.

Blessed be the fair youth of the beautiful kingdom
Of pure nature of bountiful breast.
The name of God is hallowed in all languages.
In the form of man, Mary nursed him;
Good was his bringing forth in a corporeal form,
The form of the child, the hope of mankind.
And the form of the youth was of good aspect;
He was void of reproach in his manhood,
In miracles doing great service.
The Lord was gentle and wise beyond all,
And until the day of judgment may we perform his will.
The race of the bards sing
Of what is in the world:
Of mountain, of wood,
Of the sands of the sea, of the knowledge of the stars;
Adjudged vagabonds, very great is their loquaciousness.
It would be of more service to consider the peculiar traits of the Godhead,
The beneficent King of all shores,
The heir of the great God, praise to thy high pre-eminence.

Blessed is the protection of the King of heaven,
The beneficent God (Duw dovit),
Who has created the shining sun—
Bounteous minister, the sun for the day.
Another candle of Christians,
Which shines above the waters,
The Moon for thousands of years.
And a third marvel
Is the great roaring of the sea,
Its ebbing in the evening,
Its rising and falling,
Its turning over and driving together,
Until it conceals the sky.
At the end of seven years,
Great fear of its overflow;
But it returns again to its place.
Let us give praise to the Virgin,
And the powerful God, the Son of Mary,
Who made heaven and earth.
When thou camest forth on the evening of the Passover,
From hell to the upper air there was a passage for thee.
Lord of heaven, let thy goodness redeem us.

The human mind must have been very strangely constituted in Wales if the writer of this piece can be imagined to have deliberately introduced an allusion to a Pagan deity.

This poem is not remarkable either for elegance or learning; but it is undoubtedly the work of a pious man and a Christian, who probably knew no more of Apis or Isis than he did of electric telegraphs. In truth the word *Apis*, as it is written by Mr. Williams, Ap-is, does not appear in the text of the *Myvyrian Archæology*. The word is written Ap'is, and is simply a contraction for " a peris," who made or prepared. The word *peris*, in the sense of "he created," is very commonly met with. " Peris Duw dui funnaun," God created two fountains; " Peris paradwys," he created paradise, &c.; and there is not a shadow of foundation for the Archdeacon's assertion, that here or elsewhere, in any Welsh poem, is there any trace of Egyptian mythology.[1]

[1] Such contractions as that above referred to are in common use in the

The piece itself is so manifestly Christian, and, from the way in which the Virgin Mary is mentioned, is not likely to be earlier than the twelfth century,[1] that it is astonishing how any one could have been led to suppose it could contain Paganism or Druidism of any kind. But it is a still more extraordinary circumstance that the Venerable Archdeacon Williams, himself a learned Welshmen, the author of works on these very poems, and the chairman and judge at several Eisteddfodau, should not have been aware that this very "Awdyl," arranged in lines, though with additions which do not appear in the one he has quoted, is printed at the 187th page of the *Myvyrian Archæology*, and that the contracted words which he has mistaken for *Apis* are there written at full length :—

> Cyfoethauc Dduw Ddofydd
> A BERIS lleufer llewenydd.

And the other line,

> Dduw mab Mair A BERIS new ag elvit.

We may, therefore, confidently state, that the Egyptian mystery is at an end, and that the Venerable Archdeacon has not falsified the inscription on the statue of the goddess, by lifting the veil of a Welsh Isis.

It is unnecessary to follow this author further in his views respecting the mythology of the Welsh poems, than to notice the presence of two personages in one of these pieces who are said to represent " two myths exactly corresponding with the

---

Irish manuscripts, and have been employed in some printed books in that language, of which a copious account may be seen in Donovan's and O'Brien's *Irish Grammars*. They are in principle, and often in form, the same as those which occur in Latin manuscripts of the middle ages. They are, in fact, a species of shorthand introduced for the purpose of saving time and parchment, which, before the invention of the art of printing, was an object of considerable moment.—Donovan, *Grammar of the Irish Language*, p. 429.

[1] See Rees's *Essay on the Welsh Saints*, p. 63, note.

Castor and Pollux of the Romans, the Dioskouroi and Tyndaridoi of the Greeks, in their especial character of regulators of the weather in subordination to their mystic father, the god of the electric fluid."

These two persons are Nyniaw and Pebiaw, who are mentioned in the tale of "Kilhwch and Olwen," as the two horned oxen whom God turned into oxen on account of their sins. There are other legends concerning them, but nothing that can remind us of any deity of Greece or Rome.

So far, indeed, from Pebiaw representing either Castor or Pollux, he appears really to have been an historical personage, and with his brother in misfortune, Nyniaw, to have been, like almost every other person mentioned in the Triads, a contemporary of King Arthur; for Ritta Gawr, the giant who conquered both Nyniaw and Pebiaw, and employed their beards, as he did those of many other kings, in the lining of his cloak, had the audacity to demand that of Arthur for the same purpose. In fact, the name of King Pebiaw appears in the *Liber Landavensis* as a benefactor of the church, "being penitent, with an humble heart, and mindful of his evil deeds."

Hercules is another deity said to have been worshipped by the Welsh in the sixth century, on the strength of the following piece, entitled an "Elegy on Ercwlf."

MARWNAD ERCWLF.

Ymchoeles Elfydd
Fal nos yn ddydd
O ddyfod clodrydd
Ercwlf pen bedydd
Ercwlf a ddywedai
Angeu nas riuei
Ysgwydawr y Mordei
Arnaw y torrei
Ercwlf sywessyd
Ewnin lloer egyd
Pedeir colofn cyhyd

Rhuddeur ar ei hyd
Colofn Ercwlf
Nis arfeidd bygwl
Bygwl nis beiddic
Gres heul nis godei
Nith aeth nes i nef
Hyd ydd aeth ef
Ercwlf mur fossawd
As arnut tywawd
As rhoddwy Trindawd
Trugaredd ddydd brawd.

ELEGY ON ERCWLF.

The earth turns,
So night follows day.
When lived the renowned
Ercwlf, chief of baptism?
Ercwlf said
He did not take account of death.
The shield of Mordei
By him was broken.
Ercwlf placed in order,
Impetuous, frantic,
Four columns of equal height,
Red gold upon them,
A work not easily to be believed,
Easily believed it will not be.
The heat of the sun did not vex him;
None went nearer heaven
Than he went.
Ercwlf the wall-breaker,
Thou art beneath the sand;
May the Trinity give thee
A merciful day of judgment.

The two first lines of this piece are unconnected with the rest. They give the answer to the question which constantly recurs in these songs, " Whence come night and day?" &c. Ercwlf is, no doubt, Hercules, as the mention of the columns shows; but to suppose that this ballad exhibits traces of the worship of the Grecian hero, is altogether unreasonable. Like the " Gofeisws Byd " and the " Anrhyfeddodau Alexander," this piece is an interesting specimen of the kind of knowledge which was circulating in Wales in the twelfth century.

That Hercules should be styled " chief of baptism " need cause no surprise, since in the middle-age romances the good knight Sir Hercules might have couched a spear against the worthy Sir Hector of Troy, after receiving benediction from Bishop Bedwine, without in the slightest degree shocking the chronological or historical conscience of the reader. Sir Walter Scott has presented us with an amusing example of this confusion of ideas, and of the current legendary knowledge of Scripture history, at the close of the twelfth century, in his novel of Ivanhoe.

One great mistake in these investigations has been the supposing that the Welsh of the twelfth or even of the sixth century were wiser as well as more Pagan than their neighbours. Archdeacon Williams insists that these poems contain a marvellous philosophy, or cosmogony, " which asserts the unity of the creative and upholding power, and describes the universe as infinite, or at least as not bounded by a material firmament,

not even by the 'flammantia mœnia' of the Epicurean poet."
These views are as fantastic in their way as the Helio-Arkite
superstitions of Mr. Davies, or the Neo-Druidism of Mr. Herbert. The cosmogony of these poems is derived from the Old
and New Testament chiefly, aided by such learning as might
be distilled from the monastic laboratory. We see, in fact, in
the questions on natural phenomena which abound in these
poems, some indications of the struggles of the human mind
to pierce the thick cloud of ignorance and darkness which
overwhelmed the age; still more, a pretence of learning and a
claim to superior attainments evinced in propounding questions which the contending or rival minstrels could not answer,
and to which the questioner himself could probably give replies
as little satisfactory. The following effusion appears to be from
an anxious inquirer on these subjects :—

CANU Y BYD BYCHAN.

Kein geneis canaf
Byd unddydd mwyaf
Lliaws a bwyllaf
Ac a Bryderaf
Cyfarchafi Feirdd byd
Pryd nam dyweid
Py gynheil y byd
Na syrth yn eissywyd
Neu'r byd pei syrthiei
Py ar yd gwyddei
Pwy ai gogynhaliai

Byd mor yw aduant
Pan syrth yn diuant
Etwa yn geugant
Byd mor yw rhyfedd
Na syrth yn unwedd
Byd mor yw odid
Mor fawr yn sethrid
Johannes Matheus
Lucas a Marcus
Wy a gynneil y byd
Trwy rad yr Yspryd

Taliesin a'i cant.

THE LITTLE SONG OF THE WORLD.

The song I have sung, I sing
Of the world one day more.
Much I reason,
And anxiously consider.
I address those who are Bards,
Seeing that it is not told me
What sustains the world,
That it does not fall upon the stars :
Or, if it were to fall,

Upon what would it fall,
Who would sustain it ?
The world, great its destruction,
When it shall fall into decay ;
Yet it is certain (to do so).
The world, great is the wonder
That it does not fall on one side.
The world, great its perfection,
Very great its motionless condition.

Taliesin sung this.

The four concluding lines of the poem (written probably by a later hand) give an answer to these questions, which is certainly more pious than satisfactory.

> John and Matthew,
> Luke and Mark,
> It is they who uphold the world
> Through the grace of the Holy Spirit.

The following is another of these compositions, which contains precisely the same kind of phrases, and the same amount of philosophy, as are displayed in the song entitled "I'r Gwynt," and referred to in most of the pieces of the same character :—

CANU Y BYD MAWR.

O waith Taliesin.

Gwolychaf fy nhad
Fy Nuw fy neirthiad
A ddodes trwy fy iad
Euaid ym pwyllad
Am gorug ym gwylad
Fy saith llafanad
O dan a daiar a dwr ac awyr
A niwl a Blodeu
A gwynt a goddeheu
Eil synwyr pwyllad
Im pwyllwys fy nhad
Un yw a rynniaf
A deu y tynnaf
A thri a waedaf
A phedwar a flasaf
A phump a welaf
A chwech a glywaf
A saith a arogleuaf
A ragddywedaf
Seith awyr ysydd
Uwch ben sywedydd
A thair rhan y myr
Mor ynt amrygyr
Mor fawr a rhyfedd
Y byd nad unwedd

Ry gorug Duw fry
Ar y Planete
Rygorug Sola
Rygorug Luna
Rygorug Marca
Y Marcarucia
Rygorug Venus
Rygorug Venerus
Rygorug Seuerus
A seithfed Satwrnus
Rygorug Duw dda
Pump gwregys terra
Pa hyd yd para
Una y sydd oer
A dau y sydd oer
Ar trydydd a sydd wres
Ac an bludd afles
A dyofec anlles
Pedwerydd paradwys
Gwerin a gynwys
Pymhet artymherawd
A byrth y fedyssawd
Yn dri yd ramad
Yn amgan pwyllad
Un yw'r Assia

Deu yw'r Affrica
Tri yw Europa
Bedydd gyngwara
Hyd frodic yt para
Pan farner pob traha
Rygorug fy Awen

I foli fy Rhen
Mydwyf Taliesin
Areith lif Dewin
Parahawd hyd ffin
Yng hynnelw Elphin.

THE GREATER SONG OF THE WORLD.

By Taliesin.

I praise my Father,
My God, my strength,
Who has given me in my head
Soul and reason,
And has made for my advantage
My seven senses,
And fire and earth, and water and air,
And clouds and flowers,
And wind and trees.
Other reasoning faculties
My Father has endowed me with :
One is perceiving,
The second is feeling,
The third is speaking (?)
The fourth is tasting,
The fifth is seeing,
The sixth is hearing,
The seventh is smelling.
As before mentioned,
Seven firmaments there are
High above the stars,
And three divisions of the sea.
The sea is beating on all sides ;
The sea is very wonderful ;
It entirely surrounds the earth.
God made the (firmament) above
For the planets.
He made the sun (Sola) ;
He made the moon (Luna) ;
He made Mars (Marca),
And Mercury (Marcarucia) ;

He made Venus ;
He made Venerus ;
He made Seuerus,[1]
And seventhly Satwrnus.
The good God made
Five zones to the earth
For as long as it shall last :
One is cold,
And the second is cold,
And the third is hot,
And injurious to flowers,
Disagreeable and destitute.
The fourth is Paradise,
The people shall be admitted to it.
The fifth is the temperate,
The pleasantest part of the universe ;
It is divided into three parts,
Mentioned in song.
The one is Asia,
The second is Africa,
The third is Europe
Blest with baptism :
It shall last till the day of judgment,
And all wickedness shall be judged.
Very great is my Muse
In praising my King.
I am Taliesin,
I speak with a prophetic voice,
Continuing until the end
For the deliverance of Elphin.

[1] Probably for Jouerus, Joverus, Jupiter.

We have seen in the "Canu y Cwrwf," the "Prifarch Taliesin," and other pieces already translated, a number of those questions which the Bard propounded to his audience, or the answers to which he professed to be acquainted with. But the great repertory of this lore is the piece entitled, merely because these two words happened to be written with capital initials, " Angar Cyvyndawd." It is evident that in many instances, as may be seen in the translations above given, the title of the piece is in no wise indicative of its contents, and in some cases is ludicrously inapplicable.

ANGAR CYVYNDAWD.

Inimica Confederatio.

Bardd yman ymae ni chaint aganho
Caned pan darffo
Sywedydd yn yd fo
Haelon am nacco
Nis deubi a rotho
Trwy Iaith Taliesin
Bu dydd ymellin
Kian pan ddarfu
Lliaws gyvolu
By lleith bid araith afaggdu
News dwg yn gelfydd
Cyfreu Argywydd
Gwiawn a lleferydd
A dwfn ddyfydd
Gwnaei o farw fyw
Ag anghyfoeth yw
Gwneynt eu perion
Af erwynt heb don
Gwneynt eu delidau
Yn oes Oesau
Dydyth dydyccawd
O ddyfnwedyd gwawd
Neut Angar Cyfyndawd
Pwy ei chynefawd
Cymmeint cerdd ciwdawd
A delis eich tafawd
Pyr na threthwch draethawd

Llad uch llyn llathrawd
Penilliach pawb
Dybyddaf yna gnawd
Dwfn dyfu yngnawd
Neu'r doddyw ysgygnawd
Trydydd par ygnad
Triugein mlynedd
Yd porthes lawrwedd
Ym nwfr Kaw a chiwed
Yn elfydd tiredd
Canweis am ddioedd
Cant rihydd addynoedd
Can yw ydd aethant
Can yw y doethant
Can eilewydd gant
Ag ef ei darogant
Lladdan ferch lliant
Oedd bych ei chwant
I aur ac Ariant
Pwy byw ai diadas
Gwaed i ar mynwas
Odid traethator
Mawr molhator
Mi dwyf Daliesin
Ryphrydaf i iawnllin
Parawd hyd ffin
Ynghynelw Elphin

Neur Deyrnged
O rif eur dylyed
Pan gassad ni charad
Anudon a brad
Mi ni chwennych vad
Trwy gogyweg an gwawd
A gogyfarchwy brawd
Wrthyf ny gwybydd nebawd
Doethwr prif gelfydd
Dispwyllawd sywedydd
Am wyth am edrwyth
Am ddoleu dynwedydd
Am wyr gwawd gelfydd
Cerddwn Dduw yssydd
Trwy ieith Talhayarn
Bedydd bu ddydd farn
A farnwys teithi
Angerdd Farddoni
Ef ai rhin rhoddes
Awen anghynnes
Saith ugein Ogrfen
Y sydd yn Awen
Wyth ugein o bob ugein e fydd yn un
Yn annwfn y diwyth
Yn annwfn y gorwyth
Yn annwfn is Elfydd
Yn awyr uch Elfydd
Y mae ei gwybydd
Pa dristydd y sydd
Gwell na llawenydd
Gogwn ddeddf rhadeu
Awen pan ddyffreu
Am gelfydd taleu
Am ddedwydd Ddieu
Am buchedd ara
Am oeseu ysgorfa
Am hafal Deyrnedd pa eu cyngwara
Am gyhaval ydynt trwy weryd

.   .   .   .   .

Awel uchel gyd
Pan fydd gohoyw bryd
Pan fydd mor hyfryd
Pan yw gwrch echen
Pan echrewyd uchel

Neu haul pan ddodir
Pan yw toi tir
Toi tir pwy maint
Pan dynid gwytheint
Gwytheint pan tynnid
Pan yw gwyrdd gweryd
Gweryd pan yw gwyrdd
Pwy echenis cyrdd
Cyrdd pwy echenis
Ys dir pwy ystyriwys
Ystyriwyd yn Llyfreu
Pet wynt pet ffreu
Pet ffreu pet wynt
Pet Afon ar hynt
Pet Afon ydynt
Daear pwy ei lled
Neu pwy ei thewed
Gogwn t . . ws llafnawr
Am rudd am llawr
Gogwn atrefnawr
Rhwng nef a llawr
Pan atsain advant
Par ergyr divant
Pan llewych Ariant
Pan fydd tywyll Nant
Anadl pan yw du
Pan yw oreu a fu
Buch pan yw bannog
Gwraig pan yw Serchawg
Llaeth pan yw Gwynn
Pan yw glas celyn
Pan yw barfawg myn
Yn lliaws mehyn
Pan yw baraut
Pan yw creu efwr
Pan yw meddu rolwyn
Pan yw lledf orddwyn
Pan yw brith Iyrchwyn
Pan yw hallt halwyn wyn
Cwrw pan yw Ystern
Pan yw lledrudd gwern
Pan yw gwyrdd Llinos
Pan yw rhudd Egroes
Neu wreig ai dioes

Pan ddygynnu nos
Py ddatwein y sydd yn eur Lliant
Ni wyr neb pan ruddir ei bron huan
Lliw yn erkynan newydd
Anahawr ei ddwyn
Tant telyn py gwyn
Eog py gwyn ny Gan
Py geidw ei diddan
Py diddwg Garthan
Gereint ac Arman
Py dyddwg glain
O erddygnawd fain
Pan yw per Erwain
Pan yw gwyrliw brain
Talhayarn y sydd
Mwyaf y Sywedydd
Pwy amgyffrawd Gwydd
O aches ammod dydd
Gogwn da a drwg
Cwdda cudd amewenir mwg
Mawr maint gogyhwg
Cawg pwy ae dylifas
Pwy gwawr gorphennas
Pwy a bregethas
Eli ag Eneas
Gogun gogeu Haf
A fyddant y gayaf
Awen a ganaf
O ddwfn ys dygaf
Afon cyd beryd
Gogwn ei gwrhyd
Gogwn pan ddyfeinw
Gogwn pan ddyleinw
Gogwn pan ddillydd
Gogwn pan wegrydd
Gogwn pan pegor
Y sydd y dan For
Gogwn eu heissor
Pawb yn ei Osgordd
Pet gygloyd yn nydd
Pet dydd ymlwyddyn
Pet paladr ynghat
Pet dos ynghawat
Atuyn yd ramawd

Gwawd mwy mefl gogyffrawd
Aches gwyd Gwydion
Gogwn i nebawd
Py lenwis Afon
Ar bobl Pharaon
Pwy dyddwg rwynnon
Baran achwysson
Py osgawl oddef
Pan ddyrchafwyd Nef
Pwy fu fforch Hwyl
O ddear hyd Awyr
Pet bysedd am pair
Am un am neddair
Pwy enw y ddeuair
Ni eing yn un pair
Pan yw mor meddwtawd
Pan yw du Pysgawd
Morfwyd fydd eu cnawd
Hyd pan yw Meddysg
Pan y gannawg Pysg
Pan yw du troed alarch gwynn
Pedryddawg gwaew Llymm
Llwyth nef nid ystyng
Py pedair tywarchen
Ni wys eu gorphen
Py voch neu py grwydr hydd
Ath gyfarchaf fargad fardd
Gwr yth gynnyd esgyrn Niwl
Cwddynt dau raiadr gwynt
Tracthator fyngofeg
Yn Efrai yn Efroeg
Yn Efroeg yn Efrai
Laudatum laudate Iessu
Eilgweith yn rhithad
Bum glas gleissiad
Bum ei bum Hydd
Bum Iwrch ym Mynydd
Bum cyff mewn rhaw
Bum bwall yn llaw
Bum ebill yngefel
Blwyddyn a hanner
Bum Ceiliawg brithwyn
Ar ieir yn eidin
Bum Amws ar Re

Bum tarw toste
Bum buch melinawr
Mal y maethawr
Bum gronyn erkennis
Ef lyfwys ym Mryn
A mettawr am dottawr
Yn sawell ym gyrrawr
Ymrygiaw o Law
Wrth fy ngoddeiddiaw
Am harfolles iar
Grafrudd grib escar
Gorffwysseis naw nos
Yn ei chroth yn was
Bum aeduedig feddedig

Bum llad rhag gwledig
Bum marw bum byw
Keing ydd ym Eidduw
Bum i arweddawd
Rhag ddaw bum tlawd
Am eil cynghores gres
Grafrudd am rhoddes
Odid tracthator
Mawr molhator
Mi wyf Taliesin
Ryphrydaf iawnllin
Parahawd hyd ffin
Ynghynelw Elphin.

Diwedd.

THE ANGAR CYVYNDAWD.

Is there a Bard here who has not sung a song?
When the song is finished,
If he is a learned person,
There will be from me
No denial of liberality.
According to the saying of Taliesin,
The day was yellow (waning),
When Kian finished
His numerous songs of praise.
Let my liquor be that which rightly belonged to Afaggdu.
Did he not skilfully bear away
The strains of knowledge?
Gwiawn, on whom it overflowed,
And he became profound.
He could restore the dead to life.
Though destitute of wealth,
They can make delicious things,
And boil without water;
They can make metals.[1]
In ages of ages,

---

[1] These lines clearly mean to speak of the magical powers acquired by Gwion or Taliesin on tasting the three charm-bearing drops of the Cauldron of Ceridwen.

No one can refuse to acknowledge the obligations of all Welsh scholars to

> The day remains concealed,
> For praising the profoundly eloquent one.
> Not unlovely is concord,
> To him who is accustomed to it.
> Assembly of harmonious minstrels,
> What has paralyzed your tongues?
> Why do you not recite a recitation?
> Give us over the bright liquor
> All your penillions.[1]
> He will come in the flesh;[2]
> From the deep he came in the flesh.
> Did he not ascend
> On the third day to be our judge?
> Thirty years
> He bore this earthly nature.
> In his infancy wrapped up in swaddling-bands
> In the region of the earth.[3]
> I have sung without delay,
> Before very long importunity.
> There is a song on their coming,
> A song on their going,
> A song from a hundred minstrels;
> And it is this they speak of,

Dr. Owen Pughe; but it is necessary to point out that his translations are, in numerous instances, most contradictory. The present is one of the most extraordinary.

Under the word " dylid," in his *Dictionary*, he translates these lines thus :—

" They would do their commands; they would do their duties for ages of ages." Under " telid," he translates the same lines and the two following ones :—

" Their musicians would produce a fruitless wind without sound; their instruments would ever make, from the effect of vibration, a profound flow of praise."

[1] Stanzas formed according to one of the laws regulating metrical composition. It would be interesting to know the relative antiquity of the term.

[2] Here commences a religious portion quite unconnected with what precedes and follows.

[3] The interpolated part relating to Christ ends here.

The slaughter of the daughter of Lliant.[1]
Little was her pleasure
In gold and silver,
Who is deprived of life
With blood upon the breast.
A wonderful reciter,
A great singer of songs of praise,
Am I, Taliesin.
I compose songs in true measure,
Continuing to the end
To uphold Elphin.
Is there not a tribute
Of much gold to be paid?
When shall be hated and not loved,
Perjury and treachery?
I have no desire for benefits
By yielding imperfect praise
And salutations of the brotherhood.
Compared with me, no one knows anything.
I am learned in the principal sciences,
And the reasonings of the astrologers
Concerning veins and solvents,[2]
And the general nature of man.
I know the secret of composing songs of praise.
I have sung of the existence of God.
According to the saying of Talhaiarn,
For the gifted there shall be a day of judgment,
And a judging of their qualities.
The poetic disposition
Is that which gives the secret virtue
Of a muse above mediocrity.
Seven score muses [3]
There are in the inspiration of song;
Eight score in every score
In the great abyss of tranquillity,
In the great abyss of wrath,[4]
In the depths below the earth,
In the air above the earth,

[1] Or "the daughter of the flood," or perhaps "the daughter of theft."
[2] Meaning, probably, veins of metal and the alchemical menstrua.
[3] Ogyrwen, or Gogyrwen.
[4] Annwfn, the great deep—hell.

There is a recognition of it.
What sorrow there is,
That is better than joy.
I know the blessed gifts
Of the flowing muse;
To me it brings the recompense of skill,
To me happy days,
To me a peaceful life,
And a protection in age.
I am equal to kings, whatever may be their enjoyment,
I am equal with them through redemption.[1]
When the countenance will be animated,
When the sea will be pleasant,
Whence is the growth of the seed,
Whence it grows up high,
Or whence comes the sun?
What is the covering of the earth?
How many coverings has the earth?
How the breath is drawn:
The breath, how is it drawn?
Whence is the sward green?
The sward, whence is it green?
What is the origin of trades?
Of trades what is the origin?
Do you know what is recorded,
Recorded in books?
How many winds, how many torrents,
How many torrents, how many winds?
How many rivers on the journey,
How many rivers there are?
What is the breadth of the earth,
Or what its thickness?
I know the . . . . [2]
Revolving round the earth;
I know the regulator
Between heaven and earth.
Whence the echo comes again,
And why its impulse dies away;
Whence the brightness of silver,
And why the valleys are dark;

[1] The poem breaks off here, owing to a defect in the MS. The next perfect line seems to belong to the lost passage. I therefore omit it.

[2] This line is defective in the *Myvyrian Archæology*.

What is the seat of the breath,
What is the best that has been;
Why the cattle have horns,
Why a woman is fond,
Why milk is white,
Why holly is green,
Why the kid is bearded,
Whence is the growth of the cow-parsnep
In a multitude of places;
Why wine intoxicates,
Why the mallet is made sloping,
Why the little roebuck is spotted,
Why the sea is salt,
Whence is the briskness of ale,
Why the alder is of a purplish colour,
Why the linnet is green,
Why the berries of the dogrose are red,
Or what is the age of a woman;
Whence is the commencement of night,
What melting-pot must be used to liquefy gold.[1]
No one knows what makes red the colour of the sun
On his first rising;
In an hour it goes away.
Why a harp-string is white;
Why the salmon glitters,
What preserves it without fire;[2]
What Garthan brought,
And Geraint and Garman;[3]
What brings out the polish
On hard-worked stone,
Whence the sweetness of the balm,
Whence the green colour of the young grass.
Talhaiarn is
The greatest of sages.
What is it agitates the wood,
Or fashions the froth (on the water)?

[1] Dr. Owen translates this line,

What reserve is there in the hour of flowing?

[2] That is, I suppose, the sparkling appearance of the scales; but it is not a satisfactory interpretation.

[3] Geraint was accounted a saint as well as a warrior. Garman, or St. Germanus, played an important part in British affairs in the fifth century, and is the hero of many legends.

37

I know good and evil,
The rising and motion of wreaths of smoke,
And many more equally perfect ;
Who it was emptied the bowl,[1]
Where the dawn terminates ;
What was preached by
Eli and Eneas.
I know the cuckoos in summer,
And where they will be in the winter.
I will sing a song
Concerning the deep, I will bring it
The common source of the rivers.
I know its depth,
I know whence it diminishes,
I know whence it replenishes,
I know whence it overflows,
I know whence it shrinks,
I know whence the creatures
That are in the sea ;
I know all that are like them,
All in their assembly.
How many hours in a day,
How many days in a year,
How many spears in a battle,
How many drops in a shower,
Very delicate its separation.
Excessive praise infers reproach.
A mind with the learning of Gwydion
I know in nobody ;
What caused the tide to flow
Over the people of Pharaoh ;
Who carried the measuring line
In the presence of the Creator ;
What ladder had he
When the heavens were lifted up ;
What was the fork set up
From the earth to the sky.
How many peas there are in my pot
With one in my hand.
What is the name of the two shanks
Which cannot be wedged into one pot ;
What is the cause of sea-sickness ;

---

[1] Alluding, perhaps, to the tale of the Countess of the Fountain.

Whence is the fat of fishes :
Their flesh will be of sea-food
Until it is transformed,
While the fish contains it.
Why the white swan has black feet,
Why a sharp spear penetrates.
The region of heaven has no limits.
What are the four elements
Whose boundaries are unknown.
Is the pig or the stag of the most vagabond nature ?
I ask of you, bigbellied bards,
Are the bones of man made of vapour ?
Do the winds fall down in cataracts ?
I am a reciter of information,
In Efrai, in Efroeg,
In Efroeg, in Efrai,[1]
Laudatum laudate Jessu.
A second time in transformation,
I have been a blue salmon,
I have been a dog, I have been a stag,
I have been a roebuck in the mountain,
I have been a stump of a tree in a shovel,
I have been an axe in the hand,
I have been the pin of a pair of tongs
A year and a half ;
I have been a spotted cock
Along with the hens ;
I have been a stallion in action,
I have been a fierce bull,
I have been a yellow buck,
Soft was my nourishment.
I have been a grain springing up ;
The reaper came to me,
Thrusting me into a hole,
Rubbing me with the hand
In my afflictions.
A hen became pregnant of me,
With red claws and a cleft crest.
I was necessitated to be nine nights

[1] Egroeg, Greek :—

     In Hebrew, in Greek ; in Greek, in Hebrew ;

remarkable accomplishments for the Welsh Druids of the sixth century.

In her womb as an infant.
I have been a possession of the meritorious,
I have been a gift for a king,
I have been dead, I have been alive ;
Concealed in the ivy bush,
I have been carried about.[1]
Before I received a gift I was poor.
Another welcome counsel
To me the red-fanged one gave,
A wonderful reciter,
A great composer of hymns
Am I, Taliesin.
I compose songs in true measure,
Continuing to the end
To uphold Elphin.

The end.

Some persons may see a mystery in the assertion of the Bard, that he knows the number of peas in a pot, together with one in his hand, or why milk is white, or the white swan has black feet ; we can only give the translation, and must leave comments on its philosophy to clearer-sighted inquirers.

The principal example which Mr. Williams produces of this philosophy derived from the ancient Druids, "who regarded the sun as the cause of all flow or material flux and efflux, whether the imponderables of light, heat, and electricity, or of the ponderable elements, and that without his operations all creation would be cold, dark, and rigid," is taken from a poem which has been ascribed to Taliesin, but which the editors of the *Myvyrian Archæology* tell us is supposed to have been written by Jonas Athraw or the "Doctor" of Menevia (St. David's), according to some in the tenth, more likely in the thirteenth or fourteenth, century. It is called a "A Poem of Taliesin," and is in itself sufficient to set at rest the question of a Druidic origin for this cosmogony. The writer says he obtained it from the Psalms of David, and we ought to give credit to his assertion.

---

[1] Dr. Owen gives this curious translation : —

I have been drunk before a king ; I have been a convoy.

DIVREGWAWD TALIESIN.

Goruchel Dduw golochir ym hob va
Goruchel ei enwau yn hebrea
Eli eloi ac adonai ac o ac alpha
Peryv nev parhaus gwrdda
Peris paradwys yn gynnwys i'r rhai da
Ac ufern i'r rhai drwg a gwg i'w diva
Peris ef nef parhaus wrda
Parwydydd elvydd peris privdda
O dan ac awyr a llyr a therra
Can ni bwynt un anian tan a therra
Cadwynau dyrys o dir hyd ethera
Pwy namyn cyvrwys ai cyvrwyma
A chynnil a chelvydd yn holi materia
  Achymman helis o lemaria
  Canys nid un anwyd ser a therra
Nid maen nid haearn ai cadarna
Nid cors nid calav tudded ai cuddia
Nid plwm trwm ei risg ai gorwisga
Nid mettel o waith uvel ai cylchyna
Neus gwisgwys celvydd gwr a dwvr a ia
Traethadur prophwyd pur ai traetha
Ond celvyddyd Panton sempiterna
Pan ddywed tad Selyv yn psalmodia
Quis tegit aqua superiora
Qui legis scriptura
Neus gorwisgwys gwr celvydd nev oi noddva
A syr a sygnau a haul a lluna
Peunydd cylch elvydd haul ai hwylia
Yn uchel odduchom i lleuvera
Pum gwregys lluniwys lluniedydd llawndda
Sicut in cœlo et in terra
Llawn yw y ddau eithav o eiry ac ia
A rhag eu hoervel neb nis nesaa
Ail dau a osoded o'r tu isa
Yn llawn o yngres gwres ignisia
Pumed yw y pervedd neb nis cyvannedda
Rhac maint tragwres haul yn ei redegva
Oes na gwydd na dail na neb rhyw anivail
Y ddau o boptu y dyvu tymer da
Gwres oddihwnt ac oervel oddima
Peris Duw ddwy fynnawn cyvlawn eu da
Fynnawn gwres yn awyr a haul yw ei hwylva

A'r ail fynnawn a ddail yr eigiawn yn yma
Peryv nev a peris pob da
A berys present i blant Adda
A beris paradwys yn gynnwys i'r sawl a vo da
Ac fern i'r rhai drwg er eu diva
A beris blwyddynoedd ac oesoedd a secula
Cyntav oes Addav ac oes Eva
Eiloes oes Noe a novies yn archa
Trydedd oes oes Abraham pen fydd pater patriarcha
Pedwaredd oes oes Moesen o Egyptica
A gavas y deuddeg fordd drwy Vari Rubia
A gavas gan geli voddi Pharona
A gavas dengair deddv yn y dirwestva
Mewn dan davl vaen yn mynydd Sina
Pumed oes oes ddedwydd Davydd propheta
Chweched oes oes Iesu a hyd vrawd y para
A ynddi y proved y prophesia
Dyvod o heppil enwir Eva
Mal y daw o'r drain blodau rosa
Mair wyry a ddyvu yn mru Anna
Ac Iesu a ddyvu o vru Maria
A'r nos y ganed Iesu gwr a'n iachaa
Y clywid cor engylion nev yn canu gloria
In excelsis Deo et in terra
Dyvynwys elvydd i lawer da
Ac i'r tri brenin seren lucerna
Tra vu Emanuel yn dawel yma
Gwnaeth gwyrthiau lawer a gweithredoedd da
Gwnaeth ar y neithiawr Ieuan yn Galilea
O'r dwvr y gwin melys pan erchis Maria
Ev porthes pum-mil ar y pumtorth bara
Mwy oedd o wargred nog a lewed wrth vwyta
Cyvodes y vorwyn o'r domo clausa
Cyvodes unmab mam extra porta
Y ar ei elorwydd o'i orweddva

    Cyvodes Lazar
    Y dan y ddaiar
        Brawd Mair a Martha
    Ev treiddwys tonau
    Heb geisio llongau
        Hyd y borthva
    Ev a vu veddig
    I'r parlysedig
        Yn ymyl porthig piscina

Ev a vu veddig
I'r clav nychedig
   A ddoeth attaw hyd y dyrva

Ev gwarawd deillion
Ev diddan cleivion
A charcharorion
   O bob clevyd a'u gorthryma

Nis cyvriv nebawd
Na'r holl vedysawd
   Byth nis traetha

A wnaeth ein rhiau
O anryveddodau
   Hyd tra vu yma

O'r diwedd y dyvu
Iachwyddawl Iesu
   Hyd yn Ierosolyma

Y cymmerth crog a chethrau
A frewyllau ar angau
   Y cymerth un mab Maria
   I obrynu llawer y law Satana

Ev cyvodes y trydydd dydd o'i vedd orweddva
Ac a ddoeth at ei ddisgyblon gwedi bwyta
Gwedi yspaid dieuoedd quadraginta
Neud o mewn nev y daeth pan ddaeth yma
Mewn nev bu mewn y bydd mewn y mae etwa
A dyddbrawd y daw ev attam yma
Ac a ddwg gantaw y sawl ai cofa
Y caif Mihangel y saul a vo da
I obrynu gwlad nev ys ef y sydd dda
Y gethern enwir a adewir yma
Y gethern y sy waeth ni wnaethant ddim da
Y gethern a el i ufern gan Lucifer ydd a
Pwy a wyr pwy ynt pwy a'u cofa
Pwy onid cyvrwys a'u cyvriva

Gwae a gymerth bedydd
A chred a chrevydd
   Ac ni sevis yn dda

Gwae berchenawg tir
Ni chynnalio ei wir
   Rhag un traha

Gwae er gwerth gweini
A vo cyd trengi
 Oni thrugaraa

Gwae hwynt penaethau
O chwant alavau
A dyr devodau
 Ac a'u diva

Gwae ofeiriad byd
Ni angreiftia gwyd
 Ni phregetha

Ni warcheidw ei gail
Ac ev yn vugail
 Nis areilia

Ni ddifer ei ddevaid
Rhag bleiddiau Rhuveiniaid
 A'u fon glopa, &c. &c.

A POEM OF TALIESIN.

Most high is God, prayed to in all lands ;
Most high His name in Hebrew,
Eli, Eloi, and Adonai, and Omega and Alpha.
He has created Heaven an abiding-place for good men ;
He has created Paradise for the reception of those who are good ;
And Hell for those who are wicked, and wrath shall consume them.
He has created Heaven an abiding-place for the good.
A separation of the elements he caused in the first place ;
The fire and water, and sea and earth ;
For not of one nature are fire and earth.
An entangled chain from the earth to the sky ;
Who but the Skilful One connected them together
With skill and artifice in all matter,
And collected the salt brine in the place of the seas ;
Because not of one nature are the stars and the earth,
Neither stone nor iron makes it strong ;
Neither reeds nor straw cover it with a roof,
Nor heavy lead invests it,
Nor metal or the work of fire encircles it.
Has not the Skilful One clothed it with water and ice :
A preacher, a pure prophet has declared it.
Is it not the skill of Panton Sempiterna,

As says the father of Solomon in Psalmodia,
        Quis tegit aqua superiora
        Qui legis scriptura.
Has not the Skilful One wonderfully covered over Heaven, his sanctuary,
With stars and signs and sun and moon ?
Daily the sun wheels round the circle of the earth,
On high from above he gives light to
The five zones framed by the all-good Creator.
Sicut in cœlo et in terra.
The two furthest of these are full of snow and ice,
And on account of their great cold no one can go near them.
Other two are placed on the under side (of these),
Full of parching heat and burning fires.
The fifth is the middle one, no one inhabits it
On account of the extreme heat of the sun in his course.
The two which come on all sides are of a good temperature ;
They receive heat from that side, and cold from this.
God erected two fountains of perfect goodness :
A fountain of heat in the air, the sun revolves in it :
And another fountain which produces the waters of the sea.
He created heaven, and created everything good,
And created the present state for the children of Adam,
And created Paradise as an abiding-place for whoso shall be good,
And Hell for the wicked for their destruction ;
And created years, and times, and secula.
The first was the age of Adam and the age of Eve ;
The second, the age of Noah, who swam in the ark ;
The third, the age of Abraham, head of the faith, Pater patriarcha ;
The fourth, the age of Moses the Egyptian,
Who obtained a road for the twelve through the Red Sea,
And procured from Heaven the drowning of Pharaoh ;
And obtained the ten commandments in fasting,
On two tables of stone in Mount Sinai ;
The fifth age was the blessed one of Davydd the Prophet ;
The sixth is the age of Jesus, and it shall last till the day of Judgment,
As prophets have prophesied.
He comes indeed of the seed of Eve,
As the coming of the flowers of the rose out of thorns.
The Virgin Mary proceeded from the womb of Anna,
And Jesus from the womb of Mary ;
In the night Jesus was born for the salvation of man,
Was heard the choir of the angels of heaven singing,
Gloria in excelsis Deo, et in terra,

38

Summoning the good men of the earth.[1]
And to the three kings the star was a lantern.
Whilst Emanuel was in tranquillity here,
He performed numerous miracles and good works :
At the marriage feast of the young man in Galilee,
He made sweet wine out of water at the request of Mary ;
He fed five thousand with five loaves of bread,
The fragments left were much greater than what had been eaten ;
He raised up the young maid out of domo clausa ;
He raised up the only son of his mother, extra porta ;
And from his funeral bier in the tomb
  He raised up Lazarus,
  Who was under the earth,
   The brother of Mary and Martha ;
  He walked on the waves
  Without seeking the boat
   To the landing-place ;
   He healed
   The paralytic
  At the edge of the pool ;
  He healed the sick (woman)
  Of a languishing sickness,
   Who came to him through the multitude ;
  He restored the blind,
  He comforted the sick
  And the prisoners
   In all the evils which oppressed them.
  Nobody can reckon up,
  Not in the whole earth
   Can it be related,
  The number which he did
  Of marvellous things
   Whilst he was here,
  To the end of his being
  Jesus, Saviour of all
   In Jerusalem.
He received the cross and the nails,
And the scourging and death :
This received the only son of Mary,
He who was full of merit, from the hand of Satan.
He arose the third day from his grave in the sepulchre,
And appeared to his disciples after meat.

  [1] Or, bringing to the earth an abundance of good.

After the space of forty days,
Was it not to heaven he went when he went hence?
In heaven he is, in heaven he will be, in heaven he is still;
And at the day of judgment he will come to us here.
  Woe to him who receives baptism
  And faith and religion,
   And walks not in righteousness;
  Woe to the possessor of lands
  Who does not protect his people
   Against the oppressor;
  Woe to the master
  Who, until his death,
   Is without compassion;
  Woe to the chiefs
  Who are covetous of riches,
  Who heap up possessions
   And squander them away;
  Woe to the minister
  Who does not rebuke vice,
   Nor preach,
  Nor guards his fold,
  Nor over his flock
   Keeps watch;
  Nor defends his sheep
  From the wolves of Rome [1]
   With his knotted staff.

Thirty more similar stanzas follow, all full of excellent religious and moral precepts, and the whole concludes thus :—

  I pray the gracious Son and the good Father,
  Mercy of the Trinity in the day of judgment,
  Before I go to my grave and my last resting-place,
  Complete repentance before I shall go hence.
   For what I have thought,
   For what I have done,
    Of evil or presumption,
  May I obtain mercy and a good end.

---

[1] Rhuveiniaid. If this is correct, it would seem to place the date of this portion of the poem after the Reformation.

To this we may add the " Awdyl Vraith," or " Diversified Song," likewise composed by this same Jonas Athraw, but which forms part of the Mabinogi of Taliesin, in the copy from the Red Book of Hergest.

YR AWDYL VRAITH.

1.
Ev a wnaeth Panton
Ar lawr glyn Ebron
Ai ddwylaw gwynion
    Gwiwlun Adda.

2.
A phum can mlynedd
Heb vawr ymgeledd
Bu ev yn gorwedd
    Cyn cael anima.

3.
Ev a wnaeth Eilwys
Yn llys paradwys
A'i asen aswys
    Iesin Eva.

4.
Seithawr i buan
Yn cadw'r berllan
Cyn cyvrdan Satan
    Sitiwr tartara.

5.
Oddiyno gyrwyd
Drwy ryn ac anwyd
I gael eu bywyd
    I'r byd yma.

6.
I ddwyn trwy ludded
Meibion a merched
I gael ofuned
    Ar dir Asia.

7.
Dau bump a deg wyth
Y bu yn amwyth
Yn arwain mysg-lwyth
    Masgl fœmina.

8.
Ac unwaith heb gel
Pan ymddug Abel
A Chain ddiymwel
    Homicida.

9.
I Adda ai gymhar
Y rhoed rhaw balar
I dori daiar
    I gael bara.

10.
A gwenith claerwyn
I hau'r havaryn
I borthi pob dyn
    Hyd wyl Vagna.

11.
Engylawl genad
Gan Duw uchel-dad
A ddug had tyviad
    Hyd at Eva.

12.
Hithau darguddiodd
Degved ran o'r rhodd
Hyd na chwbl hauodd
    Yr holl balva.

13.

Yno lle'r hauwyd
Yr yd a gelwyd
Medd Daniel brofwyd
   A brofeta.

14.

Rhyg du a gavad
Yn lle'r gwenithad
Er dangaws avrad
   Ar ladrata.

15.

Am hym o reswm
Rhag ovyn.dydd dwm
Mae'n rhaid roi degwm
   I Dduw'n bena.

16.

Or gwin sinobl-rhudd
A blanwyd ar heul-dydd
Ar nos loer gynnydd
   A gwymp Luna.

17.

O'r gwenith gwyn-vraint
A'r gwyn rhudd rhwydd-vraint
Y gwnair corf cywraint
   Crist vab Alpha.

18.

Yr avrllad yw'r cnawd
Ar gwin yw'r gwaedrawd
A geiriau'r drindawd
   A'u cysegra.

19.

Y llyvrau dirgel
O ddwylaw Emanuel
A ddug yr angel
   A'u rhoi Adda.

20.

Pan ydoedd yn rhen
Hyd tros y ddwyen
Yn nwvr Iorddonen
   In dirwesta.

21.

Deuddeg gweryddon
Pedwar angylion
Anvones Leison
   I lys Eva.

22.

I ddangaws cannerth
Rhag pob rhyw draferth
Pan vai anghyvnerth
   Ar brygnata.

23.

Dirvawr ovalon
A vu ar ddynion
Cyn cael arwyddion
   Misericordia.

24.

E gavas Moesen
Rhag dirvawr angen
Y tair gwialen
   Ar ddominica.

25.

Ve gavas Salmon
Yn Nhwr Babilon
Holl gelvyddydon
   Arca fœdera.

26.

Mawr gevais innau
Yn vy mardd-lyvrau
Holl gelvyddydau
   Gwlad Europa.

27.

Mi wn eu cerdded
A'u twng a'u tynged
A'u tro a'u trwydded
   Hyd ultima.

28.

Och duw mor druan
Y daw'r ddarogan
Drwy dirvawr gwynvan
   I lin Troea.

29.

Sarfes gadwynawg
Valch annrhugarawg
A'i hesgyll arvawg
    O Sermania.

30.

Hon a oresgyn
Holl Loegyr a Phrydyn
O lan mor Lychlyn
    Hyd Sabrina.

31.

Yna bydd Brython
Yn garcharorion
Yn mraint alltudion
    O Saxonia.

32.

Eu ner a volant
A'u hiaith a gadwant
Eu tir a gollant
    Ond gwyllt Walia.

33.

Oni ddel rhyw vyd
Yn ol hir benyd
Pan vo gogohyd
    Y ddau draha.

34.

Yno caif Brython
Eu tir a'u coron
A'r bobl estronion
    A ddivlana.

35.

Geiriau yr angel
Am hedd a rhyvel
A vydd diogel
    I Brytania.

O'r haul i'r ddalar, o dwvn i orchudd
Ond mi Taliesin nid oes cyvarwydd.

THE SONG OF VARIETIES.

1.

Him Panton made
In the land of Glyn Ebron,
With his two blessed hands,
    The fair form of Adam.

2.

For five hundred years,
Without much protection,
Was he lying down,
    Before he obtained a soul.

3.

He (Panton) made another
In the garden of Paradise,
From his left side,
    The bright Eva.

4.

Seven hours they were
Taking care of the garden
Before discord was brought by Satan,
    Ruler of Tartara.

5.

Driven out from thence
Through cold and chill,
To obtain their food
    In this world here.

6.

To bring forth children,
Sons and daughters,
To take possession
    Of the land of Asia.

7.

Twice five, ten, and eight,
She was bearing
A mixed burden,
    Male and female.

8.

And once without concealment,
When she brought forth Abel,
And Cain the solitary
    Homicide.

9.

To Adam and his mate
Was given a delving spade,
For breaking the earth
    To obtain bread.

10.

And shining wheat
To sow in ploughed land,
For feeding all men
    Until the great feast.

11.

An angelic messenger
From God the Great Father
Brought seeds for growing
    To Eva.

12.

But she set apart
The tenth part of the gift
Until she should have completed
    Grinding the whole.

13.

Instead of sowing it
She concealed it,
Says Daniel the Prophet
    In the prophecy.

14.

Black rye was obtained
Instead of wheat,
Discovering the treachery
    Of the she-robber.

15.

From hence the reason,
Through fear of the judgment day,
It is necessary to gives tithes
    Appointed by God.

16.

Of the dark red wine
Which was planted on Sunday,
On the night of the increase
    Or waning of the moon.

17.

Of the wheat and the red wine
It is the blessed privilege
To make the skilfully constructed body
    Of Christ the son of Alpha.

18.

The wafer is his flesh,
And the wine is his blood,
And the words of the Trinity
    Consecrate them.

19.

The secret books
From the two hands of Emanuel,
The angel brought
    And gave them to Adam.

20.

When he was in the river,
Up to his cheeks
In the waters of Jordan,
    Fasting,

21.

Twelve youths,
Four of them angelic,
Sent forth branches
    From the flower Eva,

22.

To give assistance
In all kinds of trouble,
When there should be oppression
    In their wanderings.

23.

Very great anxiety
Was there to mankind,
Before they obtained the tokens
 Of mercy.

24.

Moses obtained
In great necessity
The three rods
 Of Dominica.

25.

Solomon obtained
In the tower of Babylon,
All the secrets,
 Area fœdera.

26.

Very much I myself have obtained
In my Bardic books,
All the secrets
 Of the land of Europe.

27.

I know their arts,
Their fortunes, and their destiny,
Their going and their coming,
 Unto the end.

28.

O God! very wretched
It is to forebode
Great lamentation
 To the line of Troy.

29.

The chain-wearing serpent,
The unpitying hawk,
With winged weapons,
 From Germany.

30.

She shall subdue
All Loegria and Britain
From the shore of the sea of Llychlyn
 To the Severn.

31.

Then shall Britons be
As prisoners;
In power shall be foreigners
 From Saxony.

32.

Their Lord they shall praise,
Their language they shall preserve;
Their land they shall lose,
 Except wild Wales.

33.

Until some change shall come
After long penitence,
When shall be made equal
 The pride of both.

34.

Then Britons shall obtain
Their land and crown,
And the foreign people
 Shall vanish away.

35.

These are the words of the angel
Of peace and war;
And they shall come to pass
In Britain.

The bard then proceeds to assert that he is the only genuine "Wizard of the West" in these words:—

From the sun to the earth, from the ocean to the firmament,
There is no skilful instructor except me, Taliesin.

There are other religious poems of the same age and character in the Myvyrian collection—the Song on the Day of Judgment, the Confession of Taliesin, and the following fragment entitled "The Elegy on Madawg the Bold, and Erof or Herod the Cruel." There is no apparent connection between this Madawg and Herod, and it is probable that two fragments have been accidentally joined, owing to their having been composed in the same metre.

MARWNAD MAD DDRUD AG EROF GREULON.

Madawg mur menwyd
Madawg cyn bu bedd
Bu ddinas Edryssedd
O gamp a chymwedd
Mab Uthr cyn lleas
Oi law dy wystlad
Dybu Erof greulawn
Llewenydd anwogawn
Tristydd anwogawn
A oryw Erof greulawn
Brattau Iesu

Ag ef yn credu
Dayar yn crynnu
Ag Elfydd yn gardu
A chyscoc ar byd
A bedydd ar gryd
Llam anwogawn
A goryw Erof greulawn
Myned yn y trefn
Ymmhlith oer gethern
Hyd yngwaelawd Uffern.

ELEGY ON MADAWG THE BOLD AND HEROD THE CRUEL.

Madawg (was) very mirthful;
Before Madawg was in the grave
The city was abounding
In games and festivities.
Before the son of Uther was slain
From his hand was thy pledge.
Cruel was Herod,
Feeble in joy,
Feeble in sorrow;
And the cruel Herod caused
The destruction of Jesus.

And when He was crucified [1]
The earth trembled,
And the world was in darkness, [2]
And there was a quaking of the earth,
And the baptised were trembling.
Feeble was the step
Of Herod the cruel,
When he came in due course
Amid the cold fiends
In the depths of hell.

[1] This seems, from the context, to be a necessary correction—"croesu" for "credu."
[2] Yn arddu.

These religious compositions speak for themselves: their philosophy, cosmogony, and theology, are evidently derived from the scriptures only ; and nothing but a mistaken though deeply rooted belief in the great antiquity of these poems, could have led to the supposition that they contain evidence of another origin, and of that vague and undefined system of mythology imagined to have been current among the tribes of Britain, under the auspices of a Druid priesthood, at some epoch of unknown antiquity.

CHAPTER VI.

OF THE WORSHIP OF HU GADARN, THE SOLAR GOD, AND THE DRUIDISM
OF THE WELSH IN THE TWELFTH, THIRTEENTH, AND FOURTEENTH
CENTURIES.

THE subject of British Druidism would not be complete without some notice of the supposed worship of the Solar God, or deified Patriarch Noah, and of the existence of the Druidical institution in Wales in the fourteenth century of the Christian era.

Towards the end of the fourteenth century, a learned divine and poet, Dr. John Kent, or Sion Kent, wrote the following lines :—

> Two kinds of inspiration (Awen) truly
> There are in the world, and manifest their course :
> An inspiration from Christ of joyful discourse
> Of the right tendency, a sprightly muse.
> There is another inspiration not wisely sung,
> And they make false and filthy predictions.
> This one has been taken by the men of *Hu*,
> Unjustly usurping authority over the poets of Wales;

or, according to Mr. Stephens,

> The usurping bards of Wales.

When we inquire into the meaning of this accusation brought by the priest of Kenchurch against the Welsh Bards in the fourteenth century, we find it to amount to this.

In the Prose Triads, a compilation of various dates, there is a history of a personage called Hu Gadarn, or Hu the Mighty, who is represented as having been the divine leader of the

Cymry in their migration from Taprobane, or the land of Asia,
to Britain.   The circumstances of his legend connect this Hu
Gadarn with the deluge, and it is usual to consider him as a
deified representation of the Patriarch Noah.   According to
Davies, he lived in the age of the Deluge ; by the help of his
oxen he drew the Addanc out of the lake and prevented the
recurrence of that calamity ; he first cultivated the vine, and
taught agriculture.   This history is taken from the Triads,
but not from the poetry of the Welsh.   There is not a single
ballad, not one composition, historical, philosophical, or mythological, among all those attributed to Taliesin and Merlin,
which turns upon the history of this Hu Gadarn, or the marvellous actions attributed to him.[1]   We cannot but conclude
that the legend was entirely unknown to the age which delighted in the recital of the marvels ascribed to Taliesin.   So
excellent a subject for minstrelsy, mythic and religious, such
as we have seen in the compositions above noticed, could not,
if known, have been entirely neglected and passed over, without a single allusion by the bards who sang the history of Taliesin.   In fact, Mr. Stephens has remarked, that the mention
of Hu Gadarn first appears in the Welsh poetry after the death
of Llywelyn ab Gruffyd, the last of the sovereign princes of
Wales, who was slain in 1282.

The only pieces of evidence adduced by Mr. Davies in favour
of the notion that the Solar God Hu was worshipped by the
Welsh in the thirteenth and fourteenth centuries, are from the
writings of Iolo Goch, bard of Owain Glyndower, and from Rhys
Prydydd and Llywelyn Moel.

Iolo Goch simply describes Hu Gadarn in metre, what he is
represented to be in the prose composition.   The following is
Mr. Davies's version of the passage :—

---

[1] We have already shown the supposed occurrence of the name " Hu " in
the Elegy on Aeddon, the Llath Voesen, and the Marwnad Uther Pendragon,
to be a mistake.

Hu Gadarn the sovereign, the ready protector,
The King, giver of wine and renown,
The emperor of the land and the seas,
And the life of all that are in the world.
After the deluge he held the strong-beamed plough ;
This did our Lord of stimulating genius,
That he might show to the proud man and to the humbly wise,
The art most approved by the faithful Father ;
Nor is this sentiment false.

We quite agree with Mr. Davies that these lines are intended as a picture of the character and deeds of the Patriarch Noah, as represented in the Triads under the name of Hu Gadarn ; but no one could infer from them, standing alone, that Iolo Goch and his patron Owain Glyndower performed orgies in honour of the Solar God, or sang hymns about Pryd, before entering into their arrangements with Mortimer and Hotspur for the invasion of England. If so, they must have been the most inconsistent of idolaters, since, in "Iolo Goch's Address to Glyndower," with a description of the mansion and grounds of the latter, we find, among other objects of admiration, "a quadrangular church well built, well whitewashed, and chapels well glazed."

The next extract is from Rhys Brydydd, which Davies says furnishes "a glaring proof" of the worship of the Heathen God ; and certainly, if we did not know that Rhys Brydydd lived in Glamorganshire in the latter part of the fifteenth century, and had a son, a monk in the monastery of Margam, we might be induced to see some token of an unknown heresy in these lines :—

> Bychanav o'r bychenid
> Yw Hu Gadarn vel barn byd
> Ai mwyav a nav i ni
> Da coeliwn a'n Dduw celi
> Ysgawn ei daith ac esgud
> Mymryn tes gloewyn ei glud
> A mawr ar dir a moroedd
> A mwyav a gav ar goedd
> Mwy no'r bydoedd.

Thus translated by Archdeacon Williams :—

> The smallest of the small
> Is Hu Gadarn, as the world judges,
> And the greatest and a Lord to us,
> Let us well believe, and our mysterious God.
> An atom of glowing heat is his car,
> Light his course and active ;
> Great on land and on the seas,
> The greatest that I manifestly can have,
> Greater than the worlds.

To which must be added two lines from Mr. Davies :—

> Let us beware of offering mean indignity to him, the great and bountiful.

Unfortunately these poems are not comprised in the My-vyrian collection, but exist in manuscript only ; we cannot therefore see by the context the real significance of the passage ; but it is evident that the whole force of the passage lies in the two lines,

> Ai mwyav a nav i ni
> Da coeliwn a'n Dduw celi.

The writers who have discovered these mysteries all trans-late "Duw celi," and "Christ celi," by mysterious or concealed God, the concealed Christ. According to Mr. Herbert, the Christ celi, is the Sun, Mithras, and Elphin himself, in the higher Bardism. Dr. Owen translated the two lines from the Pseudo-Taliesin,

> Ni bu oleuad
> Cyn Celi cread :—
> There has been no illumination
> Before the Mysterious One's creation ;

but the application of common sense undisturbed by mysteries, shows the real translation to be,

> There was no light
> Before the creation of the heavens ;

and renders quite plain that " Duw Celi," and " Christ Celi," are respectively God of Heaven, and Christ of Heaven, and that the word "celi" is the Latin *cœli,* and not in any way connected with "celu," to conceal. The proofs of this statement are sufficiently abundant.

In the Black Book of Caermarthen there is an "Awdyl," commencing

> Arduireaue tri trined in celi.
>
> Yssi un a thri, uned un ynni.
>
> I will extol the three, the Trinity in heaven.
> It is one and three, one God to us.

We have seen in the whole of the poems above translated, that the minstrels were plain, pious, and some of them very ignorant Christians, who believed in nothing worse than magic and witchcraft; and this example from the oldest Welsh MS. known, is sufficient to demonstrate that no hidden or mystical meaning lurks in the word "celi," which in these poems must be translated "heaven" in the ordinary sense of the word. The same false interpretation of this phrase, occurring repeatedly in the works of the bards of the thirteenth and fourteenth centuries, has given rise to the greater part of these misconceptions, which vanish upon referring to the original poems, and considering the passages cited, in connection with the context. This will be rendered quite evident from two passages among many others in which the phrase in question occurs.

What other meaning than "Christ, of" or "in heaven," can the phrase "Christ celi" have, or what mystery or heathenism can possibly lurk, in these lines of Llywarch Brydydd y Moch, addressed to Llywelyn ab Iorwerth in the thirteenth century?

> Crist creawdyr llywyawdr llu daear
>
> A nef, am notwy rac auar
> Crist celi bwyf celvyt a gwar
> Cyn dywet gyuygwet gyuar
> Crist mab meir am peir om pedwar defnyt
>
> Dofyn awen diarchar
> Crist uab duw dym ryt ar llauar
> Y voli vy ri rwysc o dyar,
> Llywelyn llyw prydain ac phar.

Christ, Creator, Governor of the hosts of heaven and earth,
My protection from all evil,
Christ in Heaven, may I be wise and discreet,
Before I am consigned to the narrow place in earth.
Christ, son of Mary, who has created me out of four elements,
A profound and fearless muse.
Christ, Son of God, give me in abundance,
To praise my king, the ruler of the land,
Llywelyn, the chief of Britain, and her spear.

Or, in these lines of Einiawn fab Gwgawn, addressed to the same prince :—

Cyvarch om naf om neuawl Arglwyt
Crist celi culwyt cwl y ditawl
Celvyt leveryt o le gwetawl
Celvytodeu meu ny vo marwawl
Y brovi pob peth o bregeth bawl,
Y voli vy ri rwyf angertawl.
Ryvel diochel diochwyth hawl
Llywelyn heilyn hwylveirt wadawl.

I request of my Creator, my heavenly Lord,
Christ of heaven, love-prospering, ever free from sin,
A skilful utterance from the depository of knowledge,
That my poetic art may not be without animation.
Attempting all things, as Saint Paul preaches,[1]
In the praise of my king the ardent leader,
No avoider of battle, not unskilful in prosecuting his claim,
Llywelyn, the bounteous provider of bardic festivals.

This last example ought to be sufficient to explode the idea of any reference to a mysterious or concealed Christ known only to the Bards, in these poems. The reference to the preaching of Saint Paul, is quite decisive, even if the time in which these poems were written, the known condition of society, the persons who wrote and the persons to whom these poems were addressed, did not sufficiently assure us that there was no mysterious heathenism publicly proclaimed in Wales in the fourteenth century.

---

[1] Probably referring to the Epistle to the Romans, xii. 11, " Not slothful in business ; fervent in spirit ; serving the Lord."

The two lines above cited from Rhys Brydydd, must therefore read,

> He is the greatest, and a Lord to us ;
> We truly believe, and our God in heaven.

It is impossible to decide satisfactorily on the intention of Rhys Brydydd in this passage, without obtaining the sense of the entire poem ; but the third extract cited in support of the paganism in these allusions, throws some light on the mystery. It is from a composition by Llywelyn Moel, a bard who lived in the fifteenth century, and was probably a contemporary of Rhys Brydydd.   The passage as given by Mr. Davies is :—

> Ychain yn o chynhenid [1]
> Hu Gadarn a darn o'i did
> A'i bum angel, a welwch
> A pheirian eur flamdan flwch.

> The oxen who are groaning
> Of Hu Gadarn, and a part of his chain
> And his five angels, which you see,
> And golden harness with flames of fire flying about.

The allusions here are all capable of easy explanation by reference to the story in the Triads, but the five angels are an addition for purposes of effect.   The words *a welwch*, " which you see," explain that this is a part of, or alludes to, a miracle play, or dramatic performance called by the Welsh writers " Hud a Lleddrith," in which the famous leader of the Cymry, and the adventure of drawing the Addanc out of the lake by aid of the two horned oxen and the chain, as related in the Triads, were represented.   We can perceive also that the line in Rhys Brydydd which describes the chariot of Hu Gadarn as composed of particles of glowing heat, refers to the representation of his chariot and harness as covered with flames.

Mr. Davies and Archdeacon Williams discreetly abstain from offering any interpretation of the mystery of the five angels by whom Hu Gadarn was accompanied, as angels do not appear

---

[1] This is evidently a clerical error for " ochenaidiad."

40

to have formed any part of the Druidical Pantheon.   No other reasonable interpretation can be put on the words of Llywelyn Moel, than that he is referring to a miracle play.   Mr. Stephens has already shown it to be very probable that several of the dialogues attributed to Merddin and Taliesin were intended for recital in a dramatic form, and that there were a great number of miracle plays in vogue among the Welsh of the middle ages.

Several of these dialogues have been preserved : one between Taliesin and Myrddin, another between Arthur and Gwenhwyvar ; between Myrddin and his sister Gwendydd ; between Gwyddno Garanhir and Gwyn mab Nudd, between Trystan and Gwalchmai, &c.   We have one of these pieces extant in the Cornish dialect, the performers in which represented Adam, Eve, the Serpent, Death, Lucifer and the other devils, Noah and his sons, Shem, Ham, and Japhet, and the Heavenly Father ;[1] and no doubt there are many such extant in the Welsh language among the unpublished Welsh MSS.

Although, therefore, we cannot clearly comprehend the meaning of Rhys Brydydd in the lines above cited, we may be quite sure that there is no great mystery in it, and that Hu Gadarn, though a popular character in the revived traditions of the thirteenth and fourteenth centuries, was not worshipped as a god in the reign of Henry VI.

That there was some political secret attached to the party whom Sion Kent calls " the men of Hu," is very probable, from his assertion that they made lying and vile prophecies.   It is well known that this practice of making prophecies to which the name and authority of Taliesin and Merlin were attributed, was common with the Welsh Bards in the native or anti-English interest through nearly the whole of the fourteenth and fifteenth centuries, particularly in support of Owain Glyndwr,

---

[1] The MS. is in the British Museum, and is entitled " The Creation of the World, being a Cornish Play or Opera, written by W. Jordan, August 12, 1611."   See *Cambro-Briton*, vol. iii. p. 237.   It has since been printed by Davies Gilbert.   Another is noticed by Lhuyd in the *Archæol. Brit.*

and afterwards in the cause of Henry VII.   Davydd Llwyd
ab Llewellyn ab Gruffyd, Lord of Mathafarn in Denbighshire,
was the author of many of these predictions, intended to support the claims of Henry VII.   He wrote about the year
1450, and was therefore very nearly contemporary with Rhys
Brydydd and Dr. Sion Kent.[1]   One of these predictive pieces,
the author of which is unknown, called "The Confession of
Taliesin," prophesies the return of Owain (Glyndwr) in the
year 1530, for the destruction of the German race.[2]

It is scarcely necessary to reason on the absurdity of supposing Druids and Druidism to have maintained themselves
in Wales in the twelfth and thirteenth centuries, since there
is no evidence of the existence of any such institution or its
professors in the sixth or seventh century.

We find however that the terms "Derwydd," "Derwyddon,"
and "Derwyddoniaeth," though unknown to the romances, and
but very sparingly employed in the romantic ballads, which we
have examined, came into use among Christian bards residing
at the courts of Christian princes in the twelfth and thirteenth
centuries.

Mr. Stephens is of opinion that the chief Bards of this
epoch were desirous of forming some exclusive distinction for
themselves, and the traditional veneration of Druidism was
suited to their purpose; that they seized upon this, breathed
new life into the old belief, and threw a halo of mystery round
their own persons.   But of this old belief there is no evidence
whatever.   There is nothing between Tacitus in the first and
Cynddelw in the twelfth century.   The latter says, in address-
ing Owain Gwynedd,

> Beirnaid am regyd beird am regor
> Ath folant feirdion Derwydon dor
> O bedeiriaith dyfyn o bedeir or;

for which Mr. Sephens adopts Davies's version :—

---

[1] Jones's *Welsh Bards*, p. 45.   [2] *Ibid.* p. 35.

> Bards are constituted judges of excellence.
> Bards praise thee, even Druids of the circle
> Of four dialects, from four regions.

What the four dialects were, we know from the *Hanes Taliesin*, which states the Bards to have been learned in four languages—Latin, French, Welsh, and English—in all which languages they were to be ready to answer questions addressed to them.   But "dor" does not mean a *circle*, but a *door*, a *fence*, or *protection;* and by the phrase "Druids of the circle," Mr. Davies has inserted a meaning which does not belong to the original, and which involves an air of mystery and a reference to the famous "cors" and stone circles.   What the poet says to his chieftain is,

> Bards praise thee, the guardian of the wise ones
> Of four languages.

Another extract, in which the same epithet occurs, has been misunderstood by Mr. Stephens. It is from a poem in stanzas addressed by Cynddelw to Madawg ab Maredudd :—

> Nis gwyr namyn duw a dewinion byd
> A diwyd Derwydon
> O eurdorf eurdorchogion
> Ein rif yn riweirth afon;

for which also Mr. Stephens has given Davies's translation :—

> Excepting God and the diviners of the land,
> And sedulous Druids
> Of the splendid race, wearers of gold rings, there is none who know
> Our numbers in the billows of the stream.

Cynddelw is here made to refer to the number of the Druids; but on turning to the original we find that this is one of eighteen stanzas, and that the five preceding refer to the numerous retinue of Madawg ab Maredudd.   The one immediately preceding is :—

> Ym maes mathrafal mathredig tyweirch
> Gan draed meirch mawrydig
> Ar dadl cynadl ced fudig
> Arwyd iawn wladlwyd wledig.

In the field of Mathrafal the sod is trampled
With the feet of splendid horses ;
To those who converse with him he is bounteous of gifts,
The true token of a patriotic prince.

The number spoken of in the succeeding stanza evidently refers to the retinue, and not to the Druids of Madawg :—

It is not known, except to God and the diviners of the world,
And the sedulous sages
Of the golden troop, wearers of gold chains,
Our number, which is as the billows of the river :

where the epithets "eurdorf," "eurdorchogion," clearly apply to the warriors, and not to Druids or diviners.

When, therefore, we meet with the word "Derwyddon" in the poems of the known Bards of the twelfth, thirteenth, and fourteenth centuries, addressed to known individuals, we must give them credit for having meant by the expression, not Druids in the sense of Julius Cæsar and Pliny, but simply philosophers or sages, or perhaps even conjurers, persons supposed to be endowed with supernatural powers or wisdom, like Dr. Dee or Sir Michael Scott.

In fact, the moment the passages cited to prove the Druidism of the thirteenth century, are examined with the context, and with the individual history of the persons involved, the mystery at once disappears.

Thus, in a poem addressed by Cynddelw, a celebrated Bard, to Owen Cyveiliawg, Prince of Powys, in the twelfth century, Mr. Davies gives the following extract as one in which "the Bard presents us with a curious glimpse of the mystic dance of the Druids" :—

Drud awyrdwyth amnwyth amniver
Drudyon a veirtyon
A vawl neb dragon,

which he translates thus :—

"Rapidly moving in the course of the sky, in circles, in uneven numbers, Druids and Bards unite in celebrating the leader."

This passage is one of those cited by Mr. Davis as abundantly proving, " not only that there were avowed professors of Druidism in North Wales and Powys during the twelfth century, and that they regarded the same mystical lore which is ascribed to Taliesin as the standard of their system, but also that their profession was tolerated, and even patronized, by the princes of those districts."   Fortunately for common sense, and for the reputation of Giraldus Cambrensis, who represents Owain Cyveiliawe as a prince distinguished for justice, wisdom, and princely moderation, " a man of fluent speech, conspicuous for the good management of his territories," this example of the prince's toleration of Druidism is altogether misunderstood and mistranslated by Davies, who has omitted the concluding line of the passage,

Namwyn dreic ae dirper,

without which the others have no connected meaning.   The meaning of the lines runs thus :—

Courageous his disposition, his pleasantries without number,
Warriors and Bards
Praise no chief
But chiefs worthy of it.

There is here no mention of Druids[1] at all ; and the example is a very fair one of the system of extracting so much only of these passages as appears to suit a particular purpose, and then forcing them into the desired meaning by a false construction.

It would be an endless task to present all the passages which Davies and others have mistakenly exhibited as proofs of the Druidical character of these writings.   It is not without reason that Mr. Stephens protests against the system adopted by these writers, of allowing no play for the imagination of the Welsh poets, and assuming every word to be true to actual phenomena.

---

[1] The word is *Drudyon*, " courageous ones, strong ones," not *Derwyddon*, " Druids."   This word *drud* occurs no less than twelve times in the fifteen consecutive lines, of which those above cited form a part, and always with the same signification.

An amusing instance of this mode of dealing with poetic imagery occurs in Mr. Davies's translation of another passage from the same poem of Cynddelw, in which the bard extols his hero in a number of ingenious similes :—

> Yn rith rynn ysgwyd
> Rac ysgwnn blymnhywd
> Ar ysgwyt yn arwein
> Yn rith llew rac llyw goradein
> Yn rith llauyn anwar llachar llein
> Yn rith cletyf claer clod ysgein yn aer
> Yn aroloct kyngrein
> Yn rith dreic rac dragon prydein
> Yn rith bleit blaengor vu ywein.

Mr. Davies's translation of these lines is as follows :—

" In the form of a vibrating shield, before the rising tumult, borne aloft on the shoulder of the leader—in the form of a lion, before the chief with the mighty wings—in the form of a terrible spear, with a glittering blade—in the form of a bright sword, spreading fame in the conflict, and overwhelming the levelled ranks—in the form of a dragon, before the sovereign of Britain, and in the form of a daring wolf, has Owen appeared."

" Here," says Mr. Davies, " we find the Bard imitating the Druidical lore, or the mystical strains of Taliesin, and representing his hero as having made no contemptible progress in the circle of transmigration."

It would scarcely be necessary, considering the poet, the personage referred to, and the date of the composition, to refute so palpable an absurdity, were it not that even at the present day the same strange misconception of the meaning of these works of the Welsh Bards prevails. Not only do we recognize clearly in these images the mere sport of poetic fancy, but there are two circumstances which should have opened the eyes even of Mr. Davies himself to the true nature of the passage. Owain Cyveiliawe fought against Henry II., and that monarch is the " Dragon Prydein," " Sovereign of Britain," mentioned in the above lines. Even Mr. Davies would hardly contend that the Welsh prince had arrived at that point in the circle of transmigration, so as to have really appeared as a *bonâ fide* dragon before Henry II. Any doubts which might have been felt on the subject would, however, have been dissipated by a perusal of the rest of the poem. A few lines above, the Bard speaks of his patron as,

> Gelyn traws ryvel tros ruvein yd wys
> Tros y llys yn llundein.

> A foe fierce in battle against the men of Rome,
> Against the palace in London.

This alludes to the circumstance of Owain Cyveiliawe's dispute with Baldwin Archbishop of Canterbury, by whom, when preaching the Crusade in Wales, he was summoned to attend a meeting of the princes and clergy, which he refused, the jurisdiction of the see of Canterbury over the Welsh bishoprics having always been a disputed question. The plunge from such a subject into the depths of the circle of transmigration, in the space of four lines, is somewhat too sudden for the most credulous believer in the Druidism of the twelfth century.

Mr. Davies and the Archdeacon of Cardigan might have recollected that Giraldus Cambrensis was a contemporary of Owain Cyveiliawe. He was Archdeacon of Brecon, and in 1176, elected Bishop of Saint David's, through not confirmed in the see. He was legate in Wales of the Archbishop of Canterbury, and very zealous and active in the reformation of abuses in the church. Can it be for a moment supposed that such a man should have been ignorant of the existence of openly avowed Druidic superstitions and Hu-worship in Wales in his time, or that, being aware of it, he should have left it unnoticed either by action, or in his *Itinerary?*

CHAPTER VII.

WE have now given translations of more than fifty out of the seventy-seven pieces attributed to Taliesin. The remaining pieces would furnish no additional information necessary for deciding on the character and age of these compositions. Two of them, the " Gorchan Cynvelyn " and the " Gorchan Maelderw," belong to the Gododin series; the " Mab Gyfreu," " Buarth Beirdd," " Addfwyneu Taliesin," " Glaswawd Taliesin," and " Cyffes Taliesin," are of precisely the same character as those above given. The predictive pieces which carry their own date on the surface, are of no importance to the present inquiry; and the Dialogues, the Arthurian pieces, and the " Graves of the Warriors," though of great interest, belong more to the discussion of the historical questions connected with the Prose Triads. Enough has been said on the fallacy of the Druidic theories, so long connected with these compositions; it only remains to add a word upon their dates and the sources whence their materials have been derived.

It seems reasonable to admit, that some of the songs in praise of Urien were originally composed by a veritable Taliesin, a bard of the sixth century, and have been rewritten in the twelfth or thirteenth century, though the piece entitled "Anrec Urien" shows us that not only the name of Taliesin, but that of the great Cumbrian chief, was borrowed by the bards of a later period. The great difficulty in recognizing the sixth century as the epoch of any one of these pieces, lies in the fact, that the language and orthography belong to the twelfth century at the earliest, and that it is impossible to say how

41

much belongs to the bard who composed or to the clerk who transcribed the song.

Of the remaining poems which we have translated, none can be shown to be older than the twelfth century. All of them that are not religious, or merely encomiastic, appear to belong to what may be called the series of the *Hanes Taliesin*. Perhaps it is to the great name of this bard that we owe their preservation; for it seems impossible that this should have been the only romance in the Welsh language which had been reduced to that form of mixed prose and metrical recitation which adapted it to the use of the professional singers. Yet though, as we have seen, allusions and references to the other romances are sufficiently frequent, there is not one ballad or composition which has been framed upon either of them in the manner of those connected with the history of Taliesin.

For the most remarkable result of this examination of the earliest literature of the Welsh people, whatever date may be assigned to it, is, that in these, the oldest preserved specimens of Welsh poetry, there is, with the exception of those songs above mentioned which occur in the history of Taliesin, a total absence of anything like a tale, or the recital of an adventure, or even a love story. There is not, as far as I am aware, one single poem or ballad founded upon an incident or adventure, or which can be said to have a hero or heroine, if we except those descriptive of the actual combats, or written in praise of the heroic actions of historical persons. Allusions to the tales which are found in the Mabinogion collection, and to others either lost or known from fragmentary notices only, are, as we have shown, very numerous; but that we should possess a collection of more than a hundred songs without a single story of love or adventure, is very remarkable.

It is quite an unparalleled phenomenon in the history of literature and of man, to find a nation, of restless, warlike, and adventurous habits, of quick imagination and lively fancy, actually overrun with bards, minstrels, singers, and musicians, who, nevertheless, have not handed down one single love-song, or one tale of adventure, one ballad relating the exploits of some fabulous hero, supreme in love as well as in war. All this has been done in prose, but not in poetry. Some of the pieces attributed to Llywarch Hen approach more nearly to the ballad form, but are no real exception to this general statement. The compositions which chiefly have the air of a ballad are, the "Song of the Horses," which is spirited and lively, but treats of horses only; the "Preiddeu Annwn," which alludes to some adventures of Arthur; and the "Mic Dinbych."

The history of Arthur and his Knights of the Round Table, was, as we see from the *Mabinogion*, a subject which occupied the attention of the Storiawr, and furnished them with abundant materials in the twelfth and thirteenth centuries; yet not one of these adventures, so full of incident and marvel, has been made the subject of a song.

The long poem of Aneurin on the battle of Cattraeth is unrelieved by a single episode or incident in which the love of woman plays any part. The only woman supposed to be mentioned in the poem, according to Mr. Williams ab Ithel's translation, was herself engaged in the combat, "fought, slaughtered, and burned," and was ultimately slain. But this absence of the romantic element in these productions is not confined to the works of the Cynveirdd or supposed earliest bards, but also exists in those of the Gogynveirdd, or later bards, whose names and authorship of the productions assigned to them are sufficiently ascertained. Neither Meilyr, Gwalchmai, Cynddelw, the princely bard Owain Cyveilliawg, Llywarch ab Llywelyn, or any one bard of the eleventh, twelfth, and following centuries, appears to have been capable of producing a work of pure fiction. Their subjects are all religious, or elegies on the deaths of the chieftains with whom they were connected, or descriptive pieces, not without considerable merit, with a few odes or sonnets in which love supplies the theme. Their compositions, however, show that they were not wanting in genius or imagination, or the necessary poetic skill; while their frequent allusions to Taliesin, Arthur, and the personages of the romances, show that they had read and appreciated their native literature of fiction. We ought therefore, perhaps, to conclude, that the fault lies not so much with the Welsh minstrels as with the collectors or transcribers of the Welsh ballads in the twelfth and thirteenth centuries. We can, of course, speak only from the published compositions in the collection of the *Myvyrian Archæology;* and it may be that in the many thousand Welsh MSS. still in existence, other romances, both prose and ballad, may yet exist. If we are to judge by what has hitherto been printed, we must assert that, unless the *Gododin* is such, there is not, besides the *Hanes Taliesin*, which itself does not fully satisfy the required conditions, a single metrical tale extant in the Welsh or Old British language.

If this be so, the question naturally arises, who were the authors of the romances contained in the *Mabinogion?* If the Welsh Bards, then we have the curious paradox, of a nation of poets and musicians, executing all their works of imagination in prose, and that prose abounding in poetic imagery, and displaying a most exuberant fancy. Without entering on a discussion which could not be satisfactorily pursued unless the whole circle of Welsh romance were carefully examined, we may observe that the materials of these tales are not peculiar to the Welsh. That part of the story of Taliesin, which relates to the gift of prophecy and inspiration in consequence of the accidental tasting by Gwion of the magic liquor intended for another, has its counterpart in both the Irish and the Scandinavian romances. In the first, the hero of the tale is Fionn, or Fingal; in the other, the famous Sigurd of the Eddaic legends.

In the Welsh tale, Gwion, who was afterwards Taliesin, was left, it will be remembered, in charge of the Cauldron of Ceridwen. Three drops of the charmed liquor flew out of the cauldron, and fell upon the finger of Gwion. "And by reason of their great heat, he put his finger to his mouth, and the instant he put those marvel-working drops into his mouth, he foresaw everything that was to come, and perceived that his chief care was to guard against the wiles of Ceridwen. And in very great fear, he fled towards his own land." The Irish story runs thus :—Fionn,[1] being on the banks of the river Boyne, met with some fishermen who had been sent by his enemies to endeavour to take the "Salmon of Foreknowledge." The fishermen took a salmon of great size and beauty, which they placed at the fire to broil, leaving it in charge of Fionn, who was to take care that it did not burn, on pain of losing his head. During the process of cooking, a spark flew from the fire, which raised a blister on the fish. Fionn applied his thumb to the scorched part, in order to force down the blister, but the heat burning his thumb, he thrust it into his mouth to relieve the pain. No sooner had he done so, than he became gifted with prophecy and foreknowledge ; for this was the Salmon of Foreknowledge which he had been cooking ; and he at once acquired the knowledge that the King of Tara, seven years before, had expressly sent these fishermen in quest of the Salmon of Foreknowledge, in order that he might ascertain where he, Fionn, had taken refuge, so that he might seize and slay him.[2]

We have the same story, with different details, in the Scandinavian Saga of Sigurd, who, having slain the dragon Fafnir, is employed by Regin, to superintend the roasting of Fafnir's heart, which Regin, aware of its virtues, intended to eat. Sigurd having accidentally touched the heart, and then placed his finger in his mouth, becomes instantly gifted with a knowledge of the language of birds, and by their advice slays Regin, and himself eats the heart of the monster Fafnir.

Of these three forms of the same tale, the Welsh, as we have it in the *Hanes Taliesin*, is certainly the least ancient. Whether Thomas the Priest modernized a more ancient form, or adapted

---

[1] It is worthy of remark that Fionn and Gwion are the same word, according to the constant interchange of *gw* for *f* in the two dialects of the Celtic.

[2] See the "Feis Tighe Conan Ceann Shleibhe," in *Trans. of Ossianic Society*, 1854.

an Irish tale, it would be difficult to say; but the details of the story in the *Hanes Taliesin* are all modern, and all Christian. The time of the story is laid "in the beginning of Arthur's time, and of the Round Table." Gwion Bach, who afterwards becomes Taliesin, is stated to have been a man of Llanfair, *i.e.* the Church of the Virgin Mary in Caereinion in Powys; and the magical liquor consists of "three blessed drops of the Grace of the Spirit," that is, the Holy Ghost, as we see in the definition of the "Awen," by Llywelyn Sion in the "Cyfrinach y Beirdd."

The Irish stories which abound with magic and marvels, have come down from a time when the influence of Christianity was less strongly felt; and, though many have been corrupted and mixed up with Christian legends, it is to a much less extent than the Welsh. The Irish stories, moreover, contain the explanation of the fragmentary notices and allusions in the Welsh tales and ballads. In the story of " Pyll, Prince of Dyved," no account is given of the mode in which the child of Rhiannon was abstracted, nor of the cause of his being found by Teirnyon Twryv Vliant, when the latter struck off the arm of the demon who was seizing the new-born colt. But in the tale of Fionn, we find that a Fomorach used to come and carry off the newly born infant of Fergus Fionnliath, seven years in succession; and on the seventh year his arm was bitten off by an enchanted hound. The monster described in a fragment in the *Cad Goddeu*[1] was, no doubt, what the Irish legends call a Piast, and the description of the one slain by Fionn in Loch Cuan, resembles that given by the Welsh Bard in the *Cad Goddeu*.[2]

Manawydan vab Llyr, in the Welsh romance, is the brother of Bran the Blessed, whom he accompanied in the unfortunate expedition to Ireland, and cousin of Caswallawn, the Cassibelaunus of Cæsar. Under the name of Manannan mac Lir, he is well known in the Irish romance. When the three sons

[1] Translated, page 228.
[2] See the "Song of the Chase of Sliabh Truim," *Transaction of the Ossianic Society*, vol. ii. 1854.

of Uisneach are decapitated, it is by the sword of Naisi, "the sword which Manannan mac Lir gave me," and the "Crann Buidhe, or Yellow Spear of Diarmuidh O'Duibhne," was the gift of the same enchanter. In the story of Cormac Son of Art and the Fairy Branch, the same personage appears as a necromancer of power, and indeed is represented in the Irish legends as chief of the Tuatha De Danann, or Fairy race of Ireland. Four of the children of Llyr, of whom we hear nothing in the Welsh romance, were changed into swans by the incantations of their stepmother, and their adventures compose one of the three "Sorrows of Story." A whole passage of imagery, in which the contrast of colour formed by a raven drinking blood upon the snow is described, and which, in the tale of the Sons of Uisneach, is in natural connection with the rest of the story, has been borrowed and interpolated in the Welsh tale of Peredur mab Evrawc. These examples, which might be considerably multiplied, and numerous instances in which obscure or unintelligible allusions, as well in the prose tales of the *Mabinogion* as in the Myvyrian poems, receive elucidation on a perusal of the Irish legends, lead to the conclusion that the origin of the Welsh romances has not yet been sufficiently investigated. We speak here only of those romances which do not treat of the exploits and adventures of Arthur, for it is evident that the genuine Welsh traditions knew no more of Arthur than they did of the Druids. When Professor Schulz says,[1] that in the ancient poems of Aneurin, Taliesin, Llywarch Hen, Merddin, &c., we have "a direct reflection of the person of Arthur and his companions in the wars against the Saxons," he makes it evident he had never read these ancient poems; for it is by no means clear that the Welsh had ever heard of Arthur as a king before Rhys ab Tewdwr brought the Roll of the Round Table to Glamorganshire in the twelfth century. Moreover,

---

[1] "An Essay on the Influence of Welsh Tradition upon the Literature of Germany, France, and Scandinavia," which obtained the prize of eighty guineas at the Abergavenny Cymreigyddion Society in 1840.

there is not, except in the spurious verse[1] added to the stanzas on the Battle of Longborth, a single poem extant which relates any warlike feats of Arthur against the Saxons.

We need feel no surprise at finding in the Irish legends, if not the source, at least the counterparts, of the Welsh tales of sorcery and adventure, since the most celebrated necromancers of Welsh story, Math ab Mathonwy, Gwydion ab Don, and

[1] Yn Llongborth llas i Arthur
      Gwyr dewr cymmynynt a dur
      Ammherawdyr llywiawdyr llavur.

I call this verse spurious, because all the stanzas in the composition except this and the preceding one have the same form, "Yn Llongborth gwelais;" and in the Paul Panton MS. this stanza also commences in that form.   It has, therefore, undergone some alteration.   The Llongborth stanzas properly conclude with the preceding one, describing the death of Geraint, the subject of the poem; and Arthur's name is introduced without any reasonable connection with the rest of the piece.   If the stanza were genuine, there can be little doubt that it stood originally either,

                Yn Llongborth gwelais Arthur,

or   Yn Llongborth y llas Arthur;

which last would be contrary to every other tradition on the subject.   The construction, "slain to Arthur," is forced and unnatural.   Lastly, it is very improbable that the title of Emperor, "Ammherawdyr," was given to Arthur before the introduction of the Arthurian romances in the twelfth century. The most famous British princes receive the title of "Gwledig," not "Ammherawdyr," and no such title is given to Arthur by Nennius.   It is given to Arthur in the tale of the "Countess of the Fountain," though Lady Charlotte Guest has translated it "king" in that instance, and "emperor" where it occurs in the "Dream of Maxen Wledic."   If the reputation of Arthur had risen to such a height in the sixth century, it is incredible that the Welsh bards of this and the following three centuries should have left no other notices of him; and that Gildas and Bede should both have ignored his existence.   It must always be recollected that at least 500 years intervene between the supposed date of the compositions, and the earliest MS. in which they are found.   The death of Arthur took place in 542.   Llywarch Hen was his contemporary; yet we have a poem attributed to him, composed on the death of Cadwallon son of Conan, who died about 646, or, according to some chronicles, in 676.   The death of Geraint is supposed to have taken place in 530.   It is no doubt, possible, that Llywarch Hen may have written both elegies, though 116 years elapsed between the two events.

Amaethon, were themselves Irish, and were the masters of North Wales and Anglesey before they were dispossessed by the sons of Cunedda Wledig. According to the Welsh legend, Don, King of Lochlyn and Dublin, led the Irish to Gwynedd A.D. 267, where they remained for one hundred and twenty-nine years. Don had a son called Gwydion, King of Mona and Arvon, who first taught literature from books to the Irish of Mona and Ireland; whereupon both these countries became pre-eminently famed for knowledge and saints.[1] The number of romantic stories and legends yet extant in the Irish language is very considerable. "Compositions of this nature," says the learned editor of the Irish historical tale of the "Battle of Magh Rath,"[2] "were constantly recited by the poets before the Irish kings and chieftains at their public fairs and assemblies. The four higher orders of poets, namely, the Ollamh, the Anruth, Cli, and Cano, were obliged to have seven times fifty *chief stories*, and twice fifty *sub-stories*, to repeat for kings and chieftains. The subjects of the chief stories were demolitions, cattle-spoils, courtships, battles, caves, voyages, tragedies, feasts, sieges, adventures, elopements, and plunders. The particular titles of these stories are given in the work called *Dinnsenchus, or History of Remarkable Places.*" As regards the Welsh poetry, however, I am acquainted only with one instance where the minstrel alludes to his acquaintance with Irish adventures not otherwise known from the Welsh romances. It occurs in the Elegy upon Corroi, the son of Daire, of whom nothing is known from Welsh tradition. He was a famous Irish chieftain, head of the Clanna Deagaidh, or forces of South Munster, and is reported to have lived in the first century. The ruins of his castle called Cathair Chonroi, are said still to

---

[1] Iolo MSS. p. 468. 471.

We have here a specimen of the chronology of these legends. In the romances, Gwydion ab Don is contemporary with Pryderi, Pryderi with Caswallon, Caswallon with Julius Cæsar. In the legend we have Don the father of Gwydion with his date gravely affixed at the year A.D. 267.

[2] Edited for the Irish Archæological Society, by Mr. J. O'Donovan. 1842.

42

stand on the mountain Mis, between the bays of Castlemaine and Tralee, in the county of Kerry; it is a huge cyclopean building of dry-stone masonry.[1]

According to the "particular account" of his death given by Keating, "as the genuine records of Ireland particularly mention," Corroi, who was a distinguished magician and possessed the power of transforming his shape at pleasure, was treacherously slain by the celebrated Irish warrior Cuchullin, chief of the champions of the Red Branch.   It is with reference to the slaughter of Corroi by Cuchullin that the Welsh minstrel, in his elegy on the death of the former, says:—

> Tra fu vuddugre bore ddugrawr
> Chwedleu am gwyddir o wir hyd lawr
> Cyfranc Corroy a chocholyn
> Llaws eu terfysg am eu terfyn.

> Through the croaking of the raven in the morning,
> I knew the tale of men stretched upon the ground;
> In the combat of Corroi and Cuchullin,
> Great was their violence around their boundaries.

The Cuchullin here mentioned, can be no other than the famous Irish chieftain of that name.   We have here a poem ascribed to Taliesin in which the bard represents himself as being contemporary with this Irish chieftain of the first century of the Christian era.   If we adopt the reasoning of Mr. Williams ab Ithel upon the authorship of the Elegy on Cunedda, we must believe that this is a composition of the first century of the Christian era.   The subject of this piece has escaped the notice of all who have treated of these poems, or they could hardly have avoided adducing it as an instance of the great antiquity of some of these compositions.

Upon a review of all the sources of information on this subject, there can be no hesitation in asserting that the Druid is a figure altogether unknown to Welsh romance, and that at the time the *Mabinogion* and the Taliesin ballads were com-

[1] *Transactions of the Ossianic Society*, vol. i.

posed, no tradition or popular recollection of the Druids or the Druidical mythology existed in Wales. In the *Mabinogion*, not in the Arthurian romances, but in the tales which have a genuine old Celtic origin, though there is a profusion of magic and sorcery, the word Druid does not once occur. In the Irish tales, on the contrary, the magician under the name of Draoi and Druidh, a magician or Druid, "draioideacht, druidheact," magic, plays a considerable part. But this part is a very different one from that assigned to their Druids by Dr. Owen Pughe and Mr. Edward Williams. The Druids of the latter have been restored, with imaginary embellishments, from the fragmentary notices left by Greek and Roman writers; the Irish Druids are true and undoubted sorcerers and soothsayers. They were by no means men of peace and composers of tumult, but took their place as warriors in the battle, though they generally afforded supernatural assistance to the chieftains under whom they served. The Druids of opposing armies, in the Irish tales, perform counter-feats of magic, the one against the other. In the Irish edition of Nennius, the magicians of Vortigern are called Druids, "draidhe," "druidhe"; in the Latin version, Magi; in the Welsh translation of Geoffrey of Monmouth the term employed is "dewinion," diviners, which is a sufficiently correct rendering of Magi; but in the *Brut Tysilio* we actually have the "daydec Prifard," the twelve chief Bards, the same class with whom Taliesin contended in the court of Maelgwn. If the reputation of Druids for wisdom had been such in Wales in the twelfth and thirteenth centuries, as Mr. Davies and Archdeacon Williams have supposed, we should certainly have found some mention of them either in the history, the romance, or the popular literature of the age. But beyond a very few instances in the Taliesin ballads, where the word "derwyddon" occurs in the sense of "sages," "philosophers," or even "Magi," without any necessary connection with Druids, we hear nothing of them. The "syweddyd," or astrologer, is a far more important personage.

It is generally assumed that this word Derwydd is connected with " dar " and " derw," an oak. Archdeacon Williams supposes also the word " darogan," to prophesy, to have the same derivation. In the latter word, however, " dar" is merely an intensive prefix of very common employment, and so Dr. Owen esteems it in this word. We have a much more probable derivation for " derwydd," in the word " der," " dera," a fiend, an evil spirit, a devil, from whence " derwydd" would mean a person having a familiar spirit, a conjurer, or magician. But in the story of Lludd and Llevelys, the only one of the *Mabinogion* in which a magician or evil spirit, other than a witch, is expressly introduced, he is called " gwr lleturithawc," " a man capable of enlarging or changing his form," a paraphrase which seems to indicate the absence of a single word for expressing the idea of necromancer or magician.

In the Welsh version of the Bible, the word employed for the magicians of Pharaoh is " swynwyr," a charmer, or enchanter : " Ar swynwyr a wnaethant felly, trwy eu swynion,"[1] " and the magicians did so with their enchantments." This word, which is of precisely the same form and meaning as " medicine-man" of the Americans, we also find in these ballads.

We have also "gwybion," seers, and "gwidon," " gwiddan," a hag or witch, probably from the root " gwid" or " chwid," " a quick turn or revolution," or, as Dr. Owen thinks, from " gwidd," dry, withered, " a hag."

Whoever may have been the authors of the documents from which Geoffrey of Monmouth drew up his British History (and it is clear that they were derived from British sources, even if through a Bretonic channel), they knew nothing, at least have related nothing, of the Druids or Druidic worship in Britain. In the passage where Cassibelaunus, elated by his victory over Julius Cæsar, assembles all the nobility of Britain with their wives at London, " in order to perform solemn sacrifices to their tutelary gods," at which solemnity they sacrificed 40,000

[1] Exodus viii.

cows, 100,000 sheep, and 30,000 wild beasts, besides fowls without number, we hear nothing of the celebrated Druids. In the time of Lucius, the first convert to Christianity, Geoffrey of Monmouth knows only of Flamens and Arch-Flamens as the priests of the idolaters; and neither he nor the compiler of the *Brut Tysilio* has anything to say about the Druids, whose privileges were transferred to the Christian Church. Mr. Herbert, struck with this silence of the chronicler on the subject of the Druidic hierarchy, thought there was a systematic concealment of the truth; but the inference is plain, that the Druid extinguished by Paulinus in A.D. 58, had not been resuscitated in the tenth century.

From other terms significative of supernatural beings, and from numerous allusions in the Welsh romances, we know that there must have existed a widely spread belief, the source of abundant tradition and romance, in the existence of supernatural and demoniacal beings of various characters and classes. We find, moreover, that the traditions which have descended from a remote period of what may be called the fairy mythology of Wales, are still living in the mouths of the people, and see traces of their existence in the names of places, of rocks, of stones, of wells, and mountain recesses. If the memory of the Druids and their mystic ceremonies, their circles of stone, their places of sacrifice, and courts of justice, lived in the popular traditions of the sixth century, we must find them now, such is the undying character of these associations with natural or artificial objects. I am not able to state how many instances occur in Wales in which the name of Druid is attached to such objects; but of twenty-one monumental stones, stone circles, and mounds, noticed by Dr. Jones in his *History of Wales*, there is not one which bears this epithet.

Of the 208 hundreds and commotes into which Wales was divided by Edward I. in the thirteenth century, though many have names significant of events and of natural objects, and names of persons, not one is called after any Druidical establishment, or Druidical object.

In a list of the Welsh names of nearly 800 plants collected in Richards's *Botanology*, there is not one to which the name of Druid is attached, though we find "Fairy Fingers," "Fairy Food," "Dwarf's Mantle," "Taliesin's Flower," "Arthur's Sweat," "Devil's Milk," &c. Neither the Mistletoe nor the Vervain are, in the familiar Welsh names of those plants, connected with the Druid. Nor is any mention made in the Welsh poems of another celebrated symbol of Druidism, the "Glain," or Ovum Anguinum, which, according to the account preserved by Pliny,[1] was produced from serpents. The serpents, twisting themselves together in great numbers, produced this egg, and then threw it up in the air with loud hisses, upon which the Druids, who were on the watch for this event, caught it in a cloak before it fell. They then fled away on horseback pursued by the serpents, until they had reached some river, when the pursuit ceased. It is certain that such a fable was current in Gaul; and these talismans, which Mr. Herbert very reasonably concludes to have been balls of glass, were in vogue during the Roman domination, since Claudius Cæsar, who repressed the practices of Druidism, condemned to death a Roman knight who had possessed himself of one of these talismans with a view to the successful issue of a lawsuit in which he was engaged. Among the Welsh poems preserved, however, no trace of any such superstition, if it ever existed in Britain, has survived. Mr. Herbert thought that an allusion to the Anguine egg was to be found in some lines of the fragment relating to the Cattraeth combat which is mixed up with the "Dyhuddiant Elphin,"—

> Bleid y vyuyt
> Oed bleidyat rhyd
> Yn y deuredd
> Pubal Peleidyr
> Penyr pryd neidyr
> O luch nadredd;

[1] *Hist. Nat.* xxix. 12.

which he translated,[1]—

> Vivid his aspect,
> Impetuous was he over the ford;
> That which exercised his prowess
> Was the quick glancing ball,
> The adder's bright precious produce,
> The ejaculation of serpents."

The existence in these poems of a testimony to the currency in Britain of the fable relating to the talismanic "glain" would be a matter of considerable interest. It is, however, quite clear that this testimony exists not in the original lines, but in Mr. Herbert's translation of them. The fragment to which they belong, evidently a portion of a Gododin or Cattraeth poem, is extremely corrupt, and difficult to translate. But, on examining the passage in question, we see at once that the line preceding those quoted by Mr. Herbert,

> Bu edryssed,

belongs to and forms part of the sentence, and gives the key to the meaning of the whole. It is apparent that the lines contain a description of a warrior, not of a Druid, and that the "glancing snake" applies to the bright spear-head of a chieftain, not to the talisman of a necromancer. The meaning of the passage runs thus:—

> There was abundance
> Of food for the wolf;
> He was liberal to wolves
> In his valour;
> Stout was his spear;
> Its head was like a snake
> Amid glancing snakes.

We have therefore no allusion in the old Welsh compositions to any of the celebrated symbols of the Druidic priesthood, nor the slightest testimony in support of the fables

---

[1] *Essay on the Neo-Druidic Heresy*, p. 61.

promulgated as to the character, institutions, rites, and cere-monies of this famous hierarchy.

These are facts which must outweigh all the speculations possible, founded upon Cæsar's *Commentaries* and Pliny's *Natural History.*

In the descriptions of the boundaries of the lands given to the church of Llandaff by various personages, from the sixth to the twelfth centuries, a number of natural and artificial objects, trees, stones, carns, mounds, dykes, &c., are men-tioned, with their specific names. Thus, we have the Brook of the Grave of the Strangers, the Stone in the Variegated Moors, the Long Stone, the Spotted Stone, the Stone of Cinahi, the Carn Erchan; "the road along the highway upwards to the ash, from the ash across the road direct to the hawthorn;" "along Mynwy to the Red Pool, upwards to the front of the hill, downwards by the fork stone, to the influx of the Geffat;" "along the ridge of the mountain to the shaft of the Cross of Guerion;" the Stone of Lybiau, the Spring of Crug Lewyrn, the Mound of Cyfall Scoti, &c. In the great number of objects thus designated as boundary marks throughout the diocese of Llandaff, from the Severn and the Wye to the western portion of Caermarthenshire, there is only one object which can be supposed to be connected with a tradition of the Druids. This occurs in the grant of Iddon, son of Ynyr Gwent, of lands in Monmouthshire to St. Teilo, Bishop of Llandaff, in the sixth century. The boundary line runs along the Gavenny river downwards to the ford of Llechawg, " or rit dirlechluit in cruc braed diguern idrution," that is, " from the ford to the grey stone in Crug Braed, to Gwern y Dru-tion,"which may possibly mean "the Alder-trees, or the Swamp of the Druids." Druids, however, are not particularly con-nected with swamps, and it is much more probable that it refers to some traditionary combat, and means the " Swamp of the Warriors." If it be taken to have the former meaning, we may compare it with the " Cerrig y Druidion," or Rock of the Druids, in Denbighshire. Both " Drution " and " Druidion " are very different forms from "Derwyddon," especially if the word *gwydd*, "knowledge," enters into the composition of the latter. In considering these questions, we ought to recollect that the country now occupied by the Welsh or Cymry was, both North and South Wales, in possession of tribes of the Irish or Gadhelic branch of the Celtic race, before the invasion of the Northern Cumbrian Britons under the sons of Cunedda, or the conquest represented by their names. It would be impossible to enter upon a satisfactory examination of this subject without also undertaking a critical examination of the Historical Triads and the *Mabinogion*, compared with the Irish sources of history and tradition; and in this place we have only to deal with the poetry of the Welsh. The evidence of the ancient occupation of the Principality by Irish tribes has been very ably discussed by the Rev. Basil Jones,[1] and shows very clearly that the history of Britain for the latter part of the Roman dominion, and the two following centuries, yet remains to be written.

It is certainly not without significance, that the only place in Britain in which there is any distinct evidence from the Roman authorities of the existence of Druids, should be the Isle of Anglesey, the seat of the Irish population, before the migration of the Cumbrian tribes, the ancestors of the modern Welsh.

In conclusion, we may observe, that had the works of the old Welsh Bards abounded with references to some unknown mythology, and allusions to the divinities of some national but forgotten creed, a sound judgment would have afforded some more rational explanation of the occurrence, than that of the persistence of pagan superstitions, in all their force and vitality, at such an epoch, in the western and southern provinces of Britain.

Upon this point the observations of Mr. Beale Poste are worthy of attention. This learned writer, though misled by

---

[1] *Vestiges of the Gael in Gwynedd.* London, 1851.

43

the translations of Mr. Davies into believing that this Druidism existed in the Welsh poems, offered a very reasonable explanation of the supposed phenomenon. "The productions of the British Bards," he says,[1] "seem to be redolent with the ideas and dogmas of Druidism, though at the date of the poems of Aneurin and Taliesin, Christianity had prevailed in Britain for several centuries. Worn out as it was, they retained it conventionally in their compositions, appearing to think that its fictions and imagery worked up well in poetry. This is a parallel case with the reception of classic mythology among modern writers. Even down to the present times, heathen mythology may be found introduced in works of imagination, the same as if really existing. The poet invokes Phœbus, Diana, Pan, and other deities, meaning nothing by it all the time. There is likewise a further parallelism to be suspected. As we find the moderns frequently err in what they imagine the details of classic mythology, the same may have been the case with the Bards and their Druidism. At any rate, thus dealing with a defunct superstition; entering indeed but little on topics unconnected with their favourite mythology, and being at all times very mystical and obscure, the less fact can be extracted from them, and their value is proportionably diminished."

We may illustrate the above sensible and judicious observations of Mr. Poste by pointing out, that upon the principle which has usually been employed in the consideration of these poems, there would be no difficulty in proving the existence of a pagan mythology in England in the nineteenth century, from the works of the poets of that epoch. If Mr. Macaulay's New Zealander, writing, in a future age, an essay on this subject, were to support his views of the paganism of the nineteenth century by such quotations as,[2]

---

[1] *Britannic Researches*, p. 281.   London, 1853.
[2] Milman's *Belshazzar*.

God of the Thunder ! from whose cloudy seat
The fiery winds of desolation flow,
Father of vengeance ! that with purple feet,
Like a full wine-press, tread'st the world below ;

and

God of the Rainbow ! at whose gracious sign
The billows of the proud their rage suppress,—

without reference to the context and general scope of the poem, to the author who wrote, the people who read, or the social condition of the age in which the poem was written,— he would do for British poetry of the nineteenth century, very much what Mr. Davies and others have done for that of the old Welsh minstrels. We have, however, the satisfaction of finding that, when the works of our British ancestors are fully examined and fairly translated, if they exhibit no great amount of wisdom or philosophy, they are entirely free from the imputation of having inculcated the worship of Pagan deities, or having revelled in the description of mysterious abominations in the midst of a Christian people, and while exhibiting an outward conformity to the doctrines and precepts of Christianity.

If we find in the oldest compositions in the Welsh language no traces of the Druids, or of a pagan mythology, still less do we find evidence of the existence of any peculiar philosophical or theological doctrines, such as it has been the fashion to represent as lying concealed in these compositions under the somewhat vague title of Bardic mysteries. The whole tenor of the result of an investigation into the supposed evidences of this mystery leads to the conclusion that the Welsh Bards neither of the sixth nor of the twelfth century had any mysteries to conceal, beyond the secrets, such as they were, of their profession.

The " Cyfrinach," or secret of the Bards, was an artistic and not a religious mystery. It related not to the heavenly or the infernal regions, to the nature of the soul or the condition of man, but simply to the arts of music and song.

They knew of no other mystery, nor of any mystic creed, unknown to the rest of the Christian world. Their writings, as
we see, contain no evidence of any esoteric doctrines, either
Pagan or Christian. In the sixth century the minds of the
Welsh Christians were agitated with the Pelagian controversy;
in the twelfth and thirteenth, they held the doctrines of the
Church of Rome of that day. Their views of the Deity, of a
future state of existence, of a system of rewards and punishments, were those of the general body of Christians of that
age, and contained no admixture of tenets drawn from a remote patriarchal or heathen source. The notion of the "Bardic
mysteries" is a mere fable founded on a mistaken view of the
productions of the Welsh Bards of the middle ages; and the
demonstration of the want of any foundation for a belief in the
existence of such mysteries is, we may fairly hope, a step in
advance towards a true understanding of the history of the
period in question. The compositions of the Welsh of the
twelfth and thirteenth centuries which have come down to us,
and especially the romance tales in which the poetic genius of
the nation is so richly displayed, are sufficiently valuable, without investing them with an interest derived from a fictitious
mystery, which seems only to throw around them a needless
and perplexing obscurity. The Welsh nation, instead of standing aloof from Christian Europe during the period which is
embraced between the sixth and thirteenth centuries, as a
people holding, hardly in secret, while in outward conformity to
the Christian Church, a most portentous heresy, returns to the
pale of ordinary religious belief and the common Christianity
of the age.

The Welsh minstrelsy, instead of dating from a time beyond
the limits of history, or deriving its materials from a source
hidden in the obscurity of a prehistoric age, enters the circle
of the romantic literature of Europe during the tenth and succeeding centuries, and will probably be found to have received
more from, than it communicated to its continental neighbours.
It is, however, no small merit which must be conceded to the

Welsh romance-writers, that what they borrowed from others they stamped with the impress of their own genius, and gave currency, under their own peculiar national form, to the treasures derived from the mines of the stranger. In the hands of the Welsh, every tradition, every legend, no matter from what source, became Welsh,—the events localized in Wales, and the heroes admitted into the cycle of the Welsh heroic genealogies; and it is probably to this process of naturalization that we owe the preservation of the Welsh romances. The Welsh poems, such as we find them in the Myvyrian collection, we have shown to be replete with references to the extant tales, and to others of a similar nature not now known to exist; but of any other mysteries than such as can be explained by reference to the current religious philosophy of the age, or to these romantic tales, not a particle of evidence can be discovered.

Wherever such evidence has hitherto been supposed to have been discovered, investigation has demonstrated it to be a fallacy, originating in an erroneous conception of the meaning of the passages produced, or derived from documents tainted with the suspicion of modern forgery and fraud.

INDEX TO PIECES TRANSLATED.

———◆———

	PAGE
Angar Cyvyndawd	282
Anrec Urien	114
Anrhyfeddodau Alexander	253
Armes	124
Awdyl	274
Awdyl Vraith	300
Cad Goddeu	224
Cadeir Keridwen	189
Cadeir Taliesin	205
Cadeir Teyrnon	208
Can y Meirch	244
Canu Cyntaf Taliesin	157
Canu I Urien	109
Canu I Urien Rheged	105
Canu y Kwrwf	199
Canu y Medd	173
Canu y Byd Bychan	279
Canu y Byd Mawr	280
Cystwy'r Beirdd	176
Dadolwch Urien	107
Divregwawd Taliesin	293
Dyhuddiant Elphin	154—165
Englynion Cad Goddeu	223
Englynion Marchwiail	74
Fustl y Beirdd	177
Gorchan Adebon	88
Gorchestion y Beirdd	174

PAGE

Gwaith Argoed Llwyfain 99
Gwaith Gwenystrad 97
Gwawd Gwyr Israel 270
Gwawd Lludd y Mawr 255

Hanes Taliesin . . . . 155—161

I Urien . . . . 103—113
I Wallawg 93
I'r Gwynt 170

Kerdd am Veib Llyr ab Brychwel Powys 192
Kerdd i Wallawg ap Llecnawg 90
Kerdd Daronwy 237

Luryg Alexander 254

Marwnad Aeddon 129
Marwnad Cunedda 82
Marwnad Ercwlf 277
Marwnad Mad Ddrud ac Erof Greulon 305
Marwnad Milveib 148
Marwnad Owain ab Urien Rheged 108
Mic Dinbych 216

Plaeu yr Aipht 263
Pictish Stanzas 79
Preiddeu Annwn 211
Prif Gyfarch 67

Y Gofeisws Byd 248
Ymarwar Lludd Bychan 118
Yspeil Taliesin 100

London: F. PICKTON, Printer, Perry's Place, 29, Oxford Street.

Printed in the United States
94472LV00005B/28/A